The Legion Condor • Ries/Ring

A History of the Luftwaffe in the Spanish Civil War 1936-1939

Karl Ries/Hans Ring

THE LEGION CONDOR

Translated from the German by David Johnston

Schiffer Military History
Atglen, PA

Cover artwork by Steve Ferguson, Colorado Springs, CO

LEGION LEGENDS

On October 15, 1938, *Gruppenchef* Walter Grabmann of JG 88 led a fighter escort above a *Legion Condor* bomber force flying against Spanish Republican targets. On this notable mission, an interception by Rebublican "Rata" fighters was attempted and Grabmann, along with 3. *Staffel* leader *Oberleutnant* Werner Mölders, engaged the obsolete attacking bi-planes. Grabmann shot down one of the Ratas for his fifth aerial victory, placing him among the elite group of young aces in the mercenary Luftwaffe band. As for Mölders, his two Rata victims would be confirmed as his tenth and eleventh kills, even though he already carried an unofficial tenth kill marking on the tail of his Bf 109. Spain was to be the proving ground for a new type of aerial warfare and initiated some of the greatest legends in fighter lore, including the stellar career of Mölders and his command ascent to the Luftwaffe's *General der Jagdflieger* in a mere six years.

The painting depicts the Bf 109D's flown by Grabmann and Mölders as they turn off their positions over the Heinkel bombers to intercept the approaching Ratas spotted against the clouds.

The camouflage of the Messerschmitt fighters has been a point of conflict with historians for some time. The color is designated as RLM 62 in some literature sources, and actual color chips indicate the green-grey shade as shown in the painting, but no reliable color photography shows any of the Legion's Bf 109 D's in Spain.

Three types of the Bf 109 were deployed. First came the prototypes and the "B" model, which appear to be very light in color, then the "C" model, which is not always accurately identified. The "C" is not easily distinguished from the "D" model, and both were flown in the 1938 period by Grabmann and his more experienced men.

Prototype aircraft were commonly painted in a primer color designated as RLM 02, essentially a medium grey with a slight greenish tint. There is another color, RLM 63, which is very near the same paint color.

In the painting green-grey RLM 62 was chosen for the later model "D" flown in 1938, based on some reasonable speculation. There is some black and white photography that suggests a darker color was used on the "C" and "D" model Messerschmitts. The green of RLM 62 is somewhat darker than the greyer RLM 63/02. Speculation-wise, in the extremes of the Spanish mountian-desert environment, the fading of the respective greens and greys would imply the green to stay somewhat darker. Therefore, the later model fighters were very likely RLM 62 green-grey.

The Heinkel He 111B bombers are illustrated in two schemes; one of solid green-grey and the other in a tri-color of grey, green and dark brown. The colors are accurately recorded in a number of different sources. The bombers also offer a comparison of greens and greys in contrast when seen in the same photograph.

Legion Condor cuff title courtesy of,
The Military History Shop, Kennett Sq., PA

Translated from the German by David Johnston.

Library of Congress Catalog Number: 91-62741.

Printed in China.
ISBN: 0-88740-339-5

This title was originally published under the title,
Legion Condor - Eine Illustrierte Dokumentation,
by Verlag Dieter Hoffmann, Mainz.

Published by Schiffer Publishing Ltd.
4880 Lower Valley Road
Atglen, PA 19310
Phone: (610) 593-1777; Fax: (610) 593-2002
E-mail: Info@schifferbooks.com
Please visit our web site catalog at **www.schifferbooks.com**

In Europe, Schiffer books are distributed by Bushwood Books
6 Marksbury Avenue Kew Gardens
Surrey TW9 4JF England
Phone: 44 (0) 20-8392-8585; Fax: 44 (0) 20-8392-9876
E-mail: info@bushwoodbooks.co.uk
Free postage in the UK. Europe: air mail at cost.

This book may be purchased from the publisher.
Include $3.95 for shipping. Please try your bookstore first.
We are always looking for people to write books on new and related subjects.
If you have an idea for a book please contact us at the above address.
You may write for a free catalog.

Contents

Foreword

A notable feature of the Spanish Civil War was the participation of foreign troops on a scale unmatched by any previous internal conflict. Two ideologically-opposed groups were trying to seize power in Spain and this must have caused far-seeing politicians in other nations of the same color to consider what implications a preponderance of the extreme left or right in any future Spanish government might have for their own nations and strategic objectives.

As matters stood, the new face of Spain after the civil war could only bear communist or purely fascist-nationalist features. Small wonder then, that such a problem provoked the classic, if still young states of the opposing ideologies to become actively involved. Requests for aid from the two sides in Spain were only too willingly acceded to, with Italy and Germany on the one hand and the USSR on the other promising aid in the form of personnel and materiel. Without the intervention of these two power blocks it is unlikely that the Spanish Civil War could have assumed the proportions that it did, characterized by the large-scale use of modern weaponry, such as aircraft and tanks. However, a smaller war lasting some years would probably have driven the nation to economic ruin without producing a clear political result.

However it was not just the previously mentioned states which contributed to the rise in tensions in Spain, taking into the bargain the risk of the conflict a widening into a general European war. Despite their membership in the Non-Intervention Committee, or NIC, France, Great Britain, Poland, Yugoslavia and Czechoslovakia continued to deliver arms to the Republican side. There could be no question of compliance with the agreed-upon arms embargo. The absolute secrecy of such activities on the part of sympathetic governments allowed very little of the scope and nature of these arms deliveries to filter through to the outside world. As a result, the state of source material concerning the participation of foreign powers during the Spanish Civil War must be characterized as rather meager. For various reasons all of the participants still balk at making existing documents readily accessible. In particular, a release of the material held by the two Spanish archives, the *Archivo de la Delegacion Nacional de Servicio Documentales* in Salamanca and the *Servicio Historico Militar* in Madrid, would make it possible to record a truly complete history of this fratricidal war.

The less than satisfactory situation concerning access to official sources may be the reason why it has only now become possible, forty years after the events, for the authors to compile a history of the *Legion Condor*. Fortunate circumstances, access to documentary material and the cooperation of many former Legionnaires or their families has placed us in a position to compile a detailed account of the German "Legion" in Spain.

This circle of people who made available diaries, operational reports, individual descriptions, photographic material and much other material, deserve our special thanks. Without their help much would have remained the subject of dark and only vague speculation.

The following ladies and gentlemen provided us with valuable assistance:

Dr. Nikolaus Appel	Adolf Menkhoff
Dr. Wilhelm Balthasar	Victor Mölders
Otto Bertram	Edu Neumann
Eberhard v. d'Elsa	Dr. Heinrich Neumann
Wolfgang Ewald	Ernst Obermaier
Adolf Galland	Eduard Ott
Gerhard Geike	Rolf Pingel
Walter Grabmann	Douglas Pitcairn
Karin Handrick	Irmingard Prestele
Marilies Harder	Eckehart Priebe
Asta Henrici	Siebelt Reents
Paul Henze	Oskar Rumler
Hans Herold	Annelise Schallmann
Hajo Herrmann	Joachim Heirich Schlichting
Karl Hofmeister	Hans Schmoller-Haldy
Hermann Hogeback	Herbert Schob
Herbert Ihlefeld	Hans Scholz
Franz Jaenisch	Reinhard Seiler
Rudolf Jöster	Ernst Sorge
Gerd Klein-Schmeink	Hennig Strümpell
Werner Klümper	Hannes Trautloft
Hans König	Werner Ursinus
Sylvia Kristinus	Karl Wagner
Hubert Kroeck	Walter Wallinger
Alfred v. Lojewski	Dr. Gerhard Weyert
Gisela Lützow	Herbert Wittmann
Emmeran Mayer	Ilse Zemené

The expert advice and practical assistance of Hans Joachim Lind in the multi-faceted reproduction work was a welcome help during the preparation of this book; to him a special "thank you."

We hope that this book will provide the first realistic insight into the events on the Spanish peninsula during the period 1936-1939 and illustrate the madness and consequences of political power struggles. The sacrifice of nearly 300 young men, whose names fill the pages of the loss records as the dead of the German contingent, was not enough to prevent the catastrophe of the Second World War.

Mainz and Munich, October 1979

Karl Ries
Hans Ring

Rebellion of the Generals

Ju 52/3m D-APOK, *Max von Müller,* glided in over the barren approach to Las Palmas, flitted over the airfield boundary and settled onto the ground in a prescribed three-point landing. The date was July 20, 1936, the time 1137. The aircraft, of *Deutsche Lufthansa*'s South Atlantic route, *Werknummer* 5074/1936, had taken off from the DLH station at Bathurst on the West African coast. Its pilot, *Flugkapitän* Henke, was planning to make a non-stop flight to Las Palmas. Halfway there, however, Henke received a radio message directing him to land at the airfield at Villa Cisneros in the Spanish West Sahara and wait there for further orders, as the Canary Islands were under a state of siege.

As ordered, the Ju 52 flew to Villa Cisneros. After landing, Henke and his crew learned more about the events then taking place in the island group, brought about by an insurrection in Spanish Morocco, but were unable to make any sense out of the political causes behind it. The following day the *Lufthansa* crew was given clearance to continue on to Las Palmas on July 20. Permission to take off originated from General Luis Orgaz, Military Governor of the Canary Islands.

After setting down on the island airfield Henke taxied D-APOK to the airfield buildings, shut down the engines and was about to make his way to the air traffic control station when he was informed by a representative of the military government that his aircraft was being requisitioned for an unspecified period and was to be kept at the disposal of the Nationalist uprising. Although Otto Bertram, director of DLH's South Atlantic Administration, and the administrator of the German Consulate in Las Palmas, Flick, immediately protested the move, the Ju 52 was in the air again that same afternoon, dropping leaflets from the rebels over Gran Canaria. Further protests to Bathurst and Berlin also failed to obtain the release of the German aircraft. Indeed, a charter flight was scheduled against payment, in which *Flugkapitän* Henke was to fly General Orgaz and two companions to Tetuan in Spanish Morocco. The flight took place without complications, and D-APOK arrived in Tetuan at 0530 on July 23.

With this surprising seizure the German Reich found itself involved in an internal Spanish conflict, which could easily have led to a general European war as a result of the taking of sides by a whole series of European states.

But what had preceded the events in Las Palmas, what had led to the outbreak of this terrible civil war?

If one examines Spanish politics after the fall of the monarchy in 1931, one is struck by the differing directions of the various political parties supported by the very different levels of society in the country. A purely Marxist, highly cohesive mass was faced by a group comprising monarchists, liberal republicans, nationalists and extreme rightists. The efforts of separatists in the provinces of Catalonia and Asturia contributed to the internal political fragmentation of Spain, which was dragging the nation to economic and moral ruin.

It was predictable that the countless cabinet shuffles within a period of five years must lead to a struggle between power blocks, but even the most non-political citizen could see that such a pointless policy would drive the nation, which was already on a weak economic footing, to ruin.

The elections of November 19, 1933 saw the parties of the right clearly in front, however the vague policies of the following years were not endorsed by the opposition parties, who for their part were working hand in hand with the radical left. The eventual result was the proclamation of the Catalonian Republic. In Asturia, the Basque province, the first terrorist acts were registered against churches and monasteries, and the Marxist trade unions loudly demanded that the people be armed! Only with great difficulty and the assistance of troops did the government succeed in mastering these insurrections. By then the disturbances had claimed 4,000 dead on both sides.

As expected, the election of February 16, 1936 resulted in a majority for the "People's Front" (473 seats to 256). The days and weeks following the assumption of power by the proletarian forces saw an increase in excesses by the radical leftists, who must have been a thorn in the side of the more moderate elements of the government, and especially the parties of the right, in particular the fascist "Falange."

In March 1936, this "Falange," which on April 19, 1937 became the Spanish National Unity Party (*Falange Espanola de las Juntas Ofensiva Nacional-Sindicalista*), consisted of about 10,000 members, many of whom, including their leader José Antonio Primo, had been imprisoned.

The months following the election in February saw a widening of strikes, public unrest, arson and nocturnal actions against political enemies. This state of affairs reached its climax with the murder of Calvo Sotelo, the leader of the rightist block in the *Cortes*, after he accused the People's Front parties of

General Franco, leader of the military revolt in Spanish-Moroccan Mellila and Tetuan.

offenses against the Spanish people in an impassioned speech during a government session. The days that followed were marked by an escalation in tensions between the two government camps; an open confrontation appeared unavoidable.

News of the outbreak of a military revolt following the conclusion of army maneuvers on July 17, 1936 at Melilla, Spanish Morocco, led to a spreading of the revolt to the mainland. The uprising was directed and organized by General Mola, successor to General José Sanjurjo, who had been killed in a plane crash on July 20. The first open battles between Republican military units loyal to the government and those supporting the Nationalist cause broke out at various places on the mainland.

General Francisco Franco y Bahamonde, the Chief of the General Staff, had opposed the policies of the Republican government from the beginning. The latter had dealt with him by making him military commander of the Canary Islands, placing him in a sort of isolation there. Franco nevertheless pressed ahead with preparations for a revolt against the rulers in Madrid, whom he detested, encouraged by a lack of government control on the remote islands. Franco's fellow conspirators chartered a British de Havilland Dragon Rapide to fly him to Spanish Morocco, the core area of the planned military revolt. As agreed upon, pilot Bebb and three passengers arrived at Gando airfield near Las Palmas on July 15. With the news of the successful revolt in Melilla, Generals Franco and Orgaz assumed military command of the Canary Islands group. On July

Franco flew from Gran Canaria to the Spanish garrisons in the North African coastal region in a de Havilland Dragon Rapide biplane.

18 Franco departed for Tetuan in the British aircraft, arriving on July 19, 1936, after an en route stop at Casablanca.

Already informed of the objectives of the revolt by officers allied to Franco, the entire garrison of the city of Tetuan declared itself for the Nationalist side the same day. The news failed to arouse panic on the mainland, however. Following the declaration of loyalty to the Republic by the fleet and the majority of the Spanish Air Force, the government in Madrid felt certain that it could deal with the revolt quickly. There was no fear of a direct military threat from Spanish Morocco, as loyal fleet units were watching the Strait of Gibraltar, making any transport of rebel units to the mainland by sea impossible. The government saw a greater threat in the northern group of rebel military units under General Mola, which controlled the northwest corner of Spain, all of Old-Castile, the Navarra region, the western part of Aragon and the northwestern section of Estremadura. In southern Spain part of Andalusia, including the cities of Cadiz, Sevilla, Cordoba and Granada, had been occupied by the Nationalist units of General Queipo de Llano, known as the "Radio General" on account of his electrifying radio addresses. This area projected into Republican territory like a thorn. Three-fifths of the divided land was in Republican hands, including most of the nation's coal and mineral deposits as well as its industrial regions, the remaining two-fifths being occupied by the Nationalists. The government thus appeared to have the upper hand over the rebelling Nationalists

at the opening of hostilities.

The physical separation of the areas under Nationalist control and the resulting decentralized command of the northern and southern armies naturally made military action by the rebels more difficult. In addition, the Commander-in-Chief of the Nationalist forces, General Franco, was isolated in Spanish Morocco by the Strait of Gibraltar, unable to get his well-trained Moroccan units across to the motherland. Faced with these problems the Nationalists were somewhat less than optimistic about the coming struggle with the government forces; only help from the outside could lead to an improvement in the situation.

Negotiations with the German Government and Initial Aid Deliveries

On July 23, 1936 a dispatch arrived at the Foreign Affairs Office in Berlin from Tetuan via the German Military Attaché in Paris. In it General Franco and *Oberstleutnant* Beigbeder, former Spanish Military Attaché in Berlin, requested the delivery of ten military transport aircraft to Spanish Morocco.

The fact that this request was directed just toward Germany is easily explained by the political outlook of the German government of the time. However, the possibility that the Soviet Union might be flirting with the idea of establishing a bolshevik outpost in southwest Europe and would intervene could not be ignored. This possibility and the recent discovery that the French government had approved deliveries of war materiel to the Spanish Republic could not help but run counter to the interests of the fascist nations such as Germany and Italy. The Nationalist request for aid was thus issued specifically to Germany, and soon afterward to Italy, as it was thought this side was most likely to respond favorably. The recommendation of the Foreign Affairs Office to the Reich War Ministry, however, was absolutely neutral and tended to be rather negatively inclined towards Franco's request.

On the evening of July 24, however, a further telegram reached the Foreign Affairs Office. It contained an announcement from the Tetuan Consulate that the requisitioned and later chartered DLH Ju 52 was to fly to Berlin, bringing the Germans Johannes Bernhardt and Adolf Langenheim and a Spanish Air Force officer to present a handwritten note from Franco.

As *Ortsgruppenleiter Tetuan* of the NSDAP's *Auslands* Organization, Langenheim must have seemed to Franco the ideal messenger to deliver the request for aid. Bernhardt was likewise a member of the party, a press agent with the *Auslands* Organization and a former salesman. Following several illegal business deals he installed himself as a go-between on the grounds that he was well-connected to Franco through his previous dealings. His primary motivation in seeing aid begin to Spain appeared to be more business related than idealistic.

That same July 24 the Ju 52 arrived at Berlin-Gatow with the Spanish Captain Arranz, Langenheim and Bernhardt. The Foreign Office and the RKM categorically refused the delegation a ministerial or military reception so as to spare the Reich any difficulties which might arise if it became known that negotiations were taking place for the sale of German aircraft. The party was therefore taken by *Gauleiter* Bohle, head of the *Auslands* Organization, to see Deputy *Führer* Rudolf Hess. Hess immediately sent the delegation to see Hitler, who was taking in the Wagner Festival in Bayreuth.

The first discussion between the two parties took place on the evening of July 25. With Hitler were *Generalfeldmarschall* Göring, War Minister von Blomberg and a representative of *Vizeadmiral* Raeder, *Kapitän zur See* Coupette. The absence of Ribbentrop, the NSDAP's foreign affairs advisor, and von Neurath, the Reich Foreign Minister, from the nocturnal negotiations illustrated the purely military significance Hitler attached to the Spanish affair.

The view that Germany saw the civil war as an opportunity to conduct "live" maneuvers, and Spain as a military proving ground, cannot be supported at this time, as both sides had no way of predicting with certainty the duration and outcome of the conflict. However, the decisions taken during the night of July 25/26 may have been influenced by economic considerations, such as an improvement in Germany's foreign exchange situation and future trade agreements with Spain. A further consideration may have been a desire to bring about an accelerated conclusion to the war in the interests of the approximately 10,000 Spanish-Germans.

The primary motivation behind Germany's agreement to supply aid to the Spanish Nationalists, however, may have been the anti-communist attitudes of her leaders. The thought of a bolshevik bulwark in the Mediterranean region simply demanded that they go along with Franco and his interests.

Initial discussions on the organization and extent of the aid for Spain took place at the RLM on the evening of July 26, 1936 under the direction of *General der Fleiger* Milch. *Generalleutnant* Helmut Wilberg was given the job of creating *Sonderstab* W, a central office for supplying the materiel and personnel needs of the German volunteers in Spain. Wilberg was half-Jewish, but he and his family were spared any racial harassment by the regime. Using the pseudonym "Wilde," Wilberg led the *Sonderstab* until April 1, 1938. His successor was *Generalleutnant* Schweickhard, who commanded the special headquarters until the conclusion of the civil war. The mixed delegation's request for the delivery of transport aircraft had also been acceded to on July 26, but instead of the 10 machines requested they were offered 20 Ju 52 aircraft, which were to be delivered to Sevilla and Tetuan by DLH pilots via the shortest possible route.

Flugkapitän Henke took off from Berlin Tempelhof early on July 27 for Tetuan, arriving the following day. He immediately began transporting Moroccan soldiers, or "Moros" for short, to the airfield at Sevilla. Individual flights from Tetuan to Sevilla had begun on July 20 using three Fokker F VII transports, but such sporadic efforts with aircraft of limited capacity held little promise of success. *HISMA Ltda.* (*Compania Hispano-Marroqui de Transportes, Tetuan*) was formed in July 1936 as a cover organization for the agreed-upon transport of troops from Spanish Morocco to the mainland, as well as for the delivery of German aircraft and materiel. The company's registered owners were, on the Spanish side, the former Admiral Ramón Carrazana, and on the German, Johannes Bernhardt, whose participation thus turned out to be financially rewarding at a very early stage. With the later transfer of the company from Tetuan to Sevilla the scope of its activities expanded very rapidly. Until the start of work by the headquarters of the *Legion Condor* HISMA was responsible for supplying, accommodating and paying the German volunteers; in addition it was the administrative office for all German aid deliveries and the liaison center between the Spanish headquarters and "*Sonderstab Wilberg.*"

A purely German partner company of HISMA was created in Berlin on October 2, 1936. It was known as ROWAK (*Rohstoff-und Waren-Kompensation*) GmbH, and was an indication of the Reich's increasing economic interest in events in Spain. Once the groundwork had been laid for future deliveries of war materiel and the associated accounting, German aid for the Nationalist side began to flow.

Because of the admitted degree of urgency "*Sonderstab* W" was able to complete its organizational work quickly and without complications. On July 27, requests for volunteers were issued to *Jagdgruppen* based at Dortmund and Döberitz and *Kampfgruppen* at Gotha, Merseburg and Ansbach. By July 29 the first 86-man contingent had been assembled at Döberitz and was ready to be shipped to Spain. Command of the detachment was given to *Major* Alexander Scheele, a *Schutztruppe* pilot of the First World War. With his knowledge of languages and his experience abroad he seemed the ideal man for the job. On July 31, following a farewell speech by State Secretary Milch, the group embarked on the steamer *Usaramo* of the Woermann Line under Captain Heinz Stamer at the Petersen Dock in Hamburg under the cover designation "*Reisegesellschaft Union*" ("Union Tourist Party").

Operation "Feuerzauber" was under way!

First head of the Special Headquarters for German-Spanish Military Aid, Generalleutnant Wilberg, a First World War pilot and at the time of his appointment the commander of a Luftkreisschule.

Under the Spanish Sun

During the night of August 1, 1936 the freighter *Usaramo* sailed from the port of Hamburg. On board were a hastily-installed marine radio station, eighty-six volunteers, six crated He 51 fighters, twenty 20mm light anti-aircraft guns and about one hundred tons of other war materiel. All of the volunteers had been formally released from the Wehrmacht and had been provided with civilian clothing. Instructions were radioed to *Vizeadmiral* Carls, commander of the German naval forces in the waters off Spain, to escort the steamer, which was sailing without papers, from the west coast of Portugal to its destination, the port of Cadiz. The warship *Deutschland* and the torpedo boats *Leopard* and *Luchs* picked up the *Usaramo* on August 5 and, maintaining a distance of fifteen nautical miles, escorted the steamer until it sailed into Cadiz at dawn on the morning of August 6.

Unloading of the ship began at once, interrupted only briefly by inaccurate shelling from a Republican destroyer, which had not spotted the steamer and its contraband until it was entering port. The first German volunteers stepped onto Spanish soil, led by the detachment's commander, "Papa" Scheele. He was accompanied by ten bomber crews under the command of *Oberleutnant* Freiherr von Moreau and the fighter pilots Eberhardt, Knüppel, Trautloft, von Houwald, Hefter and Klein, together with technicians, mechanics and armorers. Those known from the latter group of personnel are Biehl, Buck, Eick, Gnilka, Göll, Rudolph, Schwung, Spitzhüttel, Thesenfitz and Wiegand.

After the materiel had been loaded onto rail cars, on August 7 the entire transport rolled to the city of Sevilla, which had been captured by General Queipo de Llano. In the meantime, ten Ju 52 transports had been ferried to Tablada airfield near the city by *Lufthansa* captains, so that "Bubb" Moreau and his forty-two-man group were able to begin transport flights from Tetuan to Sevilla at once. As a rule the crews made three to four return trips daily at an altitude of about 3,000 meters. Between flights the crews rested and ate their meals in small canteen tents right on the airfields. The tents bore the inscription "Personas Junkers." Flying time from Tetuan to Tablada was about ninety minutes; later the aircraft were unloaded at Jerez de la Frontera airfield near Cadiz, which reduced the flying time by about half an hour.

During the first week an average of six to seven Ju 52s were in action, in the second week five, and in the third and fourth weeks the number of serviceable aircraft fell to four machines. The rapid drop in the

Hauptmann Rudolf Freiherr von Moreau, photographed following his return from Spain. Moreau was killed in the crash of a Ju 88 on April 4, 1939 at the age of 29.

A Ju 52/3m ready to take off from Sevilla-Tablada. Weather conditions permitting, the Ju 52 crews flew the "race-track" (from the mainland to Tetuan and back) as many as four times per day.

Herr Winckler, nicknamed "Nurmi," was sent to Spain by Junkers to oversee aircraft assembly and repair operations.

Unable to fly, a group of pilots enjoy a Spanish siesta. Pictured are, from left, Hannes Trautloft, Alfons Klein and Ottheinrich von Houwald in August 1936.

number of transport aircraft available is explained by the fact that proper maintenance was impossible while the aircraft were in constant use and that even the most vital repair facilities and equipment were absent. The sporting enthusiasm of the Ju 52 crews, who loaded their tin birds to and beyond the limit —on occasion up to forty soldiers with rifles and packs were squeezed in (authorized capacity was 17) —further contributed to the running down of the aircraft.

Together with several Heinkel mechanics the volunteer fighter pilots set about assembling the fighters; Junkers foreman Winckler, who had taken over the sparsely-equipped workshop, had to lend the fighter pilots a hand on more than on occasion. Once assembled the fighters were given the fuselage codes 2-1 through 2-6, and on August 12, 1936 the first *Kette* of He 51s flew over Sevilla. It was with a heavy heart that the leader of the *Jagdstaffel*, *Oberleutnant* Eberhardt, handed over his He 51s to the Spanish pilots Rambaud, Garcia Morato, Garcia Pardo, Salvador and Ramiro Pascual as ordered; the Germans had been forbidden to fly operational sorties, except to provide escort to the transport aircraft. The sole task of the volunteer pilots was to train Spanish crews to fly and use the Ju 52 and He 51.

Among the bomber crews, in addition to pilots von Moreau, Joseph Schmitz, Rudolf Jöster, Hans Immel, observers Max Graf Hoyos, Oskar Schmidt and others, was the then *Leutnant* Hajo Hermann, who in 1943 developed the "*Wilde Sau*" method of night fighting. Like the others he flew transport runs between the mainland and Spanish Morocco by day, but he was also given an additional night job by "Papa" Scheele. Hermann's good knowledge of the French language (he had undergone training as a military interpreter) seemed to make him the ideal man to provide the Spanish troops with instruction on the 20mm anti-aircraft guns which had been brought from Germany. After flying was over for the day Hermann was briefed by a Flak NCO on the assembly and operation of the 20mm weapon. Working with the Spanish he developed practice regulations for the automatic anti-aircraft gun, and nightly he provided instruction to his charges in sweltering conditions in a hangar at Sevilla. The guns were "motorized" by coupling the light anti-aircraft guns to the Spanish artillery's horse-drawn limbers. Live firing practice was carried out on gas-filled balloons.

The result of all this was the ludicrous situation whereby *Teniente* Hajo Hermann, as the flying "Anti-aircraft Artillery Inspector in Spain," had to

Spanish gunners practice on the German 20mm Flak 30 anti-aircraft gun.

undertake inspection trips to the anti-aircraft units spread all over the country, in addition to flying combat missions against Cartagena, Madrid, Bilbao and Santander in the Ju 52.

Efforts to camouflage the German volunteers were somewhat less than successful. Some of the "civilians" had been issued the white uniforms and caps which had been worn by the security forces at the 1936 Olympic Games in Berlin. The appearance of numbers of men attired in such a fashion could not fail to be noticed by the Spanish population. In the days and weeks that followed, blinded by so much elegance and virginal white, they were now and then moved to give the Germans ovations on the open town and city streets. The remaining, normally-attired volunteers referred condescendingly to their elegantly-dressed fellows as "the soap salesmen!"

On August 18, the day which saw the completion of assembly of the first of twelve C.R.32 fighters delivered to Tablada, an He 51 was seriously damaged in a landing accident while in the hands of a Spanish pilot. In spite of intensive training the offender's latin temperament had got the better of him. On the same day, however, Morato scored two victories in his He 51, while his squadron mate Salvador returned with three. The first victories with the C.R.32 were recorded on the 21st by Sub-Lieutenant Ceccarelli near Cordoba (a Nieuport) and on the 27th by Magistrini, who shot down the Dewoitine flown by Lieutenant de Haro near Granada.

The German volunteer detachment suffered its first loss at the middle of the month (August 15): an empty Ju 52 stalled on takeoff from Jerez de la Frontera and crashed; the bodies of pilot Schultze and flight engineer Zech were pulled from the wreck, both had died in the crash.

Spanish personnel in front of one of the He 51 fighters handed over by the Germans. The aircraft still wears its original RLM-Gray finish.

The Nationalist troop reinforcements necessary for an assault on Madrid grew by another 1,600 Moros during the early days of August, thanks to the daily shuttle flights by the Moreau *Staffel*. On August 5 the Nationalists succeeded in ferrying 2,000 men from Ceuta to Algeciras through the Strait of Gibraltar in three ships. Also on board were six batteries of artillery and their ammunition. However, a blockade by Republican destroyers prevented further ship movements in this area. The advance by Franco's units made good progress through the province of Estremadura and, after linking up with

One of the first He 51 fighters to reach Spain, seen at Escalona airfield. Visible in the background is a Fokker F VII/3 of the Nationalist transport unit, formerly based at Cabo Juby in North Africa.

the Northern Army near Badajoz, along the coast in a northwesterly direction toward Madrid. But after taking Toledo on September 28 they ran into increasing resistance from the Republicans. By November 14 Franco's forces had reached the western edge of the metropolitan area. They penetrated as far as the university quarter, but there the offensive bogged down into positional warfare which was to last more than two years.

Efforts by "Red" naval units to interfere with the air link between Spanish Morocco and the mainland led to the first offensive action by German aircraft, on August 13, 1936. Since no help in combating the troublesome floating anti-aircraft platforms was to be expected from the Nationalist side, von Moreau decided to convert two of his Ju 52s into bombers by installing the conversion kits which had been provided. An attempt was to be made to put out of action the cruiser *Jamie I* in the Strait of Gibraltar. Installation work began on August 10. First, however, the interiors of the aircraft had to be hosed down to remove the evil-smelling "offerings" left by the airsick Moros. The action was planned for the first favorable opportunity.

On August 12, the *Jamie I* was reported in the Bay of Malaga; "Bubb" Moreau ordered both machines armed. Each Ju 52 carried six 250kg bombs in three DSAC 250/VIII double magazines. Von Moreau and his bombardier manned one Ju 52, while the other was flown by Henke with *Oberleutnant* Graf Hoyos. The first aircraft took off from Sevilla-Tablada at 04:10, the second at 04:15. The two flew separately toward Barbáte. After fifty minutes of flying Henke descended from 2,000 meters, breaking out of the clouds at 500 meters, and flew past Gibraltar toward Malaga, course east-northeast. Because of the low altitude — the Fl 219b bomb-sight (built by Goerz-Boykow) did not function below 800 meters — bombardier Hoyos had to make minor course corrections with the auxiliary control column in the ventral pod and steered toward the target using the auxiliary bombsight. The first approach to the target was successful, the bombs were released and seconds later there were two flashes on the *Jamie I*. Two direct hits left the ship dead in the water and it had to be towed into Cartagena harbor with close to fifty dead on board. Due to the poor weather *Hauptmann* von Moreau was unable to locate the target, apparently having strayed off course, and landed at Tetuan with his bombs still on board.

Spurred by this success, four further Ju 52s went into the workshop at Sevilla for conversion to bombers; one was from the transport unit, the other three came from Germany. The names "PEDRO 1" to "PEDRO 3" were painted in white letters behind the center engine of three of the six bombers, the remaining three received the titles "PABLO 1" to "PABLO 3." Von Moreau took over the PEDROS *Kette*, while *Oberleutnant* Rudolf Joester took command of the "PABLOS." While this half-*Staffel* now flew exclusively on combat missions, the remaining Ju 52s continued to fly troops and materiel from the small colonial airfield at Tetuan to Jerez de la Frontera. When the supply flights ended in mid-October 1936 13,500 men and 269 tons of war materiel had been flown to the Spain.

The Ju 52/3m as a makeshift bomber with extended ventral pod. The bombardier, who sat inside, could make minor course corrections during the run-up to the target using an auxiliary control column.

The commander of the "Pablos," Oberleutnant Jöster, following the homecoming parade in June 1939. Jöster went on to become a Flugkapitän and test pilot with Heinkel at Warnemünde, piloting the He 116 D-ARFD on its record-breaking flight of July 30, 1939.

Other supply ships left Germany for Spain at brief intervals. The *Kamerun* sailed from Hamburg for

Lisbon Harbor played host to visiting foreign aircraft as early as the 1920's. Pictured here is Junkers G 24he D-1230 of the Deutsche Marineleitung during a radio test flight in 1926.

Lisbon on August 13 with a load of aviation fuel, followed on the 14th by the *Wigbert* with 372 tons of bombs, two Ju 52s and fifteen bomb magazines for installation in the Ju 52s, likewise bound for Lisbon. Prime Minister Salazar of Portugal had found it easier to respond to Germany's request for permission to use the port of Lisbon when it was shown that a steady stream of war supplies for the Republicans was flowing across the Pyrenees from France. On July 26, thirteen Potez 54 bombers for Republican Spain were loaded aboard a ship in Marseilles harbor, and twelve further aircraft of this type were flown direct to Barcelona.

The fourth German freighter, the *Girgenti*, brought 8,000 rifles, 8 million rounds of ammunition and 10,000 stick hand grenades from Hamburg to La Coruna (northwest tip of Spain). Only part of this aid was delivered from German military stocks, the rest being provided by arms dealer Josef Veltjens, a First World War pilot and holder of the *Pour le Merite*. This was the first case of a private German citizen acting as a war profiteer.

British and American war supplies for the Republican side were delivered to Gijon, Bilbao and Santander, French deliveries used Barcelona almost exclusively, while Soviet freighters sailed through the Mediterranean past Menorca and Mallorca to Barcelona, Valencia and Cartagena.

Also arriving in Spain on August 30 aboard *Wigbert* and *Kamerun*, accompanied by Herr Reuter, was the first land radio station. This had been sent to replace the provisional station set up at Provisoria using radio equipment removed from a Ju 52, which was used to control flights between Tetuan and the southern tip of Spain. Reuter took over "Air Traffic Control North" at San Fernando airfield near Salamanca. "Air Traffic Control South" at Sevilla continued to remain the duty of DF operator Fläschendränger. The installations were initially one man stations, the station director himself having to carry out the duties of telegraphist and DF operator.

At Sevilla-Tablada the German fighter pilots waited following the assembly of their He 51s. Orders arrived: transfer to Escalona del Prado! There the fighters were to be handed over to Spanish pilots, who were to fly escort missions and fighter sweeps in support of the bombers supporting General Mola's Northern Army, which was bogged down at the Sierra Guadarrama. Therefore, on August 22 the remaining five He 51s were flown to Escalona via Salamanca. Two days later the Spanish flew their first escort mission for Ju 52s attacking the Republican airfield at Getafe. The result: two crash-landings and two unserviceable He 51s! One of the pilots pulled his aircraft out of an impossible skidding turn at an altitude of five meters, came down like an elevator and landed the machine flat on its belly. The Spaniards simply could not handle the rather sensitive single-seat fighters.

It was on this same August 23 that Madrid experienced its first bombing attack. The number of aircraft involved is not known, however the damage inflicted was minor. The bombers' target was the War Ministry, but it is more likely that the motivation was simply "now it's your turn."

At the urging of the German fighter pilots the *Feuerzauber* detachment leader, Scheele, held

First fraternization between German pilots and, who else, Spain's female element. The Senores, from left: von Houwald, Ekkehard Hefter, a Spanish officer and Klein.

discussions with Franco, in which he convinced him to allow the remaining three He 51s to be flown in action by German pilots in future. *Oberst* Warlimont (alias "Woltersdorf"), the RKM's representative with Franco, was able to obtain the necessary authorization in Berlin. From then on the "Eberhardt *Kette*" was over the front daily. Most of the missions were flown by Eberhardt, Trautloft and Knüppel, who dubbed themselves the "Hunters of Guadarrama."

The Germans had their first encounter with the enemy on the afternoon of August 25. What followed was described by Hannes Trautloft in his diary: "Suddenly Eberhardt gives the attack signal and dives away in the direction of Madrid. I watch him and catch sight of a Red Breguet XIX about two kilometers in front of us and a good 500 meters lower. He flies calmly toward us. I switch on the gunsight, my hands shaking from excitement. While diving, I suddenly see two more Red Breguets close by on the left. When they spot us they quickly turn about. I attack the nearest one, Knüppel the other. As I approach I see the gunner aiming his gun at me, and then the muzzle lights up as he opens fire. It all looks rather harmless. I fly to within about 30 meters and open up with my machine-guns. With the first burst the gunner disappears; his machine-gun points vertically toward the sky. The Red now pushes over into a steep dive. My second burst is brief, but on target, because all of a sudden the Breguet rears up, rolls over, roars toward the earth in a steep, uncontrolled dive and smashes into the ground north of the village of Comenar. My first victory! The Legion's first victory as well! I look around for Eberhardt and Knüppel. The second Red is flying at the same altitude, about 800 meters in front of me. Eberhardt attacks him from below in a steep climb, and suddenly a long spurt of flame appears from the right side of the fuselage. The Breguet plunges toward earth, a burning mass. Knüppel runs into trouble. His guns jam and he is forced to break off the attack. The Red makes a run for it. I try to catch him, but he dives away so steeply that I can't reach him. Below us lies Madrid, close enough to touch. We rejoin formation, laughing to ourselves and celebrating like children, and fly back."

It is only natural if today we feel a certain uneasiness over this last sentence. But any criticism should be leveled at those whose lack of reason demanded that weapons should be the ultimate means of settling political controversy. Those who allow young men to be trained to kill should not be surprised that they strive to do it well.

The "Pedros" and "Pablos," the two Ju 52 bomber *Ketten*, were employed against targets in the various regions in rapid succession. One day the bombers took off from Salamanca to attack targets on the Toledo front, a few days later Cartagena was the

A captured Breguet XIX. This obsolete biplane was forced to serve as a "maid of all work," taking on the reconnaissance, medium bomber, and occasionally, low-altitude attack roles.

Hauptmann Herwig Knüppel, one of the original pilots of the Eberhardt Kette. Knüppel was killed over France on May 19, 1940, as Kommandeur of II./JG 26.

Der Reichsminister der Luftfahrt und
Oberbefehlshaber der Luftwaffe

Der am 26. August 1936 in Gegend Papstraße Leon erfolgte Abschuß eines Flugzeuges, Typ Breguet wird dem

Oberleutnant
Herwig Knüppel

als 1. Luftsieg

bestätigt.

Berlin, den 21. April 1938.

Generalfeldmarschall

Official confirmation of Herwig Knüppel's first victory.

objective. In this case the jumping-off base was Granada. Following a transfer flight to Leon the small group of bombers flew cross-country to interrupt the unloading of vessels in Bilbao. The "Eberhardt *Kette*" often provided a fighter escort when the bombers moved to new bases. In many cases, especially on night raids, a fighter escort could be dispensed with. Italian or Spanish fighters often provided an escort during daylight bombing missions by the Ju 52s. During the night of August 18 Henke, now a reserve officer, made a lone night harassment raid on Badajoz. During the same period the Spanish bomber squadron which had been formed on Ju 52s also attacked the city several times. Understandably such weak, poorly-planned operations failed to achieve any noticeable success. The "Pedros" and "Pablos" suffered their first casualty on November 4 over Madrid, when *Leutnant* Kolbitz, who was sitting in the aircraft's ventral pod, was seriously wounded by a Republican fighter. His comrades were unable to pull him into the fuselage and he was crushed by the still-extended pod when the bomber touched down.

On August 26, Eberhardt and Knüppel each accounted for a Breguet XIX. Knüppel described the action: "We're flying west. Suddenly Eberhardt gives the attack signal. Ahead of us are three enemy aircraft! Full throttle and attack! I select one of the Breguet XIX reconnaissance aircraft. My two comrades pull up and attack the others. Now I have him in my sights. Fire! He dives away. Another attack; his motor stops, the observer is no longer firing. The Breguet crashes just behind the enemy lines. I make a loop for joy over my victory. But a Red fighter, a French high-wing monoplane, is sitting right behind me on my tail. I turn toward him and he takes evasive action. I am unable to catch him as he is faster and climbs better."

The next day, August 27, Knüppel scored again. A lone, slow Nieuport 52 fighter fell victim to a few well-placed shots and went down on fire. The enemy pilot was the Englishman Cartwright, a member of the Captain Luna's International Squadron. It is noteworthy that in this initial phase of the civil war the Russians Kopets, Erlikin and Kovalievski, the Englishmen Cartwright, de Wett, Clifford and Collins, the Italian Locatelli and other foreigners were already flying for the Republicans as fighter pilots. It should also be mentioned that the foreigners in Republican service were extremely well paid; for example, in 1937 the American Tinker received a monthly salary of 18,000 *pesetas* (in contrast, the pay of a non-commissioned officer was 800 *pesetas*). By August 1936 there was another international Republican squadron, in which flew the Frenchmen Abel Guide, Veniel, Renant, Darry, Bernay, Valbert, Thomas, Gouinet, Bourgeois, Isard, Poulain, Heilmann, Hant, Gensous and di Campo, the Czech Kozek, as well as Belgians, Italians and Englishmen. Available aircraft included Dewoitine D 371, D 372, D 501, Spad S 510 and Loire-Nieuport LN-46 fighters.

A familiar picture for the early "Spaniards," the village well in Escalona. The airfield used by the German fighters was located just outside the small town.

In spite of the very makeshift accommodations provided the fighter pilots at Escalona — the He 51 fighters sat in the open, replacement parts and ammunition were stored under tarpaulins at the wooded edge of the airfield — the hunting instincts of the small group had been awakened.

The following is an entry in Trautloft's diary from August 29:

"On our way back two French Potez bombers suddenly appear, flying to one side of us, about 100 meters higher. They have apparently already spotted us, because they beat it for home at full throttle. We gain on them slowly. Above the peak of the Sierra Guadarrama we catch up with the trailing aircraft. Eberhardt closes to fifty meters and fires until his machine-guns jam. I take his place and fire off almost all of my ammunition. I am so close to him that I can make out every detail of the Potez 54. The dorsal gunner has long been silent, his arm hangs motionless over his machine-gun. A long banner of oil spews from the fuselage and in an instant my aircraft is sprayed over and over with oil. My windscreen has become opaque and I am forced to break off the attack. However, Knüppel is now sitting close behind the Red and firing. His machine, too, is soon completely covered with oil. I watch as Eberhardt opens fire again, and at the same time observe a Red fighter appear and move into position behind my two comrades. When I cut in the Red pulls up his Dewoitine so quickly that I cannot follow. He gains height rapidly and disappears. Eberhardt and Knüppel stalwartly attack the Potez bomber, but it flies on toward enemy territory in a steep, even glide, leaving behind a long trail of oil. From this close range we can't possibly have missed. We suspect that the pilot's seat of the Potez bomber is armored. Therefore in future we will have to attack from in front."

The next day the four He 51s chased three Potez bombers. And once again the results were less than satisfying, as Trautloft reported:

"Once again I'm sitting 50 meters behind the bomber, again I fire almost all my ammunition, and instead of going down the fellow again flies away in a steep glide and sprays his oil in my face. My windscreen is badly oiled up, I can scarcely see a thing. Then I am seized by a towering rage, more than anything I would like to ram the Red. Then Knüppel and Eberhardt attack, both with the same lack of success. We are already deep in enemy territory and still the bomber does not fall. I clean my windscreen as best I can. Then I attempt an attack from in front in an attempt to knock out the pilot. But he has meanwhile got a good lead, my machine is not fast enough. In addition we are almost out of ammunition, so there is nothing left to do but break off the attack."

As it later turned out, both of the stubborn bombers crashed near Madrid on the return flight. They belonged to the bomber squadron of *Commandante* Marty, which had thus suffered badly within a period of a few days.

Just as Trautloft had scored the Legion's first victory, so too he became the first German fighter pilot to be shot down, on August 30:

"Eberhardt assembles the *Kette* just before the front. In doing so Hefter and I relax our vigilance somewhat, and a Red fighter pilot cleverly takes advantage of this. Suddenly I see machine-gun bullets striking my right wing and then there is banging all around me. I want to turn away by banking quickly, but before I can do so my machine stands on its nose and goes into a fast, left-hand spin. Shot down? All my senses are wide awake, tensed to the extreme. I try everything possible to regain control of my aircraft, but the control column flops back and forth with no resistance — controls shot away! Now there is only one thing to do: get out as quickly as possible! I unfasten my straps and dive out of my machine head first. Above me my white tennis shoes stand out clearly against the blue background of the sky. I pull the rip cord, there is a jerk and then I am hanging under my parachute with a wonderful feeling of security. Far below I see my aircraft. It smashes into the ground and a flash of flame shoots up. Sadly I look at the spot where my good old He 51 with the number 4 met its end. I can see nothing above as the parachute blocks my vision — I must be about 2,500 meters up. I hear the loud roar of an engine and the tack-tack-tack of machine-guns. It's meant for me. The Red continues to fire away at me, a small reflection of the urge to destroy, the lack of mercy with which this civil war is being fought. Fire away, you ass, I think bitterly, feeling an impulse to shout scornfully at him. In the same breath I cling to my life and would like more than anything to shrivel up into a tiny ball. But fear of death also has a limit, and once I have crossed it I become indifferent to it all. With an almost cheerful imperturbability I await what chance, fate, God's will — what difference does it make what one calls it — has decided for me.

The highly-decorated Hannes Trautloft in June 1939. With five victories he was one of the top volunteer fighter pilots of the early period of the Spanish Civil War, together with Knüppel and Eberhardt.

A Potez 54 which force-landed behind the front. Members of the recovery party have already removed the aircraft's wings and engines.

Trautloft, Oblt.
4. J / 88.

Sevilla, den 20. 2. 1937.

Betr.: Verlustmeldung einer Pistole.

An
4.Staffel.

Am 30.8.36 wurde ich abgeschossen und müsste mit Fallschirm abspringen. Meine Pistole befand sich in der Seitentasche im Fuehrersitz der Maschine. Die Maschine und Pistole ging beim Aufschlag restlos zu Bruch.

Ich bitte um Abschreibung der Pistole.

Tz.

Oberleutnant.

There could be no war without its paper train. This is a loss report submitted by Trautloft: "On 30.8.1936 I was shot down and forced to bail out. My pistol was located in the cockpit side pocket. The machine and pistol were completely destroyed on impact. I request the pistol be written off."

"All of a sudden the machine-gun fire stops, Eberhardt and Hefter have chased him away." (Trautloft was able to gain his revenge on September 1, when he shot down a Nieuport fighter.)

A day later it was the Italians who had to learn the hard way. The Fiat C.R.32s of Monico and Castellani were shot down in a dogfight with Dewoitine, Nieuport 52 and Hawker Fury fighters of the International Squadron. Squadron Leader Castellani was dragged to his death by an uncontrolled mob.

By the end of the month the Nationalists had assembled the pitifully small number of aircraft left to them, which was not quite enough to form three squadrons on various types. About twenty Breguet XIX A-2s were available for the light bombing and reconnaissance roles and six Nieuport 52 C-1s were assigned to the fighter squadron. Five or six light transports of English or American manufacture made up the rest of the Nationalist Spanish "Air Force." Also on strength with the newly-formed units were several Dornier *Wal*, three Savoia S.62 and four Macchi M.41 seaplanes. The deliveries of He 51s and Ju 52s, some by sea, some flown directly from Germany, which were getting under way, were thus a welcome and urgently needed reinforcement for the Spanish squadrons. At the same time conversion to the unfamiliar types began under German leadership.

Now and again there were uncomfortable incidents involving overflights by Ju 52s on the Dessau-Stuttgart-Rome-Sevilla route while *Lufthansa* aircraft of the same type continued to fly the same commercial routes as before. On August 9, *Flugkapitän* von Bastian strayed off course and landed his Ju 52 D-AMYM, which carried full military equipment but wore a civilian registration, at Barajas airfield near Madrid. Following a brief exchange of words with DLH representative von Winterfeldt, who hurried up to the aircraft as it taxied in, von Bastian took off again at once. Unfortunately the pilot was compelled to land prematurely when his fuel ran out after a 400-kilometer flight. The aircraft again came down in Republican territory, landing at Badajoz airfield near the Portuguese border. The crew was immediately taken into custody, the aircraft confiscated and taken to Madrid. The incident resulted in the immediate grounding of six DLH aircraft on government territory. The grounding order was not lifted until the next day, after the German chargé d'affaires had lodged a strenuous protest. The seized

Undoubtedly the oldest type in the varied collection of aircraft used by the Nationalists was the ancient de Havilland D.H. 9. The totally white fin and rudder of the W 34hi in the background, 13-3, was quite unusual.

Ju 52, on the other hand, in spite of repeated German demands for its return, remained at the government airfield at Barajas, where it was destroyed in a bombing raid in October 1936.

In contrast, the courier aircraft of *Sonderstab* W, which were navigated by experienced crews, had no difficulty in finding their destination airfields. From November 1936 these courier and long-range transport aircraft were in the air four times per week, and by the end of hostilities in February 1939 had lost only three aircraft.

On August 20, *Oberleutnant* von Moreau took off from Sevilla in a Ju 52 loaded with foodstuffs and set course for Toledo. The objective of the night mission was to drop supplies to a small group of Nationalists surrounded in the *Alcazar* in Toledo. Von Moreau

Miles M 3 Falcon Six courier aircraft in front of the hangars at Tablada. The "30" in the aircraft's code (30-55) indicated that the subject was a single-engined sport aircraft.

General Aircraft S.T.12 Monospar, a small twin-engined machine used by the Nationalist Air Force, at Sanjurjo airfield.

30-59 was the sole example of the Monocoupe 90A, an American-made, shoulder wing monoplane.

approached the objective in a glide from an altitude of 4,000 meters, with the aircraft's engines throttled back to avoid alerting the Republicans to his presence. The entire load was dropped in one pass, however it fell outside the fortress walls.

After landing at Sevilla von Moreau ordered the machine loaded again. This time he would attempt the supply drop by day, when he would have a better chance of putting the supplies down on target. On the afternoon of the 21st von Moreau swung out to the east, descended to an altitude of 500 meters and dropped the food, which was packed in metal canisters. In spite of heavy ground fire the entire load fell within the inner courtyard, whose dimensions were a mere 60 X 70 meters. The mission was a success, but von Moreau's Ju 52 had been riddled with bullets. Nevertheless, the return flight was made without incident.

In the meantime the Anti-aircraft Instructional Detachment (20mm), with its three instructors under the command of *Wachtmeister* Hakenholt, was busy training Spanish crews at various sectors of the front. Further deliveries of 20mm anti-aircraft guns had been requested by Franco, and large numbers of personnel were required. As the result of an arrangement worked out by the German Consulate, several Spanish-Germans were attached to the instructional unit to act as interpreters.

Having grown to about 30,000 men, by the end of August 1936 Franco's land forces were ready to go on the offensive. Included in this number were the *Regulares*, about 20,000 Moroccan soldiers under General Yagüe, the Spanish Foreign Legion — the

Ju 52 D-AMYM in Madrid. The aircraft's new owners give the communist salute as they pose on the fuselage.

With a few strokes of the brush from a red paint-pot the German Junkers becomes a Republican aircraft.

so called *"El Tercio,"* battle groups of the *Falange* (fascists) and *Requeté* Militia (royalists) with their self-appointed leaders. The units of General Queipo de Llano were to advance along the Mediterranean coast, supported by Italian troops. The combat value and the discipline of these units, in particular the quality of their leaders, were to be the subject of sharp criticism from the German side during the course of joint operations.

Due to the close proximity to the front of Escalona airfield, at which was stationed the Eberhardt *Kette* as well as a Spanish *Escuadrilla de reconocimiento* (reconnaissance squadron), a transfer to Caceres was ordered on September 1, 1936. Thanks to recent deliveries of He 51 fighters, there was now enough aircraft to form a complete *Staffel.* Of the total of nine Heinkel fighters, two were now assigned to the Spaniards Morato and Salvador. On September 2, Morato succeeded in shooting down a Nieuport 52 in his new machine.

Leutnant von Houwald now assumed command of the second He 51 *Kette* at Caceres. Von Houwald was later a member of the "Experts Patrol," which shot down five enemy aircraft over Alcubierre, near Zaragoza, on October 19, 1936. During the first half of September von Houwald's *Kette* was responsible for protecting the airfield against attacks by Republican aircraft.

Early in September Morato arranged to have himself attached to the Italians, with their significantly better C.R.32 fighters. Morato was to score 36 of his total of 40 kills flying the Fiat. At this point in the war the C.R.32 was superior to any fighter on the Republican side, including the imported Dewoitine, Loire and Spad machines, while the He 51 could just hold its own with the Nieuport and Hawker Fury.

On September 5, von Houwald shot down a Nieuport and a Breguet XIX, while Knüppel accounted for a Loire 46; a Potez 54 was brought down on the 6th, again by Knüppel:

"We had the Potez bomber right in the middle and placed him in a crossfire. And as we were attacking from the front this time, he had no chance to blow his oil at us and dove away steeply. Just beyond the front one man baled out. Soon afterward the bomber plunged vertically into the ground east of Talavera."

Eberhardt also shot down a Potez. Base of operations that day was Navalmoral. From there that the fighters intervened in the fighting on the ground for

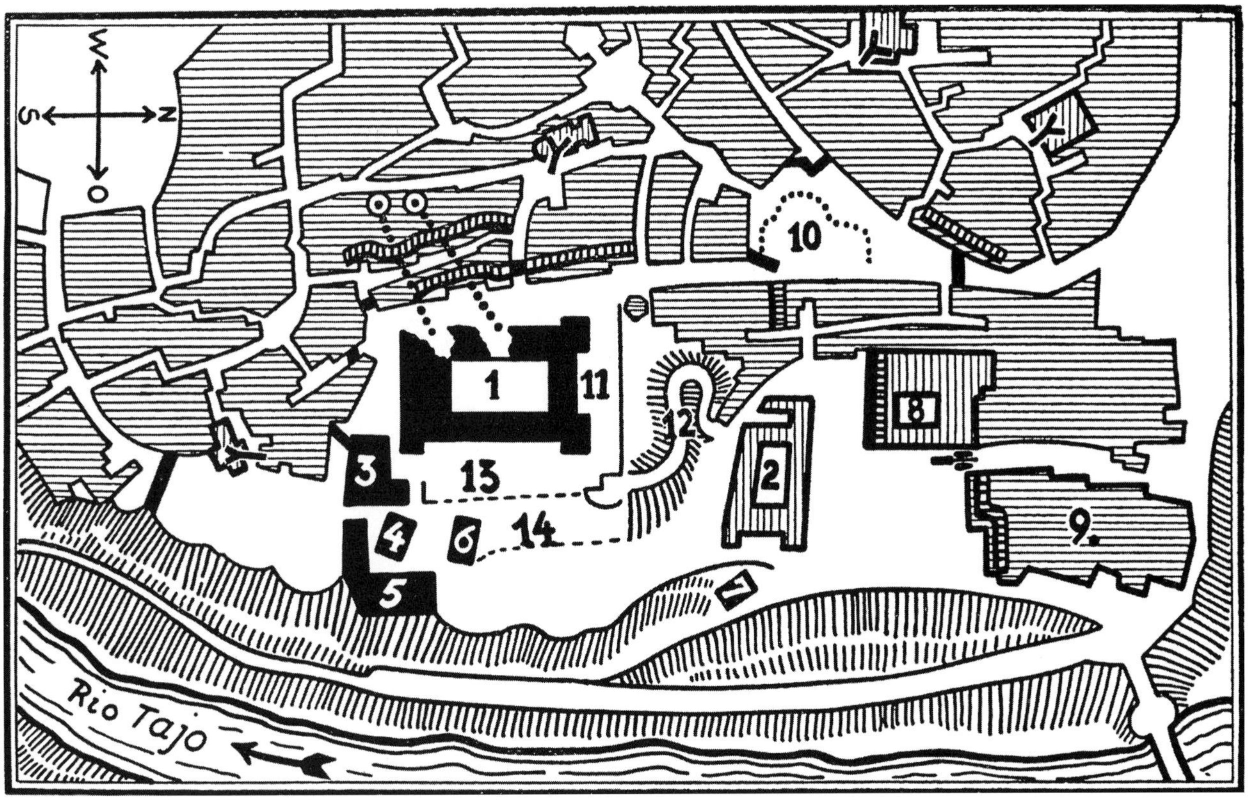

Site plan of Toledo's Alcazar showing: (1) inner courtyard, (2) military government, (3) cadet barracks, (4) kitchen and dining room, (5) stables, (6) riding school, (7) granary, (8) Santa Cruz hospital, (9) Monastery de la Concepcion, (10) Plaza Zocodover, (11) square in front of the northern facade, (12) serpentine road, (13) upper esplanade, (14) lower esplanade. ▬ barricades, ≺ machine-gun positions on buildings, ═ gun positions of the besieging forces, ⊙ entrances to the mining tunnels.

Destruction of the western facade of the Alcazar caused by two mine blasts.

Italy supplied Fiat C.R.32 aircraft for use by the Nationalist fighter squadrons. The Chirri was the most maneuverable fighter of its time.

the first time. On September 15 they carried out low-level attacks in front of the attacking infantry in an effort to add impetus to the advance.

During the advance on the Tajo the fighters also flew escort missions from the forward airfields at Navalmoral and Talavera, accompanying Ju 52 bombers to the Madrid front. Anti-aircraft guns not needed for the defense of the Sevilla-Tablada supply base were sent to this sector of the front.

In the meantime the Italian Fiats began to establish air superiority over the Talavera front. On September 11, they shot down two Breguets and five fighters, and on the 13th two fighters (for the loss of Patriarca). On the 16th a Breguet, two fighters and a Potez 54 were accounted for, but Lieutenant Franceschi was shot down and captured. The outstanding pilots during this period were Morato, Dequal, Mantelli, Magistrini and Baschirotto.

The Italians added the inscription "*Monico presente*" to their C.R.32s. As described earlier, *Teniente* (Lieutenant) Monico, their first squadron leader, had been shot down in a dogfight, came down in Republican territory and supposedly had been dragged to his death after being taken prisoner. The battle cry "*Monico presente*" illustrated his squadron mates' desire for revenge. This desire was confirmed by the numbers of Republican aircraft shot down.

As a result of pressure exerted by the English, from August 31, 1936 German supply ships were no longer permitted to use the Portugese port of Lisbon, and from then on they were forced to make the longer sea voyage to Sevilla. The first ship denied the use of Lisbon was the *Usaramo*, which was making its second trip with supplies for Spain. The ship and its cargo of twenty He 46 aircraft for the Spanish armed forces, radio equipment, aircraft replacement parts, munitions and chemicals were forced to divert to Sevilla. At the end of September the twenty tactical reconnaissance machines were still sitting at the edge of the airfield at Tablada, as there were no experienced Spanish crews to fly the aircraft.

When the Nationalist headquarters moved to Cacares, Scheel and his small staff went as well. *Major* Deichmann, as his deputy, took over the administration and offices of the main supply base at Sevilla. These functions were carried out from the Hotel "Christina," which had been made available for use by the Germans.

On September 17, German fighters again encountered enemy fighters near Madrid, as Trautloft vividly described:

"A Dewoitine races toward us in a steep dive. I just have time to warn Eberhardt and Knüppel, the fellow is almost within firing range. I turn and fly straight at him. At high speed he climbs back up to a position 500 meters above our *Kette*. Now I spot a Hawker Fury, but he quickly dives away in the direction of Madrid. The pilot in the Dewoitine, on the other hand, is a more daring fellow. His machine is superior to ours and he uses this advantage skillfully. He circles around 500 meters above us and waits for a favorable moment to dive on us. We keep a sharp eye on him. Then our *Kette* splits up, perhaps in this way we can entice him down. It works, he attacks Eberhardt. Knüppel and I move in at once. As we open fire from about 300 meters away he flies off. We race after him, firing like mad. But his machine is too fast. It's time we received faster aircraft."

Knüppel did manage to force down a Nieuport behind the lines that day. The Republican pilot set his aircraft on fire. Franco had offered 40,000 Francs to any Spanish pilot who brought down a Republican machine intact on Nationalist soil. On the other hand the Republican government offered 50,000 *pesetas* for every Nationalist aircraft shot down.

The Fiats enjoyed further success, and in the meantime the Spaniards Salvador and Salas had joined the Italians. During the fighting on the 25th, 26th and 27th the Italian squadron shot down four fighters, three Breguets and a Potez 54. The most successful pilots during the last third of September were Morato (8 victories), Dequal, Buffali, Salvador, Salas, Magistrini, Patriarca, Chianese, Mantelli, Montegnacco and Presel. Hardest hit was the International Squadron: Clifford, Smith-Piggot, Mouillinet, Maurice, Locatelli and Collins were shot down. Locatelli had brought down the first Ju 52 on September 25 over Toledo.

It was deemed necessary to station German seaplanes in southern Spain to watch over the flow of sea traffic and the ports where the ships discharged their cargoes. The first aircraft was an He 60 from a German warship, which landed at Cadiz in October with *Oberleutnant* Karl-Heinz Wolff (observer), a pilot and two mechanics. Soon afterward *Leutnant* Siegmund Storp was stationed at Cadiz with a further He 60. Operating from Cadiz the two crews patrolled the Strait of Gibraltar as far Almeria in the east.

Also sent from Germany was an 88mm Flak battery for the defense of the airfield at Sevilla-Tablada. Under the command of *Oberleutnant* Aldinger, the battery occupied positions at the edge of the airfield. Arriving on the same ship as *Hauptmann* Deichmann were an air force staff engineer and two special duties officers, whose job it was to support the activities of the still small repair facility and perform the functions of an air park. The growing organizational demands were simply beyond the capabilities of the small Scheel staff.

Following a brief side-trip to Avila, on September 23 the He 51s of the German fighter *Staffel* transferred to Vitoria on the Bilbao front. There, in northern Spain, the Republicans were still holding on to a strip of coastline approximately sixty kilometers deep between Bilbao and Gijon. Three days later the fighters scored a success: Hefter and Klein each destroyed a Breguet, while von Houwald brought down a Vickers Vildebeest.

In 1964, Trautloft received an illuminating letter from a participant in the September 26 engagement; Juan Maluquer, a former observer in the Republican Air Force, wrote:

"Dear Herr Trautloft,
It will perhaps interest you that we once met each other in the air as enemies, in September 1936 in the Vitoria area. As a reserve officer in the Spanish Army I was called up when the civil war began and during the first months saw action with the Republican air units. I was sent to Bilbao where I was employed as an observer in a Breguet XIX. While based there we exchanged fire several times with the two pairs of He 51s stationed at Vitoria, one of which was led by you. After the war I bought your book *A Fighter Pilot in Spain* and naturally read it with great interest. In doing so I learned that *Lt.* Hefter, who was later killed in a crash near Vitoria, had once shot up my aircraft, without however shooting it down as he incorrectly believed. My pilot simply dived away, as I had expended all my ammunition. We then made our way home at an altitude of ten meters. There were 21 hits in the wings of our aircraft. I do not know if Lt. Hefter took any hits from my return fire.

I was happy to read that you had survived the Second World War. It would be an honor for me to meet you if you were to come to Barcelona some time and to exchange memories.

Respectfully Yours Juan J. Maluquer Wahl"

This incident illustrates that, in contrast to the war on the ground, where both sides carried out such abominable practices as executions, torture and pillage at and behind the front, the war in the air, with isolated exceptions, was conducted with fairness by both sides.

Leutnant Hefter, the subject of the preceding letter, was killed when the wing of his aircraft struck the tower of the town hall in Vitoria on September 28. The next day the *Jagdstaffel* moved back to Avila. On September 30, Trautloft jumped a Potez bomber, which crashed into the ground at a shallow angle trailing a long banner of smoke. A second Potez was shot down by Eberhardt.

At the end of September six new He 51s and ten pilots arrived as reinforcements: Strümpel, Radusch, Henrici, von Bothmer, von Gilsa, Rehahn, Kowalski, Gödecke, Sawallisch and Mratzek. Since several mechanics had also at last arrived, it was now possible to divide the unit. The three surviving He 51s from the six which had arrived on the *Usaramo* were handed over to the Spaniards. Eberhardt led one *Kette* to Barahona, while Trautloft took the other to Leon on the northern front. There the task of the fighters was to escort supply and bombing missions to the surrounded city of Oviedo. A Fokker F VII/3m was assigned to the *Staffel* as a communications aircraft and was used to maintain contact between the two elements of the unit.

On October 19, the Knüppel half-*Staffel*, operating

Hefters' He 51 burns in front of Vitoria's town hall. As the Staffel flew over the city in formation at very low altitude, the wing of Hefter's aircraft struck the tower of the town hall, causing his He 51 to crash.

from Zaragoza, claimed five victories in a battle with twelve enemy aircraft. A Fokker, a Breguet and a Nieuport were credited to *Lt.* Henrici, while von Houwald and Strümpell each shot down a Nieuport. Henrici brought down the Breguet by ramming its wing with his undercarriage.

At that time the forces of the German volunteer detachment were equipped as follows:

14 He 51	fighters
20 Ju 52/3m	transports and bombers
6 He 45	reconnaissance aircraft
2 He 60	maritime reconnaissance aircraft
1 He 50	dive-bomber for test purposes
2 Hs 123	dive-bombers for test purposes with trials unit at Jerez de la Frontera.
3 batteries	20mm anti-aircraft guns
1 battery	88mm anti-aircraft guns

Leutnant Oskar Henrici photographed before his departure for Spain. As was usual during those years, he had received his fighter pilot training with Fliegergruppe (S) Schleissheim.

Always ready for a joke, Herwig Knüppel protects one of his flock with an umbrella, in this case Leutnant Paul Rehahn.

Following a request by the Spanish military, the first German Army units arrived at the end of September. Consisting of 122 men, the small force comprised two armored companies (personnel from the 4th Panzer Regiment, Schweinfurt and the 6th Panzer Regiment, Neuruppin) with forty-one Panzer I tanks, a transport company and an anti-tank unit with twenty anti-tank guns. Another armored company followed in October, as well as a radio intercept unit and an unknown number of guns. *Oberstleutnant* Ritter von Thoma, formerly commander of 2nd Battalion, 4th Panzer Regiment, arrived in Spain on September 20 to take command of the armored unit. General Staff *Oberst* Freiherr von Funck was named "Overall Commander Army," a post he was to hold until the end of the civil war. During his time in Spain he conducted his activities under the pseudonym "Imker."

With the assignment of the army units, *Feuerzauber*, which was purely a Luftwaffe operation, had been become "Operation *Guido*," so named after the representative of the RKM, *Oberstleutnant* Warlimont, who used the pseudonym "Guido" as well as "Woltersdorf." At first the panzer battalion was active as an instructional unit with the code-name "Drohne." On completing its duties it was to hand over its vehicles to the Spaniards. It turned out, however, that it was more valuable from the point of view of morale to allow the Germans to accompany Spanish units in offensive operations, and this practice was retained for the following campaigns.

Foraging from the food basket while at sitting in readiness at Vitoria. Unteroffizier Erwin Sawallisch (beside Knüppel on the right, with empty plate) can scarcely wait.

As previously mentioned, Luftwaffe transport operations between Spanish Morocco and Jerez ceased on October 11, 1936. The Italians had also attempted to take part in these transport operations. On July 28, 1936, eleven Savoia-Marchetti S.M.81 transports took off from Cagliari, Sardinia for Nador in Spanish Morocco. The unit was led by Colonel Vononi. However, since such transport flights seemed too unspectacular to the Italians they very soon gave up on such activities. Relations between the Spaniards and Italians were already none too good; the exaggerated Italian propaganda, which celebrated the C.T.V. as an assembly of heroes, was a constant irritant, as was the vanity of the Italian High Command. The latter were overly concerned with matters of prestige and went to great lengths to see that Italian units participated only in actions which promised success and had useful propaganda value.

Of course the Italian fighter pilots were unconcerned about such criticisms. In the meantime, together with the Spaniards under Morato, they had continued to decimate the Republican Air Force over the Madrid-Cordoba front. But rumors of the appearance of fast Russian bombers and Soviet fighters with retractable undercarriages were beginning to intensify. In fact the first I-15 *Chato* and I-16 *Rata* fighters and SB-2 *Katiuska* bombers had begun arriving at Cartagena in mid-October and were being assembled at Los Alacares. The civil war was beginning to widen.

Historically, it is not justifiable to blame the fascists alone for the fact that the civil war became two-and-a-half years of torture for the Spanish people. Southern France had become a Republican supply base, and British ships were delivering war materiel. From the Soviet Union and France came instructors, pilots and tanks. As a result of the efforts of recruiting offices all over the world the strength of the International Brigades in this early phase of the war had already grown to approximately 30,000 men. These brigades soon formed the backbone of the Republican Army. Radicals and idealists from all over the world came to join the brigades: Russians, Frenchmen, Britons, Czechs, Hungarians, Poles, Mexicans, Yugoslavians, Americans and German immigrants. In the final analysis they would be cruelly sacrificed on the altar of high politics. Trade unions, socialist parties and humanitarian organizations helped financially and influenced world opinion through clever propaganda.

Among those who flew for the Republican side were Americans Albert Bämler (4 victories) and Frank Tinker (8 victories). A true fortune hunter was the Frenchman William Laboussière (5 victories), who later also risked his life for China. Russian fighter aces included Serov (16 victories), Rychagov (15), Yeremenko (14), Denisov (13), Bobrov (13) and Lakeiev (12). The Soviet air element was commanded by J.W. Smushkevich, who was usually known only by his pseudonym of "General Douglas." As "Comrade Martin," F. Agalzow exercised the apparently necessary function of political commissar.

Still largely unknown are the activities of Austrian and German pilots with the Republican air forces. In a series of articles on the history of air warfare, an East German magazine identified the Austrians Tom Dobias and Walter Koraus and four Germans. Of the latter, Ernst G. Schacht had emigrated to the Soviet Union in the early 1930s, where he received training as a fighter pilot after obtaining Soviet citizenship. Schacht subsequently went to Spain in November 1936, where he is said to have scored several kills. Kurt Schmitt joined the International Brigade without changing his nationality. He was killed on July 20, 1937 during the fighting near Brunete, while flying with Grupo 28, a close-support unit equipped with Soviet-made R-5 and R-Z light bombers. Also killed during the Battle of Brunete was Hermann Feld of Berlin. After emigrating to France he had obtained his pilot's license and joined an I-15 squadron as a volunteer early in the Spanish Civil War; his code-name was "German Perez Lopez." The last was Wilhelm von Malinkkrodt, who had been active before the war as a test pilot with C.A.S.A./Madrid. He joined the Republicans in July 1936 and was active flying communications and staff aircraft.

One of the most successful Nationalist pilots of foreign origin was the Belgian Count de Hemricourt, who achieved ten victories. In 1940 he flew to England and fought against German fascism, until on May 21, 1941 he was shot down and killed over France. Such a man hardly fit into the standard mould, even less so than the Irish volunteer companies which fought on the Nationalist side.

In judging the civil war one should free himself of all party subjectivity and consider the idealistic motives which undoubtedly motivated the participants on both sides. It would be an oversimplification to reduce the civil war to a battle between democracy and dictatorship. A conflict between dictatorships of the right and left would probably be closer to the truth, but influences with clerical, monarchistic, capitalistic, separatist and anarchistic origins should at least be mentioned.

On October 25, 1936, the Nationalist Air Force carried out an aerial parade over Madrid as a demonstration of its strength. Forty-eight bombers and 32 fighters took part in the morning, and almost 100 aircraft in the afternoon. While hundreds of leaflets demanding the surrender of the city fluttered from the bomb cells of the bombers, the fighters put on a daring display of aerobatics low over the city's rooftops. As befitted the mentality of their pilots, the Italian Fiats put on an especially spirited display.

The demonstration had apparently failed to create any lasting impression, because on October 29 the Republicans launched their counteroffensive in front of Madrid. The attack saw the first use in Spain of Russian T-26 tanks (9.5 tons, 45mm gun) and SB-2

T 26 tank captured by the Nationalists. The B-version of this Russian 10-ton tank was armed with a 4.5cm gun and two or three machine-guns.

A Chato squadron. This I-15 wears the Republican national marking — red, yellow and violet bands — on its rudder.

The Soviet SB-2 Katiuska medium bomber provided the Republicans with an effective offensive weapon.

Katiuska bombers (known to the Nationalists as Martin bombers), with thirty of the former and three squadrons of the latter being committed. The first SB-2 was shot down by Mantelli and Sozzi on November 2. While the German fighters met no enemy aircraft for weeks, over the Madrid front the Fiats had frequent encounters with the fast Russian aircraft. On November 4 the I-15 fighters put in their first appearance, ten of these aircraft appearing over the front. They shot down a German Ju 52 and badly damaged a Spanish Ju 52, forcing it to land. Meanwhile the Italians ran into ten *Chatos*. Magistrini was shot down and killed, while Dequal was also shot down but escaped by parachute. Two other Fiats suffered damage in landing accidents. On the other side two Russian pilots lost their way on their first mission and landed at Segovia. They greeted the Nationalist "welcoming committee" with shouts of "Hail Moscow!"

These events occurred during the period of increased deliveries of war materiel to the Republican side; the first prisoners from the International Brigades were interrogated and provided an insight into the organization of this body of troops.

The German component of the international brigades comprised the following units:

"Centuria Thälmann": Commander Albert Schreiner
In October 1936 this was reorganized into the following units:

"Ernst Thälmann" Battalion: Commander Paul Hornick
"Chapayev" Battalion: Commander Klaus Becker, Otto Brunner
"Edgar André" Battalion: Commander Hans Kahle
"Hans Beimler" Battalion: Commander Heinz Schramm
"12th of February" Battalion: Commander Otto Jürgensen

Pasaremos

15. Oktober 1937

EIN JAHR XI. BRIGADE

ERSTE INTERNATIONALE BRIGADE

MADRID
CASA DEL CAMPO
BOADILLA DEL MONTE
LAS ROZAS
REMISA
JARAMA
GUADALAJARA
UTANDE
BRUNETE
QUIJORNA
QUINTO
BELCHITE
MEDIANA

All five battalions belonged to the XI International Brigade under Brigadier Richard Staimer (alias "General Hoffmann") of the Republican People's Army. The volunteers were almost exclusively members of the KPD (German Communist Party) with a very small percentage from the SPD (Social Democratic Party), who had answered a call from the central committee of the German Communist Party to join the battle against fascism in Spain.

It must be characterized as amazing that these units were capable of their military achievements in spite of the over-emphasized political work with all its unreasonable communist ideologies. As the news organ of the XI International Brigade the newspaper

Propaganda poster from the Ministerio de Propaganda in Madrid. Sitting in the boat of the Burgos junta are the clergy, monarchists, falangists, Moroccans and the German fascists, while hovering overhead is a vulture, an omen of failure.

Pasaremos transmitted combat experiences and new tactics, and repeatedly called for increased resistance against the Nationalists. Other proclamations called for and promoted the formation and operation of partisan groups based on the Soviet example. Elements of the approximately 30,000-man International Brigades were thrown into action for the first time in early 1936 against Franco's advance on Madrid.

Among those armed with pen and paper and active as reporters for the socialist press and *Comintern* were to be found such later well-known personalities as Ernest Hemingway, Willy Brandt, Walter Ulbricht and Hans Schaul, while others, like Tito, Togliatti, Maurice Thorez and André Malraux, served with active units.

Justifying their move by pointing out that General Franco had now taken possession of the greater part of Spanish territory, on November 18, 1936 Berlin and Rome recognized the General as the country's head of state. Berlin closed its embassy in Alicante and the General Consulate in Barcelona. As a result of this move *Deutsche Lufthansa,* which until now had been permitted to use Barajas and Loring airfields, was requested by the Republican government to cease its airline operations to these airports.

The first engagements with Spanish-flown Russian aircraft took place on November 5 when nine Fiats (three of them flown by the Spaniards Morato, Salas and Salvador) battled a dozen I-15s. Both sides reported a major victory: the Nationalists claimed seven fighters and a Potez shot down — the Republicans claimed five Nationalist aircraft. The fact is that at least two Italians, Picoli and Maccagno, the latter the squadron leader, were shot down. Maccagno was later exchanged for a Russian pilot. Two *Chatos* were shot down on November 6, while Captain Larrauri managed to land his shot-up Fiat at Talavera. The same day *Hauptmann* von Moreau had to make an emergency landing near Madrid in his Ju 52.

The Nationalist offensive on Madrid began on November 8. On the 9th fourteen Fiats battled two squadrons of *Chatos*. Two of the Russian fighters went down in flames, one of them Morato's 14th kill. On the 6th and 11th the Republicans bombarded Avila airfield, which was occupied by German Ju 52s, He 51s and He 46s, destroying or damaging several aircraft.

By the end of the year the situation in the air had changed. The sky over Madrid was now alive with the latest types of Russian and French aircraft (I-15, I-16, Dewoitine 510). The appearance of the *Ratas* had a depressing effect. A design of the Russian professor Polikarpov, it was the first production low-wing monoplane fighter with a retractable undercarriage to enter service anywhere. Technically, it was clearly superior to the He 51 and its outstanding maneuverability later made it a serious opponent even for the Bf 109.

In Germany the assembly of a Luftwaffe volunteer corps, the *Legion Condor,* had begun largely unnoticed under the code name "Winter Exercise Hansa." The former Operation *Feuerzauber* now came to an end or was pursued with stronger forces under new cover designations. The designation "Exercise Rügen" now appeared as a code name for the entire German intervention, including land and naval forces, in place of Operation *Guido,* which had been in effect since November 7, 1936. Franco's government in Burgos was in fact able to keep the new aid measures secret until the arrival of the German transports. On that same November 7 the Republican government left Madrid and established itself in Valencia.

At the beginning of November the disposition of Nationalist Spanish forces was as follows:

Division in Andalusia
under General Queipo de Llano: with HQ in Sevilla
Southern Army
under General Franco: with HQ in Caceres
Northern Army: with HQ in Vallalodid
under General Mola
Fleet Detachment: with HQ in Ferrol
under Captain Moreno
Air Forces
under General Kindelan (directly subordinated to Franco)

Polikarpov I-16, Type 6 Rata, known as the Mosca by the Republican side. With its retractable undercarriage, unusually small turning radius and an armament of four 7.62mm machine-guns, this fighter was far superior to the He 51.

The German fighter *Staffel* was to suffer several serious reverses before the arrival of the reinforcements.

November 13 saw the greatest test so far for both air forces. A dogfight took place above the streets of Madrid between fourteen Fiats and thirteen I-15s. The Italians had recently been ordered never to fly combat missions with less than fifteen aircraft. The Nationalist communique reported the destruction of six fighters and an SB-2 *Katiuska.* The Republicans claimed five Nationalist fighters shot down. Captains Mosca and Mariotti crash landed their Fiats at Talavera; Morato scored his 15th kill, while Salas and Salvador each shot down their fifth enemy aircraft. The Russian squadron leader Tarjov bailed out over Madrid and was mishandled by the population, who mistook him for a German. He died several days later in hospital. This incident led to an order on the Republican side not to shoot downed pilots as they might be able to provide useful information.

The He 51s made their first acquaintance with the Russians on the afternoon of November 13. Nine German fighters took off from Avila to provide escort for five Ju 52s and three He 46s, which were to attack the Republican positions on the west bank of the Manzanares. Suddenly sixteen *Chatos* and eight *Ratas* dove on the Henrici *Kette. Unteroffizier* Mratzek was able to shoot down an I-16 as it dove past. *Oberleutnant* Oskar Henrici downed a Russian fighter in the same way as the He 51s dove into the clouds. A bitter dogfight raged over Madrid at 1,500 meters. The Knüppel *Kette* dove into a cloud, reversed course in a steep turn and reemerged below the Republican aircraft. *Oblt.* Knüppel and *Uffz.* Sawallisch shot down two I-15s; Sawallisch made his way home with some difficulty with shot-up tail surfaces. The Eberhardt *Kette* had remained above the bombers as top cover. *Oberleutnant* Kraft Eberhardt collided with a Red fighter he had shot down and was killed; the Russian pilot was able to bail out. *Oblt.* Henrici took a bullet through the

EL JEFE
DEL
ESTADO ESPAÑOL

HAUPTQUARTIER DES OBERSTEN BEFEHLSHABERS

S A L A M A N C A

HEERESTAGESBEFEHL FUER DEN 15. NOVEMBER 1.936.

Der Fliegerhauptmann in der Legion Oscar Henrici hat in der Luftschlacht über Zaragoza vom 19. Oktober seine Heldenhaftigkeit und sein unübertreffliches Können bewiesen, indem er drei feindliche Kriegs-Flugzeuge abschoss, darunter eine dreimotorige, die bei ihrer Explosion in der Luft das Öl ihres Tanks auf die Maschine des Hauptmanns Henrici verspritzte, was als Beweis anzusehen ist, in wie unmittelbarer Nähe von seinem Gegner dieser sich befand. Diese Tat allein verdient eine sehr grosse Auszeichnung.

Am 13. November liess er sich mit seiner Jagdstaffel in einen Luftkampf gegen einen zahlenmässig sehr überlegenen Feind ein. Im Verlauf des Kampfes wurde der Feind geschlagen und fünf seiner Jagdflugzeuge abgeschossen. Bei diesem sehr bedeutenden Sieg war das Handeln des Hauptmanns Henrici von grösster Wichtigkeit. Obwohl er währena des Kampfes tödlich verwundet wurde, gelang es ihm auf Grund seiner unübertreflichen Heldenhaftigkeit und echt deutschen Energie, mit einer letzten, höchsten Kraftanstrengung nach Beendigung des Kampfes mit seiner Maschine den Flugplatz zu erreichen und vorbildlich zu landen, womit er sich die Unsterblichkeit gesichert hat. In dem Augenblick des Landens schied er aus diesem Leben, nachdem er den Lorbeer des Sieges, der Selbstaufopferung für die militärische Ehre, für das Ansehen seines Geschwaders und für den Ruhm seiner Nation errungen hatte.

Auf Grund der Taten, die in diesem Tagesbefehl des unter meinem Kommando stehenden Heeres erwähnt werden, und als Ansporn für Andere, verleihe ich als Oberster Befehlshaber dem Fliegerhauptmann in der Legion Oscar Henrici den Orden "Cruz Laureada de San Fernando", weil dieser Orden die höchste Auszeichnung ist, die im spanischen Heere einem Helden verliehen werden kann. Sie wird ihm angesichts des Feindes und mit den vorgeschriebenen Ehrenbezeugungen angeheftet.

Salamanca, den 15. November 1936.-

Franco

Personal letter from Franco on the occasion of the posthumous award of the "Cruz Laureada de San Fernando" to Hauptmann Henrici.

The last photograph of Oberleutnant Krafft Eberhardt, taken just before he took off from Avila on November 13, 1936. With him are the other two members of his Kette: left, Leutnant Dietrich von Bothmer, right, Leutnant Hennig Strümpell.

lung, but was able to land his machine in friendly territory. As he left his aircraft, however, he collapsed and died. The German *Staffel* became completely scattered, each pilot seeking cover in cloud and making his own way back to Avila. "Piefke" Strümpell and von Bothmer reported the destruction of two further I-15s. The Republicans claimed four kills against two losses. Following Eberhardt's death *Hauptmann* Herwig Knüppel became the new *Staffelkapitän*.

The 13th had been a black Friday for the Germans. Many had seen in Eberhardt a new Richthofen. On November 15, the entire *Staffel* had only three serviceable He 51s. From then on the Nationalist forces dared only appear over Madrid in large formations of thirty or forty machines. On numerous occasions lone *Ratas* would shoot down a machine from the closed formations of bombers and fighters formations from below, turn almost on the spot and dive away. By the end of 1936 the Russians had delivered 55 *Chatos*, 31 *Ratas*, 31 *Katiuskas* and 31 *Rasantes*. A further 92 I-15s, 31 I-16s and 30 R-Z bombers and R-5s followed by mid-March.

At this point reference should be made to the differing, even misleading designations of aircraft used by the Republican side. Since aircraft recognition, even in the later years of the war, was never a the strength of the pilots, this led frequently to confusion when discussing enemy machines. Pilots usually assigned a name to an opposing aircraft at their first meeting, in most cases the wrong one. The general similarity between the I-15 *Chato* and the Curtiss Hawk, flown by Ernst Udet at air displays in Germany, led to the assumption that the new fighter must be a type of "Curtiss." No one gave any thought to checking an existing recognition manual to set the matter straight.

It also happened that the Soviet SB-2 *Katiuska* could be mistaken for the American Martin B-12, and soon the designation "Martin Bomber" had stuck. Even the I-16 *Rata* was misidentified as the Boeing P-26, in spite of the former's retractable undercarriage. As a result, the correct designations will be used in this work, and the misleading designations will only be used when they appear in diary extracts.

A comparison of the four fighter types in use in Spain at this time reveals that the He 51 was inferior to the other three. The I-16 was the fastest and possessed the highest service ceiling, the I-15 was the most maneuverable and had the best rate of climb, while the Fiat C.R.32 was the most robust and possessed the best diving characteristics.

In mid-October the torpedo boat *Luchs*, a ship of the German Navy's security group, managed to slip undetected into Cartagena Harbor, where it photographed the tied-up Soviet steamer *Komsomol* with its deck cargo of trucks. On October 15 the Germans succeeded in capturing another Soviet cargo ship, the *Bolshevik*, on film with a load of war materiel on deck. German scruples (if indeed any existed) about increasing aid to the Nationalists must have been quickly vanished; as well such photographs could prove very useful as counter-evidence against possible reproaches from other nations. At that time the naval security group consisted of the battlecruisers *Deutschland* (*Vizeadmiral* Carls' flagship) and *Admiral Scheer*, the small cruiser *Köln* and the 2nd Torpedo Boat Flotilla with *Seeadler*, *Albatros*, *Leopard* and *Luchs*.

While the loading of personnel and materiel for the future *Legion Condor* was well under way at the ports of Hamburg, Stettin and Swinemünde under the code-word "*Cuno*," the weak German air elements at the front continued to carry out their assigned tasks as best they could. On several occasions the "*Pedros* and *Pablos*" dropped food, munitions and weapons over surrounded Oviedo (south of Gijon, on the northern front) in the face of heavy anti-aircraft fire, and attacked the city and harbor of Malaga with two Ju 52s and two Hs 123s under the protection of three Italian C.R.32s.

When Franco moved his headquarters from Caceres to Salamanca the German headquarters followed, establishing itself in the Hotel *Passages*. Salamanca was to remain a central point for the operations of the *Legion Condor* for some time.

On November 15, the Italian communist Primo Gibelli was shot down with his Breguet. The Nationalists are said to have dropped a box containing his mutilated body over the Republican airfield at Barajas a few days later.

On November 16, there was another air battle between a Fiat squadron and thirteen *Ratas* and *Chatos*. Two Russians, including the squadron leader, Captain "Palancar" (pseudonym for Rychagov), were shot down. The Italian Beretta was wounded, but managed to reach his base. The Republicans claimed five kills. On the 17th, the Fiats once again shot down two *Ratas*. On November 19, fifty Nationalist bombers, S.M.81s and Ju 52s, dropped about 40 tons of bombs on Madrid. This incursion resulted in the last major air battle of 1936, with nine He 51s and sixteen C.R.32s from the Nationalist side facing off against at least an equal number of Republican *Chatos* and *Ratas*.

Again the two sides made conflicting claims. The Fiats and Nationalist bombers claimed four enemy aircraft shot down, while the Republicans reported the destruction of three Ju 52s and three fighters against the loss of two of their fighters.

The following weeks were marked by poor weather and limited flying activity. On November 25, the German fighter *Staffel* moved to Burgos on the northern front, and then on December 4 to Vitoria. In the air the initiative had passed completely to the Republican Air Force.

Meanwhile, on October 31, 1936, a Ju 52 had taken off from Berlin for Rome and Spain; on board were *Generalmajor* Hugo Sperrle, who was to become the commander of the *Legion Condor* under the alias "Sander," with his Chief-of-Staff *Major* Alexander Holle and several officers of his staff.

The "Legion" Arrives

November 7, 1936, the very day the *Legion Condor* came into being, saw the departure of the *Fulda*, the 21st special steamer, from Stettin harbor. On board were the first elements of the Legion and about 100 vehicles for use in Spain. By the 29th no fewer than twenty-five freighters carrying personnel, equipment and weapons were to follow the *Fulda*. Franco and Nationalist Spain were about to receive the first major delivery of aid from the German Reich.

Once again the port of Cadiz and the city of Sevilla were selected as disembarkation and assembly points, respectively, for the German troop contingent in Spain. The German headquarters in Spain and its subordinate offices had already made the necessary preparations.

The plan foresaw the formation of the following units into an independent *Fliegerkorps*:

A/88	Reconnaissance Staffel
AS/88	Maritime Reconnaissance Staffel
B/88	Airfield Operating Company attached to Air Park
F/88	Anti-aircraft battalion (4 heavy and 2 light batteries)
J/88	Fighter Gruppe (3 Staffeln, at times 4)
K/88	Bomber Gruppe (3 Staffeln, at times 4)
Laz/88	Field Hospital
Ln/88	Signals Battalion (consisting of 1 radio company, 1 telephone company, 1 aircraft warning company, 1 air traffic control company)
MA/88	Munitions Depot
P/88	Park and Aircraft Group
S/88	Operations Staff

Generalmajor Sperrle, the first commander of the "Legion," during the flight from Germany to Spain.

San/88	Medical Battalion
VB/88	Bomber Test Staffel (established later)
VJ/88	Fighter Test Staffel (established later)
VS/88	Liaison Staff with Spanish and Italian Air Forces
W/88	Weather Station
Büro Grau	Office of the Air Attache

The *Staffeln,* batteries and battalions already operating in Spain were to be integrated into the new units. Existing Army and Navy units were also renamed or absorbed by the newly-created units:

Büro Anker	Office of the Naval Attache
"Nordsee"	Naval Group
"Imker"	all Army Units (also pseudonym for von Funck)
"Imker-Ausbilder"	German Training Organization for Spanish Troops
"Imker-Drohne"	Armored Group
"Imker-Horch"	Radio Intercept Company

Individual German aircraft had been delivered to Spain via Rome and Sardinia in September and October 1936. Now thirty-three Ju 52s for K/88 were to be delivered from Greifswald to Melilla via Rome. Navy warships with radio beacons were positioned in the Mediterranean to support the flights to Sevilla, which were to be made in groups of three aircraft (*Ketten*), and to provide a sea rescue service if needed. The transfer flights took place without complications, although the *Admiral Scheer* did have to recover an He 59 of the Maritime Reconnaissance *Staffel* which force-landed on the open sea. The cruiser *Königsberg* was called upon to provide the same service on December 19.

Some consternation resulted from the news that a Nationalist pilot had deserted to the Republicans with a fully-equipped Ju 52 on December 10. Such incidents were repeated during the months that followed, without, however, causing much of a stir.

By the end of October Germany had delivered the following equipment to Spain under Operation "Feuerzauber":

20 He 46 aircraft
1 He 50 aircraft
24 He 51 aircraft
2 He 60 aircraft
2 He 70 aircraft
2 Hs 123 aircraft
28 Ju 52 aircraft
3 (Me) Bf 109 aircraft
5 courier aircraft

A Ju 52/3mg3e releases a 250kg bomb. Visible just behind the right mainwheel is the extended ventral pod, and aft of the middle engine the emblem of 3. Staffel/Kampfgruppe 88.

28 20mm anti-aircraft guns
4 88mm anti-aircraft guns

Since there was no need to assemble K/88's aircraft, as they had been flown to Spain, the unit's three *Staffeln* were the first to become operational, led by:

1 Staffel	*Oberleutnant* Heinz Liegnitz at Salamanca/San Fernando
2 Staffel	*Hauptmann* Anselm Brasser at Salamanca/San Fernando
3 Staffel	*Hauptmann* Krafft von Dellmensingen at Sevilla, later Salamanca/San Fernando

Based on the evaluation of reconnaissance information brought back by *Leutnant* Balthasar, who would later become a successful fighter pilot, on November 23 the 2nd and 3rd Staffeln of K/88 flew a combined attack on the harbor and city of Cartagena. Bombs were loaded aboard the aircraft at Sevilla, however the mission itself was to be flown from Melilla on the North African coast, as the route from Sevilla to Cartagena would have taken the bombers over a broad mountainous region and through areas of bad weather. The aircraft of the two *Staffeln* flew to Melilla in small groups, refuelled there and set out individually across the Mediterranean on the 350-kilometer flight to Cartagena. Not far from the target the crews descended from 4,000 to 2,500 meters and carried out their nocturnal attacks in the face of heavy anti-aircraft fire. The two *Staffeln* returned to Melilla without loss before flying back to Sevilla the same day.

The next unit to report ready for action was A/88 under *Hauptmann* Heinsius which, equipped with twelve He 70 F reconnaissance aircraft (three-man crew), was likewise stationed at Sevilla. In addition to their reconnaissance duties these aircraft were also employed as fast bombers over and behind the front. The aircraft's bombload, 300 kg in an ELVEMAGS (electrical-release vertical magazine), was extremely limited, but at the time the Heinkel was the only high-speed bomber available.

Beginning November 18, sixty He 51 fighters for J/88 arrived in Sevilla aboard the freighters *Berlin* and *St. Louis*, camouflaged as agricultural machinery. Three *Staffeln* were formed from the available personnel under *Staffelkapitäne Hauptmann* Palm (1. J/88), *Hauptmann* Lehmann (2. J/88) and *Hauptmann* Roth (3. J/88). Among the newcomers were Harro Harder, Lützow, Pitcairn, Pingel, Schlaffer, Kley, Wilfert, Greisert, Leyerer, Riedinger, Boddem, Kienitz, Rutsch, Fenske, Hepe,

He 70 crew of A/88. Standing from left: Leutnant Kurt Strümpell, brother of fighter pilot Hennig Strümpel, observer Leutnant Bernetzeder, radio operator (unidentified).

2-24, an He 51 of Knüppel's 4. Staffel, photographed in November 1936. The unit was already using a top hat as the Staffel emblem.

Heilmeyer, Braunschweiger, Höneß, Rempel, Flegel and others. The existing "elite" in Spain and their machines formed the basis of 4 *Staffel* under *Hauptmann* Knüppel. *Hauptmann* von Merhart became commander of the *Gruppe* after the officer originally intended for the job, *Major* Baier, was forced to return to Germany with heart trouble. The former *Jagdstaffel*, which had now become 4. J/88, retained its former *Staffel* emblem, the *Zylinderhut*, or top hat. This emblem had been chosen by the pilots following their formal release from the Luftwaffe prior to their "trip" to Spain, having thus taken their "hat," or "top hat," and gone, as the expression went.

In the interests of completeness it should be mentioned that a Spanish He 51 squadron already existed at this time; however, by the end of December 1936 it had lost all six of its aircraft on the Aragon front through crashes (1), combat (1) and enemy bombing (4).

J/88 assembled its aircraft at Sevilla and by early December was ready for action. A brief quote from Harder's diary reveals the disillusionment which struck the "newcomers" after only a few weeks:

"The organization of this jackass station is awful, and we youngsters would dearly love to straighten things out. The fighters sit here and don't get anywhere. The entire operation appears more and more like a great adventure whose direction lies in the hands of incapable staff officers. Are operations even justified by the results? Why don't we have better machines? The Russian aircraft are far and away superior in their flight characteristics, the Italians have far better machines — and what does Berlin do? It orders that the He 51 is better than the Russian aircraft! The bluffing of the past three years must finally stop! What keeps us here is definitely not ideals, rather our youthful enthusiasm, lust for adventure and the 1,200 Marks combat pay."

With the acceptance of new aircraft it was possible to hand over twelve He 51s and fourteen Ju 52s from existing stocks to the Spaniards. It was planned that twenty He 46s from new deliveries would be assigned to the Nationalists.

On the northern front the "Top Hat" *Staffel* and its "old hands" under Knüppel remained at Avila. In spite of the awful rainy weather during early December, on the 8th the German fighter pilots were again successful. First Rehahn shot down a Breguet, then the Trautloft *Kette* scrambled to intercept six *Chatos* making a low-level attack on Vitoria:

"Bothmer is the second to take off and flies directly behind me, about 300 meters back. Mratzek's takeoff has been delayed. I make a right hand climbing turn to gain altitude and at 200 meters set off toward the Reds. Before I am close enough I see that they are already attacking Mratzek. A long stream of fuel spurts from his aircraft and in an instant he is on fire. In a wild rage I fly into the midst of the six Reds, who are flying in an echelon right formation. The first one is in my sights. He comes toward me at great speed, I can see clearly the muzzle flashes from his four machine-guns, and hear bullets whizzing past me. Now I open fire as well. My machine-guns fire with a regularity which gives me a feeling of superiority. The Red has taken quite a few hits, but he doesn't go down. He roars straight toward me, firing all the while. 'Come on, come on' I think, holding my course. It must be a breathtaking sight from the ground as we two roar straight towards one another. I am determined not to avoid a collision. He will have to be the one to do it, even if it's at the last second. The wheels of his aircraft sweep close by overhead. Quick as lightning I pass beneath him, pull up in a climbing turn and dive on the last Red! But before I can fire there is another Red on my tail. A terrific dogfight begins. Bothmer and I fight against the six Red fighters barely 100 meters above our own airfield. The wind is slowly driving us over the city, our bullets must land in the street. I fire with all guns whenever a Red machine rushes past in front of me, however when I try to hold him in my sights there is always another Red in firing position behind me. So it goes on, how long I no longer know, I have lost track of time. There, a Red! I am able to turn toward him. I close in behind him and have him well in my sights. I try to fire and become white with rage: Jammed! My guns won't fire! A curse escapes me. And now the Red pilot turns around, as if wanting to call to me in wonderment: now then, why don't you fire? Turning wildly, he and the others fly home singly. But I count only four. I see three machines taking off from our airfield. Ahead of me a lone machine is approaching to land. That can only be Bothmer. Thank God!"

Immediately after the first exchange of fire two Red fighters had disappeared behind the front in steep glides. It later turned out that they had crashed just behind the lines; one of the machines was supposedly piloted by a woman. Mratzek had been shot down from an altitude of 150 meters; his parachute opened at twenty meters. The two victories were credited to Trautloft and von Bothmer.

On December 9, Hannes Trautloft became one of the first to be sent to Sevilla for conversion training on the Bf 109. "Fips" Radusch was selected to test the sole cannon-armed He 112. The machine was the He 112 V 4, in which a 20mm MG C/30L engine-mounted cannon had been installed for trial purposes. Otherwise the fighter was unarmed. The few fighter pilots in Spain fortunate enough to fly the aircraft said great things of the He 112, and everyone wanted to qualify to fly the aircraft. For the time being, however, the majority were forced to continue risking their hides against the I-15 and I-16 in the now totally inadequate He 51.

By December 20, VJ/88 at Tablada had three Bf 109s on strength (V3, V5 and V6); Trautloft had a green heart painted on one of the aircraft. Radusch worked hard with his He 112 V4 and Beurer and Zitzewitz test flew a Ju 87 A-0. Also available for testing were three Hs 123s. A further Bf 109 had been destroyed on December 10 in a takeoff crash in the hands of pilot Kley.

The first sorties by the *Jagdgruppe* over the Madrid front were flown from Avila and Escalona. An over-eager 1 *Staffel* shot down a friendly reconnaissance machine. *Hauptmann* Palm scored the *Gruppe*'s first victory on December 16. He described the enemy aircraft as a "Boeing," but it was almost certainly a *Rata*. The German fighters were forced to

In Spain since mid-November 1936: from left Dipl.-Ing. Droste (first technical director of the Condor Legion), Dipl.-Ing. Scholz (alias "Commandante Rapido"), and in uniform "Fips" Radusch.

Trautloft's Bf 109V at Seville-Tablada airfield in December 1936. Trautloft had the "Green Heart," his longtime personal marking, painted beneath the cabin.

The V4 prototype of the He 112 runs up its engine at Tablada. The aircraft was armed with an engine-mounted 20mm C/30 L cannon, installed for test purposes.

fight a bitter and costly battle against the numerically and technically far superior enemy. The Republican command had concentrated all its modern fighters in the area around Madrid and on occasion the approaching Ju 52 bombers were intercepted by as many as thirty to forty *Ratas*. The Nationalist command was forced to abandon daylight operations by its bomber units and went over to evening and morning harassing raids against supply lines behind the Madrid front. Several machines were lost in the mountains as a result of icing and downdrafts. The He 51s employed various tactics in their battle for survival. One *Kette* would attempt to divert the enemy, whereupon the others would attack from a

Another test aircraft with VJ/88 at Tablada: the Henschel Hs 123, also known as "Obergefreiter" (Private) for short. This dive-bomber and close-support aircraft was never to perform in its intended role in Spain.

superior altitude in *Staffel* strength. Soon, however, the German pilots were pleased just to get their bombers home without loss.

On December 22, 2 *Staffel* transferred to Villa del Prado, 30-40 km southwest of Madrid, a desolate, sandy place. From January 3, 1937 it reinforced 4 *Staffel* at Vitoria on the Bilbao front. This *Staffel* had scored its last great success on December 12, 1936, when Knüppel, von Gilsa, Rehahn, Sawallisch and Gödecke shot down five SB-2 bombers.

During the ever-slower march toward Madrid the members of 4. J/88 gained their initial experience in the area of close-support operations. A low-level attack by the He 51 *Staffel* often took the place of absent or inadequate artillery support prior to an attack. In the beginning the Spanish were slow to take advantage of this support; instead of advancing immediately they watched the novel spectacle with fascination and showed their enthusiasm with loud shouts and hand clapping. It was to be several months before cooperation between ground and air forces was developed to perfection; however, this bound the bomber and fighter *Staffeln* to operations on the ground, causing them to neglect their strategic roles. This concept was to have disastrous consequences for the Luftwaffe during the Second World War.

By this point the heavy anti-aircraft batteries with their 88mm guns had also been forced to largely give up their air-defense role and were being increasingly used to engage ground targets in the front lines.

The *Stassfurt*, which had sailed from Stettin on November 19, arrived with two more naval aviators, *Oberleutnant* Werner Klümper and *Oberleutnant* Dieter Leicht, and their crews. The steamer had brought two crated He 59 floatplanes as deck cargo and these were assembled at a shipyard in Cadiz. As the senior *Oberleutnant*, Wolff led the small detachment. At Christmas AS/88 moved from Cadiz to Melilla in North Africa. There the floatplanes flew from a small lake located several kilometers inland. As a Spanish seaplane unit had once been based there, they were able to make use of an existing landing ramp, hangar and a primitive ground organization.

The new base at Melilla did have one advantage. No longer did the aircraft have to cross the Strait of Gibraltar to reach their area of operations. Previously every flight crossing the strait had been reported to the Republicans. Moreover they were now closer to enemy territory (Malaga-Almeria-Cartagena). With its complement of two He 59s and two He 60s, the unit was to locate, and when the occasion arose attack, enemy sea traffic. As ship movements in this area steadily decreased the unit soon went over to nocturnal attacks on the port cities. Thus the "Terror of the Sea" so often referred to in Nationalist newspapers was directed almost exclusively against land targets.

Located at Melilla was a provisional torpedo testing station with a very small number of Norwegian Horten torpedoes, which had been sent from Germany. The crews of the He 59s were under orders to evaluate the torpedo's entry behavior, running characteristics and its effect on the target when the opportunity presented itself.

The year ended with several air battles involving the Fiats. They too had developed new tactics: each five machines formed a patrol and three patrols staggered vertically formed a combat formation. When, on December 20, four *Ratas* attacked the middle patrol, three of them were shot down by the high patrol. Two days later the Italians shot down a Potez 54 and a *Rata*. The Italians now had four fighter squadrons in Spain, led by Nobili, Lodi, Viola and Francois.

In a report on the air war *General* Sperrle summed up as follows:

"At the beginning of the uprising half of the small Spanish Air Force decided for the nationalist movement and half for the government. Old aircraft types, transports and training types, dropped their makeshift bombs on friend and foe. This picture changed during the course of the month of July, when German and Italian fighter pilots gained air supremacy in the Madrid, Zaragoza, Vitoria and Leon area. At about the end of October modern foreign fighters and bombers, especially technically superior Russian fighters, appeared for the first time on the Red side, first near Madrid, later on other fronts as well. Our losses climbed and the Reds gradually won air superiority."

The cloak and dagger civilian clothes of the volunteers had been set aside with the arrival of the *Legion Condor*; taking their place was the uniform of the "Legionnaire." It was similar in cut to the Spanish military uniform and khaki in color. Under no circumstances were the uniforms to reveal that their wearers were German soldiers. These measures were brought to nothing in early 1937 by the first volunteers of the *"Imker-Drohne"* Group; they quickly replaced the silver death's head on their tank berets with a swastika, clear evidence of their German nationality. In addition, the swastika flag was often flown at German military quarters, rendering the specified camouflage measures ineffective. Nevertheless, the German media continued to remain silent on the stationing of German soldiers in Spain, and for all intents and purposes it was not until the Legion's return in May 1939 that the first reports and accounts of their actions in Spain were published.

As part of the same information blackout the Legionnaires themselves were prohibited from informing their families of their locations and correspondence was allowed to contain information only of a personal nature. All mail was to be directed to the cover address "Max Winkler, Berlin, Post-office Box." This collecting station saw to the subsequent distribution and delivery of the mail.

Spanish, Italian and German military personnel

A Feldwebel (also called Sargento or Brigada) of the army unit "Imker-Ausbilder"...

... and one such of the "Imker-Drohne," the Legion's armored component.

all used the same badges of rank, which were worn on the left breast and cap. On arrival in Spain each German volunteer moved up one grade from his previous rank; an *Obergefreiter* thus became an *Unteroffizier* (*Cabo*), an *Oberleutnant* an *Hauptmann* (*Capitan*) and so on.

The service pay of the volunteers, who at no time exceeded 6,500 in number, was considerably higher than their Spanish and Italian comrades. In addition to the regular pay which continued to be issued in Germany, expense allowances were established for all ranks in Spain. An aircrew *Leutnant*, for example, received an allowance of 1,200 Reichsmarks, an *Unteroffizier* of the ground personnel 800 RM.

The official exchange rate of 1 Peseta to approximately .31 RM meant that, from the financial point at least, the German soldier in Spain must have imagined himself in paradise.

General Franco's Fire-Brigade

Quite understandably, the first large-scale operations by the *Legion Condor* were largely dictated by the ground situation on the various fronts, and this was bleak, namely bogged down. Instead of maintaining a war of movement, the Nationalists settled down and dug in after advancing as far as the western outskirts of Madrid and the University Quarter. During the so-called "Winter Battle" of Madrid the primary tasks of the air units continued to be attacks on recognized troop concentrations and, more importantly, achieving mastery over the growing Republican Air Force through attacks on its bases around Madrid. More and more often the massed fighter defenses forced such bombing attacks to be moved to the hours of evening and night, which naturally resulted in a decrease in accuracy and damage inflicted on the target. Now and then the bombers succeeded in timing their attacks so that their bombs were falling just as the enemy fighters, which had been drawn up earlier by decoys, were landing for fuel.

As well, every mission from the sole useable bomber base near Madrid, Salamanca, had to cross the Sierra de Credos (3,000 meters), which, with the additional 1,000 meters safety altitude, led to constant icing of the aircraft and the associated danger of crashing.

The *Legion Condor*'s jumping-off base for attacks in support of the slow advance on Malaga was Tablada, near Sevilla. The target list included supply ports on the Mediterranean coast and occasionally ground targets in direct support of the offensive. As Italian ground troops were involved, the Italians had taken over primary responsibility for the air war on this front. General Queipo de Llano's so-called "olive war" was also VJ/88's battlefield for a brief period, during which its Bf 109s, He 112, Ju 87s and Hs 123s operated from Tablada.

The northern front, from Bilbao to Gijon in the west, was "stationary" at this time; only in the air were there repeated encounters between the two sides. On January 4 Harro Harder scored his first victory near Bilbao:

"Suddenly I see flames from a Ju 52, a parachute and then Red fighters, which due to their dark color are difficult to spot from above. The Ju, now a single sheet of flame, goes down in a spin, another parachute emerges from the flames. The machine crashes on a wooded slope south of Bilbao. There are combats everywhere. But I dare not leave the Ju's. As soon as I realize that no more Red fighters can attack, I go down. I see a Red in a dogfight with an He 51. I fire on him from in front, and pull up over him. Then I hear machine-guns behind me. A Red is coming at me steeply from above, his radial engine gaping at me like a giant eye. I pull my 2-64 into a turn, the Red races past, two of our fighters are already in pursuit. Far below in the valley I see one turning around. With my superior speed from above I can cut him off. I get behind him, fire, he turns, I cut him off, another turn, the smoke trails from my tracing ammunition disappear into his machine. Now he pulls up, black, with a red band in front of the tail, rolls onto his back and plunges almost vertically to the ground. I wake up — the intoxication has made me blind to everything else. I see an He 51 nearby. Exhausted, I pull up and fly to Vitoria, where I make a low-level loop over the airfield. Von Houwald and Sawallisch have shot down two more Curtisses. Of the two men who bailed out of the Ju 52 one was shot immediately because he tried to defend himself when he was captured, the other is said to be still alive."

A week earlier a Russian fighter pilot had been murdered by the civilian population. He had been unable to identify himself as an ally. As a result of this tragic incident, from then on all captured fliers had to be presented to the Russians first. As a result many German and Italian pilots escaped a terrible fate and could hope for an exchange. In fairness it should be mentioned that similar excesses also took place on the Nationalist side.

Oberleutnant Günther Lützow of 2 *Staffel* also smelled powder for the first time on January 4. He wrote:

"The machines start easily in spite of the cold; the ground crews are smooth characters! They place catalytic stoves under the intakes while the engines are being cranked, allowing them to take in warm air. When the starter is engaged, six men pull the propeller over the first difficult point and almost all the machines start straight away. We are to take off at 1110, meet two Ju 52 *Staffeln* at the assembly point and fly to Torryos. But at 1105 the Ju's fly past the airfield in the direction of the front. Start up, after them! We catch up with them on the return leg. A giant pall of smoke hangs over the front north of Brunete — they have already dropped their bombs. Suddenly they make another right turn and head back toward the front. We stay with them, to the left and at the same altitude. Of 1 *Staffel* and the Italians there is nothing to be seen.

"Suddenly, following a right turn, the formation leader rocks his wings. The signal to attack! I put the nose down slightly and — then, out of the haze over Madrid, there appears a dark dot. It pulls up, fires from 1,000 meters and dives away. Over there is another, then a third. I don't see any more. Near the Ju's there are several smoke trails, defensive fire. I descend below the Ju's and wait for the next one. Soon another climbs up. I fire from an impossible range, which causes him to dive away somewhat sooner. And then I get one square in my sights as the Ju's turn for home. I wait until he peels away and then fire hell for leather. Then he whizzes past below me and I put my nose down and set out after him. I can see his red fuselage band clearly. He is 200 meters in front of me, but my guns won't fire. What rotten luck!

"In the meantime the Palm *Staffel* and the Italians have arrived. So as not to overshoot the Ju's the Italians take up station in two rows of four, left and right, rising and falling wildly. It all looks very hectic!"

Harder's description of the shooting-down of the Ju 52 near Bilbao coincides almost exactly with the official report from the Republican side, according to which the Ju fell victim to twenty-year-old Felipe del Rio, who had taken off from the polo field in Bilbao with other I-15s. He approached the Junkers bomber head-on and set the middle engine of *Oberfeldwebel* Hermann's aircraft on fire with a long burst. Only the gunner, Karl Schmidt, who was firing back from the ventral pod, and observer Hermann were able to escape the burning aircraft and take to their parachutes. The other three crew members failed to escape the blazing inferno. Hermann came down near a village not far from Bilbao. Using his pistol, he resisted being taken prisoner by the militia. A member of the militia and an inhabitant of the village were fatally hit, after which an enraged mob trampled the flier to death.

Schmidt landed in a field outside the village of Encuri. He released his parachute and reached for his pistol to defend himself against an armed mob which was storming toward him. Suddenly a Russian fighter landed nearby. The pilot leapt from his aircraft and ran toward Schmidt. The Russian drove off the pack with his own pistol, and soon afterward the two aviators drove to Bilbao in a military truck, where Schmidt was locked up and interrogated. He informed his captors that he was a member of the NSDAP and had come to Spain to fight against Communism. "At this," reported Times correspondent Sheer, "the Basques laughed heartily."

On January 6, 1937, *Leutnant* Hans-Peter von Gallera and his wingman, *Unteroffizier* Kurt Kneiding, were shot down and killed over Madrid. While escorting fourteen Ju 52s they had allowed themselves to be lured away from the main body of the *Staffel* by the *Ratas*. Leyerer's aircraft was hit a dozen times and turned over on landing.

Although this is certainly a propaganda photo, it does illustrate the typical, hectic confusion of an Italian formation. Here six C.R.32 fighters are seen escorting an S.M.81, which has just released its bomb load.

A trio of PWS 10 fighters purchased from Poland. Powered by a 450 HP Lorraine-Dietrich engine, the PWS 10 had a maximum speed of just 240 kph.

During January, Spanish aircraft mechanics in Leon and Sevilla assembled fifteen PWS-10 fighters, which the Nationalists had purchased from Poland. Great hopes were placed on this supposedly modern high-wing monoplane. The disappointment was therefore great when test flights revealed that they had spent their money on "tired crows." Captain Salas and his pilots toiled with the Polish machines for only a brief period, before they were withdrawn from the front and handed over to the flying school at Jerez de la Frontera. There the high-wing monoplanes ended their brief lives one after another.

Active over all fronts were the "universal" He 70s of A/88, under their *Staffelkapitän, Oberleutnant*

This PWS 10 flipped over on landing while in service with the flying school at Jerez de la Frontera.

Hans Detlev von Kessel. In addition to tactical and strategic reconnaissance sorties, the crews carried out high-speed bombing attacks on airfields, supply installations and supply lines. Results were limited by the aircraft's meager bombload, although there were several notably successful missions.

Bomber operations since the appearance of Soviet aircraft deliveries had shown that there was little more to be achieved with the slow Ju 52 and that a continuation of the attacks would entail considerable losses. The He 51, which was inferior to the *Ratas* and *Chatos*, was unable to provide effective fighter cover; once combat was joined the Heinkel pilots had their own hands full and had to leave the Ju's to their fate.

For these reasons von Moreau was ordered back to Germany in December to form VB/88 as an experimental bomber *Staffel*. The three *Staffeln* of K/88, which at that time had twenty-six Ju 52s and two He 70s, were to be joined by 4. /VB *Staffel* with four He 111 Bs, four Do 17 Es and four Ju 86 Ds. Following assembly of the new machines at the Zeppelin field at Tablada, the crews worked up in quiet sectors under von Moreau. Beginning in late March, the new aircraft began taking part in the battles on the northern front. Sorties by the Ju 52 *Staffeln* were now flown only by night. The delivery of new aircraft types to the Legion was largely due to Chief-of-Staff von Richthofen, who impressed upon those in Berlin the hopeless inferiority of the earlier types.

On January 17, 1937, a Ju 52 courier aircraft crashed in the Sierra Gredos near Bejar due to icing. The accident cost eight dead, several thousand *pesetas* and the aircraft's entire cargo of courier mail.

AS/88 was presented the first opportunity to test its torpedoes on January 30, following the discovery by an He 60 on an early-morning patrol of a loaded steamer sailing west just off the south coast of Spain between Almeria and Malaga. One of the two He 59s was immediately fitted with a torpedo rack and loaded with an "eel." The mission was flown by *Oberleutnant* Klümper and his crew. Werner Klümper described what took place:

"The weather was good and the freighter was easily spotted. I made a textbook approach, released the torpedo and turned away. At the same instant my flight engineer informed me that the torpedo had not dropped. There was no indication of anything wrong on the release panel, all the control lights were properly lit. We would repeat the attack. I turned the aircraft about and made a new approach. Once again the torpedo failed to release.

"I turned away from the enemy and had everything checked in the aircraft. The flight engineer unscrewed the floorboards and reported that the release lock was not making contact — absolute carelessness on the part of the ground personnel, which could not be excused by the haste demanded during loading. The flight engineer offered to open the lock with his screwdriver at my signal on the next pass. Why not? I lined up for another approach. Freighter in my sights — signal horn — the torpedo splashed into the water! A brief look was all I needed to see that the torpedo was running in circles. Later, following a close examination on the ground, it was discovered why the torpedo had run in circles. Fractions of a second before the lock opened to release the torpedo a surge of current activated a gyro which was supposed to hold the 'eel' on course after it entered the water. This gyro had made contact on the first approach and began to run, but during the subsequent approaches it was twice turned through 360 degrees.

"Following this bad luck we returned to base and climbed into the other He 59, which was armed with two 250kg bombs, took off and set course for the freighter. I released the bombs from 1,000 meters, but once again things did not go as planned. I had selected train release but both bombs fell at the same time. But one has to be lucky sometimes, both bombs struck amidships — direct hit! There was a tremendous explosion, then we had to turn away as three enemy fighters were coming toward us from the mainland. Before we lost sight of it we saw the freighter turn toward the coast.

"Events now began to overtake one another. All the officers of AS/88 were ordered to the Spanish commander of the air base. After being sworn to secrecy we were informed that an agent had reported that a freighter carrying 200 Red Spanish volunteers was to sail the next day from Oran for Cartagena. AS/88 was to intercept and sink the ship. Because of the danger that the message might be intercepted, we were forbidden to inform our superiors in Spain of the mission. As a result we young officers alone would have to bear the responsibility for the predictable massacre. We were not entirely comfortable with the whole affair; and we therefore made an alternative suggestion to the airfield commandant, which was accepted.

"The following morning. With a torpedo under my He 59 and a good English- and Spanish-speaking radio operator on board, I flew into the waters off Oran, accompanied by an He 60. Nothing to be seen! We turned away; perhaps the ship was already en route. Twenty nautical miles from Cartagena we spotted her. She was a unique sight, her deck completely jammed with men, we estimated more than double the accepted number. Now we had to act quickly.

"I took up station to one side of the ship, while the He 60 flew low over the steamer from astern and dropped a message pouch onto the deck. Written in Spanish, the message was: 'Halt immediately — no radio communications or you will be torpedoed. Further orders will follow.' At the same time the He 60 crew dropped several light bombs fitted with impact fuses into the water in front of the ship. The panic on deck was undescribable, the ship stopped at once.

"A second message was dropped: 'Go to maximum speed, course south. If you deviate from this order you will be torpedoed at once.' I continued to circle close to the freighter so that they could see my torpedo. The ship picked up speed and turned onto a southerly course. It was working, but for how long? The accompanying He 60 had to head home as his fuel was running low. 'Klümper, you will have to handle things on your own,' I thought to myself.

"I approached and dropped another message: 'Do not use your transmitter, receiver on channel XY! Acknowledge incoming messages by signal lamp only!'

"The problem was the coming night; my aircraft could not remain on the scene much longer. Would he remain on course or extinguish all lights and make a run for a Red Spanish port? I called for the Spanish-speaking radio officer crouched in the rear. Send an order to the steamer by radio: 'Change course to X degrees. During the night you will be escorted by a submarine. If you change course you will be sunk!' Then we created a regular radio circus between the air base at Melilla, my aircraft and the imaginary submarine! Because of the 'operator's signature,' the characteristic manner in which each operator transmitted, my own radio operator, who had played no part so far, had to mimic the 'submarine.' In Spanish he signalled the steamer: 'This is submarine XY. I am directly behind you. Are you receiving me? Confirm!' Obediently the bridge signalled astern. Great, it was working. Now I had to head for home. After ten-and-a-half hours in the air I set down at Melilla with the last drops of fuel.

"The next day, February 1, I was out again at dawn, searching for our prize. I soon found her, obediently holding course, slightly displaced by a storm during the night. I sent a radio message ordering the ship to sail into Melilla, and she did as instructed. By the time darkness fell we had steered her to Melilla.

"She was the *Nuria*, 4,600 tons, with over 400 men on board. It was a fine success, and without bloodshed. The next day we found our victim from two days before. She had run up onto the beach near Nerja and only her bow was still above water."

This ends *Oberleutnant* Klümper's account.

In early February 2 *Staffel* of the *Jagdgruppe* returned to Zaragoza and Huescar on the Madrid front. The *Staffeln* of J/88 were now distributed as follows:

1 Staffel (Palm)	at Escalona
2 Staffel (Lehmann)	at Almorox
3 Staffel (Roth)	at Villa del Prado
4 Staffel (Knüppel)	at Leon

On February 11, 1937, *Leutnant* Rehahn was killed when his Bf 109 crashed from an altitude of 400 meters near Caceres. An investigation revealed that Rehahn had apparently been pushed forward onto the control column by his parachute bag as he was on final approach to the airfield. The bag, which

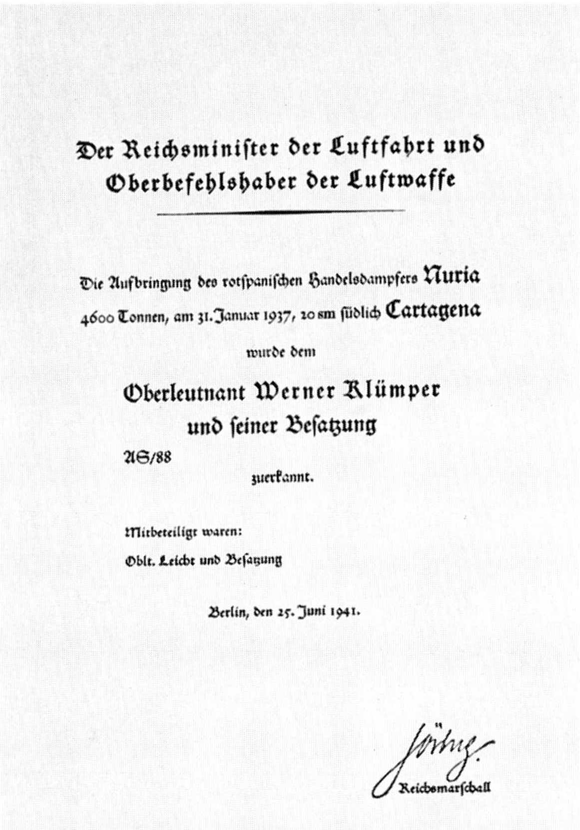

Der Reichsminister der Luftfahrt und
Oberbefehlshaber der Luftwaffe

Die Aufbringung des rotspanischen Handelsdampfers Nuria
4600 Tonnen, am 31. Januar 1937, 20 sm südlich Cartagena
wurde dem
Oberleutnant Werner Klümper
und seiner Besatzung
AS/88
zuerkannt.

Mitbeteiligt waren:
Oblt. Leicht und Besatzung

Berlin, den 25. Juni 1941.

Reichsmarschall

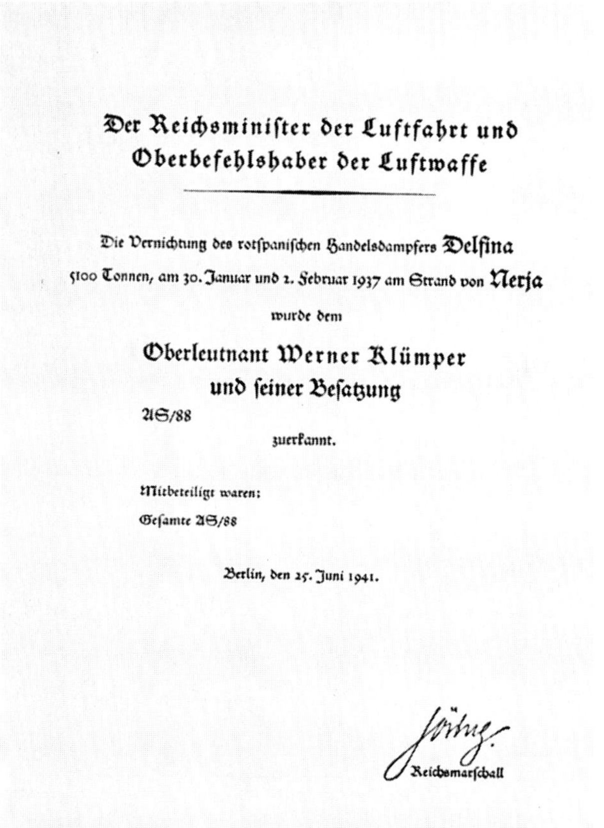

Der Reichsminister der Luftfahrt und
Oberbefehlshaber der Luftwaffe

Die Vernichtung des rotspanischen Handelsdampfers Delfina
5100 Tonnen, am 30. Januar und 2. Februar 1937 am Strand von Nerja
wurde dem
Oberleutnant Werner Klümper
und seiner Besatzung
AS/88
zuerkannt.

Mitbeteiligt waren:
Gesamte AS/88

Berlin, den 25. Juni 1941.

Reichsmarschall

Official confirmation of the destruction of an enemy ship by the Klümper crew. Strangely, the certificates were not issued to the participants until 1941.

Oberleutnant Jürgen Roth, Staffelkapitän of 3. J/88, at Villa del Prado.

was filled with dirty laundry, had been stowed in a compartment behind his back. On February 12, *Hauptmann* Palm and *Leutnant* Hepe were shot down in flames over Madrid. Both men were wounded but managed to parachute to safety. They had been surprised by Red fighters over friendly territory, and Hepe managed to take a *Rata* with him.

In the meantime things were going no better for the Italians. On January 29, four Fiats crashed on the Malaga front in a thunderstorm; one pilot was killed and Cenno, Pelo and Pesce were captured. On February 1, the Russian pilot Major "Casimiro" (Kovalevski) was shot down and killed in an engagement with an Italian bomber. On the 11th the Italian ace Mantelli was forced to take to his parachute. It was on this day that the first Spanish *Chato* squadron under Andrés Garcia La Calle flew its first combat mission. La Calle went on to score at least eleven victories. Other members of his squadron included the Americans Ben Leider, Jim Allison, Frank Tinker and Harold Dahl and Mexican Manuel Garcia Gómez.

On February 13, two Italian pilots were shot down in a battle between fourteen Fiats and twenty-four *Ratas*. One of the Italians was the squadron leader, Captain Lodi. Captain José Calderon, who had become well-known for his martial declaration: "My group will bomb tomorrow, fall who may," suffered the same fate on February 16 when his Ju 52 was shot down by Republican fighters.

Trautloft, too, almost came to grief on this day. Together with eighteen He 51s he was flying escort for ten Ju 52s when he was surprised south of Madrid by five *Ratas*, who mistook him for an Italian:

> "Suddenly one of the five peels off for an attack on me, he has no undercarriage, nor has the second —damn, they're *Ratas*. There's nothing left for me to do but dive away. I make a half-roll and point the nose straight down. The *Ratas* are above me, the shooting must start any second. Involuntarily I press myself into my machine, trying to become as small as possible. I am diving toward the earth at a terrific speed. I can see nothing behind so I keep a sharp lookout to the left and right. But I see no tracer, hear no firing or bullets striking. At about 1,000 meters I begin to pull up. Never before have I descended so fast from 5,000 meters. There is nothing more to be seen of the Reds. Once again I've been lucky."

On February 8, Malaga was taken by the Nationalist "olive warriors," and for the time being they were satisfied with this partial success. Serving as a training center and main supply base for the international brigades at that time was the city of Albacete, located between Madrid and Cartagena. A/88's "bomber *Kette*," led by *Leutnant* Runze, was sent against this important target with three He 70s. The aircraft carried out a high-level attack on the railway station and motor vehicle dispersals without loss. Visual reconnaissance during the attack revealed that Albacete-South airfield was occupied by about thirty aircraft. The He 70 bomber *Kette* flew a similar attack against the Alacar de San Juan rail junction south of Madrid; due to a determined defense by enemy fighters one aircraft attacked the secondary target, the railway station at Limares.

The most successful strategic bombing attacks by the bomber *Kette*, however, took place on February 16 and 19 under the command of *Leutnant* Runze. The targets were the power stations at Seira and Capdella, located in the Pyrenees. Prior to the attack the *Kette* had to transfer from Sevilla via Salamanca to Zaragoza, so as to be closer to the target area. In both cases, attacking at low level, the bombers were able to destroy the pipe-line leading from the reservoir to the power station in the valley. As a result of the attacks there was a considerable disruption in power supplies to the area around Barcelona. Two further power stations, Pablo de Segur and San Lorenzo, suffered the same fate in mid-February. In recognition of this feat in 1939 Runze was awarded the Golden Spanish Cross with Diamonds, posthumously.

Following these bomber escapades the He 70s were employed mainly on photo reconnaissance missions in preparation for an upcoming offensive.

In mid-February, AS/88 transferred from Melilla to Malaga, which had been occupied only a short

Two Rayos, as the He 70 was called by the Spaniards, en route to a pinpoint target in the enemy rear. In the foreground is 14-50, and at a somewhat higher altitude 14-33.

An He 70 "fallen upon by robbers!" A Chato attacked the He 70 on the way to its target, inflicting considerable damage.

time earlier. There were no operational advantages as a result of the move, in fact the opposite was true. There was no ground organization, so the aircraft had to remain tied up to buoys in the harbor. Furthermore, as the harbor basin was too small, the aircraft had to taxi out to open water and take off from there.

The *Staffel* also underwent a change of command at this time. *Oblt.* Wolff was recalled to Berlin and his place was taken by *Hptm.* Klünder. As well the *Staffel* was sent two further He 59s and an He 60.

On February 18, twenty-four Fiats in their familiar wild formation flew fighter escort for three Ju 52s and two Romeo 37s. A major dogfight developed over the front with the *Chato* squadrons from La Calle and the Russian Captain "Jose." Later a number of *Ratas* joined the fight. The Nationalists, among them the Spaniards Morato and Salvador, scored eight victories against three losses. Among those shot down were the Americans Leider (killed), Allison and Dahl. Two *Ratas* were claimed that afternoon. In spite of this noteworthy success the Nationalists were under no illusions. Franco himself wrote to the Italian representatives in Spain: "While the enemy has an air force we are not in a position to carry out the most necessary bombing attacks, because the Spanish fighter pilots have no modern aircraft. . ." Much of this irritation was due to the hesitation of the overly-cautious group commander, Major Fagnani, who was soon relieved.

Efforts to eliminate the Republican fighters through surprise bombing and strafing attacks on their airfields met with little success (The only successful effort took place during Easter Week,

February 1937: Sperrle visits General Franco at his headquarters to discuss the coming month's operations.

One of the first He 111 B bombers delivered from Germany. The aircraft was used in action by the Versuchsbomberstaffel (4 Staffel).

when three He 111s, led by *Hauptmann* von Moreau and *Oberleutnant* Graf Hoyos, destroyed twenty-four fighters and bombers at the Republican fighter base at Alcala. Six other bombers had earlier engaged the enemy fighters until they were forced to land for fuel. It was then that the *Kette* of He 111s glided over the airfield and released 96 light fragmentation bombs; a tactic mentioned in the previous chapter). The German fighters in particular were forced to avoid combat with the maneuverable enemy fighters and limited themselves to escorting bombers and, more frequently, close support missions, the latter in an effort to make up for the limited amount of artillery available.

Harro Harder characterized this critical period with the following sentences:

"We were all convinced that it was madness to continue sending the He 51s on escort missions over Madrid. The *Ratas* played cat and mouse with us. Even the Martin bombers were at least 50 kph faster than we. The morale of the pilots was excellent, but all the guts in the world were useless with this technical inferiority. So once again we were to be employed in low-level attacks. Apparently several more of us will have to be shot down before they were convinced of the stupidity of these orders." Until the appearance of the *Ratas* the German He 51s had flown in textbook *Kette* and *Staffel* formations. The critical moment came when the formations changed direction, with aircraft crossing over and under one another. This was when *Ratas* made their surprise attacks. To aid in the development of defensive tactics, performance figures for the *Rata* were requested from the Air Ministry in Berlin. The latter were unaware even of the existence of the Soviet aircraft and sent the then Chief of the Fighter Arm von Greim and *Oberst* Seidemann to Spain to see if this alarming news was true. Seidemann went along on one mission and on returning was so excited that he belly-landed his aircraft at Escalona. Gradually the pair became convinced that the He 51 was no longer anything to write home about.

Everyone was eagerly awaiting the arrival of the Bf 109 and the He 112, as well as for the Hs 123, which was being touted as an effective dive bomber and close-support aircraft. An example of the latter type had recently been tested by *Leutnant* "Rubio" Brücker. However the hoped-for deliveries of this modern aircraft were long in coming. The morale of the German pilots was not improved by the news that *Oberleutnant* Winterer had landed in Red Spanish territory on February 24 as the result of a navigational error and been taken prisoner. A few days later the Republican press published an statement by Winterer, which he had in fact given during interrogation. The text of the statement was as follows:

"I have been in Republican captivity for two days. I have been surprised by the decent and considerate treatment I have received. I have seen that many of the Spanish people here are fighting for their ideals and form of government with great determination and I have gained respect for them. I have formed an entirely different picture of the Spanish Civil War and I do not yet know where it will lead. I would not come here a second time to add to the suffering of these people."

Leutnant Hein Brücker in front of his Hs 123, 24-5. Painted on the forward fuselage is a caricature of a devil. Vitoria, April 1937.

"Rubio" Brücker (right) with Kurt Strümpel of A/88.

It is difficult to say to what extent this partial admission of guilt was an act of self-preservation by a captive. In any case it seems that Winterer was able to refute his statements on his return to Germany, as he received the same honors as the other Spanish Legionnaires at the home-coming parade in June 1939.

The day before, February 23, a Ju 86 of the *Legion Condor* was lost near Andujar. The crew were killed with the exception of one man who was taken prisoner.

After the Nationalist offensive had petered out at the Jarama River on January 28, preparations began for an attack toward Guadalajara to encircle Madrid. It turned out to be a fiasco. The attack, by four divisions, was planned and carried out by the Italians. It collapsed in the face of counterattacks by Russian T 26 and T 28 tanks, the bitter resistance of the International Brigades and, above all, attacks by the Republican Air Force. On the Nationalist side, only Italian aircraft (an S.M.81 bomber group, a Romeo 37 group and a Fiat C.R.32 fighter group) took part. The Republicans committed three squadrons of *Chatos*, led by La Calle, Captain "Jose" and Captain Kosokov, as well as several squadrons of *Ratas, Katiuskas, Rasantes* and *Nataschas*. On the 13th, 15th and 16th of March low-level attacks by fighters and close-support aircraft spread great confusion among the Italian forces on the ground. On March 18, the Italian attack collapsed under the blows of the Republican Air Force. The Italian infantry streamed back in panic, gunners abandoned their guns. Only a few officers made an effort to stem the retreat or at least conduct it in an orderly fashion. Bad weather and poor rations also contributed to this humiliating Italian defeat. The pursuing enemy were only halted following low-level attacks by the He 51 *Staffeln*, repeated bombing attacks by K/88 (still with the Ju 52) and concentrated efforts by the flak batteries of F/88. Once again the air units filled in for the missing artillery.

After this debacle the Italians became the laughing stocks of the Nationalist alliance. It is no wonder that they were gripped by a certain tiredness of the whole Spanish affair. On March 2, Trautloft, von Houwald, Klein and Sawallisch returned to Germany, the first German Legionnaires to do so. On March 6 the He 51 *Kette* from 2 *Staffel*, which had been operating from the forward airfield at Talavera since February 28, returned to Villa del Prado. A few days later, on March 10, all of 2. J/88, including the *Staffel* accommodations train, transferred to the airfield at Almorox, which was equipped with permanent buildings.

Several Americans distinguished themselves in the fighting over Guadalajara: Dahl, Tinker, Chang Selles, Bäumler and Charlie Koch. Lieutenant Blanch, who had deserted to the Republicans in December, was killed on March 13. On the 14th Tinker shot down his first enemy aircraft, a Fiat. On March 16, the Italians lost two Fiats (one to Bäumler) and on the 20th five more, while on the enemy side the Mexican Manuel Gómez was shot down and killed.

The most noteworthy event during the month of March for the German side was the reequipping of 2. J/88 with the Bf 109 B-1. The first three aircraft, flown by Knüppel, Schlaffer and Gödecke, arrived on March 14. These early Bf 109s still had wooden propellers and their machine-guns were activated byBowden cable. As well, the aircraft's 680 HP engine was very prone to mechanical troubles. J/88 was reorganized. In April, 4 *Staffel* was disbanded; 1 *Staffel* (Harder) and 3 *Staffel* (Pitcairn) retained their He 51s. Now under the command of "Franzl" Lûtzow, 2 *Staffel* took over the "Top Hat" *Staffel* emblem from the disbanded 4 *Staffel*. From now on pilots were rotated through tours of approximately nine months. Training on the Bf 109 progressed quickly; two conversion flights were the rule, with the third flight being an operational sortie.

The Spanish Nationalists formed three squadrons, each with seven aircraft, from the He 51s handed over by the Germans; as well they formed a single Fiat squadron with six aircraft.

At the end of March 1937, the Nationalist

The first Bf 109 B-1s were delivered to 2. J/88 still lacking the variable-pitch propellers of later models. With an armament of only two fuselage-mounted MG 17 machine-guns, the fast fighter was seriously underarmed.

command came to the realization that the outcome of the civil war could not be decided on the Madrid front alone. Therefore, in consultation with the headquarters of the *Legion Condor*, Franco decided to abandon the previous multi-front war and concentrate on rolling up the northern front from Bilbao to Gijon.

This photograph provides an excellent view of the wide-bladed wooden propeller of the first Bf 109 series.

Günther Lützow, Kapitän of 2. J/88 from March 19, 1937.

A Bf 109 B-1 of 2.J/88 displays the "Top Hat" emblem formerly worn by the He 51s of 4. Staffel.

The Kapitäne of the two remaining He 51 Staffeln. On the left is Oberleutnant Douglas Pitcairn (3. J/88), beside him Oberleutnant Harro Harder (1. J/88).

The Battle of Bilbao

The decision to win back the initiative in northern Spain was based on the fact that there were already sufficient local forces available there to deal with the task. With the four Navarra Brigades, the core of which consisted of *Requetés*, or royalists, the Nationalists had at their disposal well-motivated troops who were familiar with the geography of this sector.

Clearly recognizing the superior planning abilities of the German Legion headquarters, the Spaniards left total responsibility in the air to S/88. All the units involved in this theater, Spanish and Italian, were thus under the direct control of the *Legion Condor*. The first move in preparation for the offensive was the transfer of S/88 from Salamanca to Vitoria on March 29, 1937. P/88 (Air Park), until now domiciled in Sevilla, moved, together with all its technical installations, to Leon in northern Spain. As the new unloading and supply port, Vigo, located above Portugal's northern frontier, took on a

The overcrowded airfield at Burgos showed evidence of much improvisation. A wooden equipment shed belonging to the repair group. . .

. . . next to an aircraft tent, which had to be rebraced and realigned after every heavy storm.

new importance. All air units were concentrated at Vitoria and Burgos airfields.

For the first time the air forces were to be the main weapons of attack, and the *Legion Condor* was to be employed as a cohesive unit. From the beginning of operations until March 21, 1937 the Legion had dropped about one million kilograms of bombs.

The following units were transferred to the Lufthansa airfield at Burgos:

K/88 with three *Staffeln* of Ju 52s (16 aircraft)
VB/88 with He 111s and Do 17s (6 aircraft)
Reconnaissance and bomber *Kette* of A/88 with He 70s (6 aircraft)
One battery of 88mm anti-aircraft guns
Half a battery of 20mm anti-aircraft guns
Main photographic unit with one platoon from 1. BK/88
Weather reporting station

The personnel of K/88 and VB/88 were housed in accommodations trains, flying and ground person-

Among the technicians of P/88's air park were Fliegerstabsingieur Gerd Klein-Schmeink (wearing boots), who was in charge of aircraft power plants, and Engineer Junginger from the Dornier Firm, who was responsible for the recently-arrived Do 17s. Seville, March 1937.

The old city of Burgos was well compensated for providing temporary accommodation for the German aircrew.

nel of A/88 occupied quarters in the city of Burgos. Acting as airfield commandant was *Leutnant* Roth.

Stationed at Vitoria were:
(a) at the northwest, very wet field:
3. J/88 with 10 He 51s
(b) at northeast field with its 900-meter, concrete runway:
1. J/88 with 10 He 51s
2. J/88 with 7 Bf 109s
Stuka/88 with 3 Hs 123s
He 45 Kette from A/88 with He 45s and necessary signals equipment for tactical reconnaissance and artillery observation
3. F/88 - 88mm anti-aircraft battery
1 1/2 batteries - 20mm anti-aircraft guns
Headquarters F/88 - Two batteries of 88mm anti-aircraft guns were moved into position in the artillery zone due north of Vitoria. Their tasks were air defense and engagement of surface targets. For camouflage purposes twenty aircraft mock-ups were built and dispersed around the second, completely flooded airfield near Burgos.

A Bf 109 B-1 of 2 Staffel taxies out from its dispersal. At this stage the aircraft's fuselage code is separated by a horizontal bar; later the numbers would be positioned to the left and right of the black fuselage disc.

Two Hs 123s of the dive-bomber Kette, which together with the two fighter Staffeln, were based at Vitoria. Both Angelitos, as the Spanish dubbed the type, wear the "devil's head" as a provisional unit emblem.

The attached Italian air units (under General Valeni) were:

1 fighter squadron	Fiat C.R.32	at Vitoria
1 bomber squadron	S.M.81	at Soria
1 fighter squadron	Fiat C.R.32	at Logrono
1 light bomber squadron	Breguet 19	at Lasarta
1 fighter squadron	Fiat C.R.32	at Lasarta

In addition, the following Spanish aircraft also operated from the crowded Vitoria airfield:

5 He 45
1 Fokker F VII/3m
1 D.H. Dragon Rapide

Use of the concrete runway at Vitoria was reserved exclusively for aircraft of the *Legion Condor*, all others had to conduct their flying activities from the extensive grass surfaces.

On March 19, 4. Ln/88 was ordered to form an *Avila* signals detachment. The detachment's role was to handle air-ground communications. Direction-finding equipment was installed at airfields at Burgos, Leon and Logrono, and radio beacons at Burgos, Salamanca and Vitoria. Ground troops were issued air identification panels to mark the front lines; as well, each Nationalist soldier was supposed to wear a white air identification patch on his back. It was made absolutely clear to the crews that no consideration was to be given to the population during their attacks, so as not to reduce their effectiveness. The He 51s were to provide direct support to the advancing infantry and help open the way for them.

Only limited "Red" forces faced the Nationalists in the air; reconnaissance reported as occupied the airfields at Careno (12 fighters), Albericia (4 fighters) and Lamiaco (2 fighters); reported as unoccupied were La Ista, Vestare, Santona, Colunga, Llaneza, Ozales, Santander, Villaviciosa, Cuastro, Camines, Reinosa, Bilbao and Sondica. Also reported on the airfields were several Potez 54s, an old Farman and a DC-2, while the fighters were identified as Bristol Bulldogs. In an effort to reinforce these weak forces, on May 8 the Republicans tried to send sixteen *Chatos* from Lerida to Bilbao via Toulouse. However, at Toulouse the fighters were turned back by the French. On May 17 they tried again, sending fifteen *Chatos*, this time via Pau. These pilots, too, were stopped and forced to return. Not until the 22nd and 27th of May were a total of fifteen I-15s able to fly direct to Santander; two others were shot down by flak or fighters over Bilbao.

The only advantage held by the Republicans was the close proximity of their airfields to the front. As a result they did not have to make long flights over mountainous areas as the Nationalist attackers did. The Republican pilots in the north were almost all foreigners, mainly Russians.

Following flight testing at the hands of "Fips" Radusch, the cannon-armed He 112 was assigned to J/88 at Almorox. Based at Salamanca at that time was the He 70 reconnaissance *Kette*. Active with the *Kette* as observers were *Oblt.* Balthasar and *Lt.* Kaldrack (both later to become successful fighter pilots). Unable to pass pilot acceptance tests due to his shortsightedness, Balthasar had learned to fly on his own. On March 16, following a reconnaissance mission over Madrid, Balthasar's shot-up He 70 was forced to make an emergency landing at Almorox.

Several hours later fighters were scrambled from Almorox to attack an armored train near Aranjuex. Balthasar stood idly by and watched the fighters taxi out for takeoff, he was after all "only" a reconnaissance flier. Then his gaze fell upon the parked He 112. Acting on an inspiration, Balthasar telephoned the airfield commander and coolly identified himself as an experienced pilot and He 112 specialist, whereupon he was granted permission to take off. Following a brief familiarization flight in the Heinkel, during which he fired several test shots from the aircraft's 20mm cannon, he took off with 3 *Staffel* as dusk was falling to attack an armored train south of Sesena station. On the third pass he scored a direct hit on the armored train's ammunition car with the 20mm cannon, and on the return flight attacked and set on fire a Republican tank.

The reprimand he received after landing was soon followed by praise for his success. This was Balthasar's entry into the world of fighter piloting. Strategic reconnaissance was now behind him. He was given a command of a detachment consisting of three He 45s and the He 112; its role: tactical reconnaissance, artillery spotting and low-level attacks — boldness had won! Balthasar and his small unit were sent to the Bilbao front, where he continued his success.

During a sortie over the front on March 25 an Hs 123 flown by *Feldwebel* Rückert exploded in the air near Aravaca for unexplained reasons. Rückert came down by parachute between the lines and was killed by infantry fire. A "Moro" tried four times to recover the dead pilot, but was driven back by enemy fire each time.

The Nationalist offensive toward Ochandiano began on March 31, 1937. Air attacks began that morning at 0700. Fountains of fire and smoke shot up along a front of ninety kilometers as wave after wave of aircraft dropped 50kg and 250kg bombs. Fighters circled over the rear areas, often diving to ground level to shoot up vehicles, paralyzing supply traffic. Repeated attacks were made on the villages of Ochandiano, Elgueta and Elorrio. Mola's infantry followed the aerial barrage on foot and took three mountain ridges. The defenders had been numbed by the weight of the attacks and their communications had been destroyed by the bombs. Only in front of Ochandiano did the Basques offer resistance which could not be broken by the ground troops.

During the offensive J/88 flew from Vitoria. Its reckless low-level attacks made a significant contribution to the success of the operation. Impressed by the way the Heinkels swooped low over the mountains and attacked supply traffic on the roads, the Spaniards named the He 51s *Cadenas* (chains) and *Trabajadores* (workers). The term "chain" referred to the manner in which the He 51s carried out their attacks, one behind the other like a string of pearls, after which they climbed away and formed up once more in line astern formation. After exhausting their ammunition the Heinkels made mock attacks, which terrified the troops in the trenches. Confidence grew, although there were losses. The Bf 109, or *Rata Aleman*, as it was called by the Spaniards, had proved itself superior to all enemy types in air combat.

As they had done during the fighting in front of Madrid, the 88mm anti-aircraft guns provided a great deal of the artillery support in the mountainous terrain. With their flat trajectory (muzzle velocity about 800 m/sec) they were ideally suited to direct fire on pinpoint targets.

Together with the Italian and Spanish formations K/88 bombed Republican field positions and softened up the defenses for the attack's spearheads. The He 111s and Do 17s of VB/88 (based at Burgos) made their first appearance, escorted by the Bf 109 B fighters of 2. J/88. Two of the four Ju 86 bombers had already been lost, and the two survivors had been handed over to the Spanish Nationalists. The Italians came with their Savoias and Fiats from Soria and

He 111 B bombers of VB/88 at Burgos. The different camouflage schemes worn by the aircraft are noteworthy. While the aircraft on the left has been sprayed light gray overall, 25-6 wears a segmented scheme in colors 61, 62, 63 and 65.

Test running the engines of a Do 17 E. The crew entry hatch was located at the aircraft's wing root and access was provided by a ladder.

The Ju 86 D was used by VB/88 for only a short time. As with the Ju 86-equipped Kampfgruppen in Germany, engine failures (Jumo 205C) were a constant concern and often resulted in forced landings like this one.

Logrono and made several daylight appearances over the battlefield.

Several days after the beginning of the offensive, however, Sperrle was considering withdrawing the *Staffeln* of the *Legion Condor* from the area of operations. What had happened?

On April 1, the bombers and close-support aircraft once again placed their ordnance just in front of the attack forces and smashed nests of enemy resistance. On the ground, at 0800 the 3rd Navarra Brigade launched its attack on Hills 707 and 813. Beginning at 1015, nine He 51s of J/88 supported the advance with low-level attacks. The pilots were met by heavy fire and six aircraft returned with damage from ground fire. The He 51 of *Leutnant* Blankennagel was hit and crashed on a slope; its pilot had apparently been shot through the head by infantry fire. The expected attack by the ground forces did not follow; they "had no intention of attacking yet."

Afterward three Breguet 19s resumed the attacks on the positions between Hill 549 and Uncilla. Not until after it had been softened up by two 88mm Flak batteries was Hill 813 occupied by the 3rd Brigade. At 1100 nine He 51s of 1 *Staffel* bombed and strafed Corbea and Chiqui. At 1336 five machines of 3 *Staffel* attacked St. Agueda and the positions nearby. About two hours later the two *Staffeln* repeated their attacks. There was no movement on the ground!

At about 1700, four He 70s of A/88 bombed vehicle columns north of Ochandiano, blowing up a munitions truck. Three further machines bombed troop movements east of the town. At about 1800, under the protection of 2. J/88, twenty-two aircraft of K/88 closed out the day's air attacks, bombing targets west of Murubain and Oleata. The enemy was in a state of total confusion and could have been pushed back easily, but the Nationalists marked time. Major territorial gains were simply not in the plan for this day.

There was more wasted effort on April 2: useless expenditure of bombs and ammunition, risky low-level attacks in the face of heavy ground fire. And once again the infantry failed to act, there was no will to attack, and besides, "the men hadn't eaten yet"!

April 4 saw waves of attacks in the Ochandiano area. By about midday all resistance had been completely broken. The Republican troops streamed back in the direction of Bilbao in headlong flight, kept constantly on the run by the low-flying He 51s and the bombs of K/88. Survivors recounted that between midday and 1700 there were always about forty aircraft over the positions and that by sundown the figure had climbed to nearly seventy-five. Estimates placed the number of bombs which fell on the village, dug-outs and trenches at 5,000. During pauses between attacks the Basques left their shattered positions to tend to the wounded, but were constantly driven back by the machine-gun fire of the Heinkels and Fiats. The Nationalists could easily have pushed on to the "Iron Ring" of Bilbao, but the day's objective was Ochandiano. The Spanish ground forces were content to halt where they were, shout *Viva Espana!*, receive their rations and cease fighting for the day, even though the enemy was beaten and vulnerable!

The *Requeté* obviously appeared satisfied to continue with their very "individual" command of the war. The RKM bluntly confronted Franco with the problem and energetic measures were introduced to improve the discipline of the Spanish formations. Progress was slow, however. Spanish officers continued to display a lack of understanding of the situation and an inability to see beyond the present. As a result many favorable attack and pursuit opportunities were simply missed. Following a study mission in Spain *Oberst* Jaenecke's verdict was harsh. In his report filed in May 1937 he wrote: "Most Spanish officers are lazy, stupid, unwilling to learn and arrogant. They are a hindrance to the build-up (of the Army)."

Accordingly, progress on the ground was slow. It was not until May 7 that the Nationalist forces reached the "Iron Ring" in the mountains around Bilbao. On April 6 *Oblt.* Kienzle and *Lt.* Schultze-Blank were captured while scouting the front in their vehicle. A companion, *Oblt.* Karsten von Harling, was shot in the head and killed, and the interpreter Freese died later from his wounds. According to press reports Kiezle and Schultze-Blank also made statements during interrogation which were very critical of Germany's intervention in the Spanish Civil War. It is difficult to place much value in such statements in view of the indictment against the two, which charged them with rebellion and murder and demanded the death penalty. Such confessions were a proven means of obtaining more lenient sentences from ideological tribunals. In fact the death penalty was later set aside; in May both pilots were exchanged for Soviet pilots. The stiff sentence against the two Germans had not come by chance, however.

Since March 31, 1937 the *Staffeln* of the *Legion Condor* had attacked the road and rail junction at Durango several times, hoping that the rubble of the destroyed houses would block the retreat of Republican troops to Bilbao. During these bombardments and low-level attacks the population of the town suffered 127 killed, while a further 120 died later in the hospitals of Bilbao.

Only the defense's argument that "the prisoners cannot be held responsible for Germany's actions on Hitler's orders" prevented the death sentences from being carried out on Kienzle and Schultze-Blank.

On April 7, the Republican fighter bases were systematically attacked. So many aircraft were destroyed or damaged that no more than four operational fighters are said to have been left.

Under these circumstances air battles were naturally few and far between. On April 6, *Oberleutnant* "Franzl" Lützow scored his first "kill," shooting down a *Chato*. He wrote:

"1st victory. 1715 hours at 2,400 meters, northwest

of Ochandiano. Curtiss biplane. Slowly chased the other three to Bilbao together with *Hptm.* von Janson and Heilmayer. Unable to get into effective firing position as the Curtisses kept disappearing into cloud. Pilot of the downed machine landed on our side by parachute. 18 year-old, raw beginner. Stated that he had been on an overland flight Santander-Bilbao-Barcelona-Valencia."

The sudden appearance of a rainy period halted operations on the ground for eight days. April 20 brought sunshine; in the afternoon bombers and close-support aircraft were over the Republican positions clearing the way for the ground forces. Bad weather moved in again, and as a result of the poor visibility the last group of bombers dropped their loads on their own troops, which were assembled for the attack. The result was heavy casualties and a lack of desire to attack on the part of the Spaniards. Not until April 24, following the employment of all air forces, did the attack get under way, and then somewhat hesitantly.

On April 22, *Leutnant* Radusch and *Feldwebel* Heilmayer shot down two I-15 fighters. One of the pilots was Felipe del Rio, with seven victories the most successful Republican pilot on the northern front. On April 18, a few days before his death, del Rio had shot down the Do 17 flown by *Oberleutnant* Hans Sobotka. Two members of the crew were killed when they fell into the river before their parachutes had fully opened. The pilot, Hans Sobotka, went down with his aircraft. A crowd gathered at the crash site, which was located in the middle of an open, heather-covered field, and stared at the flaming wreck and the body of the pilot, who had been thrown clear. Sobotka was lying on his back, partly-burned, his body twisted. His arms were crossed in front of his face. From the papers found on him it was learned that the Do 17 had been in Spain only thirteen days; on the way it had stopped in Rome on April 5.

Guernica was bombed on April 26. As the Basque front was at the point of collapse, the command of the *Legion Condor* ordered the destruction of the railway station and the bridge over a small stream just outside the town, in order to prevent the arrival of reinforcements. The result is well known and has become part of aviation history. Harder's objective account contradicts the commonly-held view that the German legionnaires were bloodthirsty mercenaries:

"Today we flew to Guernica. It has been totally destroyed, and not by the Reds, as all the local newspapers report, but by German and Italian bombers. It is the opinion of all of us that it was a rotten trick to destroy such a militarily unimportant city as Guernica. There are certainly thousands more dead beneath the rubble, unnecessary victims. Everywhere is smoking rubble, bomb craters, empty facades."

The following quote on the Guernica attack is from an outline of the "Battles in the North" compiled by the "War Science Department" in March 8, 1940:

"On April 26 an attack was ordered against the bridge and crossroads due east of Guernica. This was carried out by nine aircraft attacking singly from an altitude of 2,300 meters. Nine 250kg and 114 50kg bombs were dropped. Observation revealed no hits on the bridge. Visibility was totally inadequate as the city was shrouded in fire and smoke. The enemy world press used the bombing as an opportunity to single out the German units as being guilty of the destruction of Guernica. A great effort was made to affect public opinion. As ordered, all fliers had spared the city. Rather it was the Reds who transformed the city into a pile of rubble through deliberately set fires and demolitions. This is further borne out by the reduced visibility encountered by the units involved, which was caused by smoke and dust from the already burning city."

According to statements by those who participated in the attack it seems today that there is no doubt that

This and the following photograph were taken shortly after the capture of the Guernica.

Damage to buildings inflicted by high-explosive bombs intended for a nearby bridge at the edge of the city.

Burning buildings in Guernica following the attack on April 26, 1937.

The city of Guernica, situated in a mountain valley.

German bombs caused the damage to the city; the number of Italian aircraft which took part is still unclear. Individual He 111s and Do 17s of VB/88 flying from Burgos opened the attack at about 1630. The first He 111 swept low over the station area dropping high-explosive and incendiary bombs. It was followed by further Heinkels, which bombed the same target. Several buildings near the station were also hit and set on fire. A good quarter of an hour had passed by the time the first Ju 52 *Kette* flew into the target area. By then the inhabitants had left their *Refugios* (bomb shelters) and had begun to fight the fires which were burning.

Approaching from the southwest, the bomber crews were unable to obtain a clear view of the target area. An impenetrable layer of dust and smoke hung over the valley in which the city lay. The first six-aircraft formation, and the second which followed 20-30 minutes later, dropped their bombs virtually blind. Once again a large percentage fell in the city, which contained about 10,000 persons on this Monday market day. Casualties among the civilian population were terrible, while the two battalions of Basque infantry at the edge of the city suffered virtually no casualties. At about 1930, after returning to Burgos to rearm, the VB *Staffel* carried out a second and final attack on the burning town, which now lay under swaths of smoke, making the chaos complete.

Taking into account the state of things and the inadequate visibility, the second attack should definitely have been called off. Nevertheless, at no time could there be any question of a terror attack. Carelessness on the part of the crews, the later inadequate visibility and the rigid command of the unit simply caused this attack on a pinpoint target to misfire. The original figure of 1,600 dead proved to be greatly exaggerated; following the capture of the city official sources revealed a figure of just over 300 dead among the civilian population. But even this dramatic reduction in the casualty figures cannot excuse this miscarried action by the air force of the German Legion.

The sole result of military significance: the rubble from bombed-out and collapsed structures blocked the avenue of retreat of the Republican forces; too little or too much to clear away the black smudges which to this day still stain the reputation of the Luftwaffe.

On the other hand, the material and even more so the moral effects of air attacks in the actual combat zone were tremendous. Once again Harder's diary:

"April 27, bad weather again. The clouds hang low in the mountains. I manage to slip past Udala with my *Kette* and find worthwhile targets on the Durango-Bilbao road. The Reds have apparently not counted on the famous 'auto hunters' coming in this foul weather. They have assembled their vehicles without camouflage. Flying low, we shoot up about twenty motor-vehicles. Repeatedly we dive beneath the low clouds. The next day we're hard at it again. I have flown four sorties with the *Staffel* in very bad weather, ceiling in the Durango valley 200 meters. We encounter many vehicles. On the third sortie Ofw. Wilfert finds three trucks with limbered guns. On the fourth sortie we once again came upon a vehicle column. Our bombs are on target. A few bursts at the church steeple in Durango, where there are supposed to be several machine-guns, then my usual low roll over the town and home past Udala over a peak where the ceiling is perhaps 20 meters. On April 31 I flew six sorties, during which we shot up about 30-40 vehicles, destroying most of them."

Marquina fell on April 27, and the destroyed city of Guernica two days later. On April 30, 1937, a Ju 52 courier machine was lost while en route from Sevilla to Rome. Killed were Hans Giesecke, Kurt von Gilsa, Manfred Fuhrke, Gustav Gaus, Herbert Demant, Ernst Ossenkopp and Ernst Mratzek. A memorial containing the names of the victims was erected on the Mediterranean coast.

On May 1 an advance from the coastal city of Bermeo completed the encirclement of Bilbao, and on May 7 the "Iron Ring" around the city was reached. Positional warfare now developed, which was to last for about a month until Nationalist forces succeeded in entering the city itself.

On May 3, seven Bf 109 fighters of 2. J/88 escorted two *Staffeln* of Ju 52 bombers in attacks on the Bermeo-Menaca road, over which the Republicans were withdrawing. No enemy aircraft were encountered. Another escort mission followed on May 7, when seven fighters accompanied seven He 70s and three Do 17s against the airfield at Santander. The bombs dropped by the He 70s were on target,

Two He 51s of 1. J/88 returning from a sortie. In the foreground is Staffelkapitän Harro Harder in his 2-64. Harder's aircraft is easily recognizable by the swastika on the fuselage side, which he applied contrary to regulations.

however all of the Do 17 bombardiers were off the mark. The same target was attacked the next day; this time the entire formation, consisting of eight He 70s, put its bombs on the target.

On May 13, *Leutnant* Wandel was shot down by 20mm flak near Bilbao and taken prisoner. He returned after the fall of Bilbao. *Unteroffizier* Kolbow bailed out over friendly territory on the 20th after being hit by anti-aircraft fire.

Oberleutnant Lützow shot down a *Chato* over Bilbao on May 22. The Fiats accounted for another the next day, and on May 28 two more *Chatos* fell to *Oblt.* Lützow and *Fw.* Braunschweiger near Santander. Targets for the bombers were Miravalles on the 25th, rail lines near Orduna on the 26th and an airfield east of Reinosa on the 27th. On May 29 twenty-one Ju 52s and VB/88 bombed Amorebieta and Pico de Gorbea.

The assault on the last defensive ring around the city of Bilbao began on June 11. On the 12th the attackers forced a 500 meter breach in the powerful fortifications, and finally, on June 19, a Spanish armored company with German Panzer I tanks rolled into the city.

In the meantime, the *Chatos* sent to Bilbao at the end of may had suffered further losses. On June 4, the Italian fighter group *La Cucaracha* claimed to have shot down five I-15 fighters; for their part the Republicans reported two Fiats shot down. Two *Chatos* were lost in air combat on the 5th, one of them falling to "Old" Rolf Pingel near St. Julian de Musques, while five more were destroyed on the ground. With these losses the *Chato* unit had ceased to exist. The Nationalist air forces also suffered losses: on June 11 an Hs 123 (*Angelito*), on the 15th an He 70 reconnaissance machine (*Rayo*) and on the 24th an He 46 reconnaissance aircraft (*Pava*). The Hs 123 was shot down during a dive-bombing attack, the aircraft's pilot, *Uffz.* Wilmsen, losing his life.

Cooperation between the close-support aircraft and the ground troops during this period had been quite outstanding. Leading the way was Harder's 1. J/88, which had been dubbed the "Marabu" *Staffel* in reference to its *Staffel* emblem:

One of the hastily-erected concrete bunkers in the "Iron Ring" around Bilbao.

Panzer I light tanks seen after the capture of Bilbao. With a top speed of 35 kph, the Panzer I was not particularly fast and its armament of two light machine-guns was inadequate.

"On May 31, flying beneath a low ceiling, we descended to a few meters above the Orduna trenches in a row of nine, while at the same time about ten tanks advanced in perfect order followed in stages by the infantry. We attacked until the tanks had broken into the trench system. Then we swept over the rear areas once again."

The He 112 had been in action with 1 *Staffel* for several weeks. Flown by *Unteroffizier* Schulz, nicknamed "Dosenmax," it specialized in hunting Red tanks. On account of its good success the aircraft was jokingly dubbed "*Dosenöffner*" (can opener). Unfortunately, in July the aircraft was written off in a crash. Schulz, who already had three confirmed tanks to his credit, was forced to return to flying the He 51. During the breakthrough toward Bilbao the He 51s flew as many as seven sorties a day, helping transform the Republican retreat into a headlong flight:

"We dove through a gap in the clouds, six machines in a row, and headed for the first position. Our salvo of bombs landed right in the middle of it. Then we flew around the nearest hill two or three times. As we circled we repeatedly entered ragged, low-hanging cloud, which mingled with the swaths of smoke rising from the burning forests and houses in the valley. A company of Moros grasped the situation. They stormed the hill under our covering fire, in the center a color bearer with a giant red-yellow-red flag. Suddenly the Reds came out of their positions, woods and houses, one group after another. Panic-stricken they ran away, heedless of cover. We came down low and machine-gunned them."

During the Battle of Bilbao *Leutnant* Kaldrack, who went on to become a *Zerstörer* pilot and win the Oak Leaves, distinguished himself as a battlefield reconnaissance pilot. He spent the entire day circling over the lines in his He 45, passing on his reports. He was

"Dosenmax" poses in front of one of his victims, an armored truck, somewhere between Ochandiano and Durango. Such vehicles were frequently used by the Republicans to transport men and munitions.

Light tanks abandoned by the Republicans during the retreat from Bilbao. On the left is a Renault FT 17.

the eyes of the Legion headquarters staff.

The following report by an officer of the Legion, written following an inspection of a captured Republican airfield, betrays a certain bond with the courageous enemy:

"Something made me truly sad. Each machine's parking place was recognizable by a small, semicircular wall of sand, whose purpose was to prevent burning oil from flowing from one machine to the next. But these people hadn't reckoned with the coming catastrophe. They must have sat in their machines all day so as to be ready to take off the moment a Nationalist aircraft appeared, not to shoot it down, but to get their machines to safety. Lonely and abandoned, the chocks still sat in front of the last three aircraft. They had one of our own on their conscience, but nevertheless I felt sorry. I would not liked to have been in their shoes. They certainly had flying spirit here. A German pilot, who had been forced to bail out over Bilbao, fell into the hands of a raging mob. A Russian fighter pilot, who had likewise been shot down and who landed by parachute not far from the German, saved him from being lynched. As well, the fallen member of my *Staffel* had been buried by the enemy with military honors. Not hate, rather a chivalrous fighting spirit seems to have prevailed here. But because of our superiority the balance had become so unequal that the Red fliers no longer flew aggressively and only tried to avoid the worst. I had respect for this enemy. In the nearby factory lay the remains of sixteen Curtiss single-seat fighters. All had been burned. We were able to count them by their undercarriages, which, as the sturdiest components, were still there. We also found many Czech Walter engines."

While the *Legion Condor* was engaged at Bilbao, the bulk of the Spanish Nationalist fighters were in action on the Ebro front in the Zaragoza-Huesca area, defending against a Red offensive. They were the Morato fighter group with its Fiats, the Corsini squadron with He 51s and the José Perez Pardo group with He 46s. They faced the *Rata* squadrons led by Ujov and Lokjev. Apart from the Americans Tinker and Bämler, all of the pilots were Russian.

On June 11, the Republicans bombed Zaragoza. The Morato group was able to shoot down five of the attackers. The next day there was an encounter between eight Fiats and a *Rata* squadron, which ended with the downing of four I-16s. In another action the Nationalist Fiats shot down two reconnaissance aircraft.

On June 18, the Republican Air Force carried out an attack on the city of Huesca with two squadrons of *Katiuskas* and three squadrons of *Rasantes*, escorted by five squadrons of fighters. The attack inflicted major damage on the city. This marked the end of the fighting near Huesca, since with the fall of Bilbao it was no longer of any significance. In this one week Nationalist fighters claimed twenty-one victories. Morato topped the list of aces with 21 "kills," Salvador now had 10 and Salas 7.

Fiat C.R.32 3-51, the aircraft of Gruppo Commander Joaquin Garcia Morato. Morato led all fighter pilots during the Spanish Civil War with a total of 40 victories.

During the fighting the signals unit had divided its 2. Ln/88 among the three Spanish Navarra Brigades (1st Brigade, Colonel Garcia Valino; 3rd Brigade, Colonel Latorre and 4th Brigade, Colonel Camillo Alonso Vega), while 3rd Company placed six ground observer teams in the attack zone. In early May the airfield at Burgos was provided with its own ground transmitter when the "furniture van transmitter" of 4. Ln/88 moved there from Salamanca. At the same time 1. Ln/88 and the rest of 2nd Company moved into new quarters in Vitoria; only a skeleton crew remained at Salamanca.

The month of May also witnessed the incident involving the German battlecruiser *Deutschland* at the roadstead at Ibiza. The *Deutschland* was the German component of the naval blockade within the framework of the non-intervention agreement which had been concluded between Great Britain, France, Germany, Italy, the Soviet Union, Belgium, Sweden and Czechoslovakia on September 28, 1936. The ironic thing about the NIC was that nearly all its members were deeply involved in the events in Spain, whether through arms deliveries or direct intervention, thus acting contrary to their own resolutions.

The *Deutschland* was lying at the Ibiza roadstead on May 29 when two Republican aircraft attacked from out of the setting sun between 1800 and 1900 and hit the deck of the battlecruiser with two bombs. A few minutes later four Republican destroyers opened fire on the coast from a range of nine nautical miles. One of the bombs pierced the deck of the seamen's mess killing 31 sailors and wounding 75. In spite of the damage the ship remained seaworthy and combat ready.

Hitler flew into a terrible rage when the incident was reported to him following his opening address at the fourth Reich Agricultural Show in Munich on May 30. He immediately ordered the bombardment of the harbor of the city of Valencia, the seat of the Republican government, as a reprisal. Concerns that there might be minefields in front of Valencia led to a decision to bombard Almeria instead. A fleet unit consisting of the battlecruiser *Admiral Scheer* and the torpedo boats *Seeadler, Albatros, Leopard* and *Luchs* approached Almeria at dawn on May 31. At 0728 *Admiral Scheer* opened fire on the harbor and railway installations. At 0733 the Republicans began to return fire. At 0745 the German ships turned away, and at 0758 the *Admiral Scheer* fired the last round. Altogether the *Admiral Scheer, Seeadler* and *Albatros* had fired 98 x 280mm, 100 x 105mm and 48 x 88mm shells, causing numerous fires in the harbor area. Shore batteries fired sixty rounds at the ships.

Krupp L3H-163 truck in service as a heavy signals truck (Kfz. 62) with Ln/88 of the Legion Condor.

For the first time since taking power Hitler had become involved in open hostilities.

While escorting Ju 52s to the Villaverde area on July 2 *Oblt.* Lützow and *Ofw.* Hillmann were forced to take to their heels; five Italian Fiats scrambled from Villarcayo and mistakenly attacked the German fighters. Unable to shake off the Italians and not wanting to return fire, they were forced to turn tail and dive away. That same day J/88's new commander arrived. Because of the Republican advance near Valdemorillo and Brunete, plans to move the *Jagdgruppe* to the recently-built, well-situated airfield at Alar de Rey had to be abandoned. On July 7, the entire unit hastily transferred to bases in the area west of Madrid to help stem the Republican advance, together with VB/88 and A/88. The same day the fighters escorted eight He 70s and bombers of VB/88 on an attack against Valdemorillo.

Relief Attack Near Brunete

While fighting raged in the north the Republican forces in the Madrid area were able to reorganize their troops and prepare a strike against the stationary front of the *Nacionales* undetected.

On July 6, Spanish Republican divisions and the XI and XIII International Brigades launched a surprise attack from the salient west of Madrid southward toward Quijorna and Brunete. The action had been conceived solely as a spoiling offensive against Nationalist preparations for an attack on Santander. Led by Republican General Miaja, in the first eight days the attack was a complete success. The weakly-held Nationalist positions, some of them shielded by only a single row of barbed wire, were unable to halt the advance of the massed forces of the Republicans.

Air units were hastily withdrawn from the northern sector and transferred to the familiar forward bases west of Madrid. The fighting was to result in a concentrated employment of the air forces of both sides. Once again Stab/88 was to command the assembled Nationalist air units.

J/88's 1 and 2 *Staffeln* arrived at Escalona and Avila, respectively, on July 7, while the *Gruppenstab* and 3 *Staffel* reached Villa del Prado on the 8th. Also mustered by the Nationalists were: two groups of Italian C.R.32 fighters under Majors Zotti and Casero, an Ro 37 group, a group of eleven Spanish He 45s, an Aero 101 squadron, the reconnaissance aircraft of the *Legion Condor*, six Spanish Ju 52 bomber groups, the *Kampfstaffel* of VB/88 and the Italian Savoia bombers, altogether about 200 aircraft.

The Republicans had assembled approximately 400 aircraft, of which about 200 were *Ratas* and *Chatos*. As well there were two groups of close-support aircraft (*Nataschas*) and two bomber groups (*Katiuskas*). The Republicans had concentrated at least five anti-aircraft batteries in the El Escorial-Valdemorillo area.

The Republicans possessed a marked superiority in the air during the initial days of the offensive. The unbearable heat (as high as 50 degrees C in the shade) made sorties an ordeal. As the battle went on air battles developed over the combat zone on a scale not before seen in the war, with up to 200 machines taking part. The pilots flew as many as four sorties per day. On July 8, *Hauptmann* Handrick took over as *Kommandeur* of J/88 from *Hauptmann* von Merhart, who was well-liked for his calm nature and thoughtfulness. During his tour of duty in Spain Handrick was known by the pseudonym "Hermann."

The Republicans had prepared plenty of surprises for their opponents of the *Legion Condor*. Harro Harder recorded in his diary:

"We were sitting quietly on the airfield at about 1900 yesterday when they came: a flight of Martin bombers suddenly appeared out of the mist at an altitude of about 2,500 meters! Before I could shout a warning we heard the sickening sound of falling 100kg bombs. It was a terrible feeling; everyone believed that the sound was coming straight for him. We lay flat in the dirt as the bombs exploded. There were towering columns of smoke, dust and dirt, splinters howled through the air, then it was all over. The bombs were on target, but I'm not quite sure why they used delayed action fuses. Three bombs fell among my second *Kette*. Two machines were slightly damaged. There was no other damage, no wounded, only a peculiar empty feeling in the stomach. Immediately afterward we took off with the

Hasty regrouping on the Brunete Front. A Mercedes 3000 serves to transport ground personnel to the new area of operations.

Limbered, with its accessories packed, an 88mm Flak 36 waits for the gun tractor.

Following repairs, abandoned Republican armored trucks were often integrated into the Legion's vehicle columns to supplement their transport capacity.

The school building in Escalona served as quarters for the technical personnel of 1 Jagdstaffel/88.

The pilot of 6-29 tried to land his Messerschmitt at the new base at Avila in a crosswind, resulting in a collapsed undercarriage.

The engine cowling of this Bf 109 B-2 has been removed, revealing the Jumo 210. Visible behind the propeller spinner are the gears of the propeller pitch control mechanism. On the right are the magazines for the two fuselage machine-guns, one of which is equipped with a leather hand grip.

remaining ten machines on a vehicle hunt east of Brunete. As we approached, several vehicles tried to save themselves by driving away at high speed. I dove on the first one, quite low, as if attacking a practice target and let him have it. As I pulled up I saw the truck roll across the ditch into a field out of control. It tipped over in a cloud of dust, tossing ten to fifteen lifeless bodies onto the road. *Hauptmann* Handrick, who was flying behind me, shot up a second truck, which then drove into a tree at full speed. A third truck suffered a similar fate. In any case we had more than avenged the two damaged aircraft."

Meanwhile VB/88 had completely reequipped with the He 111, having handed over its Do 17 E aircraft to A/88, and was later integrated into K/88 as 4 *Staffel*. During the Battle of Brunete the bombers operated from Salamanca and Avila. The reconnaissance aircraft also operated from Avila, ensuring good cooperation with the bombers.

Three Italian fighters were lost on July 6 and 7. The Russians lost two *Ratas*, one of which force landed near El Rincon largely intact. A detailed technical inspection was made of the aircraft and the pilot was interrogated at length. Twenty-eight years old, a former agricultural worker and a pilot since 1932, he had received instruction on the *Rata* in Russia. On completion of his training he had travelled by ship to Le Havre and from there by rail to Paris and then back to Spain (Valencia) by ocean liner.

On July 8, *Leutnant* Pingel and *Unteroffizier* Höneß shot down two SB-2 bombers, On July 10, the Russians shot down the Fiat of Spaniard Jesùs Rubio; the pilot parachuted to safety. Two He 70s of A/88 fell victim to the strong fighter defenses, or was it to the guns of Italian Fiats as the rescued crews surmised? Two days later Rubio's comrade Captain Bermudez de Castre was shot down and killed in combat with *Chatos*. July 12 was a successful day for the German fighter pilots. "Old" Pingel, Buhl and Boddem each destroyed a *Rata*, while an SB-2 fell to Pingel and Höneß shot down two *Pragas*. The Nationalists, five of whose Fiats had arrived at Avila, reported the destruction of an I-15, while the Italians, who had 30 to 40 Fiats in the air, claimed five I-15s and four I-16s.

The first mass bombing raid by K/88, carried out with bombers of A/88, took place on July 8 against roads and villages in the area of the Republican advance. Fighter cover was provided by the Bf 109s of 2. J/88. The towns of Brunete, Villanueva de la Canada and Valdemorillo, a supply base, sustained heavy damage. A relay attack the same night was directed against troop concentrations in a wooded area.

By July 9, the two flak batteries had arrived at the front following a fast overland drive and began to take part in the fighting. VB/88 and A/88 paid two visits to the front that day, escorted by the entire *Jagdgruppe*. After dark the Ju 52s of K/88 bombed

The "artists" of the VB-Staffel let their imaginations run wild in decorating the unit's He 111 Bs. The photos on this page, all taken at Burgos in July 1937, illustrate a selection of individual markings. The aircraft in the lower, right-hand photo is that of Albert Schreiweis.

Starting the engine of an I-16 using a Hucks-type starter. Mechanics of the Legion Condor try out the method on the captured Republican fighter.

A Type 10 Rata which force-landed in Nationalist territory. The aircraft has been finished in Nationalist colors and carries the inscription "No somos naide" — "We are no one."

Teniente "Old" Pingel, one of the most successful pilots of 2. J/88. Most of his victories were gained in Bf 109 B 6-11.

Leutnant Peter Boddem's incredible series of victories (10 kills) began in July 1937. Small of stature and delicate, his reserved style scarcely fit the image of the daredevil fighter pilot.

enemy airfields and villages in the enemy rear. The next day saw an intensification of efforts to halt the enemy offensive until ground troops could be brought in from the northern front. The Legion's light and heavy anti-aircraft guns were in action around the clock engaging air and ground targets and the results were impressive.

The Panzer I tanks of *Gruppe* "Drohne," which had been thrown into the defensive struggle, proved more useful for their effect on morale than for their firepower. These light, fully tracked vehicles, poorly armed with two 7.92mm machine-guns, were far inferior to the T-26 tanks of the enemy and therefore avoided confrontations with them. Nevertheless their rattling tracks and the martial roar of their engines provided a not to be underestimated morale boost for the infantry they supported.

Four Republican batteries made things difficult for the aircraft of *Kampfgruppe* 88 and the He 51s as they approached the battlefield at low altitude. The entire combat zone around Brunete, only a few kilometers square, was literally plowed up as a result of the constant air attacks. None of the villages in the area, most of which were jammed full of Republican troops, were spared.

On July 11, *Unteroffizier* Flegel wrote off his Bf 109 in a forced landing following an engine failure. On the 13th an air battle took place which lasted almost an hour. *Feldwebel* Boddem shot down the *Chato* flown by the American Harold Dahl, who was captured. He was initially sentenced to death but was later reprieved by Franco. *Feldwebel* Braunschweiger shot down a *Rata*. On joining 2 *Staffel* he had been assigned Bf 109 B, 6-13, which none of the other pilots wanted to fly on account of its "unlucky" number. The aircraft served Braunschweiger faithfully throughout his tour in Spain, and as a result he became especially fond of the aircraft. The Italians reported the destruction of two *Ratas*. Two Fiats collided in midair and crashed. The Republicans claimed that they had shot down nine fighters, two Romeos and a Ju 52. The previous day the Germans had lost *Uffz.* Guido Hönefs, who was shot down and killed. His Bf 109 crashed vertically to the ground from an altitude of 2,500 meters. He may have been shot down by the American Tinker.

Frontal view of a Panzer I delivered from Germany.

The Russian T-26 was a solid, aggressive-looking tank. Several examples fell into Nationalist hands near Brunete.

On July 14, Nationalist fighters shot down five *Nataschas*, two of which fell to Morato's guns. The Spanish ace scored again the next day, downing two *Ratas*. According to statements by Tinker the Republicans claimed to have shot down no less than eleven Fiats and He 51s. On July 16 *Leutnant* Pingel was able to bring down a *Rata*, which crashed near Fuenlabrada. The Republicans claimed two Bf 109s, two Heinkels and a Ju 52. The fact is, however, that no Bf 109s were lost that day.

Six SB-2 bombers attacked 2. J/88s base at Avila early on the morning of the 16th, but dropped their eight bombs a kilometer beyond the railway station. The German fighters had taken off at 0530 to escort three Spanish He 45s over the front. The *Katiuskas* therefore had only the airfield flak to be concerned about, "and they were asleep," as *Staffelkapitän* Lützow wrote sarcastically in his diary. That evening four more SB-2s appeared over the airfield, but once again their bombs were wide of the target. A Ju 52 took off for Germany at 1600 with the body of Guido Höneß on board.

VB/88 took off at daybreak on the 17th to attack Alcalá. Eight fighters of *Jagdgruppe* 88's 2 *Staffel* were flying above and below the mixed unit when two *Ratas* tried to approach the bombers. After landing Lützow wrote:

"I caught one of them beautifully, approached to twenty meters and was about to fire when I saw blue smoke trails passing beneath me. Brücker had lost sight of me beneath his wing and, thinking I had overshot, opened fire from a greater range. I pushed the nose down, but my speed was too great. Suddenly the *Rata* was only three or four meters in front of me. A pity! I was forced to break away."

In charge of providing medical care to the aircrew of the Legion until February 1938 was Stabsarzt Dr. Heinrich Neumann. He visited the various airfields in a captured enemy aircraft of an unidentified type.

Dr. Neumann's aircraft with the Red Cross and an extremely optimistic plea to enemy fighters, literally: "Don't bother me and I won't bother you!"

In the evening K/88, VB/88, A/88 and the Savoias, escorted by Fiat C.R.32s, He 51s and 2. J/88, launched the first major air attack in preparation for an attempt by the Nationalists to seal off the penetration near Brunete. The Fiats stayed with the bombers while the Messerschmitts went hunting north of Madrid. There they ran into six to nine *Ratas*. "Hermann" Handrick was forced to make an emergency landing at Escalon with engine trouble.

On July 18, Franco's troops, a large percentage of which were again Navarra Brigades under General Varela, were ready to launch their counteroffensive. At 0730 every available machine of the Nationalist air forces moved up to the front, and soon bombs were once again raining down on the Republican positions. The day began with the tactics developed on the northern front: the bombers dropped their loads directly in front of the attacking infantry, followed by close-support attacks by the He 51 units. Three minor penetrations were made into the enemy positions, but the Nationalist troops failed to reach the day's objective.

Once again there was heavy fighting in the air, during which Tinker shot down a Fiat flown by the Italian Lieutenant Mollo, his eighth and last victory. *Oberfeldwebel* Hillmann was able to bring down a *Rata*, but another of the Republican fighters shot down *Unteroffizier* Harbach. Fortunately, however, Harbach was able to parachute from his Messerschmitt and landed safely in friendly territory.

The area around Brunete was rather flat and heavily defended by anti-aircraft guns. This made things difficult for the He 51 units, as there was no high ground behind which they could approach their targets unseen. On July 19, a Spanish He 51 was lost to ground fire. Harder described the missions flown on the 18th:

"We attacked for ten minutes, flying through bursting flak the whole time. Right and left, above and below us, one burst after another. One learned to clench his teeth. Staffel discipline was wonderful, everyone stayed in line. There were bombers above us as well, and we nearly flew into the explosions from their bombs. The setting sun colored the smoke and dust blood-red. Several machines were hit by anti-aircraft fire, my own 2-64 was hit by rifle fire."

On July 19 *Unteroffizier* Schulz, the "Dosen-Max," ended the short existence of He 112 V4, in which he had destroyed three enemy tanks. On the return flight from the front engine trouble compelled him to make a forced landing. The aircraft was a total "write-off." Schulz was uninjured apart from his tongue, which was clenched between his immaculate teeth on impact. Having bitten his tongue half off, Schulz was forced to endure considerable pain, as well as a ribbing from the other members of his *Staffel*.

July 21 saw *Feldwebel* Boddem shoot down a *Rata*, a feat which he repeated on the 25th. As a result of these successes Boddem came to be looked upon as one of the *Staffel* "aces." *Oberleutnant* Galland received his baptism of fire with Harder's 1 *Staffel* on July 24 during the fighting around Brunete. Harder wrote:

"Our assignment was to suppress the flak and

In spite of its limited bombload the He 45 was also to be found over the front near Brunete and Quijorna.

He 45 15-6 flipped over on landing at Avila following a bombing sortie. The crew escaped unhurt.

afterward support the attack by the infantry. This mission will likely be remembered always by all eight of us who took part — myself, *Hptm.* Handrick, *Lt.* Reutter, *Lt.* Galland, *Ofw.* Wilfert, *Uffz.* Beurer, *Uffz.* Kolbow and *Gefr.* Terry. I divided the *Staffel* into four pairs. We flew as far as Brunete at low level, then climbed. We observed the bombing by the Spanish squadrons. Villanueva del Pardillo was almost totally obscured by smoke. Then we made our attack on the anti-aircraft positions. We were greeted by a real display of fireworks. Shells burst beside, above and below us, sometimes almost right in our machines. We went over to a low-level attack and were met by intense 20mm fire from every direction. I was able to make one of the AA positions clearly. I dove, pinning them down with machine-

The end of He 112 5-1, just short of the airfield at Escalona. The leader of the recovery party dryly diagnosed the aircraft as a complete write-off.

"Dosenmax" with pilots of J/88. From left: Lt. Heino Greisert, Lt. Rolf Pingel, Uffz. Max Schulz, Uffz. Hermann Stange, Lt. Hein Brücker.

gun fire, and dropped my whole load on the position. Everywhere one looked there were He 51s dancing and attacking through the anti-aircraft fire. The battle lasted about eight minutes, until we had dropped all of our bombs. Then we assembled and headed in the direction of Brunete to support the infantry. As soon as they saw us they launched their assault. Although we had almost no ammunition or bombs, we so shook the Red infantry through several bold attacks that they left their positions and ran away in headlong flight. We dived on them unrelentingly, but after landing we were rather all in ourselves."

The He 51s took off twice more that day. *Leutnant* Reutter was killed on the final sortie, shot down by ground fire. Also lost was a Do 17. Harder recorded what happened in his diary:

"We took off with six machines and attacked simultaneously with 3 Staffel, which was somewhat farther east than we. After four or five passes I saw one of our aircraft go down in a spin with one wing gone, crash and burn. It was Leutnant Reutter. He was my best pilot.

"Our nerves were just about shot. This latest loss just about finished me off. The staff medical officer urgently requested three weeks leave for the five senior pilots of my *Staffel*. Beurer, whose aircraft had taken numerous hits that morning, had already broken down. The rest of us were not far away from it. There was another big attack yesterday. The heavy bombers got there ahead of us. When we arrived the infantry began to advance at the double. The Reds were pulling back everywhere. Columns of wagons came out of every road and gully, the Red infantry left their trenches and ran across the open fields in rows one behind the other. Mixed in with the fleeing troops were escaped horses and pack animals, then cars, and here and there tanks, crawling slowly along, all the time firing, everything in a wild flight. We attacked unrelentingly. 3 *Staffel* dove on them after us, twice, then it was our turn again. Thirty to forty vehicles had become stuck north of Cauada. We strafed them with our machine-guns and dropped our bombs. Here a munitions truck exploded, there a bomb tore apart several cars, it was terrific chaos. To the side of the road tanks were pulling back, a terrific number. I'm sure that the enemy suffered tremendous losses on this day."

The offensive was to resume on July 24 after a brief pause. In spite of several sorties by all available aircraft, by afternoon the attackers had gained little ground. Finally, a concentrated bombing attack swung the pendulum in favor of the Nationalist side. Quite unexpectedly, and almost unnoticed, the field of rubble that was the town of Brunete fell into the hands of Franco's troops. On July 25 the morale of the Republican Army collapsed completely and the situation near Brunete was restored. *General* Sperrle wrote of this battle:

"Once the Red attack had been brought to a halt, the Red air forces had to be neutralized. The Reds had assembled about thirty of the latest bombers and about sixty modern fighters on airfields in the Madrid area, which continuously attacked the

Sperrle with his staff on "the Generals' Hill" near Brunete.

Nationalist troops and their rear communications with the most unpleasant success. Only with strong fighter cover from the two Italian fighter groups and the two German Bf 109 *Staffeln* (sic) was it possible to carry out attacks with the technically inferior Ju 52 *Staffeln*. After the Red advance had come to a halt, night attacks on the Red airfields succeeded in paralyzing Red air activity within a few days. After numerous losses over the battle zone to fighters and flak no more Red aircraft were seen over the Brunete area."

An interesting note in connection with the night attacks mentioned in Sperrle's account is the use by the "*Rojos*" of I-15s in the night fighter role, in which they claimed a number of Ju 52s. The night fighter squadron, which was led by Eriomenko, also flew by day. In addition to the Russians, its members included two Austrians, two North Americans, a Jugoslav and three Spaniards. The Russian pilots were Serov, Yakishin, Antonov, Ribkin, Karpov, Sheliganov, Stepanov, Gorojov, Kustov and Popov. Karpov was killed near Brunete. On the night of July 24/25 Yakishin shot down a Ju 52 over Nationalist territory. The following night Serov shot down another of the Legion's Ju 52s; the crew was taken prisoner.

July 25 saw a sustained bombardment of the Republican forces. Everything that could carry bombs flew at least three sorties that day. The Italians even made two flights with S.M.81s from distant Soria to add their weight to the attack. The Republican infantry were mowed down by the machine-guns of low-flying Nationalist aircraft as they fled their positions; the war was showing its heartless side. In three weeks more than 30,000 men had fallen in this restricted area; the smell of decomposing bodies hung over the ravaged countryside for weeks.

The commander of the Bf 109 *Staffel, Oblt.* Lützow, has left behind a very vivid description of his *Staffel*'s actions near Brunete, from which we will quote several passages:

"On the average, apart from scrambles, we were in action three times per day. Each sortie lasted about 1 1/2 hours and was flown at altitudes of 6,000 to 7,000 meters. We flew without oxygen then, which we soon regretted, because flying at high altitude without oxygen resulted in extreme fatigue. We had become somewhat demoralized, because in addition to the physical stress of the many sorties and scrambles there was worry over the very rare opportunities to achieve confirmed victories. We constantly had to fight against a three- or four-fold superiority. This meant that one never had time to stay behind an enemy aircraft for more than a brief period. We had to take care to hold our opponents at

The Republican bomber squadrons had meanwhile reequipped with the SB-2 Katiuska and appeared over the area of the attack in swarms.

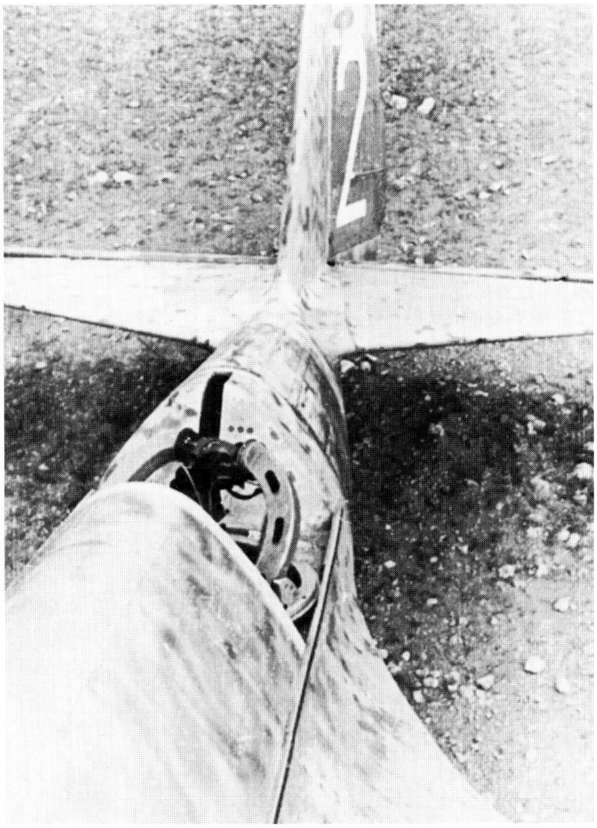

The SB-2's dorsal gunner operated a single machine-gun. When not in use the machine-gun was stowed in a slot in the fuselage spine.

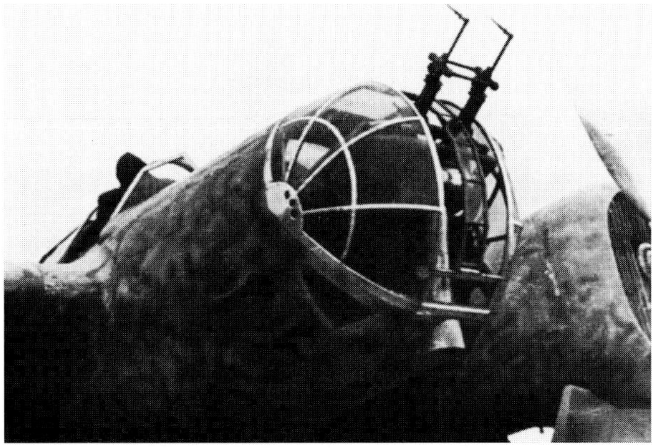

The twin machine-guns in the nose glazing of the SB-2 made things difficult for enemy fighters making frontal attacks and enabled the aircraft to make effective low-level attacks on Nationalist positions after dropping its bombs.

arm's length and keep them away from the bombers or reconnaissance aircraft were these were operating.

"Worst of all were the frequent scrambles. From dawn until dark two pilots had to remain strapped into their machines. When the ground observers or forward flak batteries reported enemy aircraft, the alert *Rotte* had to take off immediately. This was vital if the enemy aircraft were to be intercepted with certainty before they reached the bomb-dropping zone. Because of the mutual bitterness with which the battle was being fought, there was naturally a certain nervousness everywhere. Ground observers sometimes reported our aircraft as enemy ones, and the alert *Rotte* took off in vain. Such false starts did nothing to ease our somewhat overburdened state of mind. Soon the situation had reached a state of overwrought nervousness. People complained about the smallest things, not even sparing their comrades when something failed to suit them. This applied less to the younger ones, who were somewhat less affected by it all.

"One day we were sitting pleasantly beneath our sun awning beside our machines, when we heard the sound of aircraft from south of the airfield. It had to be several aircraft. In any case there was a steady buzzing. Then we could see them too. They appeared to be Italian Savoias on their way home. Suddenly the aircraft turned toward the airfield and flew straight toward us. I raised my binoculars but immediately lowered them again. They were in fact Savoias. By now we could see their nationality markings with our naked eyes. They were flying in a very neat formation, not very high, about 1,500 meters above the field. We counted ten machines. I turned away, but at once someone yelled: 'They're dropping bombs!' I turned around and thought: 'That's impossible.' As I watched, dark shapes separated from the aircraft and fell toward us at ever increasing speed. I just had time to shout, 'everyone into the dugouts!' before the first bomb struck. I saw my mechanic running to the dugout. Several threw themselves to the ground halfway there. I, too, had thrown myself flat onto the ground. I was seized by a helpless rage. I clenched my fists and thought: 'Almighty God, give me the chance to meet these fellows again!'

"The bombs were well aimed, landing in the center of the airfield. But our machines were at the edge of the field and so we got off lightly. My two readiness pilots had kept their nerve. Their faithful mechanics had also stayed with the aircraft and, with the strength of fury, had cranked up the engines. But what good was it? Although they both took off between the bomb craters immediately after the bombs had fallen and set out after the cowardly traitors, they were unable to overtake the bombers. The attack had come as too much of a surprise. No one would have thought it possible that the Reds would stoop to such a dirty trick. The aircraft had been French Potez bombers, which in fact resembled Italian Savoias (sic). It was now clear to us why these fellows had got as far as the base unreported and unmolested. They had been taken by everyone to be Nationalist aircraft.

"As a result, from that day on the ground observers and other reporting posts suspected that behind every aircraft with Nationalist markings was a disguised Red bomber. I must say that we, too, were

Savoia-Marchetti S.M.81 tri-motor, the standard Italian bomber during the Abyssinian War of 1935. By the beginning of World War Two the aircraft was not equal to the demands of a modern bomber.

The successor to the S.M.81 was the S.M.79. The S.M.79-I version equipped the 8th and 11th Bomber Squadrons of the Aviazone Legionara.

no longer sure of things after this incident. It was a terrible feeling. The various types of modern aircraft were quite similar, and many times we were uncertain whether we were dealing with friend or foe. Things had become even more complicated. One day there was a fateful mistake. It was a misty morning and I had taken off with five aircraft while it was still dark for a short patrol over the front. The past few days the Reds had been using the morning twilight to harass our front lines. I wanted to break them of this habit for good. We climbed slowly to 3,000 meters in the usual direction. The 'eyes' of the *Staffel, Fw.* Boddem, one of my most successful pilots, suddenly spotted five dots — first as always! — somewhat higher than we, coming from the direction of Madrid. He drew my attention to them and I gave the signal to attack. I should have known if they were our aircraft, as communications between the units were generally good. Therefore they could only be Red bombers, about to pay us their morning visit. We therefore had to attack first by all means! My men quickly sized up the situation. They peeled off and sandwiched the five between them. This should be a lovely chase, I thought to myself. Inside I congratulated myself for having selected this day to make a morning prowl over the front and forgot all about the early rising. Meanwhile the five bombers, which were flying in close formation, had almost reached our airfield. They flew directly toward it. As we were somewhat lower, we couln't close with them right away. I rammed the throttle forward against the stop and encouraged my brave bird. But it was all in vain, I couldn't catch the bombers before they reached our base. I saw them overfly the airfield, then soon afterward reverse course in a steep right turn and fly away over the city back toward the front. They were coming almost directly toward us. Now they couldn't escape! I turned toward them and prepared to attack. I was still debating which one to select first, when a thought struck me: 'You've seen this type somewhere before.' Suddenly it hit me: 'Man, those are some of the nine Italian high-speed bombers we worked with on the northern front!' There we had always flown along with them for a while after they had completed their mission, moving in close to their cockpits with the twin machine-guns and exchanging greetings. 'You can do that now too,' I thought, 'you can spare a moment.' I approached slowly from the side. Now I could see the Nationalist insignia. I wanted to allow myself a little fun and crossed very close, it was at most two meters, over the three leading Savoias. Then I caught sight of the grim, serious face of one of the gunners, who, with both hands on the triggers of his twin machine-guns, had trained both barrels on me. I thought: My God, he's keen! He's taking advantage of the opportunity to use me for aiming practice. At the same instant there was a thump in my machine ahead and to the right, something hard struck my right shin and I felt a stabbing pain in my right hand. I pulled up sharply, without looking about to see the effect of the hit — for that was all that it could have been — and switched on my guns and my sight. I was determined to shoot no matter what the cost. At the last moment I regained my composure, thank God. I turned around and looked at the airfield which lay behind me. There were no bomb bursts to be seen, so they couldn't have been Red bombers.

The gunner must have mistaken me for an enemy fighter. I switched off the guns and the sight and set course for base. Now I looked around the cockpit for the first time. My right pant leg was completely riddled and there was a neat tear in my shin. It seemed to be no more than a grazing wound, because I felt no more pain. The glove on my right hand had been pierced by several small splinters. Around each splinter a small, red circle was forming. These, too, appeared to be harmless, as I still had full movement in the hand. I couldn't see where the bullets had entered and exited. In any event I flew more cautiously than usual and landed as if on my first solo flight.

"I was lucky, the bullets had passed through the right wing close to the fuselage and through the cockpit. A bullet was still stuck in the control column, just below my right hand. In addition several cables had been pierced, but the damage was so slight that my machine was soon fit for action again. As I later found out, the young and inexperienced Italian gunner had in fact taken me for a Red fighter wearing Nationalist markings and had calmly opened fire on me." (10.7.1937)

"The fighting at the front near Brunete had reached its climax. In spite of our superiority in the air the Red bombers made repeated attacks. One day I was just on my way home following a long patrol over the front, which had taken me over Talavera, Aranjuez, Madrid and Escorial, when I saw flak bursts over the airfield. Stare as I might, I couldn't see any enemy aircraft. I looked at my watch and determined that I had been in the air 70 minutes already. I could therefore not allow myself a long search. Suddenly four Martin bombers appeared, to my left and somewhat lower. Immediately they turned tail and flew off in the direction of Madrid. It was they whom our flak had been firing at. I thought for a moment: should I attack or was there any point? My fuel gauge showed only a few liters left. But who could let such a worthwhile catch escape? I hauled my machine around, switched on guns and sight and set out after them. At full throttle I chased the four Martins. Still at long range, I opened fire, wanting to use all of my ammunition in the small amount of time available. Unfortunately they were flying straight into the sun, so that I saw them only as weak silhouettes. As if that were not enough, the bulb in my reflector sight burned out, leaving me without an accurate means of aiming. All I could do was aim roughly over the nose of the engine, and leave it to fate to decide whether I hit or missed.

"I didn't expect to hit anything. I was firing like a madman, without pausing, but before I could close in on the last of the four bombers my guns overheated and suddenly all three jammed. I cursed like a fishwife and hung there thirty meters behind the enemy, cocking my guns like one possessed. The gunner of the enemy aircraft seized the opportunity and fired at me like crazy. Fortunately, he was so excited that he hit nothing. I had to decide, either break off the pursuit — which I would have to do if I wished to reach my base — or continued to try and clear my guns and shoot down one of the enemy. In the latter event I had to reckon on a forced landing due to lack of fuel, which would have been an unpleasant prospect in this mountainous terrain.

"As I had relatively few aircraft available at the time, I decided to break off the engagement and take the shortest route home. With a sad heart I turned away from my victims. I didn't exactly feel like a hero, but as leader of the *Staffel* I was responsible for the aircraft entrusted to me and had to be economical with my resources.

"On landing at Avila I noticed that the two alert machines had taken off. They had taken up the pursuit of the Red bombers. One of the pilots soon returned after losing contact; the other, *Lt.* Boddem, pursued them deep into enemy territory and shot one down as it was about to land.

"I felt a twinge when he reported the victory to me. Instantly I thought back to my earlier deliberations. This man's actions had been confirmed by his success. I, on the other hand, had also been proved right in spite of my fiasco. Where was the line to be drawn here? Today I still don't know. I believe it is a question of luck, and as everyone knows that is written in the stars." (21. 7. 1937)

After returning from the first sortie on July 21, an escort mission for Spanish Ju 52s and the two Heinkel close-support *Staffeln*, Lützow described the combat strength of his *Staffel*:

"6-9 has to go to Burgos, 6-15's transmitter is shot, 6-13 is washed out, 6-9 is unserviceable, 6-10 is on patrol, I have only three aircraft ready for takeoff for the second mission at 1600."

During the night of July 25/26 the Legion lost a Ju 52 and the crew of *Lt.* Leo Falk of K/88 near Valdemorillo from unexplained causes. 2. J/88's last sorties on July 27 were scrambles to intercept five bombers on one occasion and seven on the other. On both occasions the alarm was sounded too late and the fighters were unable to intercept.

On July 28, both sides dug in along the existing front line. The bloodletting had completely exhausted attackers and defenders alike.

Uninfluenced by the fighting, during July increased efforts were made to send new, modern aircraft to the German fliers in Spain. The following is a listing of all the aircraft delivered by July 7:

Ar 66 c	6 machines as training aircraft
Do 17 E/F	12 machines as bombers and reconnaissance aircraft
He 45	29 machines as tactical reconnaissance aircraft and light bombers

He 46	21 machines as tactical reconnaissance aircraft and artillery spotters
He 50	1 machine as experimental dive-bomber type
He 51	90 machines as fighters and close-support aircraft
He 59	9 machines as maritime reconnaissance aircraft and anti-shipping bombers
He 60	8 machines as coastal reconnaissance aircraft and light bombers
He 70	25 machines as strategic reconnaissance aircraft and light bombers
He 111 B	8 machines as bombers
He 112 V	1 machine as experimental fighter and close-support aircraft
Hs 123	6 machines as dive-bombers
Ju W 34hi	3 machines as courier and mail aircraft
Ju 52/3m	59 machines as bomber and transport aircraft
Ju 52/3m/See	1 machine as transport and courier aircraft
Ju 86 D	4 machines as bombers
Ju 87 A	1 machine as experimental dive-bomber
Kl 32	3 machines as courier aircraft
Bf 108 B	2 machines as communications and courier aircraft
Bf 109 B	17 machines as fighters

To this point in time the following had been delivered as replacement engines through Park/88:

BMW 132 a	71		Jumo 205	2
BMW VI	57		Jumo 205 C	6
BMW VI U	3 engines for He 59		Jumo 205 D	1
BMW VI U	2 engines for Do 17		SAM 22 B	31
DB 600	10			

The first He 111 bombers now took the air route to Spain, flying via Mallorca to Sevilla. They remained parked there for some time, because an integration of the new type was impossible while the Brunete fighting was under way as the bomber *Staffeln* were fully committed. It was not until August that the crews converted to the new bombers and carried out acceptance flights. The same problem was encountered with twenty-two Bf 109 fighters, which were delivered in mid-July and assembled at Leon. Although urgently needed at the front, they could not be released until the pilots had carried out acceptance flights.

Virtually on its own, AS/88 under *Major* Hefele operated against the enemy fleet and sea traffic in the Mediterranean area. As well, the unit's few aircraft, usually no more than six serviceable He 59 floatplanes, were ordered to harass the unloading of ships in Republican harbors. For this purpose a flexibly-mounted Rheinmetall-Borsig 20mm cannon was installed in the nose gun position, replacing the usual MG 15. The He 59 could also carry 1,000 kilograms of bombs.

Following the Nationalist occupation of Malaga in February, AS/88 moved its base there from Melilla. The move placed the unit significantly closer to its area of operations. However, the ideal seaplane base was soon discovered on the island of Mallorca in the bay of Porto de Pollensa. From there the *Staffel's* operational area, equivalent to the radius of action of the He 59, extended along the entire Spanish east coast up to the French border. Moreover, the island group's isolated location gave the crews the comfortable feeling of being removed from the command centers on the mainland and thus allowed them to plan and carry out their operations pretty much independently. *Staffel* personnel were accommodated in the *"Mar y Cel"* tourist hotel, and they fought stubbornly to keep Pollensa as a permanent base in the face of objections from the "know it alls" on the mainland.

On July 17, 1937, the commander of the Nationalist blockade authorized attacks on all Spanish harbors, as long as there were no British ships at anchor, and all blockade runners flying the flags of Panama, Greece, Denmark and Norway. AS/88 thus had an extensive list of targets. Of the ten steamers attacked during the second half of 1937, three were sunk and two others beached. Bombing and strafing attacks against harbor installations were possible only by night on account of the strong flak defenses. Such nocturnal operations tested the navigational skills of the crews to the utmost. Attempts to engage shipping targets with aerial torpedoes had to be abandoned in August 1937, as the torpedoes supplied (imported from Norway) had proved to be of limited value in operational use.

At this point we will take a brief look at the civil operations by *Iberia* (the Spainish airline) and *Deutsche Lufthansa* . During the first months of the civil war DLH was able to continue its line flights to Barajas airfield, near Madrid, and later Loring. Not until the German Reich recognized Franco as the Spanish head of state (November 18, 1936) did the Republican authorities retract this authorization. In future scheduled airline flights were allowed to overfly Republican Spanish territory unmolested, however this may have been a special arrangement with the Republicans. Antonius Raab, the former co-owner of the Raab-Katzenstein Flugzeugwerke Kassel, had established himself as German contact man and adviser to the Spanish Republicans. All negotiations with the Republicans were conducted through him. "Black" delivery flights of military aircraft for the *Legion Condor* inserted into the civil schedule were of course illegal and completely at the risk of the Nationalists.

Internal air services, which were provided by the Spanish airline *Iberia*, were also flown largely by DLH crews. At least three DLH crews flew Ju 52 transport aircraft in Spanish markings on the Tetuan-Sevilla-Salamanca-Valldolid-Vitoria and Tetuan-Sevilla-Salamanca-Burgos-Zaragoza-Palma de Mallorca routes.

When the personnel of AS/88 arrived at Pollensa they discovered the remains of a Dornier J Wal. The aircraft was one of the Do J-Kas series, small numbers of which had been built under license in Spain.

A 20mm Rheinmetall-Borsig cannon installed in the nose position of an He 59. The weapon was a special modification for engaging shipping and ground targets.

Throughout the war Ju 52 courier aircraft made four trips per week between Germany and Spain, keeping *Sonderstab* W, whose headquarters (*Büro Kuhstall*) were in the Albrechtstrasse, Berlin, in contact with the *Legion Condor*. Three Ju 52s were lost on these flights during the war. Within Spanish territory another Ju 52 was used to maintain contact between the individual units of the Legion. Among the Legionaries the aircraft was commonly known as "*die Kleinbahn*" ("light railway").

Two He 59 floatplanes take off in the evening twilight to attack enemy supply lines near the coast.

Ju 52 transports of the Legion headquarters, such as 22-79 pictured here, maintained contact between Pollensa and the mainland.

Part of the IBERIA air park at Burgos. Visible in this photo are Spanish Ju 52s M-CABA Sanjurjo, M-CABE La Cierva and M-CABO Mola, as well as a Lufthansa machine, D-AKYS Emil Thuy.

Ju 52 M-CABO prior to takeoff from Seville for Tetuan. The aircraft's pilot was Flugkapitän Heil.

The German crew of M-CABA, from left: flight engineer Strassburger, Flugkapitän Hans Fritz and radio operator Stegner.

Equipped as an air ambulance, Ju 52 D-AVIA was frequently summoned to Spain to transport wounded to hospitals in Germany.

The emblem painted on the side of this Ju 52 offers a hint as to the functions performed by this courier, mail and long-range transport aircraft. It was one of the aircraft of the so-called "Kleinbahn."

THE NORTHERN FRONT IS ROLLED UP

Once the front in the area of the Republican attack near Brunete had been stabilized, the Nationalist commanders once more turned to their plans to eliminate the "second front," the coastal region of northern Spain between Bilbao and Gijon. The lessons learned in a year of war led Franco, in cooperation with S/88, to make very thorough preparations so as to minimize the chances of failure.

Before moving back to the northern airfields abandoned only a few weeks before, the aircraft of the *Legion Condor* were given a thorough overhaul

Transport duties were mastered with the help of Spanish truck drivers. Second from right is Uffz. Hans Herold, photographed after a minor accident.

A regrouping in the north required the entire transport capacity of the Legion Condor.

Uffz. Staege's Bf 109, 6-30, after cartwheeling on landing at Alar d'el Rey. Staege was pulled from the wreck with minor injuries.

by Park/88 at Leon. There was also time to instruct crews on the waiting He 111s and Bf 109s and allow them to undertake cross-country familiarization flights in the new types.

A few days after the fighting died down west of Madrid, 1st and 2nd Companies of Ln/88 were ordered to move back to the Alar del Rey area as quickly as possible, while 3. Ln/88 waited at Herrera de Pisuerga with a radio beacon in anticipation of the arrival of J/88.

On July 30, elements of the *Jagdgruppe* moved to Alar del Rey (Nogales) and Callahorra (Herrera de Pisuerga). The three *Staffeln* possessed eighteen He 51s and nine Bf 109s.

In the Santander area the Republicans had two squadrons of *Chatos* and two squadrons of *Ratas*. The *Chatos* were led by the Spaniards Jiménez and Riverola; the leaders of the *Rata* squadrons were the Russians Pligunov and Smirnov. The *Rata* flight leaders were also Russian. In addition there were still several dozen obsolescent aircraft such as Bristol Bulldog fighters and de Havilland Dragon light transports and machines by Gourdou, Letov, Koolhoven, Potez, Nieuport and Breguet. The Republican Air Force suffered its first serious blow on August 7, when approximately ten of their fighters were destroyed or badly damaged on the ground in an air attack.

Advancing Nationalist troops found this rare bird, a Czechoslovakian Letov S 231 fighter, at Llanes airfield.

The Czech Aero 101 was used by the Republicans, as well as by the Nationalists, to whom it was known as the Oca. Together with the R-5 and R-Z, the Aero 101 equipped the light bomber and night attack squadrons of the Republican Air Force under the generic title Papagayos.

The rather cumbersome Breguet XIX was forced to soldier on in active service with the Republican Air Force. The aircraft pictured here was abandoned in Asturia and wears hastily-applied Nationalist markings.

A brief note in "Franzl" Lützow's diary from August 13 describe's the status of the German fighters:

"6-8 and 6-9 cannot be repaired. That leaves only ten old Me's (including 6-5). What a mess."

As well as its own K/88, with eighteen Ju 52s and fourteen He 111s, and A/88, with six He 70s and three Do 17s, the *Legion Condor* once again had the Spanish air elements under its command. The total number of available aircraft on the Nationalist side was about 115. The Italian air forces flew under their own command and were supposed to support the advance by the Italian Legion from the Villarcayo area. To the west, in the area around Aquilar del Campo, were concentrated the four Navarra Brigades, which had meanwhile been expanded to divisions. Over this attack force operated the *Legion Condor*. The coastal city of Santander was the intended objective of both groups. Prior to August 7 the flying personnel were given a few days to rest and recuperate, the coast between San Sebastian and Bilbao offering the best opportunities. Unnoticed by the opposing side, in the weeks that followed the individual units moved into their jumping-off positions. Together with Colonel Vigon, the Chief-of-Staff of the Navarra Divisions, S/88 built its command post on the peak of Mount Cocotto. As well as gathering much valuable information which was to be an advantage when the attack began, intercepts of enemy front-line communications in this sector revealed that the Republicans were unaware of what was coming.

On August 5, a patrol over the front by four *Ratas* enticed the German 20mm flak into opening fire, whereupon the *Ratas* strafed the flak positions. The gun crews suffered several casualties as a result of their rashness.

Following this incident it was considered necessary to have K/88 fly diversionary attacks against Santander until the beginning of the attack. It appears that the flights achieved the desired success; in any case, no movement of reserves was observed on the Republican side.

On August 13, German fighters scored their first "kill" on this front, when *Feldwebel* Boddem shot down a *Rata* near Santander.

The attack against Santander began at about 0300 on the night of August 14, 1937, with minor skirmishes on the extreme left wing. At dawn the "flying artillery" of the *Legion Condor* crossed the front from the south and bombed Republican positions in the valleys and on the mountain slopes, while the close-support He 51s of 1. and 3. J/88 strafed trenches and nests of resistance.

The Spanish joined in as best they could with their limited resources of seven Ju 52s, six Aero 101s, twelve He 45s and nine He 51s (under Captain Montero). A second attack that day by the Nationalist air forces brought success; by evening the western group had advanced some distance through the mountainous terrain toward Reinosa. By the end of the day the *Staffeln* had made two more bombing attacks. During the final mission over the front a Ju 52 blew up in midair. An anti-aircraft shell had apparently detonated the aircraft's bombload.

Several concentrated attacks by the forces under S/88 on August 15 and 16 led to the capture of the city of Reinosa, site of Spain's largest arms factory.

Spanish Nationalist He 51s in parade formation on the occasion of a visit by General Kindelan, commander of the Spanish Air Force.

The He 51 of NCO Officer Candidate Queipo de Llano, a member of the squadron commanded by Captain Martin Campos. A mishap while taxying resulted in the aircraft standing on its nose.

Damage assessment photograph of Santander-West airfield (Albericia) following an attack by K/88. The bomb craters in the landing strip have already been filled in.

Late on the morning of August 16 *Leutnant* Rempel of 2. J/88 shot down a *Rata*. The next day *Feldwebel* Boddem achieved a double (1 *Rata*, 1 *Chato*), while *Feldwebel* Flegel scored his first "kill."

The practice of laying out of ground symbols (arrows) at the points of heaviest resistance proved an outstanding success. This method allowed air attacks to be directed at specific objectives with a correspondingly high degree of success. Following the occupation of Reinosa S/88 moved its quarters there, and on August 18 1. and 3. J/88 occupied the forward airfield at Orzales, east of the city. The companies of Ln/88 faced a great deal of hard work maintaining communications between headquarters and the individual units in the difficult, mountainous terrain.

Lützow and Boddem, both of 2. J/88, increased their victory totals on August 18, downing a *Chato* each. The pilots of the *"Zylinder-Staffel"* were acquiring a reputation as experts. That afternoon K/88 carried out a concentrated bombardment of Santander and Torrelavega airfields aimed at wiping out the enemy air force on the ground. The bombers reported the destruction of a dozen Republican aircraft. By now the *Legion Condor*'s bomber *Gruppe* had more than twenty He 111 bombers on strength. It appeared as though air-ground co-operation with the Spanish was finally functioning as intended and had provided the attack battalions with the desired impetus. An He 111 was severely damaged by Republican fighters and was forced to make an emergency landing at Reinosa.

In the days that followed the advance became increasingly arduous. Engineers were repeatedly forced to repair blown bridges and roads in the narrow mountain valleys; small units of infantry were given the job of securing the slopes on both sides of the roads against ambush. The Nationalists met scarcely any serious resistance from Republican forces.

Weather permitting, the bomber *Staffeln* crossed the front several times, day after day, to bomb supply lines, airfields and rail lines in the enemy rear (the Santander-Torrelavega area). As before, the enemy fighters put up stiff resistance. On August 20 two Spanish He 51s collided in cloud and both pilots were killed.

On August 21 and 22, the Republican fighters gave battle. According to the Nationalist communique, thirty Republican aircraft were shot down in this two day period. On the 22nd three *Chatos* were credited to Lützow, Pingel and Flegel. The lion's share of the victories were claimed by the Italian fighter group *"Gamba de Ferro"* at the cost of four of its own fighters.

By August 23, the Italians were within rifle range

Members of the ground crew take a break in the shadow of a tree. In the background He 111 25-14 waits to be prepared for the next sortie.

With several sorties being flown each day the bomb dump, located next to the dispersals, had to be replenished regularly.

There were still losses in materiel and personnel. The crew of an He 111 B-2 of 3. K/88 (note the yellow spinner tip) was forced to risk a belly landing at Burgos after the aircraft's undercarriage hydraulics were shot out.

of Santander. The Republicans had set up a strongpoint-style defensive line in front of the advancing Navarra Divisions. Exhausted from forced marching, the Spanish troops were unable to take Gredo Mountain that night as they had been ordered to do. Without hesitation Stab/88, which was accompanying the forward troops, selected a Spanish company, advanced toward the peak and occupied it; a few hours later the German command post was operational on the Gredo.

K/88 flew its first sorties against targets in Asturia and its capital Gijon that day. The attacks were aimed at the *Ratas* and *Chatos* which had withdrawn there. Fighter cover was provided by 2. J/88.

Santander surrendered on August 25, eleven days after the offensive began. About 50,000 Republican troops marched into captivity and great quantities of war materiel fell into Nationalist hands. By this time the assault group under the command of S/88 had turned west with the objective of capturing all of Asturia as far as Gijon. The flying units supported the new advance from their previous airfields.

Harro Harder had converted to the Bf 109 in mid-August and was able to score his first victory on August 27, an SB-2 over Huesca. He described the engagement in his diary:

"The Martin bomber is tough, flies wonderfully

The symbol of the falange was painted on Santander's light tower soon after the fall of the city.

Staffelkapitän Harder's regular wingman was Uffz. Ernst Terry.

6-36, Harro Harder's new Bf 109. The swastika carried on Harder's earlier He 51 has been "toned down" to a diagonal cross.

and is awfully fast. Sigmund and I peel off to attack, Terry covers the rear. I fly up quite close to him, dancing in his propeller wash, and aim calmly. Just one short burst and the large machine is in flames. I pull up and watch the bomber crash in a field."

Late in August, 1 *Staffel,* which was in the process of reequipping, together with elements of 2 *Staffel,* had been sent for a brief period to Alfamén, a large, desolate field near Zaragoza. On August 23, the Republicans had started a relief offensive near Belchite. They made some gains east and northeast of Zaragoza, but these were strategically insignificant and had no effect on the advance on Asturia.

In Aragon, where the relief attack was taking place, the Republican Air Force was able to draw on plentiful resources. The first Spanish pilots trained in Russia (about 200) were ready to see action, as were about fifty from the French class and 200 trained in Spain. There were still about 200 Russian pilots on hand. The *Rata* group was led by Ujov, and there was a *Chato* and a *Katiuska* group as well. On the Nationalist side all that was initially available

Another pilot of 1 Staffel, Oblt. Erich Woitke (4 victories). The diagonal cross remained the emblem of 1. J/88 for some time.

Supplies for the Spanish Nationalists. Ten Hs 123 Angelitos wait at Leon, assembled, serviced and ready to be collected.

was an He 46 group and a squadron of He 51s; however, on August 25 the Morato Group and the Italian fighter group *"As de Bastos"* arrived at Zaragoza with their C.R.32s.

On August 26, the commander of the He 46 group, Major Pèrez Pardo, was shot down and killed. An He 51 was also lost. The Italians appear to have lost four Fiats and a Romeo, if one can believe the Republican war communique. On September 2, the Morato Group surprised a squadron of fifteen *Chatos* and shot down seven. Morato scored his 27th kill in the skirmish, Captain Salvador his 14th and Salas his 9th. By September 9 the Red offensive near Belchite had petered out, broken in no small part by the massed bombing attacks delivered by two Spanish Ju 52 groups and an S.M.79 group.

3. J/88 continued to be purely a close-support *Staffel.* The unit's pilots called themselves the "Deep-sea Divers from the Race of the Mickey Mice." "Deep-sea diving" was in a figurative sense the daily bread of the He 51 pilots. Micky Mouse was the *Staffel* emblem introduced by *Staffelkapitän* Douglas Pitcairn. At the end of July Pitcairn handed over the *Staffel* to *Oberleutnant* Adolf Galland, who got his first taste of action in the operations in the Brunete area. A few days later *Leutnant* Balthasar joined the Galland *Staffel.* Balthasar had been grounded for a time and was forced to give up his beloved He 112 to Schulz, already well-known as "Dosenmax." During this enforced break he commanded an airfield operating company. Meanwhile 3 *Staffel* had developed its own "secret weapon." As

The new chief of 3 Staffel, Oblt. Adolf Galland, had to put his ambitions as a fighter pilot on hold in Spain. Instead he became involved in the development of close-support tactics.

A "Devil's Egg" beneath the fuselage of an He 51 of 1 Staffel. Two 10kg bombs have simply been tied to the drop tank with strips of cloth.

the Heinkels operated from airfields close to the front, carriage of the 170-liter drop-tank beneath the fuselage was unnecessary. Indeed, in the presence of heavy ground fire it posed something of a hazard; a hit from an incendiary bullet could turn the He 51 into a blazing torch in a matter of seconds.

Clever minds in the *Staffel* began experimenting with ways to expand the capabilities of the weapons release installation, which consisted of an Elvemag 6 C 10 IX in the fuselage (for 6 x 10kg bombs). They attached two 10kg fragmentation bombs to the sides of the drop-tank and carried out the first release trials. After several modifications the weapon was a success: the tank burst on impact, spraying the contents over an area of about 100 square meters, and the exploding bomb ignited the whole thing. An experiment in the field had produced an effective fluid incendiary bomb for use against positions and troops concentrations. The supply depots did wonder though about the increase in requisition forms for He 51 drop-tanks and the increased fuel consumption by the fighters. The home-made firebombs were filled with 87-Octane fuel.

Following the interlude in Aragon the Nationalists were able to once again concentrate fully on the conquest of Asturia. On September 2 the fighters of the *Legion Condor* transferred to Santander (Pontejos and Santander-West). Republican fighter strength in the north had shrunk to barely two squadrons of I-15s and I-16s. In order to minimize losses these restricted their activities to the interception of the fast Nationalist bombers (He 111s). Bf 109s soon began flying escort for the bombers and almost all of the combats in this campaign were between the German and Republican fighters. The

Visit from Berlin! Gen.Lt. Wilberg (2nd from left) with Oblt. Joachim Heinrich Schlichting, who took over 2. J/88 from "Franzl" Lützow. On the left is "Old" Pingel, right "Seppl" Seiler. This photo was taken at Santander in September 1937.

A group of notables in front of the command post barracks at Santander. From left: Gotthard Handrick, Peter Boddem, Günther Lützow, H. J. Schlichting (partially concealed), Walter Ehle, Harro Harder, Erich Woitke, Rolf Pingel.

Santander-West airfield was on located a gentle slope and could be tricky when landing or taking off. Here Fw. Norbert Flegel has let his aircraft 6-7, an early Bf 109 B-1, "come off the tracks."

He 51s and C.R.32s restricted their activities mainly to the support of the ground forces. Adolf Galland described a typical operation:

"We flew along in the last red glimmer of the sun a few meters above the calm water of the Biscaya 60 to 80 kilometers deep in enemy territory. Then we turned toward land, climbed to 1,000 meters and soon the first salvo from eighteen machine-guns and numerous bomb racks was striking communications traffic and troop, munitions and supply transport. Then we turned back in the direction of the front, attacking anything that showed itself on the roads and railway lines. We dubbed this new tactic 'evening

Uffz. Hermann Stange wrote off 6-12, another early Bf 109 with a fixed-pitch wooden propeller, in a similar fashion. Pilots making such careless blunders were usually given a dressing down and disciplined.

blessing' and were extremely pleased with our success and the merry chase."

Those who would frown upon the sentiments expressed by this carefree, cheerful hunter are touching on the basic question of the sense and madness of armed conflict; why train young men in the efficient use of deadly weapons only to express shock later when they actually put their training to use. This question could be addressed to the militaries and governments of both power blocks.

Some of Galland's sorties were much more difficult and dangerous, such as one on September 9, 1937:

"We were attacked by enemy fighters, six *Ratas* and four Curtisses. It immediately developed into a

An He 51 Staffel sneaks along the coast for a low-level attack on road traffic near Villaviciosa.

wild dogfight. A broken layer of cloud at 1,500 meters had allowed the enemy to take us by surprise. With unexpected speed we formed a defensive circle, all the while harassed by the superior enemy. One of our machines had been hit, was losing oil and had to head back across the front. Our defensive circle was broken. A wild chase began. Each of us had one of these fellows on his tail and we tried to shake them by flying low over the ground between the steep walls of the mountain valleys. The *Rata* behind me fired like mad. My machine-guns were ready, the cocking handle was in my hand. During the dogfight I had seen a parachute going down. I didn't know who it was and had no time for such thoughts. Back at our aerodrome at Santander we at first looked at other in wide-eyed astonishment and then determined that another of our number was missing. We had just finished counting the hits (37 round, 4 horizontal), when the last one appeared in the sky. *Teniente* Neumann had taken the liberty of shooting down a Curtiss. It crashed on the airfield at Llanes. Two He 70s, flown by *Lt.* Krocker and *Oblt.* von Kessel, were lost along with their crews."

The same day *Oberfeldwebel* "Seppl" Seiler scored the first kill by a German fighter over Asturia, downing a *Rata*. However, Lützow's joy over Seiler's success was dampened considerably by his anger at their Italian allies. His diary entry was brief but clear:

"Sore as hell at the macaroni eaters! None of them come to Santander — they'd rather show off, those prima donnas!"

On September 6, Boddem followed with a further *Rata*, on the 7th Harder shot down a French-made, twin-engined bomber. On September 9, he shot down a Loire 46 and an I-15, while *Lt.* Brücker downed a *Rata*. On the 15th Harder again engaged an I-15 and provided the following gripping description:

"With *Fw.* Polenz as wingman I attacked five Curtisses and three *Ratas*. The enemy were flying in close formation about 2,000 meters above us. They were alerted and came down at us. Polenz was attacked by three enemy fighters and made the mistake of trying to dogfight them. He took hits and flew home. Now I was alone. I was repeatedly attacked from above, which I parried by diving vertically followed by a vertical pull-up. A Bf 109 climbing from below is very difficult to spot, and I was able to surprise a Curtiss in a zoom climb. I closed in, placed the reticle on the center of his engine and fired from point-blank range. The Curtiss abruptly turned over onto its back and spun away. I thought I had shot him down, but then saw him recover about 500 meters below. His survival was due to his armored seat. We turned like crazy below the base of the clouds. I didn't want to lose the altitude I had gained and pulled up into the clouds. After a few moments I once again gauged the situation. I saw a Curtiss diving away steeply toward the west and home. I was able to move in behind him unnoticed. I approached slowly, my airspeed indicator showing 550 kph. Then I was in range. I aimed carefully, fired a short burst and number six crashed burning into the sea. The pilot bailed out about 300 meters below me, his parachute was badly scorched."

Burning fuel dump in Gijon. Frequent explosions hindered fire-fighting efforts, allowing the blaze to become an inferno.

At that time Harder's *Staffel* had seven Bf 109s and fourteen He 51s. On September 23, the *Staffelkapitän* of 2 *Staffel, Oblt.* Schlichting, scored his first "kill," a *Rata.* Lützow had flown back to Germany on the 14th. On September 27, Harder's *Staffel* enjoyed hunter's luck once again:

"We were flying over Gijon. Suddenly I saw the glow of a fire and a *Rata* plunged into the sea, shot down by *Lt.* Woitke. Then I saw two *Ratas* below me. I dove, then pulled up and approached from below. A burst and number seven went down spinning. I followed the doomed aircraft. Then another *Rata* turned up. I attacked and he tried to escape to his airfield, his undercarriage was already down. I attacked once again, from above and in front. He winged over and pulled out just above the ground and then set down, still going quite fast. I made three strafing runs on the rolling machine, and two more on a parked *Rata.*"

In early September, the bomber units were also moved to the marginally acceptable airfields around Santander so as to have forward bases in the same weather region as the combat zone. K/88's primary targets were now the ports of Gijon and Aviles and roads and railway lines behind the front. A precision bombing attack near Llanes smashed a well-fortified mountain position and brought about its surrender. Fighters of J/88 strafed the *campsa,* or fuel dump, at Gijon and sent it up in flames; black clouds of smoke hung over the city for six days.

Republican propaganda poster in the streets of the captured coastal city of Llanes.

On September 21, a few days after the capture of the coastal city of Llanes, 3. J/88 moved into the secondary airfield there, so as to stay on the heels of the retreating Republicans. As the roads behind the front were kept under watch all day by the aircraft of the *Legion Condor,* the enemy's supply and courier

Spanish artillery firing on nests of resistance during the advance on Llanes.

Llane's short landing field, located on a rocky plateau, made for difficult landings. The pilot of this Do 17 braked too harshly on landing, rammed a parked He 51 and ended up in the rain-softened area to the side of the strip.

Fighter pilots had an equally difficult time at Llanes. Lt. Walter Adolph touched downed too late and rolled off the end of the landing field and down the steep bank beyond.

Two Do 17 F reconnaissance bombers of A/88 on a combat sortie. In the foreground is 27-4, PABLO 1, a namimg tradition which endured throughout the civil war.

PABLO 1 again, photographed a few days later. On this occasion the aircraft's left undercarriage leg refused to lower and the pilot elected to make a belly landing beside the runway at Santander-West.

traffic moved only during the hours of twilight and darkness. A new type of close-support operation evolved under the macabre term "evening blessing." The "blessing" was conferred by an He 51 which prowled the roads commonly used by the enemy. Woe to the column or lone vehicle which did not pull off the road or take cover under trees or behind a building at the hedgehopper's approach. A dark cloud of smoke usually marked the place where an inattentive driver had steered his vehicle through the twilight. *Feldwebel* Ignaz Prestele, known as "Igel" to his *Staffel* mates, was a true specialist at this type of operation and in attacking road traffic in general, which in the vernacular of the time was known as "louse hunting."

On September 28, Harder scored his ninth victory:

"Our five Bf 109s were escorting a Do 17 to Gijon. 1,500 meters above us were four Curtisses and four *Ratas*. Suddenly four *Ratas* were behind an Me. I arrived just in time to help. One of the *Ratas* went down almost vertically, I followed him down almost to ground level. Over Gijon airfield I closed in, aimed carefully and he crashed into the ground, bursting into flames on impact.

"On September 30, we became involved in a terrific dogfight. Up and down we went against the Red fighters. *Lt.* Woitke shot down a *Rata*. Another *Rata* got on Terry's tail. I attacked and he broke away. I misread his turn and, thinking he was flying away from me, turned in the same direction. Suddenly the huge radial engine loomed unpleasantly close. I pulled up to the right. A Curtiss attacked from below in a climbing turn, firing from an inverted position and turning the most terrific figures. Another Curtiss joined in and two Me's came to my aid. We twisted and turned for about twenty minutes, repeatedly attacking the two Curtisses, which defended themselves by turning wildly and attacking bravely. Once I got right on the tail of one of them, I had him for sure, but my guns jammed. An Me ran out of ammunition and flew home. Handrick broke off the engagement. Disappointed, we flew home. They should have gone down!"

Feldwebel Flegel of 2 *Staffel* managed to shoot down an I-15 that day. The next successful air engagement was not until two weeks later, when Harder brought down a *Rata* and *Oberfeldwebel* Sigmund a *Chato*:

"Four Curtisses and two *Ratas* climbing in a tight cluster. I led one *Kette* right into the sun. We were 3,000 meters above them. A *Rata* spotted us, waggled his wings and dove away. We attacked. I selected the second *Rata* and moved in close behind him. I was attacked by three Curtisses. Clench your teeth and aim carefully, I told myself. Following the burst the *Rata* rolled slowly to the left and dove away vertically. I went down as well, the Curtisses didn't follow. A lone Curtiss was flying above me. I was joined by a Bf 109, it was *Ofw.* Sigmund. I stalked the Curtiss, then two more came from above to help. One got on Sigmund's tail. I gave up on my Curtiss and drove the others away."

Safely tucked away in a wooden shed! This I-16 is destined for Germany where it will undergo a technical evaluation.

The I-16, its wings removed, on its way to Vigo by truck. There it would be loaded aboard a cargo ship for transport to Germany.

Soon afterward Harder was promoted to *Hauptmann,* at twenty-four the youngest member of the Luftwaffe to attain this rank.

On October 21, Gijon was occupied by Nationalist troops. The fall of the city meant that the northern front had ceased to exist; the campaign in Asturia was over. The Republicans left behind four *Ratas* and four *Chatos* at Gijon. The Germans immediately whisked one of the intact *Ratas* into a shed. It was secretly dismantled and sent to Germany by ship. Three *Chatos* and a *Rata* escaped to France. The Red fighters had fought a brave but hopeless battle. All of the pilots had been Spanish, led by Eloy Gonzalo Obarro, who was killed on September 19. The two squadron commanders were Andrés Rodriguez Panadero and Tarazona Torán. Panadero died on September 30, Tarazona was badly wounded. The latter gave a penetrating description of those desperate days in his book *Sangre en el cielo.* We will quote from several places in his book:

"9. 10. I have not touched my diary for days. One lives with his comrades and dies with them. Eloy Gonzalo Obarro is dead. The day he was shot down low cloud covered the mountains. There are men who believe in premonitions, others do not. Perhaps it was the depressing atmosphere, because the small amount of light that passed through the clouds was gray and bleak, the wind cold. We looked at one another and said nothing; I don't know why, but we sensed the coming tragedy.

"I was sleeping in the cockpit of my *Mosca* when I was awakened by the sound of an automobile engine. It was Eloy. Enemy aircraft were approaching the airfield. *Major* Luna had ordered us to avoid combat with fighters. We couldn't afford to lose any more aircraft. We took off. The clouds were very low, from the base of the cloud to the ground there was barely 100 meters.

"I had to fly on instruments, something they hadn't taught us in Russia. I lost sight of Eloy and looked around for Frutos. I climbed out alone. Soon I could see nothing. The cockpit filled with microscopic droplets which smelled like smoke. The airspeed indicator fluctuated. Only the altimeter showed that I was still climbing. The clouds became thicker and the rain grew heavier. I slid back my hood. But the water droplets hurt my face, and I closed the hood again. When I emerged from the cloud I was flying over a bed of cotton wool that extended as far as the eye could see. I climbed to 4,000 meters, completely alone. I flew circles over an area below which I guessed lay Gijon. I had no other reference point but the Pyrenees. Finally, I saw something coming up above the clouds. It was smoke, rising from burning Gijon. I decided to fly out to sea. Then I descended through the clouds. In a few seconds I was below the cloud deck. I was almost skimming the waves. The clouds hung down almost to the water. From time to time I flew through heavy rain showers. There were moments when I was flying blind.

"Frutos landed just ahead of me. He had made contact with enemy bombers. As he set off in pursuit he had been surrounded by fighters. They did not fire right away, but as he was about to make off they showered him with a rain of bullets. His motor was hit and he lost altitude. He placed everything on one card and dove through the clouds.

"I asked about Eloy. . .

"The nurse showed me the body of a young man. He was naked. There were several large holes in his skin. They were bullet wounds. He lay face down. I feared that it was Eloy. The nurse helped me take hold of the man. We were able to turn the body so that the face was visible. Eloy's eyes were open. His mouth was half open, exposing his teeth. A bullet had exploded in his chest; his heart lay open to view.

"'Is this your friend?' asked the nurse in a calm voice. I couldn't answer. The moaning of the wounded and the cries of family members couldn't tear me from my numbness."

In view of the existing prescribed political phraseology, the fairness with which *General* Sperrle described the heroic resistance of the Spanish Republican forces in Asturia in a report published in the magazine *Die Wehrmacht* in 1939 is surprising:

"Even as white flags in Gijon and Aviles heralded the collapse, and prisoners from Gijon were reaching the Nationalist lines, two of our aircraft were shot down by Red rifle fire. As well, the rest of the Red air force at Gijon, about 30 modern fighter aircraft, put up a heroic fight up to the final day. Although Red fighters were destroyed daily, the tenacious Red fighter pilots continued to attack the German bombers, sometimes with success. . ."

In six weeks the *Legion Condor* alone had dropped 2,500 tons of bombs and expended 1,130,000 rounds of machine-gun ammunition, 22,500 88mm shells and 31,480 rounds of 20mm ammunition. 3. J/88's daily expenditure of ammunition was 25,000 rounds.

Finally, a brief look at what had taken place on the other fronts in the meantime.

On October 12, there was an air battle over the Zaragoza front, in which the Italian fighters came out on the short end. Five Fiats were shot down, among them that of squadron leader Captain Botto, who subsequently lost a leg through amputation. From then on the Italian fighter group called itself *Gamba di Ferro*. On the other side the 3rd *Rata* Squadron had a similar name: *Pata de palo*.

On the morning of October 15, swarms of *Katiuskas, Chatos* and *Ratas* caught Sanjurjo airfield near Zaragoza by surprise. Taking part in the surprise attack were three squadrons of SB-2s, the I-15 squadrons led by Antonov and Gerardo Gil, and the I-16 squadrons led by Aguirre, Pleschenkov, Smirnov, Ivanov and Gusier. They succeeded in destroying three Ju 52s and six Fiats on the ground and damaged several He 46s. At this time the Republicans formed a sixth *Rata* squadron under Gussaiev and a third *Chato* squadron under Comas.

In contrast to the volunteer German legionnaires of the combat units, who as a rule were sent back to Germany following nine months in Spain, some of the army instructors remained in the country for the duration of the entire civil war. Since 1937 the *"Imker/Ausbilder"* group, in cooperation with General Orgaz, had set up a dense net of schools and organized the necessary training courses.

"Imker/Ausbilder" headquarters were in Burgos, and about 130 men were active as instructors. The following German-Spanish training establishments were registered in early 1939:

1. Cubas (Madrid province) - Standing quarters

Sheds, warehouses and loading cranes in Gijon harbor.

Panzergruppe "Drohne" with (a) Oropesa (Toledo province), (b) Cassarubuelos (Madrid province), Training camp for German and captured Russian tanks, as well as anti-tank and flamethrower courses, (c) Valladolid Replacement parts depot and workshops for (a) and (b) 2. Briviesca near Burgos - Artillery training battalion 3. Cordoba - Mortar school 4. Salamanca - Gas protection school 5. Monasterio near Burgos - Signals school 6. Toledo -Infantry training camp 7. (a) Avila - Officer candidate school, (b) Granada Officer candidate school, (c) Pamplona Officer candidate school 8.(a) Miranda de Ebro - NCO school, (b) Vitoria - NCO school, (c) San Roque near Gibraltar NCO school 9. San Fernando near Cadiz - Naval cadet school

The German training methods and their results so impressed the Spanish liaison staff that, for example, they adopted the German march tempo of 114 steps/minute in place of the faster Spanish one (130 steps/min.) and adopted several German military marches for the army, adding Spanish text. By February 1939 about 56,000 Spaniards had passed through the German training centers, which were under the command of *Oberst* von Thoma.

Following the onset of the rainy period in the Asturian highlands J/88 flew to Leon for a rest. At the same time its aircraft were overhauled by P/88 at the same location. The fighter units under their commander Handrick were reorganized and 1 *Staffel* was completely reequipped with the Bf 109. J/88 was now organized as follows:

1 Staffel "Marabu" Bf 109 under Harder
(later became the "Holzauge" Staffel under Reents)
2 Staffel "Zylinder" Bf 109 under Schlichting
3 Staffel "Mickymaus" He 51 under Galland
4 Staffel "Pik As" He 51 under d'Elsa (new formation)

4 *Staffel* travelled to Spain by ship in early November 1937 and the unit was formed at Leon. As well as unit personnel, the *Karla 2,* which sailed under the code name *Golfo de Panama,* carried the *Staffel*'s He 51s as deck cargo. In charge of their assembly in Leon was Technical Officer *Leutnant* "Eckie" Priebe.

The bomber *Gruppe* under *Major* Mehnert now had three complete He 111 *Staffeln* and a few Ju 52s for use in night attacks. The majority of the Junkers had been handed over to the Spaniards and each of the flying units of the *Legion Condor* was assigned one aircraft for use as a transport and communications aircraft. K/88 was assigned to Santander-Pontejos and Leon airfields.

Newly equipped with four *Ketten* of Do 17s, one of which was a strategic reconnaissance *Kette,* and an He 45 *Kette,* A/88 began a period of rest and recuperation. The unit's He 70s had been handed over to the Spaniards. At this time the reconnaissance *Staffel* was commanded by *Hauptmann* Gerndt. The reconnaissance unit was based at Santander and, from October/November, Burgos. The crews of AS/88 continued to enjoy their long-term summer resort at Pollensa, Mallorca, and the unit retained its slow but stable He 59 floatplanes.

The five 88mm batteries, two 20mm batteries — each with a 37mm Flak platoon — and the searchlight platoon were divided between the bases at Santander and Burgos. They assumed responsibility

First parade by 4. J/88 in Leon following the issuing of uniforms.

for defense of the airfields and overhauled their equipment.

After completing their work in Asturia the 1st, 2nd and 3rd Companies of Ln/88 moved to Fresno, near El Burgo de Osma. 4. Ln/88 installed radio equipment at the new Santander-West airfield for takeoffs and landings by mail aircraft and then moved on to Fresno as well. On November 1, 1937 *Major* Saul assumed command of Ln/88 there from *Oberst* Lindner.

There was also a decisive change at Stab/88 at this time. The commander of the *Legion Condor, Generalmajor* Sperrle ("Sander"), critical, disagreeable and regarded by Berlin as a pessimist, was recalled to Germany. On November 1, 1937 his place in Commilas was taken by *Generalmajor* Hellmuth Volkmann (alias "Veith"). Dynamic *Oberstleutnant* Wolfram Freiherr von Richthofen stayed on as the Legion's Chief-of-Staff. During the brief pause before the start of the Battle of Teruel the headquarters moved to Burgos.

Personnel of the Leon Air Park carry out a technical inspection on a 20mm anti-aircraft gun.

Because of the frequent changes of position the anti-aircraft guns' exceedingly delicate range-finders had to be readjusted frequently.

The Italian Legion, now with its own, newly-created air warfare staff, concentrated its fighters in a fighter wing under Colonel Casinelli. The three groups, each consisting of three squadrons, were led by Zotti, Casero and Leotta. The squadron leaders were Nobili, Foschini, Calosso, Bianchi, Fassi, Francois, Ippodrino, Criscione and Vizotto. The Italian bomber force consisted of a group each of S.M.79s, S.M.81s and Fiat B.R.20s. In addition there was a group of liaison aircraft, equipped with the Ro 37 and a close-support squadron with Breda 65s.

The Spanish Nationalist fighter arm now consisted of four squadrons equipped with the Fiat C.R.32. The group was led by Captain Angel Salas Larrazabal. Squadron leaders were Julio Salvador Diaz, Miguel Garcia Pardo, Javier Murcia Rubio and Manrique Montero Mera. The close-support forces consisted of a group each of He 51s (José Munoz Jiménez), He 46s, Ro 37s, He 45s and Aero 101s. The bombers were concentrated in the 1st Spanish Air Brigade, which included two groups equipped with the Ju 52, three with the S.M.79 and one with the He 70.

A comparison of the Nationalist and Republican air forces shows that the Nationalists were already gaining the upper hand.

In fighters, thirteen Fiat squadrons (authorized strength 9 aircraft each) and two *Staffeln* each with 12 Bf 109s faced twelve Republican squadrons, each with 12 machines. Six of these were equipped with *Ratas* and four with *Chatos*. By the end of 1937 the Nationalists had received approximately:

250 Fiat C.R.32
50 Bf 109

the other side

158 I-16 *Ratas*
150 I-15 *Chatos*
46 I-15 *Chatos* (from Spanish production)
34 I-15 bis "Super *Chatos*"

Republican bomber strength had sunk to about fifty serviceable *Katiuskas,* compared to about fifty He 111s and Do 17s and approximately fifty S.M.81s and S.M.79s on the Nationalist side. Both sides were roughly equal in numbers of close-support and liaison aircraft. The He 51s, Ro 37s, He 45s, He 46s and Aero 101s were faced by an approximately equal number of R-Z *Rasantes,* R-5 *Nataschas,* Grumman Goblins, Aero 101 *Pragas* and *Ocas,* Gourdou-Leseurre and Koolhoven FK-51s.

Taken altogether, it looked like a continued downward trend for the Republicans. The Soviet Union had meanwhile undertaken to support China with aircraft and pilots in its struggle with Japan, and the flow of *Ratas* and *Katiuskas* to Spain was therefore no longer so abundant. The gradual withdrawal of the Russian pilots was easily made good, as about 200 Russian-trained Spanish pilots had returned to their homeland by the end of 1937, and another 400 were to follow by the end of 1938.

A Fiat C.R.32 of the Nationalist fighter group. Serial number 597 belonged to 1 Squadron under Captain Salvador Diaz-Benjumea.

Meanwhile the French government had forbidden the training of Spanish Republican pilots in French schools. Nationalist pilots were also trained in Italy (80 by war's end) and Germany (40).

The use of Vigo as the primary port for unloading shipments from Germany and Leon as the supply base for the *Legion Condor* resulted in increased difficulties with respect to lines of communication between these two important centers.

Items packed in huge crates, such as aircraft fuselages, wings and power plants, had to be moved about 300 kilometers through mountainous country from Vigo to Leon. Neither the existing rolling stock nor the many tunnels between Vigo and Leon

Meridionali Ro 37bis reconnaissance aircraft and light bomber. The Italians delivered large numbers of these aircraft to the Spanish Nationalists.

Czech Aero 101, powered by an 800 HP Praga "Asso" engine. The aircraft were fitted with bomb racks beneath the lower wing for the carriage of light bombs.

Pre-flight checks are carried out on a Savoia S.M.79 Sparviero. Above the cockpit is a fixed, forward-firing machine-gun, behind it a flexibly-mounted machine-gun.

The insignia of a Spanish bomber squadron on the fin of one of its S.M.81s. Unlike the S.M.79, this aircraft was fitted with a fixed undercarriage.

were large enough for this type of cargo. A not insignificant part of the bulky goods therefore had to be moved to Leon by private transport organizations over narrow mountain roads, which led to frequent accidents and damaged goods. Shipments soon began arriving in Leon, however. Routes were simplified, some roads were designated one-way routes and traffic was strictly regulated, eliminating most of the serious problems.

The scheme worn by this He 70 F of the Nationalist reconnaissance squadron 7-G-14 appears to have been more for shock effect than camouflage.

Unloading supply goods in the port of Vigo. This port was used almost exclusively by German freighters and warships.

The large crates containing wings and fuselages were transported by road through Orense, then through the Sierra de la Pobladura to P/88's base.

Smaller items of freight were shipped to Leon by train.

Though hopelessly overloaded and in violation of every safety regulation, this truck and its cargo nevertheless arrived at Leon safe and sound. The crate contains a section of a Do 17 fuselage.

An He 111 fuselage is lifted from its shipping crate and placed on a single-axled wagon before being towed away for assembly.

The assembly and testing of anti-aircraft guns was also carried out at the Legion Condor's supply base at Leon.

A Jumo 210 replacement engine for a Bf 109 is packed in a special crate at Albericia for shipment to Leon.

Major Schomburg, commander of the air park, together with the author Zischka.

An aerial view of Leon, its hangars, living quarters and administration buildings swept, scrubbed and tidied up. As a rule the area in front of the hangars was a jumble of aircraft, packing material and vehicles.

TERUEL

The high command of the Republican armed forces was probably well aware that the pause in fighting following the capture of the strip of territory along the northern coast by the Nationalists was only a pause for breath prior to a new offensive. There was uncertainty as to the focal point of the new offensive; from the state of affairs it could only be in the Zaragoza or Madrid area. As a result the Republicans were forced to mass troops between these two sectors, so as to be able to send reserves quickly to one front or the other. The Republicans chose the area around the city of Teruel, which lay in Nationalist-held territory, for their assembly area.

The scale, objectives and time frame of the winter offensive were laid down during the course of November by the operations staffs of Franco and the *Legion Condor* and the headquarters of the Italian Legion. The push was to be made from the area around and to the north of Zaragoza through Catalonia toward Barcelona.

Then, at the end of November, Franco overturned the entire plan of operations, probably for reasons of prestige, and ordered a major offensive against Madrid from positions at the southern edge of the Guadarrama Mountains. The offensive was to begin on December 18, 1937. The commanders of the German and Italian legions grudgingly submitted and set about making the necessary redispositions.

Stab/88 set up quarters in Almazán on the upper course of the Duero, while the bomber *Staffeln*, the reconnaissance units and two fighter *Staffeln* flew into Burgo de Osma. The two remaining fighter *Staffeln* occupied bases in Torresavina. The batteries of F/88 assumed responsibility for the local defence of Burgo de Osma, Almazán and Zaragoza. Efforts were made to convince the enemy that the attack was to come from the original build-up area around Zaragoza. To this end K/88 sent its *Staffeln* daily to bomb positions on this front and in the enemy rear.

The first contact with the *Ratas* following the

Hectic activity at El Burgo de Osma airfield during the autumn of 1937.

"Ariba Espana!" This Nationalist battle cry was an answer to the Republican slogans No Pasaran and Todo pava el frente popular.

Newly arrived at 2. J/88, Lt. Edgar Rempel.

arrival of the two *Jagdstaffeln* at Burgo de Osma on November 19 took place on the 29th. 2 *Staffel* shot down three enemy aircraft; the victorious pilots were Schlichting, Rochel and Seiler. This success was repeated a day later by Greisert, Stange and Staege. It was here that the Republicans committed the improved I-15bis "Super-*Chato*" for the first time.

On December 4, the He 111 *Staffeln* dropped thirty tons of bombs on Bujaraloz airfield. Combats with the "Super-*Chatos*, which were almost as fast as the Bf 109, were not entirely satisfactory. Harder describes the action of December 4:

"Below us there were Red machines everywhere. Here three Curtisses, there five, here a pair of *Ratas* and there several unfamiliar biplanes, very slow but unbelievably maneuverable. It was difficult to get close to these fellows, one was always too fast, had only a fleeting instant to fire and almost rammed the target. I thought I had shot one down, I saw him

Ofw. Seiler scored the third of his eventual total of nine victories in Spain on November 29 while flying Bf 109 6-32.

Uffz. Wilhelm Staege shot down his first enemy aircraft, an I-16, in late November 1937.

pitch down, then I had to get out. The Reds had excellent seat armor."

Feldwebel Otto Polenz was shot down in this action; he landed in enemy territory and was taken prisoner. His Bf 109 fell into Republican hands virtually intact and was later sent to the Soviet Union via France for technical evaluation. The next day *Oberfeldwebel* Leo Sigmund was shot down and captured. Harder wrote:

"There were about 25 to 30 biplanes climbing and a squadron of *Ratas* coming from the east. We were fifteen Me 109s. All of a sudden *Ofw.* Sigmund was not there. Below me were fifteen biplanes, climbing. I attacked alone out of the sun and got right on the tail of one of them. A clean burst and number eleven went down in a spin. The hounds rushed at me and I ran for it. After I had distanced myself I saw my victim crash not far from Bujaraloz airfield. There were combats everywhere, and the He 111s flew home unmolested. I climbed up above a flight of *Ratas*. An Me 109 was sitting behind one *Rata*. I attacked another and got in a good burst. He went down vertically, then I was attacked by two other *Ratas*. I managed to get free and flew home.

"The two losses and the difficult air battles took their toll on all of us, and we asked ourselves why and whether we should go on being foolish enough to continue to run our heads against a wall, attack recklessly and take the war so seriously. We Germans were the only ones still doing anything, the Spanish and the Italians were doing nothing at all."

Galland reported in his book *Die Ersten und die Letzten* that the catchphrase making the rounds in the Legion at the time was: "We're fighting on the wrong side." Although it was probably a product of frustration, the slogan contained a grain of truth. There was respect for the enemy's military prowess. As well, there were indications that the sources of the great social dissatisfaction which had led to the war would continue to exist under Franco, namely the absence of rights for the broad masses of the population and their inability to own property, and at the opposite pole the great influence of the major aristocratic and clerical landholders. Galland also mentioned that on the enemy side everything had been masterfully camouflaged, while on his own side troop movements, concentrations of vehicles, artillery positions and so on were uncamouflaged and clearly visible from the air and therefore would have been easy prey for close-support aircraft. Of course this lack of concern was simply a product of Nationalist air superiority and was entirely in keeping with the indifference and mentality of meridional soldiers.

During the final weeks of 1937 J/88 was transferred here and there, to Hiendelaencina, to Torresavinan and finally, at the end of November, to the Zaragoza area.

On December 10, the day of the Virgin of Loreto, the patron saint of the Spanish Air Force, the Spanish Nationalists struck. In order to camouflage a planned offensive toward Madrid on the Guadalajara, the enemy air forces were to be destroyed on their airfields east of Zaragoza. Approximately 100 fighters and 100 bombers took part in the operation. The attacks failed to achieve the desired success, however; the airfields were empty and about seventy fighters were waiting in the air. It must be said that the Republicans were very well prepared to deal with

On December 5 "Medicine Man" Dr. Neumann came to grief in He 51 2-85 while landing at El Burgo in gusty conditions. Following this incident the flying of combat aircraft was restricted to qualified pilots.

surprise air attacks. They had constructed a large number of airfields and at each was based at most a single squadron, its aircraft widely dispersed around the airfield perimeter. In addition they had built a number of decoy airfields on with mock-up aircraft.

Harder wrote of the December 10 operation:

"Another major action on December 10. The Fiats patrolled the front, we flew deep into enemy territory with fifteen Bf 109s. Fifteen Curtisses and fifteen *Ratas* climbed up in close formation. There was nothing else to do, we attacked repeatedly, but so many aircraft immediately dove on us that we were happy just to escape in one piece."

It is all the more remarkable under the circumstances that the Nationalists and the Italian fighters of the group "*Gambi di Ferro*" claimed to have together shot down fourteen *Chatos* while losing only one aircraft. An He 111 was lost, probably as a result of being struck by a bomb from another aircraft in the formation. Harder entered the following in his diary under December 11:

"December 11 was even worse. We escorted K/88. The Red fighters were already at altitude. Eight Curtisses attacked the bombers, we were able to drive them away. Over the target the bombers made a turn and became bunched up. When they dropped their bombs the *Staffeln* were one upon the other. An He 111 was struck by a bomb and blew apart. More and more enemy fighters arrived, here a unit of 18 *Ratas*, there 28 Curtisses. I gained altitude, perhaps I could attack from out of the sun. My altimeter showed 6,700 meters. Eight machines came toward me at right angles, even higher than I. Smoke trails began to come from their machine-guns while I was still debating what to do. I got out of there as fast as I could. We counted about 70 Red fighters. The Italians claimed to have shot down 20 fighters, and they hadn't flown one meter past the front."

The following days' operations were similar.

Then, completely by surprise, the Republicans seized the initiative right in the midst of the Nationalist attack preparations. During the night of December 15/16, 1937 two powerful spearheads broke through the weak positions in the north and west of the approximately 30-kilometer-wide Teruel corridor, where scarcely a shot had been fired until now. In the air the *Rojos* had mustered six *Rata* squadrons (two of them Spanish under Claudin and

Generalissimo Franco and Gen.Lt. Volkmann in conversation in the Teruel combat zone.

Zarauza), three squadrons of *Chatos* (Captains Comas and Chindasvinto Gonzàles and the Russian Stepanov), four *Katiuska* squadrons and four squadrons of *Nataschas*. A murderous prestige battle developed. Initially the Nationalists reacted very hesitantly.

By morning the mountain city of Teruel and 2,000 Nationalist troops had been surrounded and the only remaining contact with the outside was by radio. The massing and composition of the Republican units led the Nationalists to expect bitter fighting in the following days. In view of these new circumstances there could be no question of an advance on Madrid in the long term.

On December 17, the Legion's new commander Volkmann sent twenty-three He 111s of K/88 to attack the area around Teruel. Soon after takeoff, however, bad weather caused the formation to break up; the aircraft made their way in pairs to airfields west of Madrid. One He 111 was lost over enemy territory. That afternoon crews reported in from airfields at Avila, Escalona, Burgo de Osma and Talavera. In the coming weeks the weather saw to it that events in the air took a back seat to operations on the ground. It was the onset of a winter not unlike those experienced in northern Europe. Temperatures as low as -18 degrees C and heavy snowfalls made it a test of endurance for both sides. Preheating equipment was unknown, so engines were warmed with blowtorches or, as J/88 did, were started up hourly night after night.

A/88's bomb dump at El Burgo de Osma. In Germany such improper stowage of bombs would have caused the base commander to blow his top — and several times a day!

Unteroffizier Anton Kurz crashed and was killed on December 23. J/88 now transferred to Calamocha.

The Nationalist offensive began on December 29, preceded by a two-hour artillery bombardment and air attacks on the area surrounding Teruel. K/88 put into the air everything that could fly. In an air battle with six *Chatos* and fifteen *Ratas* on the evening before the offensive, the Spanish fighter group claimed four I-15s and an I-16 shot down, and on the following day two I-16s and an SB-2.

On December 30, the Nationalist air forces dropped almost 100 tons of bombs. Again there were several air engagements. This time 1. J/88 met with

Still no snow, but it's bitterly cold at El Burgo. Wearing their winter overhauls with the collars turned up, mechanics and aircrew grab a quick bite between sorties.

A New Year's toast in fitting surroundings by armorers of VB/88.

Motorized column with eight Panzer I tanks on the approaches to Teruel.

success: *Lt.* Adolph, *Uffz.* Terry and *Fw.* Prestele shot down two *Chatos* and a *Rata.* Prestele shot down another *Rata* on January 5, and on the 6th the Spanish Fiats destroyed two I-15s.

The Republicans knew very well where their worst tormentors, the *Jagdstaffeln* of the *Legion Condor,* were based, as was demonstrated by an attack on the airfield at Calamocha at 0830 on January 7, carried out by eighteen SB-2s. The bombers left behind five damaged He 51s, two of them with major damage.

Nationalist attempts to relieve Teruel failed. On January 1, 1938 the temperature fell to minus seventeen degrees. That day *Leutnant* Runzel was shot down by 20mm flak. His aircraft crashed and burned. Increased efforts by the *Legion Condor* could not prevent a surrender by the city's defenders on January 8. Only 300 men managed to escape to the Nationalist lines. In spite of this the attacks on the hilltop city of Teruel continued. The International Brigades moved into the defensive positions around the city, where they faced the Nationalists for a full month.

Apart from another attack on the German fighter base at Calamocha on January 12, the next two weeks saw little activity in the air. Handrick described the attack:

"Morning was just dawning on January 12 when I suddenly heard our anti-aircraft guns firing and rushed onto the balcony in my pajamas. I could see flak bursts in the morning sky and then the Red bombers. I could make out their flight paths clearly. Each bomber left behind a trail of gray smoke. In spite of the biting cold, I ran half-dressed to the airfield. By the time I arrived it was all over. The flak and the alert *Rotte* had done their work very well. Each brought down two of the Reds."

The successful fighter pilots were *Ofw.* Seiler and *Uffz.* Staege, who scored J/88's one hundredth confirmed victory that day.

Since mid-December 1 *Staffel* had been under the command of *Oberleutnant* Schellmann, who had relieved Harro Harder. In those weeks Schellmann was worlds away from being the leading ace of J/88, a position he would later hold for a time. He provides an honest and revealing description of a beginner's first contact with the enemy:

The new "old man" of 1. J/88, Oblt. Schellmann, following his return from a combat sortie. In the background, center, is Schellmann's Katschmarek, Fw. Ignaz Prestele.

"I was first alerted to the presence of the enemy when my people began waggling their wings. My eyes nearly fell out of my head, I simply couldn't see anything. Then, finally! An enemy squadron. Now I would show my people what I could do. After them! By this time I was seeing red. I closed in, 100 meters, 50 meters, he has to go down. The enemy was framed perfectly in my sight, then Thump! Thump! I tried desperately to escape. Where were my comrades? Where was my *Staffel*? Gone! A fine mess. Gingerly I made my way home. When I got back the *Staffel* met me beaming with joy and reported one kill. Crestfallen I looked over my machine: 7 hits!"

On January 17, Italian and Nationalist fighters shot down ten aircraft, and a Russian pilot was captured. On the 18th Schellmann scored his first "kill," which he described as follows:

"I was hanging in the sky with five machines at 5,000 meters. A *Kette* left, a *Rotte* right. I had long since spotted the enemy: a squadron of Curtisses and a squadron of *Ratas*. They were just what we wanted. But I had to be patient. It was not time to go after them yet. First we had to reach a favorable attack position. The enemy aircraft flew to and fro and appeared not to have seen us. We flew along with them nicely, I climbed to 5,500 meters and worked my way closer. When the enemy reversed course for the fourth time I waggled my wings. I attacked the machine on the extreme left. My bursts were on target. Flames shot from the *Rata*. I broke away."

A second *Rata* was shot down by *Leutnant* Woitke. But the Republican ground defenses were exacting a high price in blood. On January 20, the commander of the Romeo group, Major Négron, was fatally wounded. His observer, Captain Mira, was able to pilot the aircraft to a crash landing at their airfield. Two enemy aircraft were shot down by *Oblt.* Balthasar and *Uffz.* Rochel, a *Rata* and a *Chato*. When Balthasar returned to Germany in the summer of 1938 he had flown a total of 465 reconnaissance, bomber and fighter sorties in Spain, making him probably the most experienced pilot in the Legion. The following description by Balthasar shows that the first engagement as a fighter pilot was no walk in the park, even for an experienced pilot:

"First sortie as a fighter pilot. I still feel somewhat uncertain, but nothing will happen on my first mission and I'll have time to get used to flying with the unit. Mistake! Before I know what is happening I am all alone on a broad stage, while below me the *Staffel* is in a wild dogfight with some *Ratas*. I'm not quite sure what I should do. Unable to tell friend from foe I make a shallow turn, hoping to watch the fight and then intervene when the opportunity presents itself. This doesn't happen. Suddenly one of them turns toward me and opens fire, it can only be an enemy. What now? What had they told me to do in such cases? Oh yes, fly straight toward him and fire hell for leather. All right then. Now it all comes down to who has more nerve and holds out longer. I have become quite calm, the uncertainty has been swept away. Once again I feel one with my machine.

"The other aircraft grows larger in fractions of a second. Then he loses his nerve, banks sharply and dives away. I chase after him. We are in a vertical dive, he sits in the gunsight reticle, my incendiary ammunition reaches out for him. Suddenly he's trailing a long stream of oil. My windscreen is covered.

"He's gone. A protecting cloud has sucked him in. I go in after him, but below I have to pull up sharply, the ground is devilishly close. As I rush past I see a fire on the ground. It's probably the *Rata*. But now up and back to my *Staffel*. Everyone is gone and I fly home alone. I have lost my kill as there were no witnesses."

Everyone had to pay dearly for their wisdom, even the *Gruppenkommandeur*, *Hauptmann* Handrick. He describes his first air battle, which took place on the northern front in October 1937, in a very amusing way:

"I clamped onto the tail of a Curtiss and, as this was my first air combat, I was naturally convinced that everything would go my way and I would shoot him down. Very wrong! I can not deny that I conducted myself in a not too skilful fashion.

"I attacked the Curtiss from behind — it wheeled round. Instead of pulling up and then repeating the attack, I continued to attack and got in only about ten rounds in each attack, while the maneuverable Curtiss undoubtedly shot very well. We descended gradually until we were barely five meters above the water, close to Gijon, 50 to 60 kilometers away from the front. It was therefore high time to put an end to it. I moved closer to the Curtiss, ever closer, so close

All dressed up, and wearing civilian clothes, Wilhelm Balthasar prepares to leave flying and 2. Jagdstaffel's mobile living quarters behind for a few hours.

that finally there was a murderous crash. I had collided with him. The wing of my Me had been struck close to the fuselage and the controls were jammed. I made three or four involuntary rolls, before finally regaining control of the machine. With some difficulty I was able to fly straight and level. I flew toward land. If one of them caught me now. . .

"I finally got my struggling machine to Santander, having overcome several attempts by it to simply dive into the ground. When I touched down a piece of the Curtiss' wing flew out of my machine. My bird was in bad shape. The right wing was finished, the fuselage was dented, there were several hits aft and the tail assembly had to be replaced."

Since Volkmann had taken command of the Legion relations with his Chief-of-Staff von Richthofen had steadily deteriorated. The way the new commander saw it, the experienced Richthofen, with his knowledge of conditions in Spain, was "stealing his thunder" and he rejected many well-intentioned suggestions from his Chief-of-Staff. The latter finally grew tired of the skirmishing and on January 11, 1938 asked to be relieved. Volkmann approved the request at once. Richthofen travelled back to Germany on January 30; his place was taken by *Major* Hermann Plocher.

During a sortie over the front on January 18, 4. J/88 under *Oblt.* Eberhard d'Elsa lost *Lt.* Gerhard Klein over enemy territory. His aircraft was completely consumed by fire. As previously mentioned, most of this *Staffel*'s pilots had arrived at Vigo on November 2, 1937 aboard the steamer *Golfo de Panama.* All of the ground personnel were from the parent unit, I. (I)/JG 136, which was based at Jever. Among the papers of *Lt.* "Eckie" Priebe (*Staffel* Technical Officer) is a very informative summary of 4 *Staffel*'s inventory of aircraft at the beginning of January 1938, with data on bases and the pilots of the individual He 51s:

2-59	He 51 lost	
2-60	He 51 at Calamocha	*Lt.* Müller
2-62	He 51 at Leon	
2-64	He 51 at Calamocha	*Oblt.* d'Elsa
2-70	He 51 at Calamocha	*Lt.* Henz
2-71	He 51 at Leon (crashed)	
2-76	He 51 at Calamocha	*Uffz.* Meyer
2-79	He 51 at Calamocha	*Uffz.* Rabeneck
2-82	He 51 at Calamocha	*Uffz.* Borchers
2-86	He 51 at Calamocha	*Uffz.* Kuhlmann
2-93	He 51 at Leon	
2-95	He 51 at Leon	
2-104	He 51 at El Burgo	
2-105	He 51 at Calamocha	*Uffz.* Torner

No trees, no bushes, no houses — just sand and tents: the airfield at Calamocha. It played a decisive role in the advance on Teruel, serving as the Jagdgruppe's forward airfield.

Any sunshine is gratefully welcomed and is cause for an outdoor game of skat. Pilots of 4. J/88, from left: Uffz. Heinrich Torner, Uffz. Adolf Borchers, Lt. Helmut Henz, Lt. Eckehart Priebe, Lt. Kurt Müller.

Brief discussion before taking off from Calamocha. Lt. Priebe, Lt. Gerhard Klein (with back to camera) and Lt. Henz make up the Kette.

2-106	He 51 at Leon	
2-110	He 51 at Calamocha	*Lt.* Klein
2-111	He 51 at Calamocha	(Reserve)
2-112	He 51 at Calamocha	*Feldw.* von Cramon
2-113	He 51 at Calamocha	*Lt.* Priebe
2-114 115, 123, 124, 125, 126	all at Leon (under assembly)	

A single aircraft made headlines on January 19. *Hauptmann* Martin Harlinghausen, who had taken command of AS/88 at Pollensa in early January 1938, took off at about 0500 with his crew of *Lt.* Zenker (pilot), radio operator Hinterberger and flight engineer Schmehl to attack harbor installations at Valencia. With the engines at idle, Zenker descended from his cruising altitude of 3,500 meters to 50 meters above the still-sleeping city. Harlinghausen released his bombs over the extensive fuel dump, the *Campsa.* Flames shot into the sky, turning night into day. In moments the flak and searchlights were wide awake and searching for the He 59, which by now was flying toward the sea at maximum speed. Schmehl and Hinterberger fired on flak and searchlight positions with their machine-guns until the floatplane swept over the coast at an altitude of ten meters, leaving behind it a sea of flames.

Other seaports, such as Port-Bou, Barcelona, Palamos, San Felin, Villanueva y Geltru, Vinaroz, Alcira, Alicante, Almeria and Cartagena, remained favorite targets of the "Iron Gustav," as Harlinghausen was known, until the end of the civil war.

On the same January 19, bombers of all three air forces carried out a coordinated attack on power generating stations near Tremp on the Rio Moguera, which supplied electricity to Catalonia. The attack

Hydro-electric generating station on the Rio Segre. The total elimination of the Pyrenean power plants could have crippled the entire arms industry in Barcelona within days.

Falling 500kg bombs photographed from the belly hatch of an He 111 during the attack of January 23.

was repeated on January 23.

On January 22, *Oberfeldwebel* Reinhard Seiler shot down a *Rata*. On the 24th, the commander of a Nationalist fighter group, Major Ibarra, was shot down by Nationalist anti-aircraft fire and bailed out. As the wind carried him toward the Nationalist lines twelve *Ratas* appeared and were engaged by the Fiats. Later sixteen *Chatos* joined the melee. The Spaniards reported seven confirmed and several probable kills. Republican sources later revealed that none of their fighters had been lost, although one *Rata* was severely damaged.

The fighting in the Teruel combat zone dragged on in the air and on the ground, with the close-support aircraft bearing the major burden in the air. On January 29 the Nationalists lost an He 51 trying to repulse a Republican armored attack. By then the weather had improved somewhat, although the unusual below-zero temperatures continued.

On the advice of the commander of the *Legion Condor, Generalmajor* Volkmann, Franco decided to reduce the salient north of Teruel and advance on the city and river named Alfambra. In the process Teruel would be outflanked to the north and encircled. During preparations for this operation the He 51 close-support squadrons were called upon to halt and drive back repeated Republican thrusts against assembly areas in the rear.

On January 31, the entire headquarters staff of the *Legion Condor* moved to Banos de Fitero. K/88 was stationed at Alfaro, A/88 at Bunuel. Following the usual preparatory bombardment from the air, the Nationalist attack began on February 5, 1938 from the areas of Rubielos and Portalrubio. However, the attackers failed to reach the objectives laid down for that day. In the air, *Uffz.* Lohrer (2 *Staffel*) shot down a *Rata* and a Do 17 of A/88 was forced to make an emergency landing in friendly territory. When the Do 17 released its bombs one exploded beneath the aircraft; *Hptm.* Gerndt and *Ogfr.* Meix were injured by bomb splinters. The same day Hptm. Hentschel took command of the reconnaissance *Staffel.*

The well-known Spanish fighter pilot Luis de Frutos was killed on February 6, probably shot down by *Unteroffizier* Stange of 2. J/88, who reported the destruction of a *Rata*. Frutos had brought back the last *Rata* from Gijon. The same day Nationalist bombers dropped 120 tons of bombs, a record so far

Galland was fond of colorful markings in his 3. J/88. Here is his He 51, 2-78, with his personal insignia, a white cross paté.

Snow and desert at Calamocha. In the foreground the He 51 of Staffelkapitän Galland.

2-98, the He 51 of Lt. Kurt Strümpell of 3.J/88, displays a black and white "ying-yang" design.

in the war. The monotone drone of bombers coming and going was heard over the area of the front all day.

On February 7, the Nationalist forces landed a major blow at the Alfambra, taking several thousand prisoners and capturing a great deal of war materiel. The same day J/88 scored its greatest success of the war so far. No less than ten *Katiuskas* and two *Ratas* were shot down by the *Gruppe*. Prestele, Seiler (two), Quasinowski, Terry, Mayer (two) and Schlichting all scored victories, but the star of the day was undoubtedly *Oblt.* Balthasar who destroyed four SB-2s in the space of ten minutes. *Hauptmann* Handrick described the action:

. . . an unidentified pilot has painted a floppy hat on the side of his aircraft for good luck.

The first pre-heater to arrive at Calamocha was in constant use during the bitterly cold winter days.

The burnt-out remains of an enemy "louse" following a low-level attack by He 51s. Seen examining the carnage wrought by their Trabaderos are, from left: Oblt. d'Elsa, Oblt. Kurt Müller and Oblt. Galland.

As there was no heat, the men were forced to complete their business on the "Donnerbalken" (thunder beam) wearing their coats and gloves.

"Our bomber group had been instructed to bomb positions near Teruel. I took off with two *Staffeln* to provide fighter escort and flew with 1 *Staffel*. Far ahead of us was 2 *Staffel*.

"We had scarcely reached the front, when suddenly I spotted a large number of heavy machines flying on a reciprocal course. At first I thought our bombers had come too early and were already returning from their attack. However, one could tell by the type and a few seconds later by the blood-red insignia that the aircraft were Red bombers, Russian machines. They were attacked immediately by 2 *Staffel*. We asked the best of our engines in an effort to close the distance, because we had never before come across such a magnificent target, 22 Martin bombers without escort just behind the front. The *Rojos* veered off as

No headlines, just unremitting work for the Kampfstaffeln and ground forces. Two pilots of A/88: Subteniente (Master Sergeant) Ernst Sorge, 57 sorties on the Do 17. . .

. . . and Sargento (Technical Sergeant) Hans König, who distinguished himself by flying 95 combat sorties in the He 45.

On February 7 Hptm. Handrick came upon a squadron of SB-2 bombers, but was forced to break away when his guns jammed. A number of force-landed or captured Katiuskas were integrated into the Nationalist Air Force.

soon as they spotted us, but they were caught as they reversed course. Two machines went down trailing black smoke, broke up and were abandoned by their crews. The rest sought to escape in wild flight. But we were already upon them and in the next moment eight Reds began to burn, before plunging to earth like blazing torches.

"I myself had closed to about 150 meters behind a Martin bomber. I could make out the gunner clearly as he fired at me like a wild man. The bomber was as big as a barn door in my gunsight. I pressed the trigger, but to my despair both guns jammed after firing a total of 14 rounds. Bad luck. As I turned away from my victim I suddenly noticed three or four squadrons of *Ratas*, the bombers' fighter cover, coming down at us like a warm rain. During the brief, but intense dogfight which followed, two *Ratas* were sent to the ground. But then it was back to our bombers to protect them from the Red fighters. But these seemed to have little enthusiasm for a further acquaintance. The whole Red *mahalla* disappeared in the direction of Valencia. Our bombers carried out their attack without incident.

"After landing we heard that twelve light Praga bombers had also attacked the front without fighter escort. Unfortunately these had slipped through our fingers."

The hero of the day was *Oberleutnant* Balthasar. He provided the following description:

"The machines in front of me grow larger by the second. I can see the broad red stripes clearly. I dive through the column at high speed and approach the second vic from the front from below. They have seen me and a shower of fire reaches out for me. There is a cracking in the wings, that's the first hit. Keep your nerve, wait, get in close before firing. The aircraft on the right grows before me. The crosshairs are aligned on its right engine. My fingers are on the triggers. The range is twenty meters when my three guns begin to rattle. There, flames. I pull up sharply and the bomber explodes before me and falls to earth a mass of flames. I am quite calm. But the leader of the three-aircraft formation has apparently lost his nerve. He turns and dives away in the direction of home. I am able to cut off his turn and soon I am on the tail of the machine on the left. Once again I am enveloped by defensive fire, but I come through and

The wreckage of one of the Katiuska bombers shot down by Balthasar.

once again my machine-guns sing their deadly song. Again the flames, I hear an explosion, then my machine roars through a cloud of fire and smoke where seconds ago there was a bomber. The last of the three machines now flies on alone in front of me. Seconds later it has been replaced by a fireball, from which pieces of the bomber tumble to earth. The rest fly on in loose order. As I chase the lead vic I quickly cast my gaze over the sky. There they come, the *Ratas*. They are in a very favorable position and will soon catch up with me. Three Bf 109s race toward them. 'The formation leader must go down,' is my only thought. His vic of three flies ahead of me, still in close formation. I have to pass between the two trailing bombers. They glide past close enough to touch. The dorsal gunners aim their guns at me, I see the flickering blue flashes from their muzzles and hear the thumps as bullets strike my machine. But now my guns speak too. Once again a spurt of flame and a comet with a fiery tail plunges to earth. That was number four.

"Then a terrific blow shakes my machine. The rudder pedals will not move, dense smoke fills the cockpit. Now I will fall to earth like a comet. But luck is with me. My Me remains well in hand. My nerves settle down and I have time to look around. Behind me a heavy battle is in progress. My oil lines appear to have been hit, the oil temperature climbs steadily. I turn for home, but there are flashes behind me and once again I hear bullets striking home. I stand my crate on its nose and dive. I pull out just above the ground. Behind me all is clear, except for a long trail of oil. I fly along at an altitude of ten meters, the Teruel church steeple is my reference point. Then, from below, machine-gun fire! Several more hits! But there is the front. I am past. Now I look for a place to crash-land. I set down in a large field, my machine rolls and finally comes to a stop. Now my nerves leave me, I am unable to climb out. I look around. In the distance the black smoke clouds still hang in the sky. One — Two — Five — Nine. Exhausted and with shaking hands I climb out and examine my machine. A sieve. Rudder cables shot up. Gas and oil tanks hit. Cockpit and wings hacked to pieces. Theoretically I'm dead."

Also arriving at Calamocha on February 7 was the Stuka *Kette* under *Kettenführer Lt.* Haas. The *Kette* and its three Ju 87 A dive-bombers, or "*Stupidos*" as they were dubbed by the Spanish, had been in Spain since January 15, 1938. All three crews were from 11 *Staffel*/LG 1 based at Barth, which had equipped with the Ju 87 A in mid-1937. The men flying the Stukas soon received the nickname "*Schwartzbomber Sturzkopff*" from the sharp-tongued fighter pilots, a reference to the commander of the Stukas' parent unit, *Oberstleutnant* Günther Schwartzkopff. Following their arrival in Spain the three machines were assembled at Leon and the aircraft were assigned the following codes:

Balthasar came within a hair's breadth of not surviving his fourth victory. Bullet damage to the windscreen of his Bf 109.

1. *Lt.* Haas, with gunner/RO *Fw.* Kramer, Ju 87 A, 29-4
2. *Lt.* Weyert, with gunner/RO *Uffz.* Göller, Ju 87A, 29-3
3. *Uffz.* Bartels, with gunner/RO *Uffz.* Fleisch, Ju 87 A, 29-2

Each of the aircraft carried the same emblem on the wheel fairing, namely "Jolanthe," a fat sow. Twenty technical personnel from Germany had accompanied the aircrew to look after the aircraft. In the coming days the three Stukas were to make precision attacks on targets in the Alfambra Valley and near Teruel.

During the night the Republican troops pulled back to the east bank of the Alfambra. Flying as many as six sorties per day, the *Cadenas* from Burbaguena and Calamocha prevented the other side from halting its withdrawal. With each transfer forward of the *Legion Condor* command post, the very busy Ln/88 was called upon to extend the most important lines of communication. Air traffic control facilities had to be set up at each newly-occupied airfield, all in all a burden which was almost more than the four signals companies could cope with.

Used to more comfortable temperatures, the Moros were always on the prowl for fuel for their "campfires" and had few qualms as to its source. Thus it happened that a crew set out one morning to install several kilometers of telephone wire, only to find that the poles, which had been emplaced the day before, had simply vanished. During the night the shivering "sons of the desert" had swiped all the poles and reduced them to handy sized pieces of wood.

On February 17, Nationalist troops launched a direct assault on Teruel. This action witnessed the first operational sorties by the *Kette* of Ju 87 A dive-bombers, later to become known the world over as "Stukas." On this day, however, not only did they attack the wrong target, but their 250kg bombs fell wide of the mark as well. On February 19 Stange destroyed a *Chato*; on the other side of the coin *Unteroffizier* Heinrich Torner of 4 *Staffel* was shot

A Ju 87 A of the Jolanthe-Kette on photographed while on an acceptance flight. Within a few days the crews discovered that takeoffs and landings at the plowed field at Calamocha were easier with the lower section of the undercarriage fairings removed.

down and killed in his He 51. The Republican ground fire was very accurate. One of their specialities was setting up flak traps to catch low-flying aircraft. *Staffelkapitän* d'Elsa describes one such incident:

"Today it's a 'louse hunt,' the same old story. There's a lonely young hare! The occupants flee, but the vehicle continues to drive on. Let the jalopy have it! But what's this? Black smoke puffs in the sky? Red balls? I break away and while in the turn I see one of my machines shed a wing. It's Torner, the third pilot the *Staffel* has lost since its formation. The next day we go out on another louse hunt. It's the same story as yesterday. Suddenly we come under fire from 20mm anti-aircraft guns. Flak trap! We are going to have to try attacking with flank guards."

Once again the He 51s were committed at the critical points of the battle, repeatedly foiling Republican counterattacks. During the taking of Teruel on February 20 and 21 they even became involved in the street fighting. On the 20th "Eckie" Priebe destroyed a Republican tank with his six 10kg bombs as it was

Given the poor condition of the roads, drives into the area surrounding Calamocha frequently ended in pushing and swearing.

Uffz. Fritz Rabeneck managed to fly the sixty kilometers back to Calamocha in his He 51 (2-79), even though the aircraft's upper wing had been badly damaged by ground fire. February 1938.

attempting to escape Teruel. Having switched off his automatic bomb release mechanism, Priebe used the emergency release lever to drop his meager bombload "on the roof" of the T-26. It was his 40th combat sortie. In general the fear the Nationalist ground troops had of the "steel monsters" was balanced by their awareness of the flying skill of their pilots. A few days later Priebe was ordered to Gallur to join 1. J/88, which was equipped with the Bf 109.

Franco's troops had taken the pile of rubble that had once been the city of Teruel; the streets were choked with bodies, the cemetery had been ripped up by bombs and shells. The devastated landscape was a pitiful, chaotic scene. Everywhere there were Moroccan soldiers laden with looted goods. The city had been left to them to plunder for half a day. The atmosphere was apocalyptic.

10kg bombs dropped by "Eckie" Priebe have torn return rollers and a fender from this T-26.

On February 21, there was heavy fighting in the air with dozens of *Ratas* and *Chatos*. 1 *Staffel* (Awe, Mayer, Woitke) reported the destruction of three I-16s near La Pueble, while 2 *Staffel* shot down four *Ratas* near Sarrion and Teruel (Schlichting, Rempel, Ihlefeld, Rochel). The Italian fighter group *"As de Basto"* with twenty Fiats under Major Zotti also became involved. The well-known Spanish pilot Major Carlos collided with an I-15 which was on the tail of another Fiat and was killed. The Republicans admitted the loss of four *Ratas* destroyed and two *Ratas* and five *Chatos* damaged, while claiming seven C.R.32s, four Bf 109s, a Ju 52 and several other Nationalist aircraft.

The destruction of two I-15s by the recently promoted *Leutnant* Seiler on February 22 marked the end of the Battle of Teruel. The Spanish Nationalists lost an He 51, and had previously lost one of these aircraft on the 15th; both pilots were killed.

On the Republican side the 4th *Rata* Squadron had been completely wiped out and the 6th Squadron had to be disbanded. The 2nd and 5th *Rata* Squadrons under Vigrov and Susekalov received new equipment, the I-16 Type 10, which was armed with four machine-guns. The 3rd Squadron was now led by Bravo. Further Russian squadron leaders from this period were Caputchin, Devodschenkov, Silvestro and Smolekov. The Republican fighter force had been further strengthened by the formation of a fourth *Chato* squadron.

A "Moro" squad with its Bandera following the capture of Teruel on Feb. 20, 1938.

Dressed in a wide variety of clothing, a rather uninspiring-looking group of Moro assault troops.

Süddeutsche Ausgabe

VÖLKISCHER BEOBACHTER

Kampfblatt der national-sozialistischen Bewegung Großdeutschlands

Teruel von den roten Belagerern befreit

Vernichtende Niederlage der Bolschewisten

Roter General gefangen

Stärkung der Nation auf allen Gebieten ihres Lebens

Die Parole des Führe für 1938

A headline in the January 3, 1938 edition of the Völkische Beobachter proclaims the fall of Teruel, almost seven weeks before the city actually fell to Nationalist troops. There is no mention of the presence of German troops in Spain.

Noteworthy from a Nationalist point of view was the operational employment of two Hs 123 *Angelitos*. At the end of January, however, they returned to Sevilla where they were replaced by the recently-delivered Ju 87 A dive-bombers. Optimally the bombing accuracy of the "Stukas" was plus/minus five meters.

On February 23, the German fighters transferred to Gallur on the Ebro River, northwest of Zaragoza. K/88 left El Burgo de Osma and moved to the airfield at Alfaro. During a general briefing on February 24 the *Cuadillo*, following a thorough discussion of the situation, gave up his plans to break through to Madrid. The new objective was to be the Levant coast. Three battle groups were to strike toward the Mediterranean from the areas of Rillo, Rudilla and Carinena.

While on a trip to the front at Teruel Lt. Walter Adolph (1. J/88) is greeted by several "sons of the desert" with shouts of "Ariba Alemania."

The Advance Through Aragon

The coming days were used by the Nationalists to prepare for their great offensive in Aragon and to reconnoiter the new area of operations. It was to be a coordinated assault by four corps:

(1) Castilla Corps (General Varela)
Assembly area: Teruel to Perales
Assignment: Tie down enemy and screen the southern flank of the advancing forces.

(2) Galicia Corps (General Aranda)
Assembly area: Rillo to Rudilla
Assignment: Capture of Montalban and advance to the highway to Alcaniz.

(3) Italian C.T.V. (*Cuerpo de Tropas Voluntarias*) (General Berti)
Assembly area: North of Rudilla
Assignment: Advance on Albalate and Hijar

(4) Marroqui Corps (General Yagüe) with 1st Navarra Division (General Valino)
Assembly area: Rio Huerva, southeast of Carinena

Assignment: Advance through Belchite toward Azaila, Escatron to Caspe.

The earlier favorable experiences in cooperation with the well-disciplined Marroqui Corps, which was to play a leading role in the offensive, led the commander of the *Legion Condor* to assume responsibility for air support in the northern sector. Understandably the Italians were to operate over their own corps, the C.T.V., while the Spanish Air Force provided air cover for the offensive by the Galicia Corps. In command of the three combined air force units was General Kindelan.

The Spaniards formed two new C.R.32 fighter squadrons before the beginning of the offensive, which were incorporated into the existing fighter

General Aranda (back to camera) converses with Colonel Riva of the Italian CTV during preparations for the attack toward the Mediterranean.

The head of the Spanish Nationalist Air Force, General Alfredo Kindelan y Duany. He expressed the view several times that the Nationalists could get along without the Legion Condor.

An American Spartan 7W Executive, used by the Nationalist Air Force as a courier aircraft. The five-seater was powered by a 450 HP P&W R-985 engine.

groups under Guerrero and Barranco. The Italian Legion's air forces had reached the peak of their strength, with:

1 wing	heavy bomber	S.M.81
1 wing	heavy bomber	S.M.79
1 group	medium bomber	Fiat B.R.20
1 group	close-support	Breda Ba 65
1 squadron	close-support	Fiat C.R.32
3 groups	fighter	Fiat C.R.32

The commanders of the three fighter groups were Rossi, Aiello and Francois.

In the *Legion Condor,* on February 15 the Ju 87 *Kette* joined J/88 as 5 *Staffel.* The pilots of the dive-bombers were *Leutnant* Hermann Haas, *Leutnant* Gerd Weyert and *Unteroffizier* Ernst Bartels. Several weeks later a *Kette* was equipped with the Ar 68 and in July 1938 flew night fighter sorties against nuisance raids by Republican R-5 and R-Z bombers in the Castellon area. This experiment met with no success, however, and was abandoned. In March 1938 the first Bf 109 C and D models arrived in Spain.

On the Republican side graduates of the second pilot training course from Russia had returned to Spain and were integrated into the squadrons with the more experienced pilots.

The prelude to the attack planned for March 9 began on the 6th with bombing attacks by the He 111s of K/88. Sixteen aircraft bombed Caspe airfield, eighteen others the airfield at Bujaraloz. In the afternoon nine He 111s attacked a Republican division headquarters in Aldehuele, south of Teruel. When the attacks were over a fuel dump at Caspe was ablaze and four enemy machines had been destroyed on the ground at Bujalaroz. Late the same morning vehicle concentrations were bombed by nine Do 17 bombers of A/88; dive-bombing attacks by two Ju 87s against the Ebro bridge near Sastago were unsuccessful, however. Bf 109s of J/88 flew escort for all of these attacks, but only near Caspe was there any contact with Republican fighters. Three *Ratas* tried in vain to get close to the bombers. He 59s of AS/88 inflicted heavy damage on installations in Barcelona harbor in attacks made during the nights of March 5 and 6.

Previously assigned to protect the airfield at Alfaro, the 2nd and 6th Heavy Batteries and the 4th Light Battery of F/88 were now moved into the Villanueva del Huerva sector to support ground operations. The batteries reported ready for action on March 7.

With the transfer of the furnished train which was Stab/88's living quarters to Almonacid on March 7, the preparations for the attack to the east were concluded. In an effort to screen these actions the ground observer teams of Ln/88 had been left behind in the Guadalajara sector. These were to try and deceive the enemy as to the true assembly area through intensified (fictitious) radio traffic.

All bombers of K/88 and A/88 took off at 1300 on March 7 with fighter escort to attack the Puebla de Hijar railway station and a munitions factory situated to the north. The bomb pattern in the station area was somewhat scattered, however, the munitions factory went up in flames. The He 45 *Kette* flew three sorties checking enemy movements directly behind the front. Attacks by three Ju 87s once again failed to destroy the bridge at Sastago.

The Vultee 1A was used as a transport by the Nationalists. The Republicans used the same type as a close-support aircraft, equipped with two machine-gun positions and a bomb magazine.

On March 7, Nationalist bombers struck the war port of Cartagena and damaged the Republican cruiser *Libertad* in revenge for the sinking of the cruiser *Baleares,* which had been lost with 700 sailors in a naval engagement off Cartagena.

On March 8, two He 111 *Staffeln* accomplished what the "*Jolanthe-Kette*" had failed to do the day before. Attacking at altitudes as low as 50 meters, the bombers attacked the bridge over the Ebro at Sastago. However, in spite of hitting both approaches and the bridge itself, the bombers failed to completely destroy the bridge. By chance the nearby electrical generating station was struck by a stray bomb. The two other *Staffeln* of K/88 and the bombers of A/88 returned to

Also from the USA was the Lockheed 10 Electra. The twelve-seat aircraft was used mostly by corps headquarters as a courier and staff aircraft.

Franco's personnel aircraft, a Douglas DC-2, which had previously been flown by the Republicans on unspecified duties.

The Italians helped ease the shortage of training aircraft with the delivery of a small batch of Caproni CA.100 biplanes. Note that the span of the upper wing is less than that of the lower, a characteristic of this aircraft.

the munitions factory and railway station at Puebla de Hijar. A pair of Stukas of 5. J/88 scored two direct hits on a railway embankment with 500kg bombs, cutting the Zaragoza-Alcaniz rail line. Two of the escorting fighter pilots, *Oblt.* Schellmann and *Lt.* Awe, each shot down an I-15. Schellmann describes the action:

"I spot one little bird which is hanging back and flying slower than the others. I waggle my wings to my *Katschmarek*. We will go after this lad. However, we overtake him only slowly. I calculate: if this fellow is going to land he will have to slow down, then I'll catch him. We fly over the hilltops, then down into the valley toward the enemy airfield. We close in to 600 meters, 400 meters — fractions of a second — a burst — the enemy drops a wing and goes down. We are 40 kilometers behind the front. Pull up and head for home! Suddenly a squadron of *Ratas* 20 meters above us. Throttle forward and get out of here! My *Katschmarek* passes me, I limp along behind him. What's up with my damned engine? I scan the instruments. Idiot! The propeller is still set for diving flight! A flick of a lever and the Messerschmitt gains full speed. The enemy is already ticklishly close. I twist and turn and hug the ground, sweeping over hills, olive groves and a farm. They've already been chasing me for four minutes. An eternity! Finally, there's the front! Abruptly the enemy turns back. It's a great relief."

Twice during the night of March 7/8 Carenina was the target of Republican bombers seeking to disrupt the build-up and deprive the attack divisions of their

French Caudron C 59 biplane trainers (built 1922/23) were used by the Republicans, some still with their French registrations. Here are two captured C 59s wearing provisional Nationalist markings.

sleep.

The day of the attack, March 9, 1938: Due to the poor visibility caused by dust raised by the supply columns and the refraction of the rising sun, the infantry was unable to begin its attack at 0600 as intended, moving out instead two hours later. *Hauptmann* Neudôrffer and his four *Staffeln* of K/88 took off from Alfaro at 0641. Coming from Gallur, 1. J/88 rendezvoused with the bombers and escorted them as they bombed the road and nearby positions at Villanueva del Huerva-Fuendetodos in the attack lane of the 5th Division. 42.9 tons of bombs were dropped in this raid. Hill positions on the Herrera massif were the targets of nine Do 17s of A/88 from Bunuel. Six Bf 109s flew escort for the "flying pencils." The bombers attacked the target

Almost all of the flying personnel of the Ju 87 Kette are present in this photo. From left: Uffz Fleisch (radio operator/gunner), Uffz. Bartels (pilot), Fw. Kramer (radio operator/gunner), Maj. Graf Fugger of Stab/88, Lt. Weyert (pilot), Lt. Haas (pilot).

He 111 of 2. K/88 with propeller spinners in the Staffel color, red. Compared to the earlier B version, the E could carry twice the bombload, or 2,000 kilograms.

An MG 15 with mounted Dt 15 double magazine in the dorsal gun position of an He 111.

Ventral gun pod of He 111 B 25-17 in the extended position — a very windy spot for the gunner. Visible on the right side of the pod is the locking lever with indicator.

from high altitude, achieving good results. Two Ju 87's armed with 500kg bombs attacked some "tougher nuts," concrete positions four kilometers east of Aguilon. In a second sortie the nine Do 17s plastered Entredicho Hill with SC 50 bombs. Two *Staffeln* of He 51 close-support aircraft rounded out the air forces which started off the attack with a bang. 3. and 4. J/88 supported the tanks as they advanced across the gently rising terrain, and at about noon they strafed Republican positions, pinning down the defenders. The He 51s reappeared in the 5th Division's attack sector, the Fuendetodos-Herrera area, at about 1400, to provide close support. The Ju 87 *Kette* flew three further sorties that day with fighter escort: between 1200 and 1300 they dive-bombed columns which had been sighted in the town of Azuara, at about 1400 their bombs tore up

Loading a Do 17 E of A/88 with 50kg bombs.

Do 17 27-25 in formation flight. On the fuselage nose next to the emblem of A/88, a bearded devil, is the pilot's personal emblem, a figure riding on a bomb.

crossroads west of Belchite, and after reloading they attacked the strongly fortified fortress of Casilta, six kilometers west of Belchite. The twenty-four hour total of 210 tons of bombs dropped was a record which stood for the rest of the civil war. This deluge of bombs abruptly smashed the resistance of the Republican units.

The clear success of March 9 prevented the enemy from establishing a cohesive defensive line which would have justified further attacks by the bomber units. On the 10th, therefore, the plan of operations for the He 111s, Do 17s and He 51s called for attacks against enemy airfields reported as occupied. Taking off from Alfaro at 0600, Neudörffer's four He 111 *Staffeln* began this special assignment. At about the same time the Do 17s of A/88 were lifting off from Bunuel and all four *Staffeln* of the *Jagdgruppe* were taking off from Gallur and Sanjurjo. At 0700 the bombers of *Kampfgruppe* 88 arrived over the Republican airfields at Caspe, Sarinena and Candasnos. Conditions were hazy. At Caspe five enemy aircraft on the ground went up in flames. The airfield at Bujaraloz was bombed by the Do 17 *Staffel* and soon afterward was forced to endure a low-level strafing attack by several He 111s. Returning from a high-level attack on Candasnos, the Heinkel bombers roared over Bujalaroz airfield with all guns blazing. The He 111 unit set course for home,

Do 17 crew at Bunuel, March 1938. Lt. Philips, the observer, is flanked on the left by his pilot, Ofw. Sorge, and on the right by his radio operator, Uffz. Wawrock.

leaving one parked aircraft in flames, but the aircraft commanded by *Leutnant* Kettner turned back for a second attack. Heinkel 25-7 had just crossed the airfield when it was attacked from behind by an I-15. Flight engineer Hofmeister in the dorsal position was unable to fend off the attack as his gun had jammed. Within seconds the He 111's fuselage, wings and engines had all been hit numerous times and the bomber was unable to maintain altitude. The only choice left was a crash-landing at the edge of Bujalaroz airfield. The crew of *Leutnant* Kurt Kettner (observer), *Feldwebel* Willi Hesse (pilot), *Unteroffizier* Theo Kowollik (radio operator), *Unteroffizier* Karl Hofmeister (flight engineer) and *Obergefreiter* Heinz Clacery, who had gone along on the mission as an observer, were taken prisoner, some with minor injuries. All of these men were exchanged for Republican fliers on January 2, 1939. Handrick sent his J/88 against Belchite and Jatiel, where three parked *Chatos* were strafed and set on fire. *Feldwebel* Prestele was able to shoot down an I-15, while Rochel and Schlichting each destroyed a *Rata*. A Spanish He 45 was shot down by Republican ground fire.

About 2.5 kilometers east of Belchite the 88mm guns of 6. F/88 shot up an enemy anti-aircraft battery, allegedly manned by French International Brigadists. The village fell the same day, March 10, following several attacks by the *"Jolanthe-Kette"* on

Photographed in front of the first He 111 delivered to 4. K/88 is Uffz. Gruetzmacher, flight engineer in Lt. Kettner's crew. The entire crew was captured on March 10.

The red-yellow-red turret stripes reveal that this T-26 belongs to a Nationalist tank company.

The Republicans abandoned this Bronieford BA armored car on the Belchite—Azaila road after it developed engine trouble. The vehicle weighed 1.8 tons with a crew of three and was capable of speeds of 50 kph on roads.

crossroads in the area and Belchite itself. The infantry and accompanying tanks had been supported all day by the He 51s of 3. and 4./J 88 as they advanced along the Fuendetodos-Belchite road. The day was also marked by extremely heavy artillery preparation and support by anti-aircraft guns in the Marroqui Corps' battle zone.

Here too, as on other fronts, the International Brigades were engaged in the defensive battle against the Nationalists, among them the XI International Brigade which included German units. It was here that the first Germans fighting on the Republican side were captured. Two units equipped with Panzer Is, "Imker Drohne" and a Spanish tank company, took part in these battles. Strengthened by the addition of several captured T-26 tanks, they participated in the subsequent operations which saw the Nationalists advance to the Ebro. Two motorized batteries fell into the hands of the advancing Nationalists after their vehicles had been shot up by He 51 close-support aircraft.

Following attacks against airfields beyond the front late in the morning, K/88 took off again at 1200, this time to attack the town of Lecera and nests of resistance to the north. A Bf 109 *Staffel* guarded the bombers against attack by Republican fighters. The second Bf 109 *Staffel* accompanied Do 17 bombers as they attacked the railway station in the city of Escatron on the Ebro. At about 1700, after being quickly rearmed, thirty-one He 111s took off on their third mission of the day. Their targets were the towns of Azaila and Hijar, while A/88 carried out a high-level attack on Vinaceide.

Other than defensive sorties over Azaila and in the Hijar area, the Republican fighters were conspicuous by their absence. That afternoon the He 51 *Staffeln* of Galland and d'Elsa were over the front like a swarm of hornets for the fourth time that day. Their attentions were focussed on the battle zone around Azuara and Almonacid de la Cuba.

AS/88 risked a flight into the interior with its slow He 59 floatplanes to attack crossings over the Ebro near Tortosa. Special attention was paid to the large road bridge near Amposta, which had been completed only a few years before. This 140-meter suspension bridge had to handle almost all the road traffic between the two banks of the Ebro, as the bridge near Tortosa was under an almost continuous hail of bombs from Italian and German bombers and Stukas. AS/88 had been sent against this important link once before, on November 24 and 25, 1937, during the Teruel offensive, but had scored only near misses with 250kg bombs fitted with delayed action fuses. One 250kg bomb in fact pierced the concrete roadway, but detonated eight seconds later in the water of the Ebro.

On March 10, AS/88 returned to finish the job. Three He 59s arrived in the target area at about 2015 and approached the Amposta bridge in *Kette* formation. Each He 59 released five 50kg bombs from an altitude of 2,500 meters. The entire salvo landed next to the bridge. Fifteen more bombs were released on the second pass and several hits were observed. As the destruction of the bridge could not be confirmed in the weak moonlight, the floatplanes made a third pass and once again dropped their

Three Zapatones (He 59 floatplanes) en route from Pollensa to their target.

bombs in unison. All fell into the water. Not until the following day did damage assessment photos reveal that the roadway and the suspension section of the bridge now lay in the water of the Ebro River. The transportation link so vital to the enemy had been severed.

At the command post of the *Legion Condor* on the Cruz Heights that evening and night were spent working out the attack orders for the following day, March 11. At 0730, in warm sunny weather, all thirty-three serviceable He 111s took off from Alfaro. They overflew Zaragoza and by 0815 were over the target, the villages of Albalate del Arzobispo, Hijar and Azaila. After dropping a total of 42.4 tons of bombs the formation turned northwest toward home. About thirty Republican fighters tried to interfere with the bombers as they approached the release point, but were engaged by the escorting Bf 109 fighters. The Legion fighters lost one Bf 109 without inflicting any losses on the enemy. Graf zu Dohna, who was to have relieved Schlichting as *Kapitän* of 2 *Staffel*, was shot down by a *Rata* on his second combat sortie. His Bf 109 struck the ground near Caspe with the pilot still aboard. Five He 111s returned to base with major battle damage. The enemy had once again shown his teeth!

The second mission by K/88 that day was the first to be led by *Major* Mehnert, successor to *Hauptmann* Neudôrffer, who had returned to Germany on March 15. The bombs began falling on Albalate and Hijar at 1300. The escorting fighters had nothing to do as no enemy aircraft showed themselves. The Do 17s of A/88 were despatched twice against the heavily-fortified crossroads near Kilometer 54 of the Belchite-Azaila road, at 1000 and again at about 1700. In between the Dornier bombers flew another strike against the town of Azaila. The *"Jolanthe-Kette"*, which was operating as 5. J/88, carried out an attack against the town of Sastago during the noon hour. The dive-bombers each made two diving attacks, scoring hits on the center of the town, which was now filled with retreating troops.

During their advance between Belchite and Lecera the 5th and 150th Divisions once again profited from the continuous low-level attacks by the 3rd and 4th *Staffeln* of J/88. The He 51s, the *Cadenas*, attacked and destroyed a Republican battery. The He 51's limited fuel capacity, good for only 70 minutes flying time, allowed only 15 minutes of combat at

The intact Amposta suspension bridge, whose support towers were designed in the shape of archways. In spite of its narrow width this Ebro crossing was the supply lifeline for Republican forces fighting on the south side of the Ebro.

The bridge has been hit and a section has fallen into the river.

Damage assessment photo of the severed transport link. The city of Amposta lies on the south bank of the Ebro, which flows from left to right in the photograph.

the front, after which the aircraft had to break away and begin the long flight back to their base at Gallur.

As always, road surveillance and photo reconnaissance were the daily bread of the He 45 reconnaissance machines. They went about their duties with no prospect of spectacular success, such as the fighters brought home daily. Also in the shadow of the "Aces" were the He 59s of AS/88, which achieved good results in attacks on rail junctions south of Vendrell and rail installations near Tarragona and Tortosa.

The constant air attacks denied the Republicans any chance of reorganizing their forces and mounting an effective defense; the breakthrough to the Ebro could now only be a matter of a few days.

On March 12, the day Escatron was reached and occupied, there was a major air battle between eighteen Fiats of the Spanish Salas Fighter Group and twenty *Chatos*. The Spaniards claimed seven I-15s and an SB-2 shot down as well as several probables. Two of the kills were credited to Morato. The Republicans reported an air battle between twenty *Ratas* and nineteen *Chatos*, which were providing escort for *Katiuska* bombers, and twenty-five C.R.32s. They claimed three Fiats destroyed against the loss of two *Chatos* shot down. Two further I-15s made forced landings. There are extremely dubious elements in both accounts; in contrast to the strict requirements of the *Legion Condor*, confirmation of victory claims was given too lightly, in spite of the absence of the necessary proof and eye-witnesses.

On that day the *Legion Condor* command post was located on the Valadico, one kilometer east of Belchite; from there 3. and 4./J 88 were the first to receive orders to suppress resistance in front of the 5th Division. Constantly changing positions, the artillery and flak kept pace with the spirited advance, which on the early afternoon led to the capture of the city of Azaila.

A/88 flew its first reconnaissance sorties at 0500, located enemy concentrations and during the forenoon attacked these with six of its own Do 17s. During the period between 0800 and 0900 thirty-three He 111s of K/88 successfully bombed Hijar and the railway station near Pueblo Hijar with high-explosive bombs. Between 1200 and 1300 a second attack was directed against the Samper de Calanda rail crossing and the town of Castellote.

Two Ju 87s of 5. J/88 carried out a dive-bombing attack on the Ebro bridge near Sastago in an effort to halt the Republican retreat across the river; results were unsatisfactory, as all bombs fell wide of the target. Traffic across the bridge was halted for a brief period while the attack was in progress. The He 51 *Staffeln*, the true "water bearers" of the ground

88mm anti-aircraft guns of F/88 engaging surface targets before Azaila.

Pilots rest on one of their aircraft before the next takeoff. The He 51 Staffeln became indispensable on account of the effectiveness of their low-level attacks.

forces, flew five strafing missions against positions and road traffic near Escatron. The attacks left two trucks burning and three destroyed at the side of the road.

That evening He 59s of AS/88 prowled along the Vendrell-Tarragona rail line and shot up two locomotives before turning toward the sea and heading back to Pollensa.

By the time darkness fell the command post had been moved forward again, to a point four kilometers south of Azaila; in contrast to the offensives in the spring and summer of 1937, the Germans were satisfied with the cooperation with Spanish and Italian divisional headquarters. Previously, it had not been at all unusual for German liaison officers to have to rouse Spanish staff officers from their beds in the morning to see to the assembly of their units; meanwhile the bombers and close-support aircraft were already attacking in the forefield, expecting an attack by the ground forces. "Good troops and miserable generals who are fit to be battalion commanders at best," von Richthofen wrote in his diary. A few exceptions, like the Chief-of-Staff of the Navarra Division, Colonel Juan Vigon, its commander, General José Varela, or the commander of the Moroccan Corps, General Juan Yagüe, enjoyed the respect of their German officer comrades.

Early on the morning of March 13 A/88 was already reconnoitering the area around Montalban, located at the foot of the Sierra de San Just and in the attack sector of the Galicia Corps. The first strike, launched by thirty-three He 111s of K/88 at about 0925, was directed against the city of Caspe and its airfield, and was escorted by two *Staffeln* of Bf 109s. Republican fighters reacted strongly and two of 2.

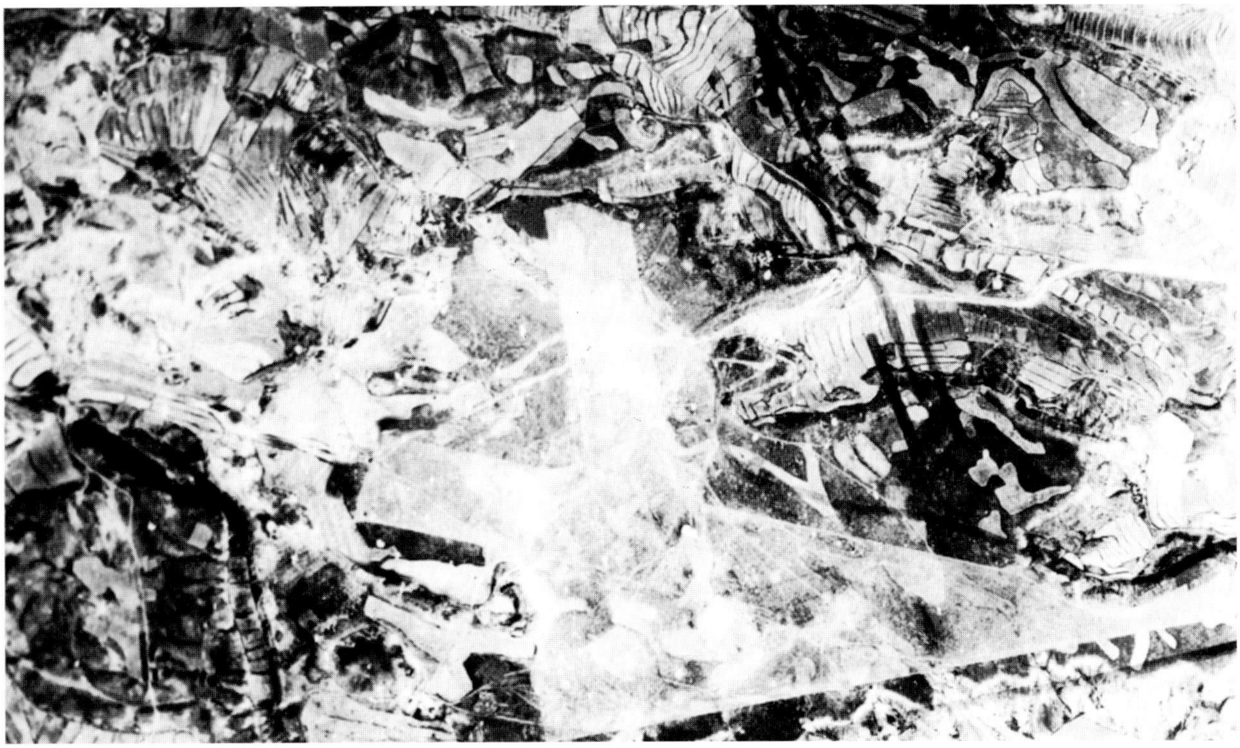

On March 13 Kampfgruppe 88 bombed the Republican airfield located 10 km northwest of the city of Caspe. The two diagonally overlapping runways are situated in typical Los Monegros countryside.

J/88's pilots, *Leutnant* Ettling and *Unteroffizier* Ihlefeld, each shot down a *Chato*. K/88 repeated the attack between 1300 and 1400. Four He 45s sent to observe troop movements in the Sastago area returned with proof that the Republican defensive front was firming up on the other side of the Ebro.

Once again the "bats" of AS/88 used the night for attacks on road and rail supply traffic. At about 1900 an He 59 made a low-level attack on the track system at Vinaroz, dropping ten 50kg bombs. It was followed

Aerial photo of Vianroz railway station, an important station on the Barcelona—Valencia line.

Located right at the edge of town, Ulldecona through-station. It was here that the Republicans unloaded the troop and freight trains bringing reinforcements from Valencia.

by a second Heinkel floatplane which released twenty 50kg bombs at a train near Vinaroz station. A third He 59 approached Ulldecona and at 1920 bombed the railway station with eight 50kg bombs. All of the sorties flown during the month of March were intended to choke off supply traffic along the coast. In most cases, however, they only succeeded in interrupting traffic for two to five hours, after which the generally limited damage to railway installations had been repaired and the rubble cleared away.

At attack altitudes of between 60 and 200 meters the fragmentation effect of the bombs used (with 15 second delayed action fuses) was far less than expected. On more than one occasion bombs released from these low altitudes struck the ground in a flat attitude, bounced several times and then lay along the tracks as duds. Only release heights of 100 meters or greater could ensure a sufficiently steep impact angle, with the resulting ground penetration and increased explosive force.

Later questioning of railway personnel revealed the astonishing fact that during attacks by the "*Hydros*" most fled at most 100 to 200 meters into the fields and felt themselves absolutely safe there. As most of the stations were some distance from the towns and villages, most of the civilian population

One of the losses suffered by the Italians on March 14, a Fiat C.R.32 of the 4a Squadriglia, which crashed near Hijar.

remained calmly in their beds. Several people were of the opinion that the "railroaders," as they called the He 59s, warned of their approach by dropping hand grenades before reaching their target; they were probably referring to 50kg bombs dropped on sections of open track.

Although the Legion's entire air strength and two 88mm batteries of F/88 were standing ready to provide support, in the early hours of March 14, 1938 General Yagûe could not make up his mind to attack Caspe. As a result of the Spanish General's indecision, at about midday *Generalmajor* Volkmann cancelled any further participation by the *Legion Condor*. Renewed pressure subsequently moved the commander of the Marroqui Corps to launch the attack; but without air support the Spanish troops became bogged down after some minor gains.

On March 14, it was the turn of the Italian Fiat fighters. Forty-five of them tangled with about fifty Republican aircraft. Two *Ratas*, five *Chatos* and four Fiats were lost. On the 15th the Republican fighter pilot Claudin was able to shoot down a Fiat; his friend Tarazona was forced to make a belly landing due to battle damage. The Republican fighters lost their airfields at Caspe and Escatron in the first week of the offensive and were therefore out of necessity somewhat more cautious in the period which followed.

Embittered by the experience of the previous day, on March 15 the Legion moved its command post back to Banos de Fitero. In spite of further support from the He 51 *Staffeln* the day's objective, the city of Caspe, could not be taken; the newly-arrived XIV International Brigade and the remaining elements of the XI and XIII Interbrigades inflicted heavy losses on the attackers. The Do 17s of A/88 felt the effects of the enemy's revived fighter defense as they bombed troop concentrations in the town of Maella; a straight and level approach to the target was virtually impossible and the persistent fighter attacks forced several pilots to jettison their bombs. The escorting Bf 109s had their hands full trying to protect the Do 17 unit from the *Ratas* and *Chatos* attacking from above. Ju 87s twice dive-bombed the bridge south of Guadelope, but were unable to destroy the span.

Following an unopposed attack by an He 59 on the railway station at Vinaroz with five 50kg bombs at about 1930 the previous day, March 15 was to cost AS/88 one of its aircraft. The machine dropped twenty 50kg bombs on a military transport train at 0430, destroying several cars. An attempt to shoot up the locomotive on the same pass brought the crew to grief. The He 59 flew directly into the defensive fire of the train's guns and was hit in the fuselage and left engine by several bursts of machine-gun fire. An attempt to reach the sea failed. Steadily losing altitude, the He 59 crashed in an olive grove beside the Vinaroz-San Carlos road. All five members of the crew escaped unhurt. They managed to set their aircraft on fire before they were challenged by civilians from Alcanar, taken prisoner by a local constable and brought to Castellon de la Plana.

March 16 also failed to bring about the eagerly-awaited capture of Caspe. Large numbers of Republican artillery, tanks and bombers prevented a further advance by the Nationalists. F/88's 2nd (heavy) Battery was in action from the early morning near Caspe, helping beat off enemy counterattacks. It was hoped that an attack by a *Staffel* of He 111s

The only clue that this is the wreckage of an He 59 floatplane is the still-intact tip of one float, visible on the left. The aircraft was set on fire by its crew following a forced landing in enemy territory.

would crack the defensive lines near Maella. The attack was made at 1500 but failed to achieve the desired results. Stukas with fighter escort bombed enemy batteries near Caspe and a munitions column on the road to Maella; afterward about thirty I-15s appeared over the battlefield, but by then the Germans were on their way home and there was no contact.

Without informing Franco, Italian bomber squadrons carpet bombed Barcelona that day, killing nearly 1,300 civilians and injuring another 2,000. When he learned of the raid Franco was furious, and he reproached the Italian commander sharply for this unauthorized action.

Not until March 17 did the Republicans begin evacuating their positions around Caspe. Attempts to occupy new positions east of the city were frustrated by sticks of bombs from six He 111s; trucks bringing in reserves from the direction of Alcaniz were driven from the roads by repeated attacks by low-flying He 51s. All of Caspe was taken that day, but the Nationalists dared not launch a further advance toward the sea. On the evening of March 17 the entire *Jagdgruppe* 88 was assembled at Sanjurjo, near Zaragoza, to allow the pilots and aircraft a brief rest for the coming operations.

From March 16 to 18, the city and harbor of Barcelona were bombed repeatedly by the Italian bomber groups, this time with the approval of the Spanish General Staff. By night six He 59 floatplanes also took part in the attacks on Barcelona using their proven tactics: a climb to altitude after takeoff, a virtually noiseless gliding approach to the target from 4,000 meters, a release of bombs from low level and subsequent strafing then a dash out to sea at full throttle. Harassing raids were also made on rail installations near Tortosa, Benifallet, Vendrell, Vinaroz and Alcanar. The standard bomb load was twenty 50kg bombs, which the Heinkel floatplanes rained down on railway embankments, tracks and signal boxes.

Oberleutnant Jürgens and his crew were listed as missing on one such night raid over the Levant coast on March 21, 1938, probably a victim of the very active Republican night fighters.

North Ebro

The fact that their forces had encountered stiffening resistance in the final days before the capture of the Ebro city of Caspe brought the Nationalist commanders to the realization that a further advance toward the Mediterranean on a narrow front could only achieve the desired success at the cost of great sacrifice. The new strategy of an advance toward the Mediterranean on a broad front was intended to disperse the main Republican force massed on the Ebro and thus thin out the defensive front.

According to plan, by March 22, the day of the attack, the Nationalist forces had spread themselves along the approximately 250 kilometer front from Teruel to the Pyrenees. General Vigon requested the entire *Legion Condor* for the northern front, so that it might bomb a way clear for the Navarra Corps (General Solchaga) and the Aragon Corps (General Moscardo), which were to open the offensive from the Huesca area. The Marroqui Corps had orders to advance northeast across the Ebro between Caspe and Quinto, supported by Spanish air units. Assembled in the southern sector of the front were the Galicia Corps (General Aranda), the Italian C.T.V. (General Berti) and the 1st Navarra Division (General Varela); air cover for these formations was to be provided by the Italian air forces.

Banos de Fitero, home to the headquarters staff of the *Legion Condor* since it had moved there in mid-March, was to be the nerve center of the operation; the forward command post was set up near Huesca. A light and a heavy battery of F/88, under the command of *Oberstleutnant* Lichtenberger, were placed in the assembly area to provide direct support to the Spanish corps.

On the morning of March 22, precision attacks on forward positions and lines of communication in the rear by K/88 opened the second major battle of movement of the Spanish Civil War. In spite of repeated low-level attacks by He 51s and day-long support by the anti-aircraft guns in a ground role, the Nationalists were able to gain little ground in the face of bitter resistance. The following day brought bad weather which hampered operations on the ground and in the air. Only General Yagüe managed to get his Moros across the Ebro and establish a bridgehead. A Spanish He 45 reconnoitering at low altitude was brought down by rifle fire. *Hauptmann* Hering, who was to take over 3. J/88 from Galland, arrived in the combat zone that day to familiarize himself with conditions in Spain.

Clearing weather on March 24 permitted an increase in air activity. Eighteen Nationalist Fiats encountered twelve *Chatos*; several Bf 109s later joined the skirmish. The Spanish pilots shot down four I-15s and lost one machine. 1. J/88 also scored, with *Lt.* Awe, *Oblt.* Schellmann and *Uffz.* Stark each shooting down an I-15. Salas reported that he had damaged an I-15 and appeared to have wounded the pilot. Flying alongside at low altitude, he directed the Republican pilot to fly to the Nationalist lines. At that moment a Bf 109 (Schellmann's 6-51) attacked and shot the I-15 down in flames. The Republicans admitted the loss of six of their fighters, as well as one which made a belly landing.

On March 25, Salas scored a spectacular success. He observed three Republican training aircraft landing at Mas de las Matas airfield, which was still being fought over. Covered by his fighter group he

March 25, 1938. Direct hit by a Ju 87 crew on the Alcala de Obispo crossroads. The bombing had no lasting effect as the Republicans simply routed traffic around the bomb crater.

landed and took the pilots prisoner. The next day two Spanish Fiats were lost to ground fire. A description of just how tough a battle the close-support pilots were fighting is provided by the pen of Adolf Galland:

"Five of us were to attack enemy battery positions near Balaguer. One had to turn back prematurely with engine trouble. Suddenly, about 20 kilometers behind the front, we were attacked out of the sun by two squadrons of Curtisses. A wild dogfight developed at once. Two of my men slipped away across the front; that was the only right thing to do to avoid being overcome by the enemy's superior numbers. I still thought I saw friendly aircraft in the dogfight. The Curtisses fired like mad and stacked up behind us one after the other. My *Katschmarek*, a capable *Unteroffizier*, stuck doggedly behind me. Suddenly he roared away straight down. Behind him was a Curtiss and then me. One of my machine-guns still fired occasionally, and then only when operated by hand. Nevertheless I finally forced the Curtiss to break away from my *Katschmarek*. He landed smoothly behind our lines with thirty hits in his machine and a nasty wound through his shoulder and the tip of one lung."

The He 51s had transferred to Sarinena at the end of March.

The northward-advancing units under General Yagüe were able to reach the line Candasnos-Fraga on March 26, and the Aragon and Navarra Corps had reached the west bank of the Rio Alcanadre in several places. The Spanish He 51 group 1-G-2, led by Captain José Munoz Jimènez, lost one pilot killed and four wounded in its close-support missions.

A Spanish battery occupies positions in front of Fraga. The wooden-wheeled light artillery piece is being towed behind a truck on a rubber-tired trailer.

The battery in firing position; the gun tractors have withdrawn.

The city of Fraga, with its destroyed bridge over the Rio Cinca, photographed a day after its fall.

This Falange propaganda loudspeaker truck followed on the heels of Nationalist units as they moved into Barnastro on March 29, 1938.

Lt. Hans-Karl Mayer (8 victories in Spain) and Oblt. Eberhard d'Elsa, Staffelkapitän of 4. J/88.

Three S.M.81s and an S.M.79 returned from missions over the front with flak damage.

On March 27, the heavily-fortified positions around Fraga were the primary targets for the four He 111 *Staffeln* of K/88, under *Staffelkapitäne Hauptmann* Hans Schultz (1 *Staffel*), *Oberleutnant* Rolf Schröter (2 *Staffel*), *Hauptmann* Heinz Fischer (3 *Staffel*) and *Hauptmann* Dietrich von Ziehlberg (4 *Staffel*). Indicative of the success of the bombardment was the capture of Fraga that evening by Yagüe's troops. The two He 51 *Staffeln* moved to the forward airfield at Bujalaroz, where the reduced transit time to the front allowed them to remain longer over the target. A/88 was also busy all day, flying the reconnaissance sorties needed to create a photo mosaic of the area. This was prepared the same day by the staff photographic section (Stabia) for the headquarters of the Spanish corps. On the basis of information gained from these mosaics, the Aragon and Navarra Corps were able to successfully conclude their attacks in the direction of Rio Cinca and the city of Barbastro; both objectives were reached on March 28 and Barbastro was captured.

A further target for K/88 that day was Lerida airfield, where several *Ratas* were destroyed at their dispersals. On March 29, *Leutnant* Hans-Karl Mayer ("Downhill Mayer") destroyed an I-15 near Lerida, his fourth kill.

Well-armed, but too slow for its intended role as a close-support aircraft, the Breda 65bis was flown by the 65a Squadriglia d'Assalto of the Italian Legion.

These two He 51 fighters collided in mid-air and struck the ground still locked together. Help came too late for Hptm. Hering and Lt. Michaelis.

During the night of March 29/30, several heavy explosions shook buildings in the city of Barnastro. It was initially thought that a heavy raid by Republican bombers was under way, but this soon proved to be false when a major swelling of the Rio Cinca was reported east of the city. In an effort to delay Nationalist troops crossing the river the Reds had blown up the dam associated with a power station north of Barnastro. Nevertheless, once the flood had ebbed the leading elements of the two Nationalist corps crossed the river and advanced to the Canal de Zaidin. An Italian Breda 65 was lost that day.

While returning from a close-support mission, two He 51s of 3. J/88 collided in mid-air and crashed on the east bank of the Cinca. *Stabsarzt* Schauwecker, who was flown to the crash site by Fieseler *Storch* as soon as the news came in, could only confirm that both pilots, *Hauptmann* Hering and *Leutnant* Michaelis, were dead.

The rapid advance in the northern sector demanded the utmost of the men of signals battalion Ln/88. The continual extension of telephone lines, the erection of new radio stations and repairs to lines taxed this sub-unit of the Legion to exhaustion.

Toward the end of March Benicarlo railway station was the preferred target of the *Aufklärungsstaffel See*. At 0430 on March 27, a day later at 1945, and at exactly the same time on the 30th and 31st, an He 59 appeared over the station area and unloaded twenty 50kg bombs on the track system and the engine house with its turntable. Considerable damage was inflicted but there were no human casualties, as the station personnel had adequate time to flee to the shelters.

The discovery by A/88 of concentrations of enemy troops on the Guadalajara front, northeast of Madrid, made it advisable to send the *Staffeln* of K/88 there on March 31 before the Republicans could launch a relief offensive from this area. The bombers made one attack, pouring a hail of bombs on the area around Cifuentes.

Undisturbed by this threat Yagüe fought on toward Lerida, while south of the Ebro the C.T.V. and the 1st Division began their race toward Gandesa and reached the Matarana River. On the evening of

A Fieseler Fl 156 Storch, deliveries of which had just started in Germany. The liaison aircraft was used exclusively by the headquarters staff of the Legion Condor.

Several Junkers W 34hi aircraft were delivered from Germany for use as light transports, and as navigation trainers for training Spanish pilots.

S.M.79 28-43, the personal aircraft of the commander of the Italian Cuerpo de Tropas Voluntarias (CTV), General Mario Berti. Franco also used this aircraft on occasion, instead of his usual DC-2. Burgos, December 17, 1938.

April 2 Yagüe's forces occupied the provincial capital of Lerida, the initial objective of the North Ebro offensive. Returning from a bombing mission, two He 111s of K/88 collided over their base at Alfaro. One of the pilots managed to land his damaged machine, but the other crashed in flames in the city. The entire crew, consisting of *Lt.* Herbert Hoyer, *Fw.* Walter Hoyer, *Fw.* Herbert Brüggemann and *Uffz.* Kurt Kondziela, were killed.

1. and 2. J/88, which were operating from Zaragoza, received orders to transfer to Lanaja, located south of Huesca, on April 4. During the afternoon of the 4th, while visiting the *Staffeln* at their new base, Commander-in-Chief Volkmann received the sad news that *Leutnant* Fritz Awe had been killed during the transfer flight. "Eckie" Priebe describes the fatal moment of the crash:

"It was a transfer flight to Lanaja. We made an overlapping turn according to the new scheme, with pairs of Bf 109s spaced far apart, the nearest pair to the side, the next one higher, and so on. Leading the *Schwarm*, Fritz Awe made a 90 degree turn, and his wingman dutifully overlapped him. As the second *Rotte* in the *Schwarm*, I likewise turned 90 degrees to the left and saw to my horror that Borchers was

The large railway complex outside the city of Benicarlo. As well as the usual facilities it featured a locomotive shed with turntable, all of which appeared on AS/88's list of targets.

When Benicarlo fell the bomb damage from the March attacks had not yet been repaired. On the left the locomotive shed, in the foreground the station workshops.

The forward fuselage of Awe's 6-20. The aircraft was cut in two at the cockpit by the propeller of an accompanying aircraft.

One of the last photos of Fritz Awe (left), showing him packing with Staffelkapitän Schellmann.

The remains of the unfortunate Awe were sent to Germany aboard a Ju 52. An honor guard presents arms as the coffin containing their fallen comrade is loaded into the aircraft.

turning in too close above Awe. Either Awe climbed slightly or Borchers approached too close, possibly blinded by the sun, but in any case his propeller struck Awe's cockpit and cut the Bf 109 in two. The tail of 6-20 spun to earth, while the engine, wings and cabin fluttered to the ground like a falling leaf. We thought at first that Awe might have escaped death, but then we saw him sitting headless in his cockpit, and so he crashed with his aircraft. *Uffz.* Borchers was forced to make an emergency landing. His aircraft turned over and he was rescued slightly injured by a pair of farmers."

A preliminary briefing on Operation "Neptun", a massed bomber raid against Republican naval forces in the ports of Cartagena and Almeria, took place on April 7; the crews learned that the harbor installations and the ships there were to be the targets of all

The provincial capital of Lerida before its capture on April 3, 1938. Clearly visible are the fortress and sand banks downstream in the Rio Segre. The bridges were not blown by the withdrawing Republicans.

four *Staffeln*.

During a farewell party for *Hauptmann* Hentschel and *Leutnant* Klinkicht, news arrived that a Do 17 of A/88 was missing over the front. At 2300 the Republican Army communique reported the shooting down of the aircraft three kilometers southwest of Artesa. The crew of *Lt.* Kendel (observer), *Uffz.* von der Driesch (pilot) and *Uffz.* Birkhofen burned to death in their aircraft.

While there was little air combat in April the close-support units continued to see heavy action. *Leutnant* Otto Bertram, who had arrived in Spain on March 22, where he was transferred to 4 *Staffel* and assigned He 51 2-82, described his initial experiences:

"First mission: The *Staffel* is to attack the infantry positions near Huesca! I don't understand much of what everyone is talking about, I know only one thing: stay close to my *Kettenführer*! The *Staffel* is in the air. My *Kettenführer* peels off and fires. Stay with him, stay with him! is my only thought. There's not much to see — nothing at all. A few trenches and a few men at most. Throttle forward! The *Kette* climbs, turns and prepares to attack again. Stay with him! Bertram, do you see anything? — Not much. In silence I think: This is not at all as I had imagined it! Throttle forward, climb, turn, again.

"Tack-tack-tack-bang! My machine receives a lovely knock and makes a hop — what the hell? A thousand questions race through my brain in fractions of a second. A damned mess! As I glance to the right my eyes become a little bigger: the aileron and landing flap are gone, a few tatters still dangle in the slipstream. A fine state of affairs! I turn away in the direction of home.

"My engine continues to run bravely, the machine still flies. Nevertheless, I loosen my straps. I am

Posters on the walls of Lerida reflect efforts by the Communists to fill up their units with volunteers.

Two Moroccan soldiers of the Marroqui Corps (General Yagüe) following the occupation of Lerida.

ready to get out should something happen. My machine climbs. I have gotten over my initial fright. It could have been much worse. But will I be able to get down alright? The landing comes off fine, man you've been lucky!

"The war assumes hard shapes. It is really no fun flying in this awful cold.
0800: first sortie
1100: second sortie — refuel, lunch break while we wait, new ammunition loaded.
1400: third sortie
1700: fourth sortie — fall into bed dead tired.
Lerida offensive: the low-fliers give the infantry room to breathe. It's a damned proud feeling to see how the Spanish *Bandera* is carried into the enemy positions. That things succeeded so quickly today is our work! The *Staffel* roars over the captured positions: waving jubilantly, the Spaniards shout into the air: '*Viva Allemania.*'
The enemy front is certainly reeling, but is still stubbornly defended. The enemy has dug himself in again on the heights of Fraga.

"Otsch" Bertram flew his first combat mission with 4. J/88, the Pik-As Staffel under Oblt. d'Elsa.

This could have turned out much worse. Small wonder that Bertram stared wide-eyed at his battered 2-82 after landing.

The He 45 was still capable of inflicting damage on the enemy. Oblt. Lampertsdörfer, known to his friends as "Lampi," was the jokester of A/88. He was well known for his humorous operational reports, such as: "We've prepared another Cannae for the Reds."

'After them, you low-fliers — give them no rest!' 1130: The infantry have taken the first position. My *Kette* lands at Bujalaroz airfield, 65 km east of Zaragoza. 'Refuel them quickly — rearm them as well — we're taking off again immediately — they're on the run!'

"A half hour later I'm flying along the floor of the Cinza depression peppering the retreating enemy. The cluster of troops trying to get back to the road has been scattered. They will fight no more. Now on the road to Fraga: Louse hunt! No sign of life on the road. There's one. After him! A steady tack, tack

"Californian Crash" of an He 45; this term was used by the crews to describe a total write-off in which the occupants escaped with little more than a black eye.

from my guns. Reload! Click! Out of my reverie. Ammunition gone! Head for home.

"The enemy has settled down again near Lerida. The Segre River forms a difficult natural obstacle.

"'4 *Staffel* will attack the positions along the river.'

"They're tough nuts, made of concrete! The other defenses aren't made of cardboard either. Losses become heavier and heavier — the attacks more bitter.

"The breakthrough to the sea has succeeded, the low-fliers are deployed to the Levant front.

"When the *Staffel* returns from a mission those on the ground count the machines: 1, 2, 3. . . 8, again there is one missing.

"We all say: 'Flying the Messerschmitt is the best form of life insurance, our ground attack business is shit!"

Oberleutnant Balthasar, who flew in Galland's *Staffel* for a while, described one of these reckless sorties:

"The Reds have established themselves at the edge of a high plateau in very well fortified positions. We have already made two attacks on this trench system. Those people up there are heroic defenders and good shots. Galland had the cards shot right out of his hand on the last sortie. We almost always had reason to regret coming up against these fellows. We have thought out a completely new approach: we'll smoke out this nest. Galland hasn't loaded any bombs this time, instead a drop tank full of gasoline fitted with a detonator. As I am flying the last machine I have a good view. Flying in a line, we wind through the terrain like a snake, exploiting the cover offered by every small valley, every tree, every hedge. Up front Galland flies so skillfully that I frequently lose sight of him. Now he pulls up, wings over to the left and goes down in a steep dive. Is he going to pull out? My God — he's going to ram the target! Then the tank separates and falls right in the center of the position. There is a dull thump, a bright flash reaches into the sky. A glowing firestorm pours into the trenches. Anyone who doesn't flee must burn in agony. They're already running, forced to flee back across the broad, flat plateau. Forcibly I gather my thoughts. Tack, tack, tack, machine-gun fire sweeps over the fleeing men. The stream of fleeing soldiers becomes ever thinner, now the grass is sprinkled with dark, lifeless shapes. Way out in front a figure runs with panther-like strides, a red scarf flapping behind him. Brrt — he collapses and topples to the ground. The plateau is dead now, only the glimmering fire and the dark forms speak the grim language of war. There, close to the fire, a red-yellow-red flag waves over the plateau.

"In the evening twilight we drive forward to have a look at the plateau. The evening breeze sweeps gently over the burnt-out, winding trenches. There is a sweet smell which tickles the throat. We all stare thoughtfully at the scene, then each turns and walks away quietly, lost in thought. Before me lies the one with the red scarf. He is a well-built, brawny lad with work-roughened hands. I bend over the dead man, carefully loosen the red scarf and stuff it in my pocket. Since then I have worn it on every flight."

Who will argue here? In spite of all the sorrow over the basically senseless sacrifices of both sides, the death of one did mean life for the other. *C'est la guerre.*

On the ninth day of the month the Italians once again found themselves in trouble with their Spanish hosts. With the objective of the Mediterranean in mind, an all-out race to the coast had broken out in the area south of Gandesa between the Galicia Corps (Gen. Aranda) and the C.T.V. (Gen. Berti). When the spearhead of Aranda's forces were west of Cherta, several kilometers ahead of the Italians, General Berti approached General Franco with a request that he halt Aranda and allow the Italians to take precedence. Wordy justifications such as being permitted to be the first in the east to salute the Italian homeland from beyond the Mediterranean horizon failed to move the *Caudillo*. Disappointed, Berti returned to his headquarters like a wet poodle.

Having concluded that they could break through to the Mediterranean more quickly in the battle zone south of the Ebro than in the north, and thus split Republican territory in half, the leaders of the Nationalist Army decided on a continuation of the offensive from the Lerida area into Catalonia. The new objective was Valencia.

Once again it was the He 59 floatplanes and their 50kg bombs which were given the job of trying to cut off the flow of men and materiel to the front from the direction of Valencia. The area around Benicarlo station was the target for lone He 59s at 2000 on April 3, 2005 on the 6th and 2050 on the 9th. As well, near Magdalena Station, which was situated in open country, a military transport train was hit by five 50kg bombs at 2015 on April 6. In spite of heavy rifle and machine-gun fire from soldiers who had fled into the open fields, the He 59 returned to Puerto Pollensa undamaged.

On April 10, an advance party was ordered into the Tortosa-Vinaroz-San Mateo area in preparation for the transfer there of all the units of the *Legion Condor*. At first the He 51 *Staffeln* continued their activities in the north, going about their daily routine of low-level attacks on positions and road traffic. Two of the biplanes were hit by ground fire that day; one He 51 caught fire after a forced landing, the second sheared off its undercarriage in rough terrain (40% damage). Fortunately both pilots were unhurt.

Two days later, on April 12, 1938, *Uffz.* Gerstmann's He 51 was hit during an air battle. He managed a forced landing west of Balaguer but suffered a broken collarbone in the process. Heavy enemy attacks were reported on the northern front on the 13th, but these were repulsed. Perhaps in an attempt to yet beat General Aranda, General Berti

Quartet of J/88 Staffelkapitäne in April 1938. From left: Oblt. Schellmann (1 Staffel), Oblt. Galland (3), Oblt. Schlichting (2) and Oblt. d'Elsa (4).

made a request to the commander of the *Legion Condor* for one of F/88's heavy batteries, stating that otherwise he would not be able to reach the Mediterranean at all. Berti got his "eighty-eights."

Nevertheless, it was General Aranda who, on Good Friday, April 15, was the first to enter the city of Vinaroz and look down on the *Mare Mediterraneo.* Immediately afterward the Italians slowed their pace; the chance for glory had been lost, they would just have to look for another nearby objective which offered a good chance of success.

Atop the list of Nationalist fighter aces was Morato, with 30 kills, followed by Salvador with 15; Salas and Guerrero had 10 each. At this point the

Pilots of 3 Staffel with their Staffel leader at readiness at their dispersal at Zaragoza-Sanjurjo.

3. J/88's accommodations train at Sanjurjo airfield; the cars contained sleeping quarters and offices. Galland and his Staffel comrades enjoy the first April sun.

most successful German fighter pilots were *Hauptmann* Harder with 10, followed by *Feldwebel* Boddem and *Leutnant* Seiler with 9 each.

On the morning of April 16 at Alfaro, the engines of the He 111s were run up, routes laid down and flight bags stowed away. On the program for the next day, the 17th, was *Neptun*. This meant a transfer flight to southern Spain, in order to place the targets, Cartagena and Almeria, within range of the bombers. After being wished good luck by the commander the *Staffeln* taxied out and took off, destination Sevilla-Tablada. Following a refuelling stop, some at Salamanca, some at Avila, only a few of the bombers managed to reach Tablada without incident. One bomber suffered undercarriage damage after making an emergency landing at Villafranca des los Barros due to engine trouble, but the crew of the He 111 which crashed thirteen kilometers west of Monasterio had no chance to escape from the fully loaded aircraft. Killed were *Lt.* Siemsen (observer), *Fw.* Kruschbersky (pilot), *Fw.* Spieler (radio operator) and *Fw.* Matz (flight engineer) as well as two mechanics, *Ogefr.* Schmalfuss and *Ogefr.* Frielingsdorf. Due to the low ceiling the majority of the forty He 111s turned back, and after refuelling set out once more to try and reach Tablada. Nine He 111s landed at the airfield near Sevilla on the first attempt, while 25 more followed on the morning of April 17.

The first target was Cartagena. On April 17, thirty-four He 111s took off for the city; the attackers were met by heavy anti-aircraft fire, but only three *Chatos* took off to intercept, and indication that surprise had been achieved. Late in the afternoon twenty-five He 111s repeated the attack on Cartagena, while one *Staffel* was sent to bomb the city and port of Almeria. A total of 82.5 tons of bombs was dropped. Observations by the crews and photographs showed three direct hits on the quay and railway station at Cartagena, a direct hit on the *Jamie I* and another on a torpedo boat, which sank in the harbor. 25-27 was hit several times by anti-aircraft fire and was forced to ditch in the sea near Motril; the crew were rescued. 25-15 was hit by machine-gun fire from an attacking I-15. With the return by the bombers to their home base at Alfaro on April 18 Operation "Neptun" came to an end. In view of the extensive preparations the organizers of the operation had hoped for greater success.

On April 20, a conference took place at headquarters in San Mateo, near Vinaroz, between the commander of the *Legion Condor*, Volkmann, his staff and General Aranda. The topic of discussion was the employment of the *Legion Condor* to support the Galicia Corps in its advance on Valencia.

Part of a loose formation, an He 111 J flies above the landscape of Old Castille during Operation Neptun.

Serviced and armed, He 111 bombers stand ready for the next attack on harbor installations at Cartagena.

Officers of the Legion headquarters staff: Chief-of-Staff Obstlt. Hermann Plocher (far right), Ia Hptm. Torsten Christ (center) and Kptlt. Bendler (left).

Maj. Deichmann listens with furrowed brow to the concerns of Hptm. Schulz (center), Staffelkapitän of 1. K/88, and Oberstabsingenieur Fritsche.

Drive on Valencia

On April 23, 1938, Nationalist troops began their offensive toward Valencia. Initially it was conducted with relatively weak forces and made only slow progress. Interrupted several times, partly by bad weather, the operation dragged on in stages until July 25.

By July 24 the *Legion Condor* had completed its move. The tactical operations staff was now located at Benicarlo, south of Vinaroz. The flying units occupied airfields in the new combat zone:

J/88	to La Cenia
He 45 *Kette*	to La Cenia
F/88	to La Cenia
	with tactical operations staff at St. Magdalena

K/88 remained at Alfaro, while the bulk of A/88 stayed at Bunuel. Three 88mm batteries and a light battery were attached to the Aranda Corps to provide fire support; one heavy and part of a light battery

Transfer to La Cenia completed! From left, Medical Officer Dr. Nikolaus Appel, Gotthard Handrick, Reinhard Seiler and Eberhard d'Elsa in front of their new domicile.

were grouped around La Cenia to provide local defense. Another heavy and half a light flak battery guarded the tactical operations staff in Benicarlo.

Almost all of Ln/88 occupied quarters in Geviert La Cenia, San Mateo, St. Magdalena and Vinaroz. Its primary tasks were putting in order the existing telephone and radio net, as well as occasionally repairing telephone lines cut by saboteurs.

The attack was also supported by the two Nationalist fighter groups and two Spanish close-support groups equipped with He 45 and He 46 aircraft.

On the Republican side there were three *Rata* squadrons and at least one *Chato* squadron deployed on the Levant front. The remaining three *Rata* squadrons remained in Catalonia, from where they occasionally took part in the fighting.

On April 25, the *Staffeln* of K/88 set out on the long flight from Alfaro to the new combat zone and bombed the city of Castellon de la Plana and Sagunto harbor. Attacks on airfields around Castellon revealed that these were unoccupied.

As it advanced on Vinroma the 83rd Division encountered heavy resistance, which was not broken until the 26th following the commitment of He 51s, Ju 87s and two batteries of Flak 88s. In making their attacks the aircraft of J/88 ran the gauntlet of fire from four Republican heavy anti-aircraft batteries. *Hauptmann* Harlinghausen, the "Iron Gustav," met with the Legion's tactical operations staff to discuss how his He 59 *Staffel* was to be employed. In future it was to supplement K/88 as much as possible by bombing targets in the coastal area.

For two days the attacking columns marked time, as the continuous rain made air support out of the question.

April 29 also saw only limited activity in the air, in the course of which the Spanish Nationalists lost another He 45 to ground fire. In spite of continued bad weather the Varela Corps went to the attack near El Pobo and Allepuz, northeast of Teruel, on May 2. The units of the *Legion Condor* were still grounded, as rain-soaked runways precluded all flight operations. Only the anti-aircraft guns were in a position to carry out their assigned tasks by engaging enemy movements on the ground.

Not until May 4 were individual flights made in support of the Aranda Corps. While strafing roads in

A bogged-down He 111 is towed to firm ground by an 8-ton Krauss-Maffei KM m9 tractor (SdKfz. 7) at Alfaro. These tractors were assigned to most heavy anti-aircraft batteries.

A new crew prepares to take off on its first familiarization flight over the front.

A/88's base at Bunuel-Tudela. From here the reconnaissance aircraft flew over Zaragoza and Alcaniz into the new area of operations in front of Valencia.

Recent rains have caused this Do 17 E to sink up to its axles in the mud. Planks have been placed in front of the aircraft's mainwheels, over which it will be rolled to a new parking place.

A force-landed "sewing machine," in this case a Soviet R-5. During the Second World War these biplanes were a veritable plague over the front lines and rear areas in Russia.

the Cuervas de Vinroma area the He 51 of *Unteroffizier* Hester was hit by ground fire, caught fire and crashed near Albocáer. Hester had no chance to bail out and was killed when his He 51 struck the ground. May 5 saw two massed sorties by K/88 over the battle zone south of Vinaroz. Individual He 59s also played their part in attacking the enemy's lines of supply, bombing the Alcira-Silla and Cullera railway stations south of Valencia.

The entry in the Legion's war diary on May 6 was brief: "Continued bad weather, attacks halted, no sorties flown by the units." May 7 also saw only isolated reconnaissance sorties by A/88, which moved into Vinaroz on the 8th and remained there temporarily. For the first time lone SB-2s appeared in the cloudy skies, dropping poorly-aimed bombs on La Cenia and Vinaroz. Anti-aircraft guns fired on the lone intruders without success.

Encouraged by a slight improvement in the weather, on May 11 the leading elements of the Castilla Corps (Gen. Varela) forced their way into the village of Villarluengo, northeast of Teruel. The poor, rain-softened roads prevented any further advance. The first air combat occurred on the 11th, when Legion fighters flew increased numbers of sorties escorting reconnaissance aircraft. *Uffz.* Ihlefeld of 2. J/88 was able to bring down a *Rata.*

May 13 and 14 saw a regrouping of the Castilla Corps for a resumption of the assault and increased efforts by the Republicans to disrupt this from the air. On two occasions the "night ghost," probably an R-5 harassment bomber, dropped its "eggs" in open country south of the *Legion Condor*'s command post. No damage was inflicted, but the night's rest was spoiled.

While the Legion kept most of its aircraft on the ground on the 14th, the Spanish squadrons were all in action. Two He 51s and an He 45 were lost to ground fire. On May 15, *Leutnant* Priebe destroyed an I-16 near Sagunto. He worked his way to within 20 meters of a three-aircraft formation and shot

Puzol airfield near Sagunto. Two Rata squadrons were based at the airfield, which was situated right beside a Mediterranean beach.

down one of the unsuspecting *rojos.* In spite of heavy losses the close-support aircraft continued to fly and fight.

On the 15th, the *Cadenas* smashed a counterattack by a Republican battalion near Cuervas without loss. On the other hand the Nationalist flak missed a sure chance to shoot down an enemy biplane, which calmly approached Benicarlo and released two bombs. Not until the bombs were falling did the gun crews realize that it was an enemy aircraft. The intruder then turned tail and ran for home, pursued by ineffective 20mm anti-aircraft fire.

K/88 moved closer to the front, transferring from Alfaro to Sanjurjo, hoping to leave behind the long periods of rain and its softened airfield.

Hauptmann Harder's second tour of duty in Spain lasted from April to July and for several weeks he led the *Jagdgruppe* in an acting capacity. He brought with him the He 112 V9, armed with two 20mm wing cannon and two fuselage-mounted MG 17 machine-guns. In February he had demonstrated the aircraft in Belgrade, Bucharest and Budapest. On

May 18 Harder took part in the "largest air battle" he had ever experienced. He was flying at an altitude of 3,000 meters when two squadrons of I-15s flew past below him in textbook formation. He immediately dove into the midst of the enemy to break up the formation. "As I was diving away I realized there were *Ratas* in the area, a few at first, then more, probably 25 *Ratas* and as many Curtisses. I tried to climb back up into the sun. The Reds assembled in a large cluster and milled about wildly. Repeatedly I tried to get into the pack and pick one out, but every time I ended up with *Ratas* on my tail, which forced me to take evasive action. Slowly we succeeded in forcing the swarm of enemy fighters over Castellon, clearing the way for the bombers. *Uffz*. Rochel was able to shoot down a *Rata*. Over Castellon the Reds broke off the battle and quickly disappeared. Three further *Ratas* had been shot down by Ihlefeld, Seufert and Handrick. Handrick's opponent, an American pilot, was killed, his back armor was riddled."

On May 18, the activities of the air units were devoted exclusively to supporting the advance by the 4th Division (Gen. Alonso). The attacking forces suffered heavy losses, however, and the advance was halted by a determined Republican counterattack.

Obviously quite at home at La Cenia, Handrick and the personnel of the Gruppenstab, including Edu Neumann (2nd from left), enjoy a sumptuous repast in the shade.

The "sofa circle" in front of the Gruppe command post. Enjoying the comfortable upholstery are (from left) Lt. Wolfgang Ewald (2. J/88), Dr. Appel and Maj. Handrick.

The *Staffeln* managed only one concentrated attack on the 19th; high winds with gusts to 120 kph kept the crews on the ground for the rest of the day. The meteorologists promised "flying weather" for the following day and they were proved right.

The dates May 21 (target Albocácer), May 24 (target Ares del Maestre), May 25 (target Benasal) and May 26 (target Villar de Canes) were reserved for precision attacks against troop and vehicle concentrations as well as enemy headquarters by the Stuka-*Kette*. The aircraft of the *Jolanthe-Kette* each carried a single 500kg bomb beneath the fuselage for these attacks. Precise damage assessment photographs were taken and these were used to improve future dive-bombing attacks.

On May 23, the Republicans attempted a relief attack in the north against the Nationalist bridge-

The small city of Albocácer, situated north of Castellon de la Plana.

The terraces leading up to the village of Ares del Maestre have been traversed by trenches; the village itself was occupied by a division headquarters.

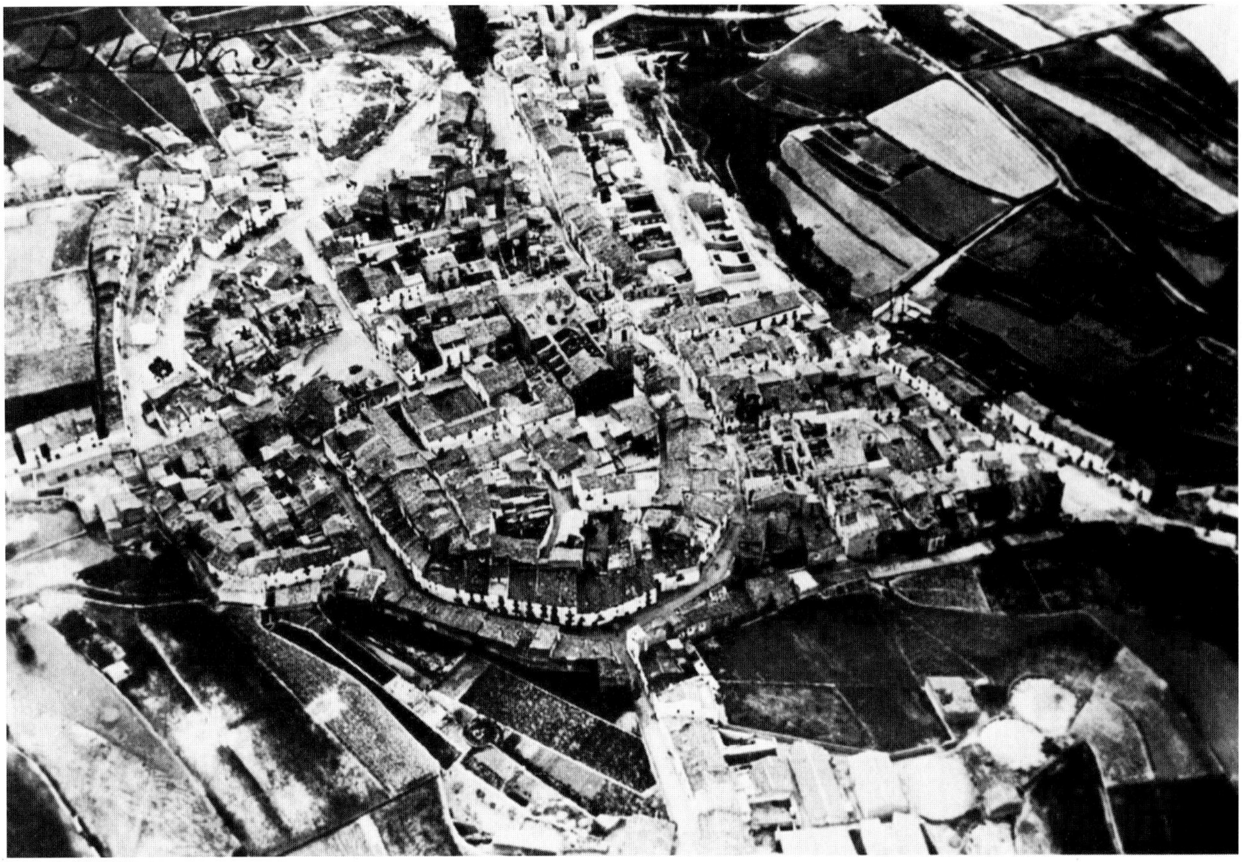

Resting vehicle columns in Benasal were the targets of the 500kg bombs of the Stuka Kette/88 stationed at La Cenia.

Stuka target: Villar de Canes. The Republicans surrounded the villages of the Sierra Maestrazgo with defensive positions.

head on the Segre. To support the effort the three *Rata* squadrons stationed in the Levant were transferred to Catalonia. Both Spanish Nationalist fighter groups were also moved into the area. On the following day the Italian fighter groups *As de Bastos* and *La Cucharacha* ran into three squadrons of *Ratas*. Later the two sides furnished widely-differing accounts of the encounter. The Republicans claimed 22 kills, including two S.M.79s and seventeen C.R.32s. In reality only three Fiats were lost. On the other hand the Italians claimed to have shot down five I-16s and six I-15s; it appears that the actual Republican losses were three *Ratas* and an SB-2. If one is to understand these claims one should keep in mind that the air battles at this time bore a striking resemblance to the confused swarms of biplanes familiar from the First World War, where everyone fired at everyone else. In contrast to the German practice, in Spain a machine was considered shot down if it came down away from an airfield, even though the kill was not confirmed until it could be proved that the aircraft had been destroyed. As a result there was a great disparity between the victory claims made immediately after an engagement and later confirmations.

Republican attacks against the Balaguer and Tempre bridgeheads on the Segre front continued with strong tank and air support. In the south the *Staffeln* of the *Legion Condor* were pinned down on their rain-soaked airfields and were unable to assist the defenders at the Segre.

Not until May 31 was 3. J/88 again able to support Aranda's advance toward Valencia in *Staffel* strength. *Leutnant* Losigkeit's aircraft was damaged by 20mm flak and he was forced to bail out. He was carried into no-man's-land and a search for him turned up nothing. Reports from the other side revealed his fate; Losigkeit had been taken prisoner.

Once again the Spanish Fiats were involved in a hectic scrap with about 25 *Chatos* and 10 *Ratas*. They succeeded in keeping the Red fighters away from the bombers. The Republican fighter pilot Tarazona wrote in his diary that after landing they could have kissed their *Ratas* — the Latin mentality! Eight I-15s and two I-16s were shot down, three of which were credited to Salvador. One of his kills smashed into the ground, the pilot of the second took to his parachute and the third he strafed and set on fire after it had landed at Sarrion airfield.

These losses were a serious blow to the Republican fighter force. No new *Ratas* were delivered from Russia during June and July; the factory in Alicante, which was to assemble 100 I-16s under license, had not yet started production. Where the *Chatos* were concerned the situation was somewhat more favorable, as production of this type was in full swing at the Sabadell and Reus factories, one I-15 being built per day. On the German side the difficult flying since the winter had had a noticeable effect on the *Jagdgruppe*'s operational strength, which had sunk to sixteen Bf 109s. At the moment all efforts in Germany were being concentrated on preparations for the *Anschluss* with Austria, resulting in a markedly reduced flow of materiel to the *Legion Condor*.

On June 2, the Republican Air Force undertook to raid La Cenia airfield with nine SB-2s, but took a serious beating in the process. *Lt.* Heinrich shot down two of the bombers, while *Uffz.* Meyer and *Uffz.* Ihlefeld destroyed two more. A fifth *Katiuska* was brought down by the airfield's anti-aircraft guns. In an effort to avoid the constant threat of bombing raids on La Cenia the fighters made increased use of secondary airfields at Alcala de Chivert and Cabi. During the final years of the Second World War such moves to secondary airfields by Luftwaffe fighters were carried out under the code-name *Blindschleiche* ("Blindworm").

In the meantime the situation for the German fighter pilots too had become more threatening. Following the capture of Losigkeit, on June 2 *Lt.* Haupt was shot down and killed by ground fire and he was followed on the 8th by *Lt.* Erich Beyer ("Fakir"). Harder refused to accept responsibility for further He 51 operations. The command staff agreed; the two *Staffeln* (3. J/88 Galland, 4. J/88 d'Elsa) were stood down temporarily.

On June 3, the command post at San Christobal came under attack from nine *Katiuskas*. Having learned from the previous day's hard lesson, they were escorted by about 30 *Chatos*. As the bombers flew away the fighter escort strafed the area, however there were no personnel losses on the ground. On June 4 an Italian pilot lost his life when he was fired on from the ground by machine-guns as he hung beneath his parachute. The 8th was a big day for the Italian fighter group *Gamba di Ferro*. The group's fighters claimed the destruction of ten *Chatos* and an SB-2.

In an effort to break the considerable resistance being mounted by the enemy on the approaches to Adzaneta, on June 9 He 111s of K/88 and Do 17s of A/88 bombed roads and positions in this area. The escorting Bf 109 *Staffeln* made contact with a group of thirty-one *Chatos* but stayed close to the bombers. As a result the German fighters claimed no victories.

Temporarily equipped with the 37mm Flak 36, 4. F/88 was responsible for the defense of the fighter base at La Cenia.

A bird's eye view of La Cenia. Every Legion flier will surely remember the characteristic layout of three crossing runways, as well as the even more typical "sandstorms" raised during takeoff.

An He 51 of 3. J/88, the "Mickey Mouse" Staffel, with an aircraft of 4. J/88 Pik-As in the background. Each of the twelve cylinders of the BMW VI engine had its own exhaust stack instead of a collector installation, a somewhat complicated solution.

Approaching Republican bombers were greeted by barrage fire from the heavy batteries of F/88, which forced the *Katiuskas* to turn back across the front. On two occasions they jettisoned their entire load of bombs on their own positions.

Again on June 10 the enemy held the initiative over the battlefield, but at a high cost. Late that morning J/88's alert *Schwarm* scrambled to intercept a group of enemy bombers with fighter escort. The enemy formation was not found until it was on its way home; anti-aircraft fire had forced the Republican aircraft to climb above a solid cloud deck. Two *Ratas* and a *Katiuska* were shot down in the brief engagement. Lt. Heinrich also reported a probable kill.

Late in the afternoon, six *Katiuskas* with fighter escort appeared over the attack sector near Adzaneta. This time success went to the anti-aircraft guns. Under accurate fire from F/88's 6th Battery the enemy aircraft broke off their attack at about 1720 and jettisoned their bombs. Two of the SB-2s struggled to reach their own lines while steadily losing altitude. However, the two bombers caught fire one after the other and, trailing black plumes of smoke, crashed east of Costur. The 4th Battery claimed the destruction of a *Chato* that day.

On June 11, *Leutnant* Edu Neumann and *Leutnant* Heinrich each destroyed a *Rata* while on a *freie Jagd* mission. The Aranda Corps occupied Albocácer and Torreblanca and the 4th Division took the heights around Villafames.

On June 12, an unusually cold day, K/88 and the Do 17s of A/88 tried to halt road traffic south of the coastal city of Castellon, however results of the bombing were uncertain. J/88, on the other hand, was able to report a major success on the evening of June 13 after flying escort for K/88. Six He 111s suffered considerable damage; two of them just made it to La Cenia where they landed without incident. The Republicans, who had sent several squadrons to intercept, waited in vain for the return of six *Chatos* and two *Ratas*; they had been destroyed in combat with the Bf 109s of 1. and 2. J/88 in the Castellon area. The destruction of an SB-2 was awarded to the 6th Battery of F/88.

On June 14, ater 140 missions, *Lt.* Priebe of 1

The first Nationalist ships sail into Vinaroz harbor on June 2, 1938, led by the mine-layer Vulcano.

Staffel came to grief. This is how he described the incident:

"Stuka escort, altitude about 4,000 meters; in front of us and above us a squadron of *Ratas* and many Curtisses. The command *Schwarm* turns to the left to climb into the sun. The *Rata* squadron dives on them. I intend to follow and after completing a turn I look around for *Lt.* Rech; instead I see a Curtiss close behind me. I dive away and in doing so I am struck a blow on my left shoulder. This is the end. My arm falls from the throttle lever, my left side is completely stiff, great pain — a curtain begins to fall before my eyes! Then I pull myself together: the 109 is tumbling like a falling leaf, one moment the nose is up the next down. I don't have the strength to

"Take your hat and go!" Practical jokes and humor as Staffelkapitän d'Elsa's comrades bid him farewell in June 1938. Enjoying the party are, from left: Wolfgang Ewald, Edu Neumann, d'Elsa, W. Schellmann and G. Handrick.

Lt. Eckehart Priebe in the cockpit of his Bf 109 B-2, 6-33.

reach over to the left with my right arm and jettison the canopy. That is my salvation, as I would have bailed out over Red territory. Orientation is simple: the Mediterranean to the right, to the left land and home!

"Then I see Villafames, friendly territory, I become wide awake. I begin preparations to land, but I am unable to operate the throttle lever which is on my left side. With the last of my strength I push the red button to kill the engine, so as to land with a stationary propeller and, as it turned out, one flat tire. I come to as someone pounds on the canopy and shouts: '*Herr Leutnant*, open up, what's wrong?' We are just behind the line of advance. They pull me out of the cockpit and report my condition to the *Kommandeur*. That's *Hptm.* Harder, as Handrick is on leave. Harder comes rushing up, sees me spitting blood and laying on the hot Spanish earth surrounded by Spaniards and says in greeting: 'Well, the big-mouth Berliner is going to be taking a little rest.' Covered in blood, I reply: 'Thanks very much for the flowers!'

"Zaragoza hospital: A bullet has pierced one lung, another is lodged in my shoulder blade. I receive excellent care and am given leave to recover. Several times I try to obtain permission to return to action, but nothing doing. I am sent home."

The same afternoon Harder, too, was hard pressed by Republican fighters:

"There come the Red fighters, first several Curtisses, then swarms of *Ratas*, spiraling upwards. By turning tightly we are able three times to keep them from attacking the bombers. Suddenly the Reds are gone. There are still two Curtisses south of Sagunto at 4,000 meters. I attack one of them. In the instant I begin to fire he pulls up and opens fire at me while on his back. I pull up and at the same instant I am attacked by four *Ratas*. One is already on my tail in firing position. I dive away but can't shake him off. I try everything to lose him: full throttle, shallow dive, radiator flap up, propeller pitch set for diving flight. The *Rata* sits somewhat off to my left and tries to get below me by diving steeply. There are machines in front of me, many Red fighters! The way is blocked!

"I try to count them. 10, 20, then a new swarm approaches, I can only estimate their numbers at 10 to 20. I try to slip past them at the coast but that fat radial engine is still behind me. The Reds fail to notice me until I'm at their altitude, too late for them. Not far from Castellon, at an altitude of 1,000 meters, my pursuer gives up. How would things have turned out if I hadn't had the fastest machine in the *Gruppe*?"

Leutnant Henz was shot up by a formation of *Ratas* south of Castellon, and after crash-landing on the north bank of the Rio Mijares was taken prisoner. The Republican pilot Tarazona wrote of the day's events:

"We had just had a terrible battle with Heinkel bombers and Bf 109s. During the air battle I flew in a pair with Claudin. As I was looking at the destruction the fascists had wrought in Nules I spotted something near the beach which caught my attention. An aircraft was flying away toward the north trailing a white plume behind it. We descended and recognized it as an Bf 109. We made one pass without firing. The machine landed on the beach on the right bank of the Mijares River.

"After landing at Sagunto I was given the job of recovering the Bf 109. We drove off in a truck, several mechanics, an armorer and me. 'There's the great bird,' said one of them. The pilot was close by, in a ravine near Villareal. He was a young lad, probably no more than 18 years old. I was impressed by this fine product of German aviation technology. I admired the machine from the outside until I was tired from staring at it. Proudly I climbed into the cockpit. The oxygen equipment, the radio, the main tank which served as the pilot's seat . . . we must fly her, study her unique characteristics, we must compare her precisely with our fighter aircraft. The machine was intact. As we talked there was the rattle of our machine-guns and the raw voice of the cannon of both sides in the background. The front was barely 15 meters away, within sight of Castellon. The buzzing of aircraft caused us to raise our heads. The noise grew louder; apparently they were coming along the road but we couldn't see them. Suddenly there they were!

"Six Bf 109s appeared over the sea, almost touching the water. When they came to the mouth of the Mijares they made a slight turn to the right. They were coming straight towards us. On the ground, quickly! The monoplanes circled round the shot-down aircraft. They came down and showered it with machine-gun fire. On their second pass the machine burst into flames."

This ends Tarazona's account. The Republicans had rejoiced to soon over their acquisition of a nearly-intact Bf 109.

J/88's equipment situation had become catastrophic. 1 *Staffel* now had four Bf 109s, 2 *Staffel* seven; in spite of this the units often had to fly as many as ten sorties per day. There were no deliveries of new aircraft as Germany was in the midst of the Austrian and Czech crises. The only reinforcements to arrive was a military band!

There were scarcely any changes in the front in the days that followed; as during the operations before Caspe the fighting was now marked by increased resistance and occasional Republican counterattacks. The *Staffeln* of the *Legion Condor* remained on the ground from the 17th of June until the 22nd. At the front artillery duels were the first indication of the beginning of positional warfare.

A military band brings the "ancient Spaniards" tunes from home.

Uninfluenced by events on the ground, "Iron Gustav" Harlinghausen sent his "rattle-traps," as the He 59s were known, against shipping and harbor installations. On June 23, a Republican sailing vessel was bombed and sunk off Sagunto. On June 24, pairs of AS/88 aircraft operated in conjunction with Nationalist warships taking part in the seizure of the Columbrete island group, located in the Mediterranean about 60 kilometers east of Castellon.

Not until June 25 did the aircraft of K/88 and A/88 reappear over the Levant front, attacking trenches and artillery positions in the Sagunto area. Assigned to provide fighter cover, "Gedalje" Schellmann and Ihlefeld were able to shoot down two *Ratas*. Their victims were the Spaniard Ruiz and the well-known Russian pilot Romanov. Ruiz took to his parachute but was shot and killed as he descended. At the end of June there were several organizational changes in the Nationalist Air Force. Morato, who had spent several days at La Cenia testing Harder's He 112, was placed in command of the Ibarros fighter group. At this time the first of the long-awaited new Bf 109s began reaching J/88. This enabled 3 *Staffel*, which since May had been led by Mölders, who had relieved Galland, to be equipped with Bf 109s. As the number of aircraft grew, three Spanish fighter pilots, José Munoz, Miguel Garcia and Javier Murcia, were transferred to the *Staffel*. The bloodied 4 *Staffel* was disbanded and its He 51s handed over to the Spanish Nationalists, enabling them to form another squadron.

Aerial reconnaissance and reports from agents pointed toward a relief attack by the Reds from the Tortosa area, near the mouth of the Ebro, probably sometime near the end of June 1938. The Lister, Campesino and 35th (International) Divisions had been identified there, and it was obvious that the Republicans were preparing to launch a thrust toward the southwest, or into the rear of the Nationalist forces advancing on Valencia. The Spanish High Command was well aware of developments at the foot of the Sierra Balaguer; however, they allowed efforts to capture Segorbe and Sagunto to continue, a reckless attitude which was to cost the Nationalist side dearly.

Railway lines around Segorbe were the targets for the Legion's bomber units on June 30; a munitions train was blown up on the tracks, resulting in an impressive fireworks display. On the last day of June General Solchaga's corps broke out of its positions south of Teruel in the direction of the Rio Turia. Cubla and Villarstar were taken on July 3 and Solchaga's left wing stood poised in front of the village of Villel.

On July 4, Tarazona's "Red Flight" was able to shoot down two S.M.79s which were bombing

Several Republican stragglers surrender to the Nationalists during the capture of the village a village near Castellon.

The civilian population comes out to meet the conquerors with white bed sheets attached to sticks.

Alicante. The Nationalists gained revenge the next day when Comas destroyed an I-16. Its pilot, the Republican group commander Claudin, one of the veterans of Asturia and Belchite, was killed. Together with Aguirre, Bravo and Zarauza he was one of the first Spaniards to command a *Rata* squadron.

The focal point for the flying units of the *Legion Condor* remained the approaches to Valencia, where the primary targets were lines of communication. On July 5, it was the turn of the Nules-Sagunto coastal road and positions near Vall de Uxo. All of K/88 participated in this action. The use of air

Nationalist infantry moves into the bitterly fought-over mountain village of Ares del Maestre.

Staffelkapitän Schellmann in his element. Like all aircraft of 1. J/88, 6-51 has a white propeller spinner and wears a diagonal cross on a black disc, as introduced by Harder.

Even Wolfgang Schellmann was not spared the universally disliked paperwork.

power was a vital part of the efforts to crack the virtually impregnable defensive positions in the Sierra de Espadan. In the past this would have been a job for the low-flying *Cadenas*; now, however, the task fell to the He 111s of K/88, which practiced significantly less-accurate horizontal bombing. On July 7, A/88 and K/88 sent their Do 17s and He 111s over the mountain range south of Castellon; the effects of the bombs in the rugged mountains was probably limited, if not zero.

It was vital that this ring of positions be cracked, however, so another bombardment of the difficult terrain was ordered for the next day and again on July 9. On the latter date bad weather forced the He 111s to return to Zaragoza. The aircraft landed with their bombs still in the bomb cells and the cursing ground crews worked late into the night unloading them.

By early morning of July 10 the weather had improved somewhat and the bombs which had been laboriously removed the day before were loaded back into the bombers. In addition to the rocky nests in the Sierra de Espadan the attacks by all four *Staffeln* were also directed against positions near Vall de Uxo. All Nationalist ground corps were able to report minor gains that day.

Preparations for the offensive blow against the port city of Valencia were concluded on the evening of July 12, 1938. That day Keidel and Ihlefeld each destroyed a *Chato*.

On July 13, the Solchaga and Berti (C.T.V.) Corps broke out of the assembly area around Teruel toward Valencia. It was a warm sunny day and the columns advanced along both sides of the road to Sagunto and captured the city of Sarrion. The Italians, who were providing air cover, reported the destruction of four *Chatos* and an SB-2 at the cost of one Fiat. A Spanish He 51 was hit by light flak and crashed.

Manzanera was taken by the Solchaga Corps on July 14. Berti and his Italians advanced as far as the road fork north of Albentosa. A Spanish C.R.32 failed to return after combat with the maneuverable, snub-nosed *Ratas*. The two Spanish fighter groups were withdrawn from the Teruel front a few days later and transferred to western Spain. Their new base was Merida.

Flying Bf 109 6-79, on July 15 Werner Mölders shot down his first enemy aircraft, an I-15, from the Spanish skies. Within four months he would work his way up to become the most successful German fighter pilot in Spain. While escorting He 111 bombers the Messerschmitt fighters fought a sharp battle with forty *Chatos*. Nine were shot down in flames. Among the victors was *Leutnant* Oesau. He described the encounter enthusiastically:

"Man — Oesau, first contact with the enemy: three squadrons of Curtisses! There they are, the enemy fighter insignia. Hunting fever seizes me. Now show them what you can do! I close in on the right-hand flight, but other of our fighters beat me to it: the enemy's right wingman goes down.

"After its victory the Me turns away. The enemy seems not to have noticed anything. The flight leader flies on calmly. Now I see red and close in as if in gunnery practice. A burst — a spurt of flame — the machine falls. A body falls from the aircraft and a few seconds later a parachute opens — *Holzauge*! Don't watch so long! Shame! Now I've been caught

Feldwebel Herbert Ihlefeld beams following his sixth victory on June 25, 1938. His aircraft, 6-6, is a veteran Bf 109 B-1.

With full right rudder an He 51 dives on its chosen target. These times were now over! Orders had been issued to hand over all the He 51s to the Spaniards.

The Trabaderos were flown to Sanjurjo for a complete overhaul prior to being handed over to the Spaniards.

napping, there are two Curtisses on my tail. Bank steeply and down I go. I reach 1,500 meters and look behind. There's no *Rata* there. My good *Katschmarek* Uffz. Bauer has got rid of him for me."

Feldwebel Ihlefeld scored his 8th and 9th kills in this engagement. The same day the Italians lost an S.M.79.

Far removed from events at the front, at 1600 on July 15, a Friday, the Headquarters Company of S/88 opened a "German bordello" in St. Magdalena, a necessity which should not go unmentioned. The Spanish mentality and the strict manner in which young Spanish women were brought up by mostly orthodox families allowed direct contact with foreign soldiers (German and Italian) only on very rare occasions. In such circumstances sexual relations between the daughters of Spain and the foreigners were the great exception.

In this situation what other choice did the command authorities have but to create appropriate establishments to meet the sexual needs of their soldiers. For 25 *Pesetas* every German Legionnaire could gain entrance to the bordello during its operating hours of 1600 to 0100. For this sum he received a token, which he was to hand over in advance to the lady of his choice. Before leaving the house the visitor had to undergo an inspection by the attending medical sergeant. Drunks were refused admittance.

A construction team of 1. Ln/88 laying an FFK (field telephone line) on the approaches to Nules, at the foot of the Sierra de Espadan.

It is interesting to note that J/88 had set up a similar establishment, referred to by the soldiers simply as "*Puff*" (soldiers jargon for whorehouse), on its own six months earlier.

Nationalist forces crossed the Rio de los Paraisos, a somewhat larger stream, on July 16, and reached the town of Albentosa. The Italian close-support squadron lost three Fiats in low-level attacks. Herbert Ihlefeld of J/88 was promoted from the ranks to *Leutnant* following his ninth kill.

A day later Möders and Oesau each scored their second victory during an escort mission in which five *Chatos* were shot down from a group of thirty; the other successful pilots were *Lt.* Resch, *Uffz.* Bauer and *Uffz.* Quasinowski. Nationalist bombers were sent several times to attack the Segorbe and Soneja railway stations as well as road and rail traffic in the Segorbe-Sagunto area.

There was a large dogfight in the Segorbe area on July 18, the anniversary of the beginning of the Spanish Civil War. The Germans accounted for three *Ratas*, while the Fiats of the Italian fighter group *As de Bastos* claimed two *Ratas* and five *Chatos*. Three C.R.32s were lost, including that of squadron leader Captain Raffi. An S.M.79 was hit by anti-aircraft fire and crashed just short of the lines. The Republicans (12 *Chatos* and 25 *Ratas*) reported the destruction of two Bf 109s and eight Fiats against two of their own fighters shot down. Targets for the bombers were positions near Algimia de Almonacid and once again the system of positions in the Sierra de Espadan.

The bombers of K/88 were assigned the same targets on July 19 as well as road traffic between Segorbe and Liria. Near Sagunto the Mölders *Staffel* ran into 18 *Katiuskas* escorted by three squadrons of I-16s. Five *Ratas* were shot down, one of them becoming Mölder's third kill. The Republicans claimed the destruction of five Fiats. German Situation Report No. 541 from July 20, 1938 proudly stated:

"In the five days since the delivery of the 22 new Bf 109s the German *Jagdgruppe* has shot down 22 Red fighters without loss."

Republican preparations for a breakout from the bend in the Ebro continued to grow in scope. Aerial reconnaissance and intelligence agents estimated the assembly of forces at about six divisions. The Marroqui Corps was positioned to intercept them. On July 20, the Italian legionnaires pushed on along the Teruel-Sagunto road toward Viver. Solchaga's forces captured the village of Begis. While escorting bombers attacking positions north of Algimia de Almonacid (north of Segorbe) *Oberleutnant*

Lt. Fuhrhop's crew made a practice of taking their mascot along on combat sorties. However the dog's luck ran out over Sagunto, when it was killed by bullets from a Rata.

Fuhrhop's aircraft, He 111 B (25-15) of 1. K/88. The aircraft still wears the emblem of its previous owners, 4 Staffel.

Still an unwritten page. Oblt. Werner Mölders during his first weeks with the Legion.

A four-leaf clover, 25-12»s good luck charm.

The chimney sweep on He 111 25-17 has done his duty. The crew managed to bring their aircraft home in spite of numerous bullet holes.

Schellmann scored a double, destroying two *Ratas*, his 7th and 8th victories. *Uffz.* Brucks accounted for a third *Rata*.

There was little change on the Mediterranean front on July 21 and 22, with the Nationalist corps making some minor gains. In contrast, on the Estremadura Front, to the west of the Pyrenean Peninsula, the attack groups captured the town of Monterubio de la Serena and advanced irresistibly toward Campanario. They had been given the task of eliminating a large salient in the front. The fighting lasted until September 15, with air support provided exclusively by Nationalist units, which consisted of: one Aero 101 group, two squadrons of He 70s, an understrength Ju 52 wing, an He 51 group, two Ju 86 bombers, two Hs 123 close-support aircraft and the two Fiat fighter groups commanded by Salas and Morato. The latter unit, less two squadrons, returned to the Ebro for a time (July 29 -August 24).

The Spanish fighters now began a series of successful aerial engagements. On July 29, the Guerrero Squadron managed to shoot down four *Chatos* and a *Papagayo*. On August 12, the Fiat squadrons led by Guerrero and Pazo tangled with 35 *Chatos*; once again four of the Republican fighters were shot down. The struggle for local air superiority brought almost daily encounters with Red fighters which we have summarized briefly:

Newly-delivered Bf 109 fighters are inspected by technical personnel before being assigned to the Staffeln.

. . . before the "new mule" can join the "old sleds" at the Staffel dispersal.

August 25: two I-15s shot down, one Fiat lost
August 26: two I-15s and an I-16 shot down
August 31: three I-16s shot down, one Fiat lost
September 1: two Grumman Delfins shot down
September 2: three SB-2s and an I-16 destroyed by Major Salas. Four I-16s and an SB-2 by other pilots in a battle with 15 *Ratas*, 7 *Chatos*, 9 *Katiuskas* and 8 *Papagayos*. The pilot of the I-16 shot down by Salas was squadron leader Redondo, son of the mayor of Madrid. Salas circled his parachute until it touched down and as he flew away raised his arm in salute. Redondo returned the gesture. This was Salas' 15th kill.

The weapons have to be adjusted and bore-sighted on the target range. . .

On September 18, following the conclusion of the fighting in the Estremadura, the two Nationalist fighter groups returned to Escatron on the Ebro front.

For the first time during the civil war the growing strength of the Nationalists allowed them to conduct major operations simultaneously on two distant fronts.

Six SB-2s which attempted an attack on Nationalist spearheads on July 21 were driven off by the heavy batteries of F/88; the guns were credited with two enemy aircraft shot down and one probable. The Do 17s of A/88 reported the construction of foot and pontoon bridges across the Ebro south of Mirabet, indicating that offensive action by the Republicans was imminent.

The Italians lost a Fiat on July 21 and two more the following day. Four Ro-37s and an He 45 suffered major damage. In recent days the Italians had suffered heavy losses. The squadrons led by Tessari, Remondino and Rossi now included large numbers of new, inexperienced pilots.

On July 23, all three Messerschmitt *Staffeln* were involved in a battle with about forty Republican fighters, which resulted in the destruction of four enemy machines. Mölders noted in his diary:

"Today was a great day. Toward the end of my flying time I saw 2 *Staffel* engaged with about forty Curtisses and *Ratas* north of Viver. I joined in the dogfight with my 3 *Staffel.* The Curtisses had learned a great deal. Twisting and turning they dove away and circled about at 1,000 meters in between the *Ratas,* which kept climbing. In the meantime 1 *Staffel* had also turned up. I wanted to bring Jaenisch into position to fire at a newly-arrived group of Curtisses which I had just spotted; but he came a bit too late, and in any case 1 *Staffel* swept in and upset our whole attack.

"All the Messerschmitt's were now above this circus, diving into the swarm of bees and firing repeatedly from endless distances, but without success. I saw none at all go down. As soon as one of our fighters dove on an enemy aircraft three or four others opened fire. There were some devilish situations, often one found himself in the middle of such a group and could only escape their fire by rapid changes of direction!"

On July 27, Oesau destroyed two SB-2s. The enemy had a good view of the German base and were therefore immediately aware of the Messerschmitts taking off. They very rarely encountered enemy aircraft over the front, even though the area had been crawling with enemy aircraft just a short time before. *Gruppen* Adjutant Oesau therefore devised a new tactic. Two *Staffeln* were sent aloft and when they landed following a fruitless hunt, the remaining *Staffel* took off undetected under cover of the great dust cloud, and set course for the sea at low level. The fighters flew sixty kilometers toward the sea, climbed to 6,000 meters and entered enemy territory from an unexpected direction, behind. Many unsuspecting bombers fell victim to this tactic.

On July 23, *Unteroffizier* Boer made a forced landing and a Spanish close-support aircraft was shot down.

Toward the end of July *Leutnant* "Otsch" Bertram was transferred from close-support flying to Schellmann's *Staffel,* where he was assigned Bf 109 6-67.

Schellmann commanded 1. J/88, the *"Holzauge-Staffel." Holzauge* (wooden eye) What did it mean? It was a typical Spanish gesture: when caution was demanded, the Spaniard pulled down his lower eyelid with one finger, hence the term "wooden eye." For a fighter pilot being able to see the enemy was half the key to success and survival. A budding fighter pilot had to learn to be always on the lookout. Bertram learned this lesson during his first sortie as a fighter pilot:

"The *Kettenführer* waggles his wings. Attack! He dives, I race after him. I haven't seen a thing and still can't see anything. Then, large and clear: an enemy squadron. Yes, wooden eye! Gunsight on — there's the reticle — inside sits the enemy machine! I press the buttons! But he doesn't fall; I almost ram him

He 70 F 14-40 rolled into a trench while taking a short-cut to its dispersal. The aircraft spent several days in the repair shops as a result.

Firing position of a German 88mm anti-aircraft battery beside a road in the Gandesa area.

4-meter shipping crates serving as bench, writing table,dinner table and cloakroom.

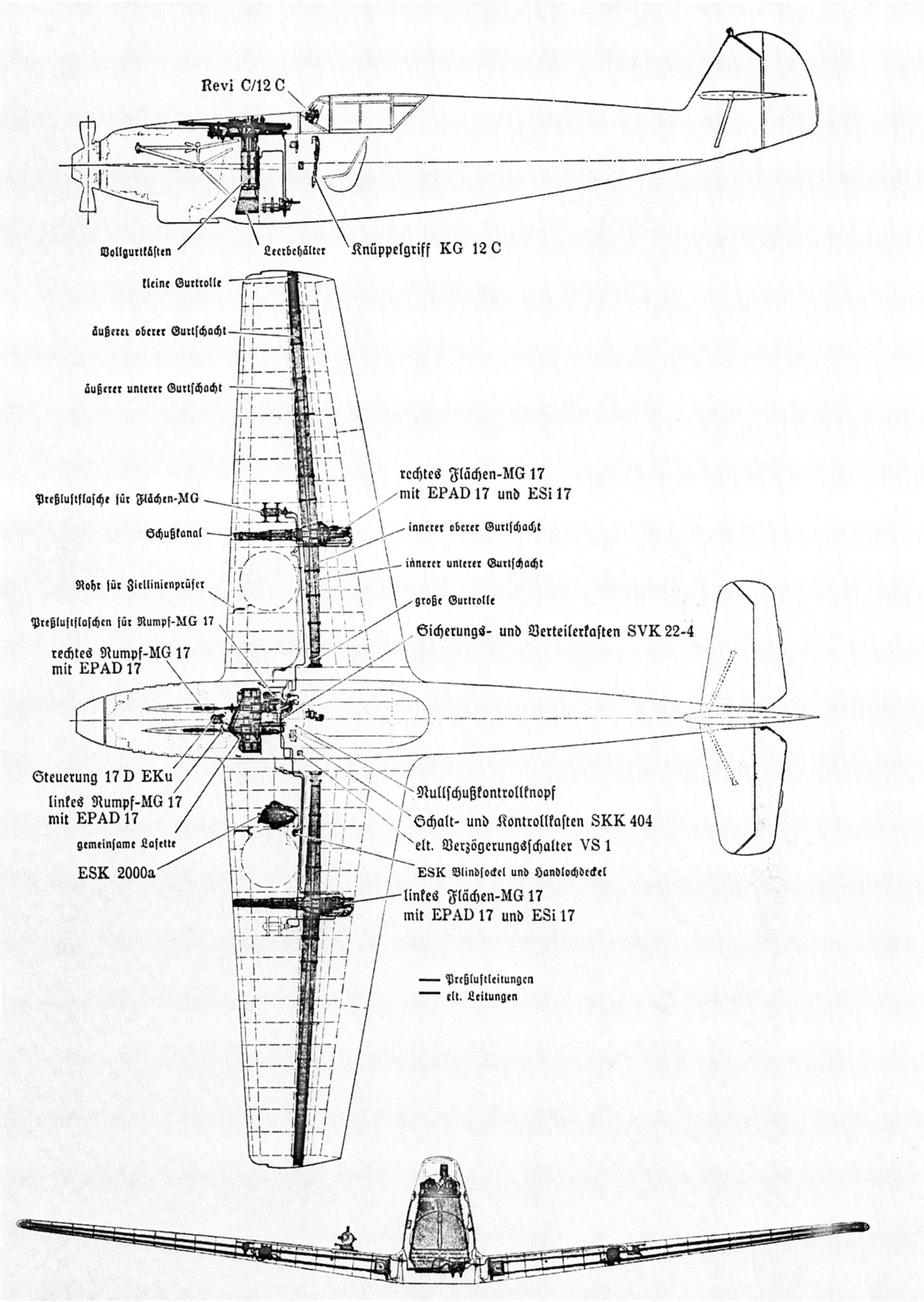

Three-view drawing showing the weapons installation of the Bf 109 C-1 and D-1.

Werner Mölders in front of his Bf 109 D. The raised panel gave the armorers easy access to the MG 17, which was fed by an continuous ammunition belt running to the wingtip.

Mölders' Katschmarek, Uffz. "Francisco" Jaenisch, who took over Ihlefeld's Bf 109.

The pilots of the Stabskette J/88 with the Kommandeur, the slender Lt. Walter Oesau, and the somewhat heavier Lt. Wilhelm Ensslen.

and race past the enemy aircraft. Now it's quiet, still. Where are the others? I look around and am simply flabbergasted: behind me hangs a cluster of five Curtisses! Stick in the corner and get out of here! I return to base somewhat crestfallen, after all I behaved like a scared rabbit."

Instead of ordering the bomber *Staffeln* to change targets to the assembly areas spotted at the Ebro, on July 24 these once again dropped their loads on the Algimia system of positions, which the Nationalists were storming in vain.

On July 25, 1938, "Veith" (*General* Volkmann) sent the following radio message to "Sven" (Schweickhard), the new chief of *Sonderkommando W*: "At daybreak the enemy launched a surprise attack across the Ebro near Amposta, Mora de Ebro, Flix, Fayon and Mequinenza." It could hardly have been a case of "surprise": for days reconnaissance flights by A/88 had been bringing back clear proof that a Republican attack on the lower Ebro was imminent; but Franco's headquarters was so engrossed with its objective, Valencia, that it denied the danger from the north or underestimated it.

The greatest penetration by the Republicans was in the sector held by the Nationalist 50th Division. Composed mainly of raw recruits, it was forced to fall back to a line Cherta-Gandesa-Villalba-Fayon.

A bitter battle was now to develop in this confined area, 30 km wide and 20 km deep, to restore the Ebro front to its former course which was to last until mid-November 1938 and claim about 25,000 men killed from both sides. An area on the near side of the Ebro won at great cost was sacrificed to a prestige operation (Valencia).

Only now were the *Staffeln* of K/88 redirected to make mass attacks against the Ebro crossings. J/88's operational order read: "This evening the enemy has broken through between Amposta and Mequinenza. Through the course of the day the Legion will be committed against the breakthrough points. K/88 will fly its first sortie at 0800. J/88 will provide fighter cover and attack ground targets if the situation permits."

Red Success at the Ebro

The "surprise" of July 25 turned into a real surprise when the balance for the month was drawn up on the 28th. Within three days Republican forces had captured 600 square kilometers of territory. It was not until the first week of August that the Nationalists once again had the situation under control; from then on there was a succession of attacks and counterattacks. The battle lasted until mid-November with some interruptions and ended with the withdrawal of the Republicans.

Nationalist air strength was as follows:

Force	Unit	Aircraft	Base
Spanish Nationalist			
	2 fighter groups	Fiat C.R.32	Escatron
	2 bomber wings	S.M.79	
	1 close-support group	He 46	
	1 close-support group	He 45	
	1 close-support group	Ro 37	
	1 close-support group	He 51	
Legion Condor			
	1 fighter *Gruppe*	Bf 109	La Cenia
	1 bomber *Gruppe* (one third with Spanish crews under Major Rambaud and Captain Zabala)	He 111	Sanjurjo
	1 reconnaissance *Staffel*	Do 17	Bunuel
Italian Legion			
	fighter group *As de Bastos*	C.R.32	Escatron
	fighter group *Gamba di Ferro*	C.R.32	Sarinena
	fighter group *La Cucaracha*	C.R.32	Caspe
	1 bomber wing	S.M.79	
	1 bomber group	B.R.20	
	1 close-support group	Ro 37	
1 close-support group	Breda 65		

On the Republican side fifty *Ratas*, fifty *Chatos* and twenty-four *Katiuskas* had been delivered from Russia during July/August 1938. There were seven *Rata* squadrons during the Ebro battle, two of which were still Russian. However, not all of the squadrons saw uninterrupted action during the fighting at the Ebro. There was also a *Chato* group with three squadrons.

During the initial stages of the battle both sides concentrated their efforts on the Ebro bridges and troop concentrations. The *Jolanthe-Kette* was in action four times on July 27 against enemy concentrations on both sides of the river; bridgeheads and mobile crossings (foot-bridges) were also on the list of targets for the Stukas. K/88 also carried out systematic attacks on the Ebro foot-bridges. After a few days the Republican engineers lowered the foot-bridges, so that they were as much as 70 cm beneath the surface of the water, rendering them invisible from the air.

This time it was the Nationalists who opened up the floodgates of the Segre power station at irregular intervals, increasing water levels in the Ebro. The lightly built foot-bridges were regularly swept away by the current and afterwards had to be rebuilt.

Until the end of July the operational orders for all the air forces of the *Legion Condor* followed the same theme: Ebro crossings, assembly areas! Understandably the Ju 87s were kept busy against such pinpoint targets.

On July 29, the batteries of F/88 arrived in the new combat zone and were immediately integrated into the ground defenses.

At La Cenia the pilots of J/88 could hear the exploding bombs delivered by their comrades of the other faculty, K/88, which flew its missions from

Zaragoza (Sanjurjo). Handrick's pilots had to share their large, sandy airfield with elements of A/88. A *Schwarm* or a *Staffel* could only take off from La Cenia in line abreast, as the great dust clouds raised during takeoff precluded staggered departures. The other half of A/88 was based at Bunuel, northwest of Zaragoza.

On July 30, poor navigation by a group of He 111s tasked to attack positions east of Villalba de los Arcos resulted to an unpleasant surprise for Nationalist ground forces. The radioed order for the formation release by the He 111 unit was given too soon, and as a result the trailing *Ketten* dropped their bombs over Nationalist territory. Fortunately the attack had been followed closely by the Nationalist troops on the ground. The troops were under cover when the bombs exploded and thus suffered no casualties.

The first air combats took place on August 1. The Spaniards reported the destruction of seven *Chatos*, among them Morato's 35th victory and Salvador's 23rd. 3. J/88 had an encounter with 25 *Chatos* and scored three kills. *Leutnant* Tietzen was compelled to make a forced-landing in friendly territory. The Nationalists lost a Fiat and an He 51. Once again K/88 flew several sorties against the Ebro crossings and stockpiled bridging materials.

On the Sierra de Espadan and near Villavieja the Republicans attempted a diversionary assault toward the north with limited forces, in an attempt to draw forces away from the Nationalist defensive front to the south. However the advancing Republicans were intercepted by the remaining security forces and thrown back.

The Republican assault against Gandesa was blocked, and from August 2 the Ebro front slowly stabilized. Crossings and roads in the Ginestar and Flix areas were bombed by K/88 with J/88 providing fighter escort. *Oblt.* Hubert Kroek was able to bring down a *Rata* in a dogfight with three of the Republican fighters.

He 59s of AS/88 carried out a harassing attack against industrial targets in Paitrosos (SE of Tortosa), in the course of which one of the twin-engined floatplanes was forced to make an emergency landing on the sea near Vinaroz. A coastal vessel rescued the crew, who were unhurt except for the pilot, *Uffz.* Euen, who had sustained minor injuries.

August 3 saw the Legion's bombers over the same target area as the day before, and the Republican anti-aircraft fire was as effective as ever; seven aircraft landed with flak damage and an He 51 was shot down. This time J/88 met no opposition. On the other hand an SB-2 fell to the gunners of 6 Battery F/88 near Gandesa.

On August 5, A/88 reported the loss of a Do 17 of the long-range reconnaissance *Kette*, after it flew into a flak barrage near Flix. Observers on the

The start of the enemy counterattack meant hard times for the technical personnel. The large number of sorties flown per day demanded servicing of the aircraft around the clock. The photo shows the morning briefing of technical personnel at La Cenia.

Ju 87 A 29-4, crewed by Lt. Haas and Fw. Kramer. At this time the Jolanthe-Kette was attached to the Jagdgruppe as 5 Staffel.

Briefing of flak officers. Maj. Lichtenberger (with back to camera) explains the situation to Hptm. Wäntig and Lt. Wilhelm Werner.

Two of the air-dropped weapons which could be carried on the ETC 500/IX fuselage bomb rack of the Ju 87 A: the SC 500J (1.97 meters long) and the SC 250 (length 1.64 meters).

In August 1938 the battery chief of 1. F/88, an 88mm battery, was Hptm. Heitzmann. His men distinguished themselves in the fighting in front of Villalba.

Nationalist side watched as two men bailed out, after which the aircraft crashed into the Ebro. *Oblt.* Fach and *Ofw.* Mende came down by parachute and were captured. The third member of the crew, *Uffz.* Lehmann, died in the crash of the Do 17.

Supported by two panzer companies from "Drohne," on August 6 Nationalist forces drove the enemy back almost to the Ebro in the Fayon-Mequinenza sector. Meanwhile, on the Mediterranean front the two opponents were content to eye each other across the lines; no forces could be spared by either side from the battle going on 120 km to the north.

Day after day the *Staffeln* of K/88 and the Italians hung over the Ebro, which the crews soon came to know like the back of their hand. Every tributary, every foot-bridge, every pier became engraved in the memories of the bomber crews, enabling them to

Seated at the "green table," Graf von Kerssenbrock (A/88), also known as "Schmissing," discusses with General Antonio Aranda (right) cooperation with the latter's Galicia Corps.

immediately recognize and mentally transpose even the most minor change. The Republican Air Force opposed the daily incursions with everything that could fly, even dipping into their reserves on occasion. As a result contact with the enemy and air combat became more frequent.

On August 12, 1 *Staffel* J/88 destroyed three SB-2s and two I-16s; two SB-2s were credited to *Oblt.* Schellmann, his 9th and 10th victories. Bertram reported:

"I'm flying in the *Staffelkapitän*'s *Kette,* to his left and behind. Schellmann waggles his wings: a squadron of Martin bombers! Attack! The two aircraft flying on the right go down. Damn, Schellmann can shoot! I go after the third one. A short burst — there, one of them is bailing out, a cloud of fuel swirls around the right engine. Break away. Five *Ratas* move in slowly. They are trapped by the neighboring *Kette,* a stupid attack. — Where is my wingman? He has just attacked a bomber, the crew bails out, small figures swinging beneath their white parachutes. *Ratas* poke their noses in. An odd feeling to be chased by those fat, radial engines. Break away. Dogfight. A single thought rules me: just get one of them! There's a lonely hare! Man, why don't you keep a better lookout? I get behind him and loose off a burst. The *Rata* continues to climb. I become incensed! He must go down! My bullets saw through the left wing of the *Rata* until it breaks away. Suddenly bullets whiz past my cockpit. Now I'm going to get it. Keep calm! Wing over and run for it! All of a sudden divine stillness. My first kill! I shout to myself. But where is the *Staffel*? The rest are assembling for the flight home. I stamp my feet and would dearly like to put my fist through the canopy. Then I'm over the airfield. Now comes the greatest moment in the life of a fighter pilot: those who have come home with a kill are allowed to waggle their wings. I roar over the airfield and waggle my wings. Land — taxi in — cigarette, my mechanic is grinning from ear to ear. Soon the paint pot is brought out and the first white bar is painted on."

On August 13, the Bf 109s encountered the "Super-*Ratas*" of the *3a Escuadrilla de Moscas,* which had recently reequipped with twelve of the new "sleds." Tarazona described the action in his book:

"A wonderful day. Over Reus we saw the 'Messers' taking off from La Cenia. In the distance we could make out several groups of dots, it was the Fiats of Alcaniz, Caspe, and so on. The sun was on our left, and we had time to work our way into position as the German fighters had just taken off. Bravo was of a different opinion. Before the Ebro we climbed through a wall of iron extending from 1,000 to 7,000

"Target in sight!" Concentrated effort at a heavy flak battery's 4 MR 34 data computer.

The battery's guns are aimed at the aerial target using the firing data provided by the data computer. A loader (K3) of 8. F/88, his fist protected by a loader's glove, pushes a shell into the breech.

meters. Nevertheless we were able to cross the airspace over the Ebro without loss. Now I saw why Bravo had flown as he did: flying at an altitude of about 3,500 meters were three close formations of He 111s. Somewhat higher were the Spanish Fiats. Above them the Italians. We dove on the He 111s. A Fiat crossed my path and I had to veer off to avoid a collision. I was so surprised that I had no time to fire. Soon I was surrounded by a cloud of enemy fighters. The remaining *Moscas* of my squadron were in the same situation, our unit was scattered. The bombers released their loads on the Ebro bridges. Then even more fighters raced about the sky. There were no fewer than 100 machines in the air. Parachutes hung like light bulbs in the vastness of space. The four machine-guns of the *Super-Mosca* spat like mad. The new I-16 behaved well. Who was hanging beneath the parachutes?

"When I returned to Pla de Cabra I counted only eight of the twelve machines which had taken off. I went to the telephone. Bravo let himself fall heavily into the armchair, one could see how exhausted he was. Fortunately no one had been killed. Montilla had landed at Reus, Margalef had joined the Merono squadron and was at Vendrell. Pitarch was in

Pilot Ofw. Mende of A/88 before his last flight with Oblt. Fach's crew.

Rear view of a German Panzer I, Ausf. A. Removal of the forward and aft fenders give the vehicle a rather tall appearance.

Tarragona, his Mosca riddled like a sieve. Sirvent had collided with an enemy fighter, but escaped by parachute. There was talk in the wing that we had shot down two bombers and several Fiats. None of us could claim with certainty that we had shot down an aircraft; there was no time to follow them after firing.

"I had tested my new fighter in action. It was wonderful. I felt like someone in a new pair of shoes that didn't pinch. I wanted her to understand me when I spoke to her, and it seemed to me as if she knew. Even before I applied pressure on the stick she was already laying on the side where I wanted to go. She handled sweetly. But then when she received a full control deflection she executed the maneuver powerfully. We two had to become an unbeatable team."

On August 14, the sky was again full of aircraft. Three *Rata* squadrons and a number of *Chatos* tussled with about 90 Fiats and Messerschmitts and 27 He 111s. The Republicans claimed three Fiats and an He 111. One Fiat was in fact lost, two others landed away from their home fields. On the other side of the coin the Nationalists shot down five *Ratas*; according to Tarazona at least two *Ratas* were lost, two pilots were wounded and squadron leader Merono had half his elevators shot away. The German fighters claimed six kills in a battle with twenty I-16s. The following account was made by *Uffz.* Szuggar:

"The Schellmann *Staffel* has been given the job of escorting reconnaissance machines over the area of the enemy penetration. At 5,000 meters they thunder in the direction of Tarragona. The *Staffel* is flying in two *Schwärme* of four aircraft each and a *Rotte* of two machines. I fly in the first *Schwarm* to Schellmann's right. There, the mouth of the Ebro. We know there are Red fighters at the front. 30-35 were reported just before we took off. We have to catch them before they can form up into a defensive circle. There, below us, the Red fighters! They haven't spotted us yet. Schellmann is first off the mark. He pushes the stick forward and goes into a dive. Schellmann's Me dives on a *Rata* like a winged bullet. With the first burst bright flames spurt from the Red fighter. The *Rata* spins away. I cover Schellmann's tail against the other *Ratas*. One attacks the *Staffelkapitän*. A sharp left turn places him in the reticle of my gunsight. The *Rata* dives away vertically and escapes my burst. I dive after him. There are still *Ratas* behind me. Motors howling we dive vertically toward the earth. I take aim. Three times I have the *Rata* in my crosshairs. Bursts hammer from my machine-guns. After the third burst the *Rata* begins to smoke. Flames leap out. His fuel tank has been hit. The left wing breaks off. Burning, the *Rata* spins away. Pull up and climb. I watch the spinning enemy. Will the pilot get out? I am distracted for a few seconds. Then . . .! The air is filled with long, thin streaks of dark smoke, whizzing past my machine. Tracing ammunition. Sitting behind me are three *Ratas*. Half-roll and dive! I escape the bursts of machine-gun fire then pull out and turn to face the Reds. But the *Ratas* have all disappeared. I head for home. The *Staffel* roars over the base at low level. Three aircraft waggle their wings. That means three kills, and it was ten against thirty!"

Armorers of J/88 test fire a machine-gun between the legs of one of their number, who has apparently grown tired of living; less carelessness than evidence of a devil may care attitude.

At this point a detailed look at of one of K/88's combat missions may shed some light on the activities of the Legion's bomber crews and the type of operation they were called upon to fly daily:

Operational Order 115: Attack on bridge south of Mora la Nueva on 14. 8. 1938.

Hptm. Wolfien, *Staffelkapitän* of 2. K/88, scheduled the takeoff of his *Staffel* and the command *Kette* (5. K/88) so that the unit arrived over the target at 0905 at an altitude of 3,800-4,000 meters.

Takeoff sequence:

Accommodations for the personnel of 1. J/88, a vegetable oil processing facility near La Cenia.

2. K/88 with nine He 111s

25-45	25-51
25-52	25-53
25-26	25-47
25-50	25-49
25-46	

5. K/88 (command *Kette*) with three He 111s

25-3
25-24
25-28

The twelve-aircraft formation reached the target area over Gandesa and attacked the bridge from south to north. After two passes, at the end of which the bombers broke away in a left turn each time, the attack ended at 0920. A total of 12 250kg, 250 50kg and 48 BSK 36 (bomb dispensers with *Elektron* incendiaries) bombs were dropped on the target.

Two direct hits were counted on the center section of the bridge and further hits on the road leading away to the east; medium and heavy flak fired everything they had throughout the attack without, however, damaging any of the bombers.

The same afternoon 1. K/88 took off to attack construction work on the bridge near Mora de Ebro, led by *Staffelkapitän Hptm.* Heyse. Nine He 111s took off, carrying 9 250kg, 180 50kg and 36 BSK 36 bombs:

25-2	25-9
25-15	25-10
25-4	25-6
25-22	25-1
25-12	

Like 2 *Staffel* earlier in the day, 1 *Staffel* chose to approach over Gandesa and attack while flying southeast to northwest. The *Staffel* made two passes over the target between 1725 and 1743, dropping half its bombs on each pass, then made a left turn and left the target area, pursued by bursting anti-aircraft shells. All the while the Bf 109 fighter escort had its hands full keeping about 15 enemy fighters away from the bombers. He 111 25-9 was hit a number of times and turned for home after the first pass, returning safely with one engine out; 25-6 returned with two hits from machine-gun fire in its wings. All other aircraft landed back at Sanjurjo undamaged.

Attacks on crossings over the lower Ebro went on throughout the month of August in an effort to cut off the flow of supplies to the hotly contested front. The weight of bombs dropped is an indication of the importance assigned to these lifelines to the front. Stab/88 recorded:

on the bridge north of Flix, 250.45 tons of bombs
on bridges near Mora de Ebro, 671.10 tons of bombs
on the bridge north of Ginestar, 545.00 tons of bombs
on foot-bridge west of Ginestar, 32.25 tons of bombs
on foot-bridge at Benifallet, 26.75 tons of bombs
on ferry landing near Asco, 39.00 tons of bombs

As well as the He 111s of K/88, A/88 and the Stuka-*Kette* also participated in the bombing of the bridges and the approaches on both sides of the river.

The German fighters changed bases several times during this period, taking off from airfields such as Zaidin and Poma, which were very well camouflaged. A lane was cleared in the bushes from which the fighters could take off unseen. They immediately flew into the nearest valley and remained at low level until just before the mountains, then climbed into the sun and headed for the front. Employing this tactic, on August 15 1 *Staffel* surprised three squadrons of SB-2s at 4,000 meters and three squadrons of I-16s at an altitude of 1,000 meters, forty kilometers behind enemy lines. The Messerschmitts attacked at once and returned home with three kills. Oesau, Bertram and Küll each received a case of beer, the standard congratulatory offering for downing an enemy aircraft. Tarazona reported the loss of four *Ratas* and one Fiat shot down on August 15.

On August 19, seven Nationalist divisions attacked Villalba de los Arcos, in the direction of Fatarelle, to clear the area of the Republican penetration; strong support was provided by units of the *Legion Condor*. This major operation resulted in only minor gains

An aerial photograph showing the area of operations of the Nationalist bomber units: the city of Mora de Ebro with its destroyed bridge.

2. K/88 flies toward its target, Mora la Nueva, in Staffel V-formation. From the foreground are 25-49, 25-50, 25-52.

He 111 25-17 of 1. K/88 was unavailable for the August 14 attack due to damage suffered in a one-wheeled landing.

on the ground, with the attackers failing to get anywhere near the day's objective. In the air German fighters destroyed four I-16s, while the Nationalists lost an He 45 and an He 51.

On August 20, "Gedalje" Schellmann scored his twelfth kill, a *Rata.* It was to be the last during his time in Spain. Northwest of Gandesa He 111 25-41, part of a *Staffel* formation, was shot down by anti-aircraft fire. *Lt.* Willer sustained fatal head injuries while bailing out, while *Uffz.* Schwarz and *Uffz.* Frischling received minor injuries. The fourth member of the bomber's crew, *Uffz.* Naumann, was initially listed as missing in action; in fact he had been captured.

The final days of August saw the Nationalist forces make slow progress in the face of bitter resistance by the Republicans. On August 23, there was once again a series of air battles. Mölders shot down an SB-2, his fifth victory; three I-16s were also destroyed. The Italians claimed eight I-16s and an SB-2 destroyed while losing three C.R.32s.

A day later Mölders found himself in a sticky situation when he attacked a formation of *Katiuskas* alone and was then jumped by a *Rata* squadron:

"A *Rata* came toward me from the right. I turned towards it, then two more *Ratas* dove on me from the other side. I evaded them and as I did so spotted two more *Ratas* racing toward me. I curved and spun down between the enemy aircraft like a hunted wild animal. They sat on my tail like a swarm of bumblebees. Then they lost me in the ground between the valleys. Flying low, I raced home across 50 km of enemy territory."

The Republicans were able to make good some of their heavy personnel losses at this time as graduates of the third pilot training course in Russia began arriving at the front.

On August 24, sixteen Spanish Fiats ran into a group of *Ratas* and *Chatos,* shooting down an I-15 and an I-16 while losing two of their number. Tarazona described this action:

"We positioned ourselves in the sun. We were unable to make out the bombers, but could see the explosions of the bombs they dropped on the bridges.

Two 250kg bombs are towed to the Ju 87s of 5. J/88 on hydraulically-activated bomb trollies.

The "bulldog face" of the Ju 87 A, made even more aggressive looking by the broad, forward-extending mainwheel fairings.

When we were closer we caught sight of them and tried to cut off their retreat. A cloud of fighters blocked our path. The whole sky was full of tracer. I saw a *Mosca* with several Fiats on its tail and rushed in to help. I drove them away and attacked one of the Fiats. My attention was diverted for a moment, then a burst of fire shot past my ears and shattered the glass in my windscreen. There was a Fiat only about 50 meters behind me. I stood my machine on its nose and rammed the throttle forward. I pulled out at 650 kph and climbed steeply. I had shaken off the Fiat, which had given me a terrible fright and put several holes in my right wing. Back in level flight I sighted a shot-up Fiat. It was trailing a banner of smoke and flying toward the coast, steadily losing height. I positioned myself behind him and had to throttle right back to avoid chewing up his tail. No gunsight was needed, the Fiat filled my windscreen. I pressed the trigger — not a bullet left the barrels of my machine-guns. I rammed the throttle forward to avoid stalling, pulled up over the Fiat and tried to clear the stoppage. I had the uncomfortable feeling that the enemy might open fire on me from close range from behind. Soon my machine-guns were in working order again. I attacked from ahead and the Fiat went into a dive. My burst struck the fighter's cockpit. A moment later the machine plunged to the earth out of control. Bravo also shot down a Fiat. In spite of everything the bombers had destroyed two important Ebro bridges."

Both Spanish Nationalist pilots survived and were taken prisoner.

The Nationalists got their revenge on the 26th, shooting down two I-16s and an I-15. An Ro 37 was damaged, but in spite of his serious wounds the pilot was able to land the machine safely.

An He 59 crashed and was written off while returning from a nocturnal harassment raid on the Levant coast on August 29. The aircraft nosed in on landing and broke up in the Bay of Pollensa, AS/88's home base. *Uffz.* Prengemann (pilot) and *Uffz.* Bülling (flight engineer) escaped with minor injuries, however the badly-injured *Oblt.* Römisch had to be pulled from the water.

A severe storm swept along the coast during the night of August 29/30, severely damaging an He 45 and a Ju 52 at La Cenia and inflicting less-serious damage on a number of others.

All dressed up for a "freie Jagd" in the town of La Cenia. Waiting for a ride are (from left) Unteroffiziere Hien, Resch, Boer, unidentified, Bauer and Jaenisch, all of 3. J/88.

Near Vinaroz the Mediterranean serves as a beer cooler. The fighter pilots are obviously enjoying the refreshments from one of the breweries "back home."

Oblt. Rudolf Unger, 1. J/88 (right), on an outing with friends and his mongrel dog.

Exploding bombs shattered the peace in Vinaroz at about 2200 on September 1; several Republican bombers struck the city's harbor quarter, setting on fire a fuel-laden sailing vessel and a arehouse.

An Italian Fiat landed on the Republican side of the lines on September 4. On the 5th fifty *Ratas* and *Chatos* attacked German fighters and bombers. An I-16 was shot down by an He 111 gunner, while *Lt.* Ensslen destroyed an I-15. Two days later "Otsch" Bertram scored a double, shooting down a pair of I-16 fighters:

"I'm on patrol with two *Rotten.* I am dead tired and fed up. 6,500 meters, oxygen tube in my mouth, my mouth is dry, no saliva. I see an enemy squadron and then the whole *mahalla* rolls in: five squadrons! Handrick and Oesau attack, a wild dogfight develops. I force myself to be calm, because to attack too soon is rubbish. I'm just about to tackle a squadron of Curtisses flying at 4,500 meters, when a lonely trio of *Ratas* comes along at 5,500 meters. Change of target! Soon I am hanging behind the right one. It falls with no sign of fire, no one bails out. Time to go home, or is it? Where is my wingman? Not there! Should I try it again? I am alone, but it's taking me straight to the front. And it works: another one goes down, this time in flames!"

Oblt. Mölders scored his 6th victory on September 9, destroying a *Rata. Uffz.* Kiening made a forced

Using all his skills as a mimic, Lt. Wolfgang Lippert (5 victories) initiates two curious Senores into the tactics of air combat.

landing north of Gandesa after taking several hits from an I-15 which attacked him from below in a vertical climb. *Lt.* Lutz was also shot down that day while on his 25th sortie:

"I couldn't believe my eyes — a Curtiss squadron a thousand meters below us. In the same instant the *Staffelkapitän* waggled his wings and we banked steeply and dove on the enemy. Just before I reached firing range on a Curtiss he made an about face. I dared not allow myself to be drawn into a turning contest, as the Curtiss was superior to the Messerschmitt in a dogfight. I pulled up in order to gain a favorable position for an attack on another Curtiss. Far in the distance, somewhat higher, I saw other machines and, because of their formation, took them to be another *Staffel* of Bf 109s. This soon proved to be a mistake. I stopped looking ahead and concentrated on the Curtisses, which had formed a defensive circle. I looked down and then, acting on an inspiration, forward and above as well. That was my salvation. Eight to ten *Ratas* roared down at me from above and opened fire. Following my initial fright I hauled the machine around in the direction of the front. My motor was no longer pulling as before. I saw that the right side of my cabin was smeared with oil. My motor had been hit. Now it was good night!

"The front was some distance away, while I was at 4,000 meters with *Ratas* in front of me and *Chatos* below. A dive to ground level would have been tantamount to a landing in Red territory. I tried to make my way toward Nationalist territory by making shallow turns while diving more steeply.

"Two or three *Ratas* pursued me. It was a disgusting feeling, to be weaving helplessly toward the front in front of their guns. The right side of my cabin was completely covered in oil. My engine misfired continually. A *Rata* roared past me and then dove away in a steep left turn. At the same time the dance began all over again. The altimeter showed 1,500 meters. I recognized the front. The evening sun glittered. All quite lovely if my engine hadn't been smoking so heavily. But perhaps this had an advantage. The Reds thought I was on fire and left me alone. I breathed somewhat easier, concerned now only about my engine. I tried everything possible to keep it going. Meanwhile I was down to 300 meters. Hurray! I had reached the front! My altitude dropped: 200 m, 150 m, 80 m. Would my engine hold out until I reached my airfield? 50 m, 30 m, nowhere for an emergency landing, only olive groves, nothing but olive groves. A bang — a crash — that's the last I remembered. I woke up in hospital."

On September 10, *Hptm.* Handrick was relieved as *Kommandeur* of *Jagdgruppe* 88 by *Hptm.* Grabmann; at the same time the *Kommandeur* of K/88, *Maj.* Mehnert, was relieved by Haerle. Schellmann's replacement as leader of 1 *Staffel* was Reents. The other two *Staffeln* were under the command of Kroeck and Mölders. Walter Oesau remained as adjutant of the *Jagdgruppe* until November 4, 1938. Half of the experienced fighter pilots were relieved, as they were urgently needed in Germany on account of the Czech crisis.

There were also drastic changes among the Italian units. On September 15, 10,000 Legionnaires embarked in Cadiz for return to Italy. Mussolini was annoyed with Franco, who had given England a promise of neutrality, and had therefore ordered the withdrawal of an infantry division and the fighter group *Gamba di Ferro*. The fighters were handed over to the Spaniards, as were all S.M.81 aircraft, whose crews likewise returned to Italy. This allowed the Spanish to form a seventh fighter squadron. At this time the first Caproni Ca.310 *Libeccio* low-altitude attack aircraft arrived in Spain from Italy.

On September 28, the first 3,500 members of the International Brigades left the Pyrenean Peninsula from Barcelona. One hundred Republican fighters paraded over the city in their honor.

On September 13, Mölders once again shot down an I-16, while another landed at a Nationalist airfield near Lerida. There were frequent occurrences of Republican pilots going over to the Nationalist side, and most were immediately incorporated into front-line units. Such a civil war has its own rules, so

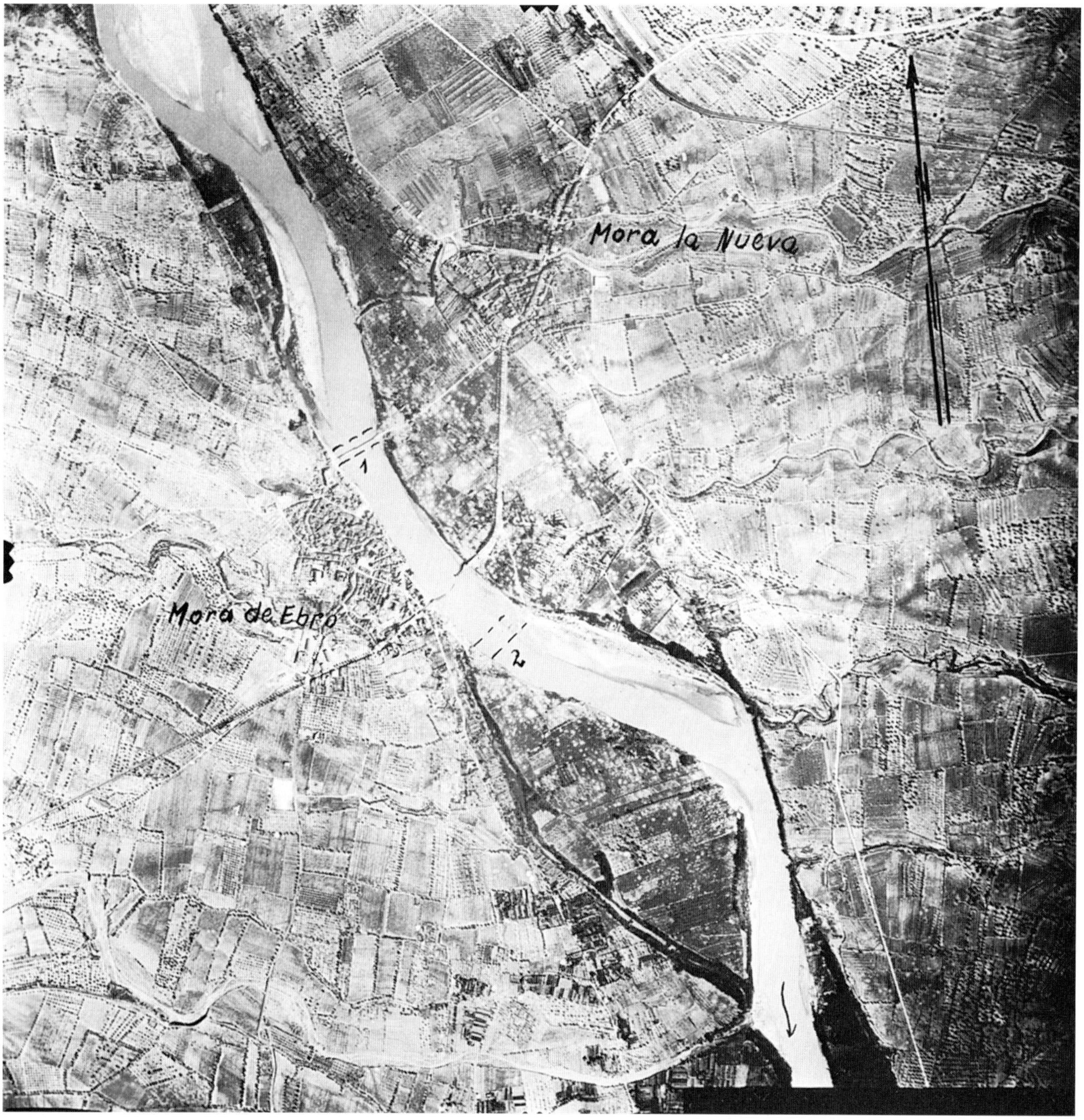

Once again the target is enemy crossings at the Ebro. The attack concentrates on bridges and foot-bridges between Flix and Mora de Ebro. This aerial photograph was taken on September 6, 1938 from an altitude of 4,000 meters.

the Spaniard Aresti took advantage of his first combat sortie to desert with his *Rata*. On September 18, *Lt.* Fözö destroyed a *Rata*, and on the 20th German fighters claimed four kills.

In this period the situation at the front remained virtually unchanged. Minor gains by the Nationalists were partly offset by Republican counterattacks. Over the next two weeks there was a series of daily air battles, with the Republican fighters becoming more aggressive. Nationalist fighters alone shot down 25 enemy aircraft, while their own losses were light. It should be mentioned that, when opposing the *Ratas*, the Fiats were in the same disadvantageous position as were the *Ratas* against the Bf 109, namely that they possessed an inferior rate of climb and ceiling. September 21 and 22 saw the loss of one Fiat each day. In the book *Air War over Spain* by J.S. Larrazabal are to be found two descriptions of air battles on September 22 from the pens of two Spanish pilots. We wish to reproduce parts of these accounts here, because they illustrate clearly the highs and lows experienced by a fighter pilot in such an air battle, in a literal and figurative sense. The first account is by the Nationalist fighter pilot José Larios:

The Jagdgruppe's new CO, Hptm. Grabmann, enjoying a welcoming drink with his predecessor Handrick. Beside him to the left are Walter Oesau and Wilhelm Ensslen.

"I stood my machine on its nose. The entire aircraft shook and shuddered, but I managed to position myself behind the *Rata*. I held my fire until I was very close. The tracers disappeared into his fuselage, and it looked as if the two machines were joined together by strips of tinfoil. The *Rata* began to stagger and suddenly went into a spin. I followed her down, still firing. Suddenly I heard the sharp rattle of machine-guns. Two *Ratas* had got onto my tail. I plunged downwards, rocking my machine from one side to the other. I continued to make abrupt control movements, so as to keep the machine on its zigzag course. Suddenly they broke away, one of our Fiats must have intervened just in time. . .

"I spotted several dots in the distance, milling about like a swarm of bees. I climbed still higher, the sun at my back. I dove on the first *Chato* to fly in front of my guns, attacked from behind and clung to its tail. After my burst of fire she swung from side to side, sluggish and lifeless, until she went down in an uncontrollable spiral. Suddenly, another *Chato* appeared from below my right wing, climbing. I pulled up quickly and made a half-loop, which placed me on the *Chato's* tail. I stuck with her and fired burst after burst from point-blank range. The *Chato* tried desperately to defend itself, then the nose rose slowly, the aircraft hung helplessly for a moment, turned and went into a spin. Then, in less time than a cock-crow, three *Chatos* dove toward me. For the second time in this air battle I heard the deadly rattle of machine-guns directly behind me, an unforgettable sound. I stood my machine on its nose and dove away vertically, employing all the tricks I had learned. I was certain my last moment had come. The ice cold feeling which creeps along the spine, the fearful contraction of the stomach and the knowledge that certain death is aiming at you from behind: I wouldn't wish this on my worst enemy. I felt done for and powerless.

"The *Chatos* clung to me like a leech, my heart

A gold medal winner at the 1936 Olympic Games, Handrick applied appropriate symbols to the spinner of his Bf 109 (6-56). . .

. . . as well as the first letter of his name on the fuselage side.

was in my throat, which was as dry as sandpaper. There was nothing I could do but dive, dive, turn left, turn right and wait for the fatal shot. The earth came whirling up toward me. Suddenly I spotted a dense cloud low over the Ebro, but it lay at 45 degrees to the direction of my dive! I had to pull up at once in order to reach it. The *Chatos* remained stubbornly behind me. Seconds later I plunged into the cloud, leveled off and set course for our lines.

"At low speed, so as to spare the engine, and with very gentle control movements, I snuck home.

"My machine had about 30 bullet holes in it. Several wing spars had been shot through and both tires were flat. The fuselage and tail were riddled. One bullet had just missed my windscreen and was stuck in the engine."

The new Gruppenkommandeur, Grabmann, took charge of 6-56, overpainting Handrick's "H" with a "G."

While Handrick turned to physical training for relaxation, Grabmann used the occasional outdoor nap to "preserve his physical well-being."

As befitted his station, the "old man" introduced himself by shooting down an SB-2, a Chato and a Rata on September 23.

And now the other side, represented by Tarazona:

"I had just learned that the pilot of the 6th Squadron who bailed out had been shot in the air. I couldn't believe that the Spanish fascists had done it. Certainly they differed from us ideologically, but they were still Spaniards.

"The machines of the 4th Squadron, which were equipped with oxygen equipment and superchargers for operation at high altitude so as to enable them to dive on the 'Messers' from above, gave us an awful fright. At certain angles, from three or four thousand meters below, the blue bellies of the I-16s caused us to mistake them for the Germans. The Germans flew singly or in a line, while the *Moscas* flew a squadron vee formation.

"We took off with seven machines, accompanied by the Pereiro squadron with eight machines. I wasn't happy about this, because Pereiro was too reckless and lacked judgement. His squadron flew from one side to the other. My neck hurt terribly, as the constant turning of my head had caused the skin to be rubbed off. When we reached the front we saw at least sixty fighters and three squadrons of Savoia-79s and Heinkels. Pereiro came over and gestured with his head toward the enemy. His face revealed a mixture of joy and astonishment.

"I formed my planes into a line and we fell on a formation of twin-engined machines. Before we reached them tracer flashed across our path. I fired at a silhouette which flew by barely twenty meters in

Armed with two 7.7mm machine-guns in the wingroots, two weapons of the same caliber in a shallow under-fuselage bath and fragmentation bombs, the Caproni Ca.310 was a well-armed close-support used by the Aviazione Legionara.

A welcome object for study: the new I-16/Type 10, which was unexpectedly "served up" to the Nationalists in mid-September 1938. Test and comparison flights were conducted far from the front at Badajoz airfield near the Portuguese border.

Oblt. Siebelt Reents assumed command of 1. J/88 on September 2. His aircraft, 6-86, was a recently-delivered Bf 109 D.

front of me. It was a Fiat. I followed her as my tracers disappeared into her white fuselage. Several short thumps caused me to look around; a Fiat was glued to my tail. Montilla, to my right, tried to drive her away and pulled up and over, almost colliding with the Fiat in the process. The Fiat dropped away. It was impossible to get close to the bombers, so well were they covered by the Fiats. Suddenly I saw a pair of *Moscas* climbing up through the middle of the bomber formation. They climbed up, half-rolled and dove on the Heinkels. After the attack there were several Fiats waiting for them. The *Moscas* regained altitude and we cut off the Fiats. The trailing *Mosca* seemed to have been hit; it went down pursued by several Fiats. Four of us raced after them. The Fiats immediately abandoned their prize and dove away. Montilla and I caught one of the Fiats in a steep turn and shot it down.

"As our fuel was running low, I gave the signal to head home. We dove in a line from 4,000 meters to ground level. The swarm of Fiats could not follow. After landing we counted 58 hits in Sirvent's machine."

A German He 45 and a Romeo were lost in air combat in this period. On the other hand, on the 24th Herbert Schob destroyed an I-16. A Spanish He 51 failed to return on the 27th; the same day Tietzen returned with two bullets in his shoulder after shooting down an I-16 and had to make a crash-landing.

The first combat sortie by *Lt.* Hogeback and his crew (1. K/88) almost became their last, when the starboard engine of their He 111 was hit by flak and burst into flames soon after a *Staffel* attack on targets near Mora de Ebro. Hogeback immediately dropped out of formation and tried to reach his home field of Zaragoza with the "stinking" engine. However the bomber steadily lost altitude and commander Hogeback gave the order to bail out. Radio operator Pacht, apparently fatally wounded by shrapnel, went down with the pilotless aircraft. After bailing out Hogeback struck the antenna mast and fin and landed in no-man's-land with a fractured skull and broken ribs. He lay there until darkness fell, when he was recovered by a Moro patrol. On the other hand, flight engineer Hermann and observer Poppenhagen

Two Arado Ar 68 E fighters at their dispersal at La Cenia. They were originally intended as twilight and provisional night fighters, however the aircraft lacked the necessary instrumentation.

were blown over friendly territory and landed unhurt. The rest of the *Staffel*, under *Hptm.* Heyse, returned to Zaragoza unmolested.

At this time *Kampfgruppe* 88 was under the command of *Major* Fritz Haerle. However, Haerle was killed on a mission over Madrid on March 12, 1939, when a 250kg bomb which had failed to release detonated in the aircraft's bomb bay. His successor was *Major* Nielsen.

On October 2, the Nationalists scored six air victories, all *Ratas* and *Chatos*, against one loss. Once again a description by Larios:

"A large group of *Ratas* attacked us from above. I raised the nose of my machine to take aim at a *Rata* which was diving at me from ahead, its four machine-guns spitting flame. This was always a terrible feeling, but I kept my nerve. As the *Rata* raced past above me I was able to put a short burst into its fuselage. It turned in behind me, which was not a good move, because the Fiat could fly tighter turns than the *Rata*. As I gained ground in our turning contest he broke away. I was about to follow him when I spotted a Fiat being chased by two *Ratas*. I dove on them with all the power my engine could give me and opened fire from a long way off to distract them. They put their noses down and fled. It was Ibarreche to whose aid I had come. I climbed to 6,000 meters. That was the Fiat's ceiling. Control reaction was very sloppy at that altitude and breathing very laborious; because of lack of oxygen reactions became slower. Suddenly I saw a *Rata* on its way home, only a few hundred meters in front of me. It had been in my blind spot while I was climbing. He seemed completely unconcerned and flew along at cruise speed. I approached the *Rata*, somewhat lower, with the sun at my back. A shadow crossed in front of the sun, I froze in terror; luckily it was a Fiat, which was closing in on the same prize. But I was closer. I forced myself not to fire too soon, the temptation was torture. I opened fire from 30 meters. One burst after another bored into his fuselage. The *Rata* flew on without changing direction, but began to wobble. Then thick, black smoke belched out. Soon afterward it struck the ground and exploded."

Uffz. Herbert Schob, known to his comrades simply as "the fat one." He scored his first victory in 6-60 on September 24, 1938. The motto NNWW (Nur-Nicht-Weich-Werden, or "Don't Give In") also appeared on the Bf 110s flown by the later Knight's Cross winner during WW II.

Oblt. Hermann Hogeback (2nd from left) before the fateful mission of October 1, 1938. Hogeback went on to become one of the Luftwaffe's most successful bomber pilots and was decorated with the Knight's Cross with Oak Leaves.

On October 4, German fighters shot down two *Ratas* and a *Chato,* but suffered a painful loss. *Leutnant* Bertram, with eight kills one of Mölders' most stubborn competitors, was shot down and taken prisoner. Bertram described what happened:

"Scramble! It's five o'clock. Out of the bunk. A short time later the *Staffel* is over the front. It begins: a squadron of Curtisses. I pick out my eighth victory and prepare to attack! Select propeller pitch. Radiator flap up. Supercharger on. Look left and right, my wingmen are there, in we go! — Ten seconds later: stinging impacts on my face, a rattling and crashing, flames spurt from the engine. Instinctively I throw my arm in front of my face, which burns like fire. I jettison the hood with my left hand, while my right releases the safety belt. Subconsciously I notice that the ground is above me, the earth is going to land on my head. I pull the parachute release. A jerk, and I am swinging as if on a giant swing, the huge canopy is above me. I reproach myself as I descend: 'You ass, letting yourself be shot down!' Down below is the Ebro —and there spins my faithful 6-67, there will be no eighth victory bar painted on you today! Farewell!

"The enemy fighters circle round me. This is probably my final hour! I am a living target. I rummage in my pockets as I have plenty of time. I was at 4,000 meters, that means a descent of a quarter of an hour. The Red fighters don't shoot at me, instead they wave and disappear. I destroy my Legion identity card, letters — do I have any insignia anywhere? My helmet is who knows where, and my leather vest won't tell them anything. It is the *Staffel*'s traditional vest and has lived through twenty victories already. Below an auto follows my progress, the welcoming committee. Watch out! I draw up my legs. I crash against a wall in the middle of an olive grove, my knee hurts terribly. Two soldiers free me from my parachute, I stagger to my feet and, supported by the men, hobble to the car. Captured!"

What had happened? A Republican fighter had climbed vertically onto Bertram's tail and shot him down from below. The pilot was the Spaniard Cortizo. The same day SB-2 bombers destroyed a Bf 109 and damaged four others on the ground at La Cenia airfield. The *Katiuskas* appeared over the field early, at about 0745, escorted by twenty *Ratas.* After the bombs had fallen they roared over the field at low altitude and raked the dispersals with machine-gun fire. An automobile was destroyed and one man sustained minor injuries.

On October 7, *Lt.* Ehrig and *Fw.* Menge destroyed two *Ratas*; *Hptm.* Grabmann and *Oblt.* Gamringer (subsequently force-landed) each sent down an SB-2 on October 10, while Mölders reported the destruction of a *Rata.*

From October 5, a Spanish Do 17 *Staffel* was assigned to K/88 and placed under its tactical control. The Spanish crews were to amass experience with the new aircraft while flying with the larger German unit.

There were large air battles once more on October 15, in the course of which Nationalist fighters destroyed two *Ratas* and German fighters four; Mölders led the way with two kills. The following day an He 111 exploded in the air southeast of Fatarella over enemy territory; only two members of the crew were seen to bail out: radio operator *Fw.* Keppler and flight engineer *Ofw.* Ernst, both of whom were captured. *Oblt.* von Janson (observer), *Lt.* Rödel (pilot) and *Uffz.* Hoevener, who had gone along as second pilot for familiarization, were killed when the aircraft blew up. Probable cause was the premature detonation of a 250kg bomb following activation of the automatic bomb release mechanism.

Bad weather set in on October 18 and limited air activity for the next several days and thus the intensive attacks on the enemy's supply routes. As a result of the heavy rain La Cenia airfield was under water for two days.

On October 25, a Ju 52 mail aircraft, 22-86, narrowly avoided crashing into the Mediterranean as a result of the horrible weather. The aircraft took of from Zaragoza bound for Palma de Mallorca. The crew made it to the island, but low cloud made a landing impossible. They then set course back to Zaragoza, in the hope that visibility there would be good enough to land. But the cloud cover over the mainland had also intensified and there was no radio contact with the wandering aircraft after 1915. On the morning of the 25th headquarters finally received the news that the aircraft was down near Carinena and that the crew had escaped with more or less serious injuries.

The Nationalist offensive at the Ebro began on October 30 and saw the entire Nationalist air force in large-scale action. In spite of this the attack made little initial progress. Numerically the Republican Air Force was still a considerable force. For example, on October 28 one hundred fighters paraded over Barcelona to mark the departure of several International Brigades. The Republican fighters fought a series of major battles from October 30 to November 3, but suffered heavy losses. During these five days the Nationalists claimed 30 enemy aircraft shot down and J/88 eighteen.

The Republican fighter pilot Tarazona described these battles in such detail that we will turn to him again for several passages:

Otto Bertram (left) photographed with two comrades, Lt. Helmut Lenz and Lt. Fritz Losigkeit, on February 8, 1939 on French soil.

"30. 10. Suddenly two squadrons of Fiats appeared. With the sun at our backs we dove on them from a superior altitude. Unfortunately they were warned by anti-aircraft fire and quick as lightning the Fiats broke up their tight formation. One squadron turned left, the other right. Our 6th Squadron was meanwhile in battle with the 'Messers.' We chased the Fiat squadron, which turned for the sea. As we closed we spotted three further Fiat squadrons ahead of and above us, undoubtedly the Italians. I attacked the leader of the squadron, followed by Paredes, Montilla and Calvo. The Fiats turned away and we shot past them like meteors, machine-guns blazing.

Exchange of information between Staffelkapitäne. Hptm. Mölders (2nd from left) and Oblt. Reents (far right) analyze the situation. Interested listeners are Lt. Wolfgang Lippert (far left) and Lt. Rolf Strossner.

We turned back and attacked from the front. We raced towards one another with a relative closing speed of 1,000 kph. Neither gave way. Cannon shells from the Fiats hammered into our motors, shattering our windscreens. I had the feeling that I had lost control of my actions, my cramped fingers clutched the trigger of my machine-guns. The powder smoke intoxicated me. The nose of the Fiat grew in my sight. My tracers chewed their way into its fuselage, which now loomed huge in front of me, spitting fire. I could feel the impending collision, death was near, he was right in front of me . . . a moment later . . . empty sky.

"Several hefty blows against my seat armor brought me back to my senses. Barely 50 meters behind me sat a Fiat. I stood my *Mosca* on its nose and dove through the clouds. The Fiat followed, and I pulled back on the stick and raced upwards, out of the sea of foam. I looked around; I was alone. Once again I dove through the layer of cloud, back into this battle for life and death. A Fiat was attacking a *Mosca* which was heading back toward our lines. I cut in from the side and the Fiat abandoned its prey. I followed her, coming ever nearer, and loosed off two long bursts. At once I was enveloped in a ball of fire. I pulled up sharply to avoid a collision. The pilot of the Fiat bailed out. I flew toward the other *Mosca*. The right side of its fuselage was smeared with oil and a piece of the engine cowling was missing. I moved in close and saw the pallor in the face of the pilot. He had been badly wounded. I gave him the signal to follow me. An aircraft of the 3rd Squadron joined us. We escorted the crippled machine as far as the sea and he landed on the beach. We saw people running to the aircraft. I was about to return to the front when my engine began to sputter. The oil pressure dropped. I gained altitude slowly. The engine finally quit in the vicinity of the airfield. I pushed the nose down and dove at a fairly steep angle to maintain flying speed. I lost height very rapidly and it seemed I would not be able to make the airfield. I was close to setting down in a field, but I felt ashamed to do so, after all I was the squadron leader. Should I make a belly landing? If I landed with my gear down there was a danger of nosing over . . . I started a gentle turn. I lowered the landing gear and passed over the airfield boundary rather high. Then I dove, pulled out and began to float. The trees in front of me grew alarmingly. With all my strength I forced the machine lower and touched down. I tramped on the brakes and pulled the stick back into my chest. Still racing toward the trees, I released the left brake and the docile *Mosca* turned to the right. I rolled to a stop a few meters in front of the squadron hut."

On October 31, 50 *Ratas* and 30 *Chatos* were in the air; they manged to shoot down an He 111 but suffered heavy losses. Squadron leader Beltrán was killed. German fighters reported the destruction of nine I-16s and one I-15. Mölders and *Fw.*

Kuriere at Salamanca. In the foreground is Ju 52 22-82 of the "Kleinbahn." Behind it is a second Tante Ju, one of those which maintained service between Spain and Germany. Airfields in the rear, too, were provided with light anti-aircraft guns for protection against air attack.

Among the Nationalist bomber squadrons was the He 111-equipped 10-G-25, whose informal motto "We come from the brewery" appeared on the amusing squadron emblem painted on the tails of the unit's aircraft.

The emblem of the Spanish fighter squadron 5-G-5. Its battle-cry "Searching for luck and the bull" reappeared in 1942 on the Eastern Front with the four Spanish volunteer squadrons.

Fleischmann each scored doubles. German accounts repeatedly spoke of the appearance of a new "Curtiss" type, which was almost as fast as the Bf 109 and possessed an excellent rate of climb. The new fighters operated at high altitude and had "bounced" German fighters several times. That day Mölders and his 3 *Staffel* surprised a squadron of these new birds while they were still climbing.

On November 1, the Republican fighters once again received orders to avoid combat with Nationalist fighters. On this day an I-15 landed at the Nationalist airfield at La Cenia. On November 2, the two Spanish Nationalist fighter groups celebrated a major success; they reported the destruction of seventeen enemy aircraft in two missions.

On November 3, the day the town of Pinell fell into the hands of the Nationalists, marking the first major breakthrough at the Ebro, the German fighters enjoyed another successful day, scoring six kills, five of them I-16s. Mölders got his 14th victory that day, Oesau his 9th. The following is a description by a German fighter pilot, probably *Obergefreiter* Freund:

"We flew escort for the bombers followed by a fighter sweep. We had been in the air fifty minutes already and were at the point of heading for home, when suddenly my *Rottenführer* waggled his wings briefly: enemy in sight! A second later he was diving. I placed myself in the proper position and raced along after him. We descended from 6,000 meters. Not until we were in the dive did I see the Curtisses below us. Two squadrons, one at about 2,500 meters, the other somewhat lower. Apparently my *Rottenführer* hadn't seen the higher squadron, as he dove right by it. Suddenly he pulled up and attacked the higher squadron from below. He must have seen them at the last moment. When I pulled out I was in the middle of the squadron being attacked, at exactly the same altitude. A Curtiss came straight toward me from the left and opened fire. His burst of fire passed just to my left. I had no time to turn left, so we flew past each other, missing by a hair's breadth. I now found myself in an ideal attack position, when a Curtiss appeared about 50 meters in front of me in a very shallow left turn. He flew straight into my burst of fire. Now all I could see was this fighter and my only thought was that I must shoot it down. My second attack was better. I saw pieces fly off, then I had to pull up otherwise I would have roared right through the short, fat-bodied fuselage of the Curtiss. I immediately banked hard left, almost placing my machine on its back. I saw the Curtiss go down, smoking heavily.

"When I looked around again I was shocked. I had never seen so many Red machines. Blue smoke trails from incendiary and tracing ammunition flew past my cockpit. Repeatedly the Reds came toward me. I climbed, but that was no help. Three *Ratas* dove at me from directly above. The flashing of machine-guns from their huge radial engines eliminated almost all hope of getting out of this alive. Then three shadows shot past me.

"It was wonderfully quiet. I was amazed that the motor was still in one piece. But then smoke suddenly began pouring from it. I was at 3,500 meters. Had the motor been hit? I looked for the front. I couldn't make it. What now? Inspiration struck me like a bolt of lightning: I had forgotten to open the radiator flap, which I had closed while diving. The coolant temperature was now 100

6-79, Luchs, Mölder's aircraft. After Mölders had been relieved the aircraft was assigned to newcomers in an attempt to give them confidence and awaken their sense of responsibility.

degrees. I immediately eased back on the throttle, opened the radiator flap and went into a dive to cool off the glycol. There was nothing more to be seen of the Red fighters."

On November 5, *Gefr.* Mirminger was slightly wounded and had to crash-land his fighter. 2. J/88 reported three kills. The same day the commander of a *Chato* group, Captain Comas, was seriously wounded in a bombing raid on Monjos airfield, as a result of which he lost a leg through amputation. The bombers concentrated on enemy airfields that day, with the *Legion Condor* being assigned those at Reus and Valls. During one of the ensuing air battles *Uffz.* März was shot down south of Valencia and captured.

During the night of November 6/7 the Republicans launched a surprise attack across the Segre river in an attempt to relieve the pressure on the shaky Ebro front. Several local penetrations were made, however these were cleared up within a few days. There was large-scale action in the air again on the 12th, in the course of which the Nationalists shot down a *Rata* and a *Katiuska* and the Germans four enemy fighters.

By November 16, Nationalist forces had regained the old front all along the Ebro, and this day is generally recognized as the conclusion of the battles to eliminate the Republican gains.

An object of much curiosity is CA-108, an I-15 Chato which landed at La Cenia. Clearly visible are the aircraft's red wingtips and the red-yellow-purple stripes on the rudder.

Thoroughly camouflaged. Even the propeller blades of this captured SB-2 have been sprayed in a mottled camouflage pattern. Zaragoza, October 1938.

The 3 1/2 month battle in the bend of the Ebro had cost the Republicans more than 300 aircraft. The Spanish Nationalists accounted for a third of these and J/88 a further third, with Mölders' 3 *Staffel* alone claiming 42 victories. Morato led the list of Spanish aces with 36 kills, followed by Salvador with 24, Vasquez 20, Salas 16, Aristides and Guerrero 13, and Bayo and Garcia Pardo 11. Mölders was now the legion's top scorer with 14 enemy aircraft to his credit, while Schellmann had 12 and Harder 11. The most successful of the Spanish Republican fighter pilots were Garcia La Calle and Aguirre with 11 each; Zarauza, Bravo, Comas and Zambudio all had 10 kills.

The older Bf 109 B-2 was still a capable weapon in the hands of a skilled pilot, as the eight victory bars on the rudder of Oesau's machine confirm.

The End in Catalonia

On November 17, the units of the *Legion Condor* received orders to begin a period of rest to last until December 1, during which the *Staffeln* were to be brought to full operational readiness. The only aircraft to remain at combat readiness during this period were one *Staffel* of K/88 and J/88, as well as one Do 17 and one He 45 of A/88.

At this time the air units were distributed as follows:

A/88	at Tauste
AS/88	at pollensa/Mallorca
J/88	at La Cenia
K/88	at Zaragoza (Sanjurjo)

This pause before the beginning of the final offensive saw only infrequent meetings between the opposing air forces and was also used to make organizational changes.

The three *Jagdstaffeln* were now commanded by Reents (1. *Staffel*), von Lojewski (2.) and von Bonin (3.). In mid-December the *Jagdgruppe*'s strength stood at 37 Bf 109 B, C and D fighters, and word had been received that the first of the new E-series would soon be arriving. The remaining elements of the *Legion Condor* consisted of about forty He 111 bombers, four Ju 87 dive-bombers, five Do 17 reconnaissance-bombers, five He 45 tactical reconnaissance aircraft and eight He 59 floatplanes.

The three Spanish pilots who had converted to the Bf 109 with J/88 in October now began the process of forming two Spanish squadrons to be equipped with the Bf 109 and He 112. The squadron leaders were Murcia and Garcia Pardo. Initially only two He 112s were available, but an additional thirteen had been bought by January 1939, allowing the squadron to be committed in Catalonia in January. The He 112 was to claim only one aerial victory, on January 19. The Spanish Bf 109 squadron was not fully equipped until early March 1939. By then J/88 had received forty new Bf 109 E-1 and E-3 fighters and had handed over its remaining Bf 109 Bs and surplus C-series machines to the Spanish Air Force. Morato flew his first combat sortie in the Bf 109 on March 10.

The two Italian fighter groups, still equipped with the C.R.32, formed a fighter wing under the command of Remondino Tessari. Squadron leaders were Mezzetti, Crosara, Favini, Gasperi, Meille, Valerio and Jannicelli. The Nationalist fighters were also concentrated in a fighter wing under the command of Morato. It consisted of two fighter

Departure of Oblt. Hubert Kroeck, Staffelkapitän of 2. J/88 from May 28 to October 31, 1938. Kroeck and his CO Grabmann enjoy one last "Legion Condor Special" (Beck's beer) in front of the decorated gas-powered carriage which will convey him to the Ju 52 transport.

Good humor is an excellent cure for homesickness. Standing from left: Lt. Heinz Bretnütz (2. J/88), interpreter Mode, in the car Dr. Appel and an unidentified driver of the Gruppenstab.

A bird's eye view of the Gruppe command post. In front are two light machine-guns for defense against low-level attacks.

groups equipped with the Fiat C.R.32 under Salas and Barranco as well as a mixed group under Munoz. The Spanish and Italian fighters were based at Escatron, Caspe and Sarinena, two further squadrons being spread between the Balearics, Granada and Seville. At mid-December Nationalist fighter strength stood at 155 C.R.32s, two He 112 and three Arado Ar 68 E aircraft. Additional deliveries by the end of the war included the thirteen He 112s already mentioned, seven Romeo Ro 41s and fifteen Fiat G.50s. A squadron was formed on the G.50 under Captain Bonzano, but saw no action.

Excluding the *legion Condor*, Nationalist bomber strength consisted of:

A close-up view of the command post bunker at La Cenia — nothing fancy, but efficiently camouflaged beneath some trees.

26 S.M.81	23 Ju 52
62 S.M.79	2 Ju 86
14 Do 17	2 Hs 123
11 B.R.20	

Available close-support and reconnaissance aircraft (excluding those of the *Legion Condor*) were:

22 He 51	7 Br 19
2 He 46	11 Ba 65
4 He 45	10 Ca.310
10 He 70	4 Aero 101
18 Ro 37	

The total numbers of fighters to see service with the nationalist Air Force by the end of the war were:

130 (136?)	Bf 109 V, B, C, D, E
380	Fiat C.R.32
15	He 112
18	Romeo Ro 41

A less well-camouflaged location was 1. J/88's workshop shed with shipping crates, paint and oil cans scattered about picturesquely.

The two new Jagdstaffel leaders. Left "Loje" von Lojewski, next to him Hubertus von Bonin.

131	He 51 (including close-support aircraft)
3	Arado Ar 68
10	Nieuport Ni-52

Republican Air Force totals were:

380	Polikarpov I-15 *Chato* (Curtiss)
287	Polikarpov I-16 *Rata, Mosca* several Polikarpov I-153
8	Bristol Bulldog
28	Dewoitine fighters of various types
10	Letov fighters of various types
50	Nieuport Ni-52
25	diverse types such as the Koolhoven, Hawker Fury, SPAD 510, Nieuport-46, etc.

Accommodations for the pilots of 2. J/88, built on stilts to protect against vermin and framed by a veranda for use on sunny days.

A veteran Nationalist transport aircraft, D.H. 89A Capitan Vela, photographed during a stop at La Cenia.

The new generation of liaison aircraft, represented by the RWD-13 (here 30-4), a small number of which were delivered from Poland. The aircraft was powered by a 120 HP Walter Major engine.

The Meridionali Ro 41 fighter could not match the performance of the C.R.32 and only a few reached Spain. This aircraft (7-7) has had its streamlined wheel fairings removed.

By mid-December the roughly 200 Nationalist fighters were opposed by about 140 *Ratas* and *Chatos*. There was a growing shortage of I-16 fighters as deliveries from Russia had by now virtually ceased. By war's end a factory in Alicante had built 12 of a planned series of 100 *Ratas*. Losses of *Chatos* could more easily be made good as the factory in Reus was building one I-15 per day. 600 pilots had been trained in Russia and 100 in France, as well as a further 300 in Spanish flying schools, so that there was never a shortage of pilots.

By now all the Russian pilots had left Spain as a result of the Soviet Union's commitments to China and the waves of political purges. It also appeared that the Russians considered the war lost and were therefore unwilling to invest further men and resources in a lost cause. Increasingly Spanish fightersaccepted combat with the Bf 109 only when numbers and the tactical situation were in their favor.

The bombers of K/88 returned to action on the Ebro front on November 26; none of the *Staffel*'s bombs fell on enemy territory however, all landed among forward Nationalist positions, inflicting a number of casualties among the infantry. Pending the next offensive the bombers were assigned targets in the Peralejos, Montalbos and Onda areas.

The new commander of the Legion, *Generalmajor* von Richthofen, former Chief-of-Staff under Sperrle, arrived in Spain on November 30, 1938 to take over the offices of *Generalmajor* Volkmann, who had left Spain on November 13. Accompanying him as new Chief-of-Staff was *Oberstleutnant* Seidemann. There was not much left for the dynamic, technically gifted von Richthofen to do in Spain. For all practical purposes the Nationalist breakthrough to the sea had decided the outcome of the civil war. Ultimate victory would already have been achieved had the Nationalists followed a logical strategic plan. The main task facing "Roland," as von Richthofen was known in Spain, was to work to bring the war to a conclusion as quickly as possible. He spent the first few days inspecting the forces under his command, familiarizing himself with the changes which had taken place in Spain during his absence. X-Day, originally set for mid-December, had to be postponed until December 23 for unspecified reasons; ostensibly the Spanish and Italians could not agree on which cities were to be taken by their forces.

On December 8, the aircraft of K and A/88 began familiarization flights over the new combat zone, while the tactical operations staff transferred to Estacion de Tamarite, northwest of Lerida.

Two Bf 109s were destroyed on the ground during an attack on La Cenia airfield by Republican bombers on December 16. The startled German fighter pilots made good the loss, however, by shooting down two SB-2 bombers.

According to the plan the last great offensive was to roll up the Republican front to the north, in the direction of Barcelona, and on as far as the French frontier. The original objective, Valencia, was written out of the plan.

An "old fox" and very familiar with conditions in Spain, Gen.Maj. von Richthofen assumed command of the Legion Condor in late 1938. His first activities: visits to the front for a first-hand look at the situation.

At 0800 on December 23, in clear weather, Nationalist batteries began ranging in on the enemy positions. The first attacks by K/88 on targets in the attack zone near Lerida took place between 0845 and 0915. The German bombers were followed at 0930 by the Italian squadrons. These were intended to smooth the way for the Italian troops of the C.T.V., which was to begin its advance at 1015. The Spanish He 51 close-support aircraft operated in front of the Navarra Corps, which advanced east out of the Granja de Escarpa area.

North of Lerida the Aragon Corps set out toward the northeast; still farther north, near Balaguer, was assembled the Maestrazgo Corps. The most northerly force was the Urgel Corps, which launched a drive in the direction of Basella.

Several days before the beginning of the attack General Yagüe had ordered his troops to simulate preparations for an offensive from the area of the mouth of the Ebro through increased patrol activity with air support. It was hoped these measures would draw Republican forces away from the area of the planned offensive. Ln/88 completed the deception by maintaining a high level of radio traffic in the Ebro area. The ruse in fact succeeded in tying down powerful Republican forces in this area, which were

This Republican SB-2 squadron was forced to share its dispersal with a light harassment bomber unit.

thus absent when the actual offensive got under way along the Rio Segre.

Poor weather set in on December 23, with up to 10/10 cloud cover. The only aircraft to get airborne were He 111 bombers of K/88, which attacked targets in Mayals and Granadella at about 1230. By 1500 the skies had cleared, allowing the Stuka *Kette* to get airborne and attack and destroy a munitions dump near Mayals. Mayals, Llardecana and Granadella endured the last air attack of the day, which was carried out by K/88, at about 1600. On this the first day of the offensive the 20mm and 37mm platoons of F/88 distinguished themselves in action against ground targets, playing a decisive role in the success of the attack. The enemy air force was totally absent, as their airfields lay under the area of bad weather which had passed over the front in an easterly direction late in the morning.

Fog and snow on Christmas Day 1938 limited combat operations to the ground; the squadrons of both sides were grounded by the bad weather. The previous day Nationalist fighters had wiped out a complete squadron of R-5 *Nataschas* before the fighter escort could intervene. The Spaniards scored nine kills, nine of these being credited to Morato alone. Squadron leader Captain Mendizábal was forced to bail out over enemy territory and was taken prisoner. He was later murdered by a Republican mob.

On December 26, the *Staffeln* of K/88 poured a hail of bombs onto troop concentrations, preventing the Republicans from establishing a defensive line against the advancing Nationalist corps. The latter made only minor gains, however; the necessary massive air support was simply not available.

On December 27, a Spanish-crewed Do 17 was shot down by enemy anti-aircraft fire. As it made its final plunge the stricken bomber collided with a second Do 17 and both aircraft went down. High water

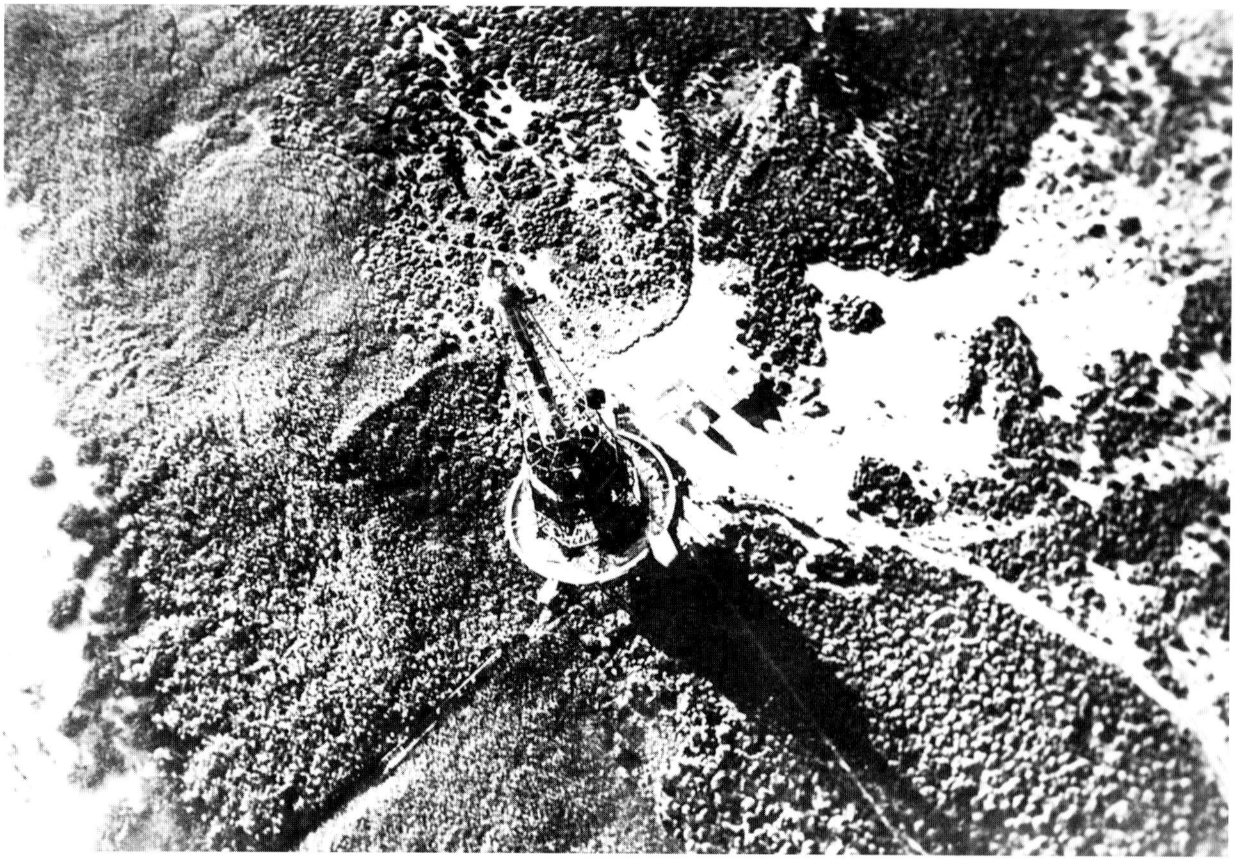

The light tower in the Ebro delta served as an orientation point for Republican as well as Nationalist air units.

R-5 Natascha light harassment bomber. Toward year's end increasing numbers of these aircraft were sent over the front by the enemy, resulting in sleepless nights in rear area quarters.

levels in the Ebro prevented the Marroqui Corps from intervening from the south and bringing some relief to the hard-pressed attack forces.

The only element of the *Legion Condor* constantly in the air during this period of poor weather was AS/88. The experienced crews of the He 59 *Staffel* flew day and night against the ports of Tarragona and Barcelona, providing the Republicans with some unpleasant surprises. The aircraft usually attacked at intervals of 1 Î to 2 hours, throttling back their engines before gliding silently over the harbor and releasing their bombs, then applying power and heading for the open sea. Once back at Pollensa they were rearmed immediately and sent back out to attack the same target.

The Maestrazgo Corps reached its objective of Artesa de Segre on January 3/4, 1939. On the third day of the new year German fighters carried out a low-level attack on Montblanch airfield, destroying and damaging several *Ratas* and shooting up ground installations. On January 5, while the Segre offensive was making slow progress, news broke of a Republican relief offensive near Pozoblanco in the province of Estramadura, aimed at the city of Sevilla. Should General Queipo de Llano's weak forces be unable to halt the Republican attack, consideration would have to be given to a transfer of air forces into the area. The Spanish command centers, as well as the headquarters of the *Legion Condor*, began the necessary preparations with great haste in order to avoid a second Brunete. By January 7 the "Reds" had succeeded in smashing a breach in the front 30 km wide and 20 km deep and were advancing from the Sierra de Almaden toward Cordoba. Not until January 7, when the first signs of irresolution in the further conduct of the relief attack began to appear, was the tension broken. The Nationalist squadrons which had been assembled for transfer remained in Catalonia. The only air resources active in support of the defensive effort were the few He 70s, two Ju 86 bombers and Hs 123 close-support aircraft, as well as a squadron of Fiats, which were stationed in the area. These were reinforced by two further fighter squadrons from January 12.

A *Chato* was shot down on January 9 and two more of the same type were destroyed the following day. Operations were severely curtailed by poor weather. Nevertheless, on January 23 the Nationalist ace Captain Vázquez was shot down and killed in combat with *Chatos*. The severely-wounded pilot bailed out successfully but died of his wounds. As he was carrying a cigarette case bearing Morato's monogram, the Republicans at first thought they had shot down the top Nationalist ace. At the time of his death Vázquez had 21 "kills" to his credit. A *Chato* was shot down in the same engagement. Four I-15s were destroyed on January 24. Two Fiats collided in mid-air, their pilots bailing out over enemy territory. Five more I-15s were brought down on February 9, by which time the Republican offensive had failed; by February 4 the former front line in Estramadura had been restored.

In spite of snow and adverse weather, on January 8 Nationalist forces crossed the mountain range (Sierra de Montsant) before Tarragona. The successful assault was carried out by the Navarra Corps, which fought its way through stiff Republican opposition.

Foggy weather failed to prevent K/88 from bombing Tarragona's harbor and railway station on January 9. The Marroqui Corps crossed the Ebro that day. Its objective was to cut off the surrounded enemy from the sea and capture the important port of Tarragona as quickly as possible.

On January 12, the Bf 109s of J/88 carried out surprise low-level raids on Republican airfields at Valls, Vendrell and Villafranca. Approaching from over the sea, the fighters turned toward the coast east of Tarragona and attacked their assigned targets. Thirteen enemy aircraft were destroyed on the ground. The same day the Italians shot down four I-15s, losing two of their own machines. A Republican artillery battery in the midst of changing positions was caught on the road between Montblanch and Valls. The Flak 88s of F/88 fired high-explosive shells into the column, scattering the gun crews. The entire battery and all its vehicles fell into the hands of the advancing Nationalist infantry, which was also able to occupy Montblanch.

The increasing numbers of deserters were a clear indication to the Nationalists that Republican morale was on the decline, but also reinforced their desire to seize the moment and not allow the retreating enemy a chance to regroup. After the capture of Valls on January 14 the race was on for Tarragona. The previous day attacks by the Stuka *Kette* had interrupted loading operations at the port several times and destroyed three freighters. Work at the port was also repeatedly interrupted during the night by AS/88; the He 59s fired on any visible light with their 20mm cannon.

The heavy batteries of F/88 were no longer able to keep up with the high tempo of the advance on Tarragona, the continual changes of position simply

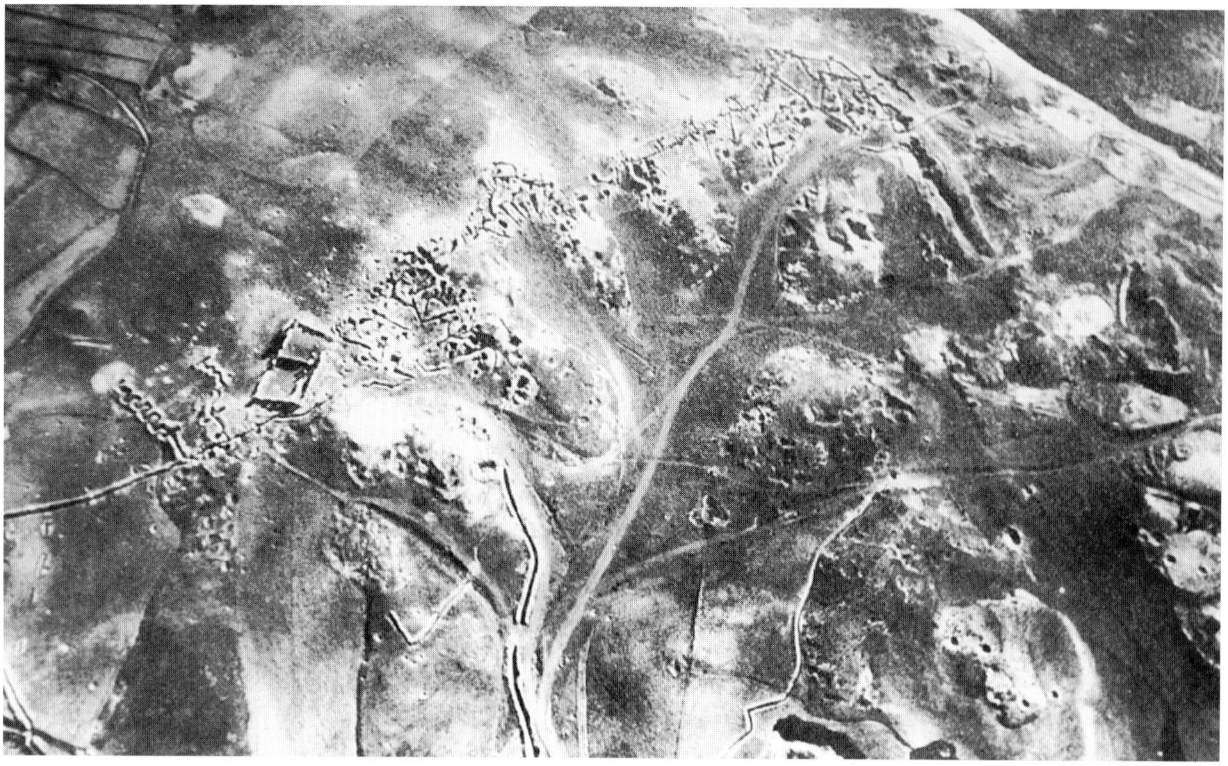

Republican trenches and positions in the Sierra de Montsant north of Tarragona. Such systems of positions were usually bombed by Nationalist bomber units before being assaulted by the infantry.

Engineers have thrown a pontoon bridge across the Ebro next to a blown bridge to allow the Marroqui Corps to cross.

Air raid shelters (refugios) like this one were built at Valls airfield by the Republicans to protect personnel during Nationalist air attacks.

Following the low-level attacks on Vendrell the airfield perimeter was littered with burnt-out wrecks like this Grumman Delfin. It was during these months that the Republican Air Force received its death blow.

took too much time. A light battery under the command of *Oblt.* Deventer was therefore assigned to the Navarra Battalions. The light anti-aircraft guns with their tracing ammunition proved very effective in breaking enemy opposition and they entered the city at the head of the corps. On January 15, the Nationalists closed the pocket; inside was a third of the Republican Catalonian army. The evening of that memorable day also saw the arrival of the Marroqui Corps, which had force-marched to the city on the Mediterranean coast.

What followed was more of a mopping-up operation, not at all like the battles of 1937 and 1938. The enemy's efforts were now directed toward reaching the French border before their line of retreat was cut off at the Pyrenees. It was therefore vital for them to hold open the western flank, and so the Republican forces tried to summon their will to resist once more.

On the Nationalist side motorized columns took up the pursuit of the shattered remains of the Republican divisions as they fled toward the north. No one was concerned about the Republican-occupied territory in southeastern Spain; it would simply fall into the laps of the victors like a ripe apple.

During air battles on January 19 Morato shot down a *Chato* for his 40th victory, a tremendous score by the standards of the civil war. Flying his He 112 Garcia Pardo shot down a *Rata*; this was to be

Ju 87 A 29-2 was in Leon for repairs and was thus not available for the attacks on shipping targets in Tarragona harbor.

The first Ju 87 B Stukas to arrive in Spain. As before the dive-bombers were attached to Kampfgruppe 88, and their sorties were coordinated with those of the bomber Staffeln.

the sole victory credited to the He 112 in Spain. On January 21, J/88 moved to captured Valls airfield, while the Italians transferred to Vendrell and Reus. On the 26th the *La Cucharacha* fighter group reported the destruction of four *Ratas* for the loss of one of its own machines. On January 29, *Leutnant* Böttcher's Bf 109 was shot down by anti-aircraft fire, Böttcher losing his life. The following sentences are from a J/88 report written during this period:

"Shortly before the fall of Barcelona the Reds were still very active in the air. Our reconnaissance aircraft were attacked with deadly certainty if the escorting fighters were not extremely alert. There were almost daily air battles, most of which took place over the sea in full view of the inhabitants of Barcelona. The Reds had only a few *Ratas*, but their pilots were seasoned veterans and were fully a match for us."

Barcelona, the last bastion, fell on January 26, leaving only scattered pockets of resistance in several suburbs. Members of the *Legion Condor* were forbidden to enter the city; the Spaniards were to be allowed to feel that they had achieved the victory on their own. Their friends from the other side of the Mediterranean took a different view, however. They demanded that their Legionnaires be allowed to enter the city with the first Spanish battalions. Ciano noted in his diary: "The victory in Spain bears only one name, that of Mussolini, who led the operation with courage, confidence and firmness!" The war diary of the *Legion Condor* refrained from contradicting this vain self-assessment by its Italian allies — why should it?

During the final days of January the air units of the *Legion Condor* participated in the pursuit of the

Aerial photograph of the port of Barcelona taken on January 22, 1939. The reconnaissance photo shows a hit freighter (1), two tankers (2), 26 large freighters (3) and a beached transport (4).

J/88 found this abandoned I-15 Chato (CA-229) at Valls airfield. Many Republican aircraft fell undamaged into the hands of the Nationalists at this time.

Gil-Pazo GP-1 training aircraft, previously in service with the Republican training center. Its training duties ended with the fall of Catalonia.

Jagdgruppe 88's temporary command post at Valls, a small hut with a hastily-built radio shack attached.

beaten enemy units fleeing toward the Pyrenees.

A brief entry under January 27 noted: "K/88 took off at 0900 with 17 He 111s for Massanas railway station and rail crossing near Tordera, bombing altitude 3,800 meters, total of 28.9 tons dropped, good results. A/88 flew two sorties to reconnoiter roads, railways and airfields in the Barcelona-Vich-Clot-Figueras area. J/88 registered four escort missions with K/88 and A/88. During a night attack on Jan. 26/27 AS/88 dropped a ton of bombs from an altitude of 800 meters on road traffic near Malgrat. F/88 not involved in combat operations."

A large military parade took place on the main street of Barcelona between 1100 and 1200 on January 28. The Bf 109s of J/88 flew overhead just in case the enemy should attempt a surprise bombing raid. At 0820 seventeen He 111s of K/88 dropped 28 tons of bombs on the Palamos harbor area. The only opposition was machine-gun fire from the ground. At about 1330 the He 111s bombed a steamer north of Tossa; once again the bombers were escorted by Bf 109s. Because of heavy cloud cover over the enemy rear A/88's morning reconnaissance (from 0700) was limited to lines of communication along the coast. AS/88 was active until dawn, making four attacks on road traffic between Arenys and Malgrat. Three Republican fighters attempted to intercept, but they quickly lost contact with the *Hidros* in the darkness. A deserter landed his *Rata* at Prat de Liobregat, Barcelona's airport. The aircraft was immediately collected by a Nationalist Air Force technical team. Initial work began to prepare Sabadell airfield for use by J/88 and A/88. Since the capture of Barcelona the flak had been released from its ground support role; its sole responsibility now was the defense of the city and the surrounding airfields.

January 29 saw the Marroqui and Navarra Corps in rest positions; by evening the remaining units were manning a line Mataro-Granollers-Caldas de Montbuy-Castellar-Moya-Avinyo-Balsareny-Naves. The situation at the foot of the Pyrenees remained confused for the next few days. An early morning reconnaissance by A/88 reported empty harbors and limited road but heavy rail traffic. At 0850 two *Staffeln* of K/88 attacked the Figueras railway station and one *Staffel* rail facilities at Gerona; the bombers were under expressed orders to spare the towns themselves.

At about 1000 a *Staffel* of Bf 109s returned from strafing road traffic north of Arenys del Mar. Fourteen He 111s and two Do 17s carried out a second attack on the Figueras and Gerona stations between 1215 and 1230. An He 111 flown by the Böttker crew was shot down by flak and crashed near Mollet. The bombers took off at 1400 for a third attack on the two transportation centers, this time escorted by the fighters of J/88. The escort promptly became involved with three squadrons of *Ratas*, however both sides came away unscathed.

Cloudburst-like rainfalls severely limited action in the air and on the ground on January 30. The only action by the Legion was a patrol by two He 59 floatplanes over the waters around Cap de Creus.

In spite of the rain-softened ground, on the last day of January the Do 17s of A/88 transferred to Sabadell; the crews were sorely disappointed at the poor condition of the airfield. Late that morning two *Staffeln* of He 111s attacked the railway stations at Gerona and Figueras yet again. A second attack, with a planned takeoff time of 1140, had to be cancelled; the heavily laden bombers became bogged down in the mud as they taxied out for takeoff. Instead every available Do 17 of A/88 took part in another attack on Gerona station at 1330.

On February 1, *Jagdgruppe* 88 joined the reconnaissance unit at Sabadell; completion of the transfer was reported to headquarters at 0945. By then K/88 had already returned from its first attack on the Gerona railway station; its aircraft were immediately rearmed for another strike against the same target. Throughout the late morning the area of the railway station was obscured by thick dust clouds stirred up by exploding bombs; He 111s in *Schwarm* and *Staffel* strength were over the long-suffering city all morning. After completing their escort duties Bf 109s of the *Jagdgruppe* swooped down on Gerona airfield and strafed an I-16 parked there, leaving it in flames.

Harbor installations at San Feliu de Guixols were the chosen targets of the He 59s of AS/88, which carried out attacks by individual aircraft during the hours of darkness on February 2 and 3. A *Rata* squadron trying to escape to the south was intercepted by the Italian *Asso di Bastoni* fighter group and lost two aircraft.

A Do 17 E (27-27) of A/88 at Sabadell. Daily reconnaissance sorties were flown over the northern areas of Catalonia and Ampurdan as far as the French border.

Nothing raises the morale of the crews like success! Lt. Lommel of A/88 greets the photographer with a "Hail Moscow!" salute; on the right, looking on somewhat skeptically, Lt. Gasten; left, enjoying the show, is interpreter Mode.

J/88 and Italian aircraft carried out a combined low-level attack on the Republican airfield at Banolas early on February 3; the degree of success achieved is impossible to tell from surviving records. He 111s bombed Figueras station four times that day; the three *Staffeln* appeared over the target area with their fighter escort at one hour intervals. The last *Staffel* released its bombs at 1615. The *H-Kette* (equipped with Hs 126 tactical reconnaissance aircraft) photographed the target area before darkness fell, so that the effects of the day's efforts could be assessed.

On February 4, there were combats with several *Chatos* and *Ratas* in the Figueras-Rosas area; the German fighters were escorting A/88's *F-Kette* (Do 17 long-range reconnaissance aircraft). Progress by Nationalist forces pursuing the retreating Republicans was slowed by the increasing numbers of

Assembly shops in Sabadell for the license production of Chato fighters.

Packing crate and partially-assembled I-15 Chato near the production facility's railhead. Most of the fighters under construction were later completed by the Nationalists.

With seven victories Lt. Horst Tietzen (right) was among the most successful German fighter pilots in Spain. A souvenir photo with Lt. Hubertus von Holtey taken at Albatarech, near Lerida.

blown bridges and railway lines they encountered. Much time was lost in laborious repair work.

February 5 saw a total of 46 He 111s of K/88 attack Figueras station three times and shipping targets in Ouerto de la Selva harbor twice, each time escorted by J/88. As their home field of Lerida was covered by ground fog, the He 111s were instructed to land at Sabadell. He 111 25-65 crashed into a mountain near Cervia in dense fog. *Lt.* Brückers (observer), *Uffz.* Hoffmann (pilot) and *Uffz.* Schnabel (flight engineer) were killed on the spot; the radio operator, *Uffz.* Wissmann, was thrown from the aircraft on impact and sustained only minor injuries.

The Nationalist fighters, Fiats as well as Bf 109s, were ordered to carry out a low-level attack on Figueras airfield. They shot down several *Chatos* and destroyed four *Ratas* on the ground. Tarazona described the attack from the Republican side:

"The entire field was in a colossal disorder. The large fuel trucks sat about uncamouflaged. No one did anything to conceal them. Nobody knew where the personnel of the various work groups were, or indeed who they were. I tried to make contact with wing, but my efforts were in vain. I rolled my aircraft into cover. A noise in the sky caused me to stop and listen. Several squadrons of Fiats were approaching from the southwest. The airport personnel hurried to cover. We had just returned from a mission with four *Moscas* and had landed between the bomb craters. Our aircraft were still without fuel and ammunition as an air attack had taken place just before we landed.

"Several *Chatos* were still circling over the field. The Fiats dived on these unfortunates, who were also out of ammunition and low on fuel. Manolo and I tried to cover the landing of the *Chatos* with two machine-guns. They twisted and turned a few meters above the ground. One of the five, his engine stopped, tried to land with a Fiat on his tail. He touched down, bounced high into the air and collided with a fuel truck. There was a brutal explosion. In less than two minutes half the field was burning. Meanwhile we had moved almost to the center of the field and opened fire on the Fiats. Our *Chatos* came down one after another. Two of the pilots had been wounded. We hurried to get the aircraft away from the landing strip, but a flight of Bf 109s appeared to add the finishing touch to this hell. They wiped out everything, fuel trucks, aircraft, trucks . . ."

1. J/88 group photo. From left: Uffz. Halupczek, Uffz. Holitzke, Uffz. Nirminger (hidden), Oblt. "Fürst" Wilcke, Lt. Roedel, Staffelkapitän Reents, Oblt. von Holtey, Lt. Sandmann, Lt. von Minnigerode, Oblt. Hollweg, Lt. Schumann.

Sitting about with nothing to do. From left: Lt. Ursinus, Lt. Schumann, Lt. Lutz, Oblt. von Lojewski and, perched on the ladder wearing a melancholy expression, Lt. "Joschko" Fözö.

On February 6, it was the turn of Vilajuiga airfield. An evening reconnaissance mission the day before had reported the field occupied. Two *Ratas* and three *Chatos* managed to get airborne, but fifteen fighters and two bombers were destroyed on the ground. A Bf 109 was shot down by Lieutenant José Falco, commander of the night fighter squadron. The German pilot, *Uffz.* Heinrich Windemuth, was killed. A German fighter pilot described the attack:

"To the left below my wing the snow-covered zigzag of the Pyrenees is visible in the first rays of the sun. Below us to the northeast there's a bright patch in the gray landscape. That must be it. The *Staffelkapitän* makes a gentle turn to the right, we cross over. Then a turn to the left. Battle formation. The action is about to begin. The *Capitano* wings over. Staying close, I select radiator flap up, low-ratio supercharger on, set the propeller pitch and switch on my gunsight. We go down like an elevator. One eye is on the man in front of me to the right, the other on the target. The airfield is difficult to make out due to the presence of a thin mist. Soon I am able to judge my range using the gunsight. 1,500 — 1,000 — 700 — 600 — I aim carefully! Stay to the right side of the airfield! Suddenly, small, dark shadows, barely visible. Curtisses to the left. One — two — three, another farther away — to the right and behind me an Me.

"A Curtiss in front of me and to the left, he pulls around and approaches from below. I turn left and dive toward him. Insolent dog! Zoom — we roar past one another. I pull up just above the ground and climb. Using the speed built up in the dive my bird shoots into the sky like a bullet. The speed gradually bleeds off and I scan to every side, above and below, no Reds in my vicinity. I put the nose down and approach the field at right angles. There — I can see the parked aircraft. I flip off the safety and open fire. Four machine-guns spray the Red aircraft down below with bullets. The target grows quickly in my sight. My aim is good; there — small flames! About time — I pull the stick back into my stomach. Raising my head I see that he's still not burning. I climb steeply and make a left turn. A quick look to the right. Behind me is my wingman, right where he is supposed to be. Below us our Me's are everywhere. Their white insignia flash briefly in the sunshine.

"Down we go again. The same target! Aim carefully. The white tracers race into the fuselage of the *Rata* like glowing nails. The reticle is centered on the engine. There, hurray! Smoke, a burst of

Following a night approach to Sabadell, Ju 52 22-90 landed too long and rolled over the bank at the airfield boundary and into the adjoining field. The aircraft's undercarriage was damaged but otherwise it escaped relatively intact.

The attacker's view of Villajuiga airfield.

flame! Pull out. Again I look back. The airfield is burning in several places. I count the fires: three, four, seven. It's very warm in the cockpit. In all the excitement I have forgotten to take the oxygen tube from my mouth; I have been chewing on it like a lunatic. *Lento, lento*! Time to get back. At low altitude I set course for home along the coast. Reconnaissance confirms our success: eleven enemy fighter aircraft burning on the ground, one shot down in the air by *Uffz.* Herzog. One Bf 109 failed to return, number 98 flown by *Uffz.* Windemuth. It crashed onto the airfield at a steep angle. The machine was on fire when it crashed, the pilot was not observed to bail out."

Windemuth's body was found when Nationalist forces occupied the airfield. A machine-gun bullet had pierced his heart. Not until the airfield was overrun did the Nationalists realize the extent of the damage wrought on Vilajuiga.

The Urgel Corps became the first to reach the French frontier, near the Sierra del Cadi. The other four columns advanced slowly northward, meeting occasional pockets of resistance.

The delivery of bombs to K/88, which was stuck at Sabadell, became a real problem. By employing every available means of transport 500 SC 50 bombs were delivered to Sabadell. On February 7 10,000 SC 50s were loaded into a transport ship at Palma, which immediately sailed for Barcelona. Two heavy flak batteries had to be moved back to the front to help overcome pockets of stubborn resistance. The gun crews were especially active during the crossing of the Rio Ter and with the spearheads of the Navarra and Maestrazgo Corps.

On February 8 and 9, Stab/88 once again ordered all of the bomber *Staffeln* into action; the target was road and rail traffic in the Figueras-Navata-Rosas-Llansa area. The objective of the attacks was to cut off the Republican forces' avenue of retreat to the French border. The fighters of J/88 flew escort for the bombers. Nocturnal attacks by AS/88 delivered further damaging blows against the port of Rosas and Puerto de la Selva, as well as to shipping in the waters around Cape Creus. During the nights of February 8/9 and 9/10, the He 59s hauled approximately 15 tons of high-explosive and incendiary bombs to the mainland.

A rich booty in war materiel fell into Nationalist hands as a result of the paralysis of the transportation system behind the Republican front. Nationalist forces reached the French border at several places on February 10, 1939, completing the occupation of Catalonia.

A group of Nationalist prisoners crossed the French border with the fleeing Republican forces on the evening of February 7. There were ten captured pilots of the *Legion Condor*, thirty Italian fliers and

The wreckage of Uffz. Windemuth's Bf 109 E 6-98, photographed after the capture of Villajuiga airfield. Around the airfield perimeter are the remains of destroyed Ratas and Chatos.

sixty members of the Nationalist Air Force. Bertram, who was among the prisoners, placed great emphasis on the assistance provided by members of the "*Aero Club de France,*" who immediately provided the foreign fliers with necessary food and clothes. Separated from the Republicans (who were installed in a barracks camp), Bertram and his comrades were housed in permanent barrack blocks, before being sent home a few days later.

Peace had returned to Catalonia. During the final offensive the fighters had flown as many as six sorties per day, shooting down 47 enemy aircraft and destroying at least 31 on the ground.

Staffel serviceability reports indicated the following aircraft available on February 12:

A/88	2 Do 17 E	Sabadell
	2 Do 17 P	Sabadell
	3 He 45	Sabadell
	1 Hs 126	Sabadell
AS/88	7 He 59	Pollensa
	1 He 60	Pollensa
J/88	22 Bf 109	Sabadell
K/88	31 He 111	Lerida

Nothing But "Days of Roses"

The *Legion Condor*'s part in the planned attack on Madrid was to be limited to photo reconnaissance and coastal patrol sorties. While A/88 and AS/88 carried out these tasks J/88 and K/88 were kept busy overhauling their equipment.

There was a sudden increase in enemy air activity over the Teruel front on February 13, and an He 59 on patrol without fighter escort was shot down by three Republican fighters. On February 18, the Legion's tactical operations staff moved from the desolate quarters in Sabadell into its better-equipped barracks train, which had moved to Prat de Llobregat. Following the move the staff felt much more "at home."

All personnel of A/88, J/88 and K/88, as well as some from F/88 and Ln/88, were ordered to Barcelona for a major parade in front of the Generalissimo, which took place on February 21, 1939. A few *Katuschas* could easily have dampened the enthusiasm of the victory-intoxicated Nationalists, but

The final phase of the Spanish Civil War. The newly-arrived Bf 109 E fighters encountered enemy aircraft only rarely.

Staffelkapitän Reents in his new Bf 109 E 6-119. In contrast to the B, C and D series, the E arrived in Spain with full radio and oxygen equipment.

While at readiness the pilots ate their meals at the dispersal; simple one-pot meals were most suitable. In spite of this Oblt. Karl-Wolfgang Redlich seems to be enjoying his meal.

Oblt. Hans Schmoller-Haldy's 6-123. As well as the Staffel emblem of 3. J/88 his Bf 109 features the foaming beer mug of the "Order of Cardinal Paff," an international pilots association devoted to alcoholic pursuits.

The Spanish fighter squadron 5-G-5 has received its first Bf 109s. The pilots had their hands full converting to the modern "Emil" as this landing in the Ebro near Lograno might suggest.

6-130, the last of the E series machines to reach Spain, was flown by Gruppenkommandeur Grabmann. The aircraft was destined not to see combat before the war ended.

the sky remained quiet.

There was shocking news on February 24: a German courier Ju 52, D-ALUS, had disappeared over the Mediterranean. No trace of the aircraft was ever found.

On February 28, K/88 began bombing attacks on roads and bridges on the approaches to Madrid under the somewhat macabre title of "Practice Missions." Significantly no resistance was met in the air. These "practice missions" were directed exclusively at arterial roads outside occupied towns and the inhabitants were not threatened. However, the "practice munitions" used were live, and the targets were anything but a collection of shacks like those used on practice ranges in Germany. The unmolested bombers attacked in *Schwarm* and *Staffel* strength. Later, during World War Two, Allied bomber crews were to dub such unopposed flights "milk runs."

March 1 was "The Day of the German Luftwaffe." An order of the day was issued, instructing the *Legion Condor* to assemble in Sanjurjo for a parade in front of the Legion's commander and honored guests such as General Davila, General Vigon, General Kindelan, and so on.

On March 2, a Republican courier aircraft was expected to deliver military representatives to Burgos, the seat of the Nationalist government, for negotiations. However, the aircraft failed to show up.

There were more "practice missions" on March 3 and 4, some with fighter escort, some without. During an attack on a bridge west of Torre Baja by five He 111s a light anti-aircraft shell burst in the nose compartment of 25-61, the aircraft of *Oblt.* Ramming and his crew. Everyone on board suffered minor injuries, but the crew managed to get their battered He 111 home, where it made a smooth landing. At 1230 on March 4, the Stukas of the *Jolanthe-Kette* made their first appearance over enemy territory in some time. However, the bombers failed to hit their target, a bridge in Salvacanete; the fighter escort met no opposition. The attack was repeated about 3 1/2 hours later, at 1551, but again the Stukas placed their "eggs" in open country instead of on the bridge.

The regrouping of forces for the assault on Madrid began in early March. On March 5, J/88 took off on a fighter sweep over Alicante, with an intermediate stop at Calamocha. *Oblt.* von Bonin shot down a *Chato* over Alicante, the last victory by *Legion Condor* fighters during the Spanish Civil War. On the 11th the German fighters transferred to Barcience-Torrijos, the bombers to Avila, Escalona and Salamanca.

The Italian fighter groups went to Escalona and Delta. The Spanish fighters were based at Posadas (near Cordoba), Grinon (near Madrid) and Almaluez. At this time the Nationalists formed a close-support group with *Chatos* captured in Catalonia.

The Republican side no longer possessed any air

". . . and hereby opens this year's gliding season!" Mightily impressed by the new base at Barcience, Joschko Fözö forgot to extend his landing gear before touching down.

forces worthy of note. Three squadrons of R-5 light bombers, two squadrons of SB-2s, about 30 fighters — that was all. A series of 100 *Ratas* was in an advanced stage of construction in Alicante, a dozen had already been delivered. However, some of the components necessary for the completion of the rest were not available. The Republicans were also expecting the delivery of 70 *Ratas* from Russia via France, as well as 50 "Super-*Katiuskas*." Several Seversky and Bellanca machines purchased in the USA were on their way to Spain by sea, but all of these deliveries came too late. The collapse could no longer be prevented.

It was at this time that the first reports began filtering out of Madrid of conflicts between radicals and the circle around General Miaja, who favored

Captured I-15s on strength with a Nationalist close-support unit.

peace negotiations with the Nationalists. The latter naturally watched such developments closely, as they might contribute to a rapid end to the war. In the days that followed, these battles between those weary of the war (certainly the more sensible) and the communist idealogues spread through all of Republican-controlled Spain. The N.V.A., the side for peace, appeared to be slowly gaining the upper hand.

On the morning of March 7, aircraft of A/88 reported that the Republican fleet had sailed from Cartagena. The ships were already 30 km from their former base, bound for the French port of Bizerta on the Algerian coast. Although the He 59s of AS/88 were immediately armed with bombs and flown to the reported location, they were unable to find the fleet. The ships reached Bizerta, where they were met by French authorities who had been informed of their coming in advance. All of the ships' personnel were interned; the vessels themselves were handed over to the victor Franco following the conclusion of the civil war.

Thirty-three He 111s of K/88 carried out a series of attacks on enemy positions in the Viver-Segorbe-Sagunto area and ships in the port city of Sagunto on March 7 between 0930 and 1600. The bombers dropped 49.6 tons of bombs from altitudes of 2,000 and 6,000 meters in the face of heavy anti-aircraft fire. The Bf 109 escort was not challenged.

There were more "practice missions" on March 8. Twenty-seven He 111s dropped 43 tons of bombs on roads and bridges southwest of Teruel, a total just slightly below that of the previous day. The returning crews reported light anti-aircraft fire but no fighter opposition. The list of targets for March 9 included the airfield at Alcala de Henares, railway stations at Colmenar and Collado and bridges near Salvacanete and Moncofar. This time the Heinkels were opposed by flak and fighters. In spite of this the bombing was accurate.

Further missions of this type followed. On March 12, the machine of the formation leader exploded in mid-air shortly after the bombs were dropped. A 250kg bomb had become stuck in the bomb magazine and exploded during attempts to jettison it. *Major* Haerle and his entire crew were killed and wreckage from the shattered bomber rained down on the bombed-out airfield at Alcala de Henares. Since March 10 the Legion Headquarters had been in Toledo, where preparations were being made for the taking of Madrid.

Following preliminary photo reconnaissance on March 16 the *Staffeln* of the *Legion Condor* took off on the last major attacks before the conclusion of hostilities.

The Messerschmitts were sent on a *"freie Jagd"* mission in the Madrid area, while twenty He 111s and two Ju 87s spent two hours attacking road underpasses near Guadalajara, a bridge at Meco, a crossroads near Los Santos and a bridge at Fuentiduena de Tajo. Two Bf 109s collided in mid-air near Toledo. Both pilots managed to bail out and came down in friendly territory. One of the two, *Lt.* Strössner, suffered minor injuries while bailing out.

The following is a summary of the Legion's activities on March 17, 1939:

0930-1015:
J/88 mission: escort reconnaissance aircraft and *freie Jagd* in Toldeo-Madrid area (1 Bf 109 only)
1100:
Attacks by K/88 on railway junction northwest of Arganda and Las Rocas-El Escorial road.
1130:
Attack by K/88 on infantry positions northwest of Quijorna
1300:
A/88: two Do 17s and two Hs 126s photo reconnaissance and familiarization flights in Madrid-Toledo area.
1400-1500:
J/88 *freie Jagd* over Madrid area, no enemy contact
1500:
Attack by K/88 on infantry positions bear Valdemorillo. On March 17 K/88 had a total of 28 He 111s and 2 attached Ju 87s in the air.

A similar brief summary of flying activity for March 18 follows:
0930:
A/88 photo reconnaissance south of Toledo and around Madrid; enemy battery located 1.5 km southeast of Titulcia
1200-1300:
J/88 *freie Jagd*, no enemy contact
1230:
Five Hs 126s of A/88 bomb Collado-Manzanares road, some anti-aircraft fire
1300:
Attack by K/88 on infantry positions west of Quijorna, very good bomb pattern
1300-1400:
J/88 *freie Jagd* over Madrid area, no enemy contact
1430:
Attack by one *Kette* (3 He 111) of K/88 on battery spotted earlier near Titulcia
1430:
A/88 photo reconnaissance south of Toledo
1400-1500:
J/88 *freie Jagd* over Madrid area, no enemy contact all day

F/88 harassing fire on outskirts of Aranjuez and enemy battery near Aranjuez.As this brief summary shows, by now the Republican Air Force had either ceased to exist or its pilots had lost the will to fight. Its aircraft sat in their camouflaged dispersals, and even the most necessary maintenance work could not be carried out as many of the technical personnel had already returned to civilian life.

The only unit active during the period March 19-22 was A/88, whose Do 17s and Hs 126s flew photo reconnaissance sorties and kept an eye on enemy airfields. Two He 59 floatplanes of AS/88

Two Ketten of Hs 126 aircraft took over reconnaissance duties from the long-obsolete Heinkel He 45 Pavos. The Spaniards dubbed the new aircraft Super-Pava.

were in the air from 1130 to 1430 on the 22nd, patrolling the waters off Valencia. One of the floatplanes was forced to make an emergency landing north of the island of Ibiza and was written off. A British destroyer found the crew paddling about in their life vests and picked them up. They were put ashore at Palma, where (now quite drunk on Scotch whiskey), they bid their new-found travelling companions farewell with much hearty shoulder-clapping.

On March 23, Hs 126 19-4 of A/88 spotted for Artillery Group Lucht. The artillery unit had originally come to Spain strictly as an instructional unit, but soon found itself supporting Nationalist batteries with precisely directed fire, beginning with the campaign to capture Catalonia. The Hentschel made an emergency landing with engine trouble and there was no aircraft to spot for the 105mm battery until later in the afternoon. That day A/88 at Barcience reported three serviceable Do 17s and four Hs 126s.

A Republican negotiating team landed at Burgos on March 25. The outcome of these negotiations would determine whether the attack on Madrid, scheduled for March 26, would go ahead as planned. At about 2000 the waiting press representatives were informed that talks had broken down.

Operational orders for "D-Day," as it was designated in the *Legion Condor*'s war diary, went out to the *Staffeln* the same evening. Ground crews began arming the aircraft. The *Generalissimo* ordered the attacks to begin as follows:

Attack from the south 26. 3. 1939
Attack from the center 27. 3. 1939
Attack from the Levante 29. 3. 1939

Events at the end of March proved that Franco's martial bearing during the negotiations in Burgos had had the desired effect on the other side.

The advancing Southern Army, which moved out of its assembly area north of Cordoba, met no significant resistance; thousands of deserters and prisoners were sent to the rear to be registered in camps.

On March 27, the bomber *Staffeln*, escorted by Bf 109s, flew over the forward positions for the last time. The Heinkels bombed in close formation, shattering the few Republican positions still mounting effective opposition on the ground. Afterward the Toledo front was broken by the Toledo, Maestrazgo and Navarra Corps and the Italian C.T.V. and completely rolled up.

The same day an Hs 126 reported seeing white flags flying in the streets of the Spanish capital, a signal that all resistance had ceased. From then on units of the German Legion took to the air only to participate in aerial demonstrations. The fighters continued to fly fully armed, however, they were under orders to intercept any aircraft which appeared and escort them to Nationalist airfields. The German pilots were expressly forbidden to carry out further low-level attacks.

Two He 115 floatplanes, a type which was just entering service with the *Küstenfliegerstaffeln* in Germany, arrived in Spain too late to see operational use with AS/88. Assigned the civil registrations D-AOHS and D-ANPT and flown by *Leutnants* Fiehn,

Jandrey and Wachsmuth, they landed at Puerto Pollensa on March 26, 1939. The three pilots had received instruction on the new aircraft in Travemünde from *Lt.* Gerhard Geike and were eagerly awaited by the *Staffelkapitän of AS/88, Hauptmann* Smidt, and his adjutant, *Major* Reppchen. Now, however, the two new arrivals bobbed idly at their moorings at Pollensa. The two He 115s were among the few German aircraft which did not remain in Spain, and were sent back to Travemünde during the course of 1939.

One of the four Bf 108 B aircraft delivered to Spain, seen at Llanes. The Taifun was an ideal courier and liaison aircraft between the German, Italian and Spanish headquarters.

Sacks of bread and food in place of bombs. Following the first signs of surrender the He 111s of K/88 began dropping such loads over parks and open spaces in Madrid.

With its docile handling characteristics the Storch could be put down on any field. To the troops it was "the sacred bird of the headquarters." They were rarely entrusted to unfamiliar pilots and the headquarters pilots watched over them jealously.

The *Legion Condor* played no part in the occupation of the remaining parts of Spain still under the Republican flag. All of its units were ordered to assemble in the Toledo area in preparation for their return to the Reich.

At 1200, on March 28, 1939, news reached the Legion's tactical operations headquarters that Madrid and Aranjuez had surrendered that morning, surprising the staff officers in the midst of their lunch. An hour and a half later the technical personnel had already begun dismantling the command post — the Germans were in a hurry to close the door on three years of civil war.

Between War and War

A European drama had come to an end; yet, tragically, the final days of the war saw a number of veteran fighters, participants in many battles, lose their lives.

On March 28, Captain Garcia Pardo (12 victories) and a Lieutenant crashed and were killed while returning from their last mission. On April 4 Morato, the ace of aces, crashed and was killed at Sevilla while giving a demonstration of aerobatics in his famous Fiat, number 3-51. The same day Major Ibarra died while on a transfer flight.

The following weeks were to see the deaths in flying accidents of Group Commander Baranco and the successful fighter pilots Muntadas and Manrique.

The *Legion Condor* received the tragic news that Rudolf Freiherr von Moreau had been killed in the crash of his Ju 88 at Rechlin. He was awarded the Spanish Cross in Gold with Diamonds posthumously.

The following weeks were filled with victory parades:
April 17, 1939, in Sevilla May 3, 1939, in Valencia May 12, 1939, in Barajas (About 500 aircraft took part in the Barajas celebration, from ancient Breguet 19s to captured *Nataschas* and *Chatos*). The biggest parade of all took place in Madrid on May 19, 1939. The air force overflew the parade site in an imposing formation, with the fighters spelling out Franco's name.

The following aircraft were captured by the Nationalists or returned by the French government following the Republican collapse: 36 *Nataschas*

The first victory parade passes through the extravagantly-decorated streets of Seville on April 17, 1939.

(R-5), 9 *Rasantes* (R-Z), 9 Grumman Delfins and Goblins, 5 Vultee V-1A, 19 *Katiuskas* (SB-2), 22 *Ratas (I-16), 44 Chatos* (I-15), 20 "Super-*Chatos*" (I-15bis), approximately 50 other military machines and 100 civil aircraft.

The Italians handed all their equipment over to the Spaniards at Tablada on May 21. The Nationalists took charge of the aircraft at the air park. November 9, 1939 saw the creation of an independent Spanish air force, the *Ejercito del Aire.*

Franco bade farewell to the men of the *Legion Condor* with a parade in Madrid on May 22, 1939. It had originally been scheduled for May 20, Hitler's birthday. As part of the send-off the Legion's com-

Triumphal arch ready to receive the Legion Condor in Leon.

The large parade through Leon on May 22, 1939 was led by the band of the Legion Condor.

mander presented a donation of one million *pesetas* to help support the dependents of members of the Spanish Air Force killed during the civil war. Further, the German ambassador to Spain, Eberhard von Stohrer, announced that the ships currently on their way to Vigo to transport the Legionnaires home were bringing 700 tons of food and medicines for the Spanish civilian population.

German war materiel was also left behind in Spain, with the exception of the latest and therefore still secret developments. Responsibility for arranging the terms and manner of compensation fell to Bernhardt's office, the HISMA/ROWAK.

By May 26, the passenger ships lying at anchor at Vigo had embarked the personnel of the *Legion Condor*. The ships left Spanish territorial waters the same day.

Not until the day the returning fleet sailed into Hamburg harbor did the name *Legion Condor* appear in the German press. Right after the fall of Madrid German newspapers published accounts of deeds performed by German volunteers in Spain, but an incomprehensible security complex forbade mentioning the name of the volunteer unit.

In official terminology the German participants in the Spanish Civil War are always called "volunteers"; it is about time that this inaccurate designation was corrected. There is no doubt that those Germans fighting in Spain before the *Legion Condor* was dispatched, or prior to early November 1936, were volunteers. However the rapid buildup of the existing troop contingent and the stipulation that only soldiers of suitable qualifications and character be sent could not be achieved on a volunteer basis alone. A considerable percentage of the Germans who participated in the 3 1/2 year civil war were ordered there. It must be said, however, that most of those affected were quite happy to go, considering the good pay and the opportunities for promotion, as well as the chance to get to know a foreign country.

Among the Legionnaires welcomed in Hamburg by Göring on May 31, 1939 were those who had been released from captivity after the collapse of Republican resistance or handed over to the Nationalists by France. Throughout the war the International Red Cross had worked to bring about the exchange of prisoners, but often it ran into unexpected difficulties. In general the Republican government was only prepared to exchange pilot for pilot. This was a real problem, as only a few Republican fliers were available for exchange. The small numbers of Republican Air Force prisoners was due to the defensive role in which the Republican Air Force found itself after a certain point in the war. As a result Republican aircraft operated mostly over their own territory and pilots who parachuted from their aircraft usually came down behind their own lines. The risk of being captured was much greater for the Nationalist, Italian and German fliers, as they were generally engaged in offensive action over enemy territory. The ratio of captured Republican to Nationalist aircrew was in fact 1:4. It was not uncommon for one side or the other to threaten to execute an important or prominent captive in order to bring about or accelerate an exchange.

Enough has already been written about the mutual practice of looking at prisoners as a negative in-

Bf 109 E-1 fighters of 1. J/88 parked at Leon in preparation for handover to the Spaniards.

The final day on foreign soil. Three Oberleutnante in front of the Jagdgruppe's motor pool, recently handed over to the Spaniards: Hans-Jürgen Ehrig, Alfred von Lojewski and Hubertus von Holtey.

Home to mother! Photographed on deck during the voyage home, from left: Lt. Gustav Rödel, an interpreter, Hptm. Siebelt Reents, Oblt. Wold-Dietrich Wilke.

fluence during a bitter battle. At various times directives were issued to take no prisoners during this or that engagement. Such arrangements are known to have existed on the Nationalist side. A typical example occurred during the retaking of Teruel by Nationalist forces. Enemy troops were shot or bayonetted until dead or incapacitated; attempts to surrender were usually futile and most were ignored. Statements from reliable sources indicate that the soldiers of the Nationalist parties behaved no less bestially than those of the Republicans.

Waiting in Vigo harbor to take the Jagdgruppe home: the passenger steamer Der Deutsche.

Members of the International Brigades stood little chance of being taken alive or of surviving more than a few days after interrogation. The commonly-held view in the Nationalist camp, which saw international brigadists as criminal and corrupt characters serving the hated objectives of world communism, made the members of these units little better than wild animals. The few prisoners from the German or Austrian battalions not left to the Spaniards "for liquidation" disappeared into concentration camps after being returned to Germany.

An official list of casualties suffered by the *Legion Condor* during the war years was compiled in Spain. It lists 298 men killed. Of these 298 dead Germans 173 were killed in action, 97 died as the result of accidents and 28 through illness. Official German sources record the awarding of 315 "Honor Crosses for Surviving Dependents of German Fighters in Spain." This figure includes the survivors of those killed aboard the battlecruiser *Deutschland,* which was not a part of the *Legion Condor.* As far as can be ascertained most of the dead German Legionnaires were returned to Germany and interred there. A brief ceremony was held in Hamburg by the returning troops in honor of their fallen comrades.

Following the initial reception in Hamburg the members of the Legion were transported to the Reich capital, Berlin, where "*Sonderstab Döberitz*" had prepared the barracks at the troop training grounds and a tent camp to accommodate the Legionnaires. Here those just returned from Spain were joined by former Legionnaires of previous years for a few days rest before the ceremonial entry into Berlin and a marchpast in front of Adolf Hitler. Because of a lack of space former officers and officials of the Legion had to be quartered in the Olympic Village (now an infantry school).

The variety of programs offered the men as well as the free use of extra trains laid on by the *Reichsbahn,*

The homeland's first salute at St. Pauli pier.

which allowed them to freely visit Berlin with its theaters, bars, variety shows and points of interest, caused the days leading up to the parade on June 6 to fly by. A total of 14,000 men were assembled for the Berlin parade.

Late on the morning of the last day in the life of the *Legion Condor,* bus after bus delivered the "Legionnaires" and "former Legionnaires" to the Reich capital for the marchpast in front of Hitler, the three commanders of the *Legion Condor* and heads of the military and government. It was an uncomfortable occasion for the Legion's former members, who had been hastily outfitted with khaki-brown uniforms from Reich Labor Service stocks. They had never worn the uniforms before and it was hot June day. Those lining the streets, which had been closed off to allow the columns to form up, were treated to the sight of crowds of itching and scratching Legionnaires. The latter were only too happy that the spectacle was soon to be over.

Finally, the individual blocks of troops, drawn up in ranks of nine, paraded past their senior commanders in Berlin's *Lustgarten.* Although use of the "goose step" had been waived, the Legionnaires nonetheless were soon sweating profusely and many lost their hard-earned decorations during the snappy parade. A special detachment was formed to follow the parade and collect the glittering, and often trampled, crosses.

The "Legion," which had made such a significant contribution in preventing the establishment of a communist enclave in the Mediterranean region, ceased to exist on June 6, 1939. The khaki-brown uniforms went into closets and footlockers, and from then on "Luftwaffe Blue" was the color in which the participants of *Winterübung Hansa* went about their daily duties. There remained only a brief respite of four months until Operation *Ostmarkflug,* the entry into the Second World War.

Three Spanish memorials to fallen members of the Legion Condor.

Main entrance to the quarters at the Döberitz troop training grounds.

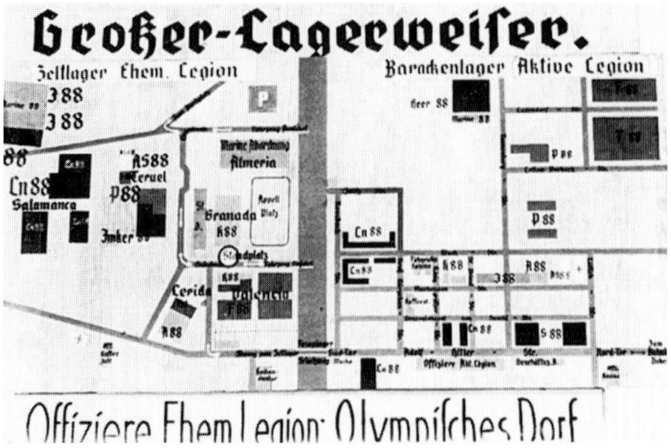

A good look at the map avoided stupid questions to the camp police.

Spartan simplicity, close quarters and well-ventilated closets!

Groups of tents in the camp housing the former Legionaries. With coffee out-of-doors and special rations, the troops would gladly have seen this "summer vacation" go on forever.

Presentation of decorations. Well and good, if only the wait in the blistering heat while everyone had his turn hadn't been so long.

The last Chief-of-Staff of the Legion, Oberstlt. Hans Seidemann, in conversation with Oblt. Bertram. Seidemann still wears the uniform of the Legionnaire, while Bertram is back in his Luftwaffe uniform.

Officers are forbidden to sit! Unfortunately it's impossible to ban sweating in the hot summer sun.

The Legionaries wait in the side streets of the Reich capital for the parade squares to form up.

Mass of personnel at the formation site. The individual march squares were directed to their places using loudspeakers.

June 6, 1939. The parade past senior Wehrmacht and party officials. A chapter in German history has closed.

MERKBLATT

FÜR DEN 6. JUNI 1939

1. Antreten und Meldung in der Marmorgallerie.
   Mütze aufbehalten. Koppel umgeschnallt lassen.
   Aufstellung in Linie zu 2 Gliedern.
   Am rechten Flügel die 3 Befehlshaber der Legion Condor, Admiral Carls, Admiral Boehm Oberst d. G. Warlimont und die Offiziere des Sonderstabs W.

   Dann nebeneinander
   - die spanischen Offiziere
   - die italienischen Offiziere
   - Sonderstab W
   - die Kommandeure und Kommandanten
   - die Offiziere mit Spanienkreuz in Gold mit Brillanten
   - die Offiziere mit Spanienkreuz in Gold
   - die Unteroffiziere mit Spanienkreuz in Gold.

   Innerhalb der einzelnen Blocks nach den Wehrmachtteilen antreten.
   Reihenfolge: Luftwaffe, Heer, Kriegsmarine.
   Innerhalb der Wehrmachtteile dem Dienstalter nach aufstellen.

2. Der Führer betritt die Gallerie von der Mitte der Nordseite der Gallerie.

3. General der Flieger Sperrle meldet dem Führer. Dabei grüßen alle Generale und Admirale, während alle anderen Offiziere und Unteroffiziere in Grundstellung bleiben und Augen rechts bzw. links nehmen.

4. Der Führer geht die Front vom rechten Flügel aus ab. Er wird begleitet von den Oberbefehlshabern der 3 Wehrmachtteile, Generaloberst Keitel und Generaloberst Milch. Die Befehlshaber der Legion Condor und Oberst d. G. Warlimont schließen sich an.

5. Nachdem der Führer die Front abgeschritten hat, begibt er sich in sein Arbeitszimmer. Es folgen ihm alle deutschen und ausländischen Generale und Admirale. Die anderen angetretenen Offiziere und Unteroffiziere begeben sich sofort in den Mosaiksaal und Speisesaal und verteilen sich dort auf die Tische. Die auf der Rückseite namentlich aufgeführten Offiziere und Unteroffiziere nehmen an den numerierten Tischen Platz. Es bleiben alle Herren an ihren Stühlen stehen bis der Führer den Marmorsaal betreten und sich gesetzt hat.

6. Der Führer wird zuerst an einem Tisch in dem Mosaiksaal, dann an einem Tisch im Speisesaal Platz nehmen. Wenn er den Speisesaal betritt, haben sich alle Herren von ihren Plätzen zu erheben.

7. Nach dem Essen kann zwanglos herumgegangen werden.

8. Das Rauchen ist in sämtlichen Räumen der Reichskanzlei nicht gestattet, auch nicht im Ehrenhof und Garten.

Instructional leaflet for participants in the Führer reception on June 6, 1939.

SUMMARY

The soldiers of the *Legion Condor* returned to their parent units in Germany, bursting with pride over their achievements, their skill and their superior weapons. Their experiences were soon to have a profound effect on the early campaigns of the Second World War.

Leading German fighter pilots — first Lützow, then Harder and Schlichting, and finally Mölders —had perfected the operation of fighters in *Schwarm* formation. This formation proved so superior to other tactical formations that it was later adopted by the enemy out of necessity. In the wide-open battle formation used by German fighters, the individual *Rotten*, *Schwärme* and *Staffeln* flew with increased lateral and vertical spacing compared to the formations used by other air forces, allowing them to cover a great deal of airspace. Individual pilots had to concern themselves less with maintaining formation and could thus concentrate on the enemy. The loose formation was not as pleasing to the eye, but it provided the aircraft within the formation with a better view. Even the smallest fighting unit, the *Rotte*, had great freedom of decision, without which the grouping of *Rotten* and *Schwärme* to suit the existing situation in the air would not have been possible. The Spaniards and Italians often fought in close formations of twenty or thirty aircraft. In such formations the aircraft frequently got in one another's way or lost contact when the formation was broken up.

It was the fighting in Spain, influenced somewhat by the superior qualities of the Bf 109, that determined the typical mode of operation of the German fighter pilot: the seeking of a height advantage and the tendency to escape attack by diving and then regaining altitude. The ideal was the surprise attack and kill, if possible from out of the sun. The fighters approached to firing range unnoticed in the smallest formation, element leader and wingman; the leader opened fire from close range, covered by his wingman. This tactic was developed to take advantage of the excellent speed and diving ability of the Bf 109 as well to minimize the negative effects of its somewhat poorer turning characteristics. Under these tactical restrictions the requirements for a good fighter pilot were good eyes, accurate shooting and calm nerves, so as not to open fire too soon. During the course of the war most fighter pilots developed their own fighting style to suit the situation in the air, the enemy and their own natures.

Some of the most valuable tactical experience gained in Spain was the development of close-support operations, in which Harro Harder, Adolf Galland, Pitcairn and d'Elsa played leading roles. Continuous, overlapping operations in *Kette* and *Schwarm* strength were developed to a peak of perfection. The Chief-of-Staff of the *Legion Condor*, Wolfram von Richthofen, was the spiritual mentor of this development. Close-support missions were so closely coordinated with the ground forces, that by the time the low-level attack was over the advancing infantry were within hand grenade range of the enemy position. The close-support units even employed a primitive form of napalm bomb, whereby drop tanks coupled with high-explosive or incendiary bombs were dropped on enemy trenches. Undoubtedly the lessons learned by German fighter pilots in three years of war Spain placed them far ahead of their later opponents in the Second World War. All the tactical lessons they had learned there in combat, whether relating to fighter sweeps (*freie Jagd*), the protection of bombers (close escort and sweeps ahead of the bombers), the escorting of reconnaissance aircraft, intercepting enemy bombers, conduct while under anti-aircraft fire, defensive patrols, alert and cockpit readiness, engaging enemy fighter escorts, formation flying, rapid transfers, armament, loading, and so on, were incorporated into training manuals. It was to take the Allies some years and a great deal of blood to make up for this tactical advantage.

Lest one be blinded by all this external brilliance, it should be stated that it was in Spain that the seeds were sown of a development which was to have such fateful consequences from 1943 on, during the bitter years of the Allied bombing offensive against Germany. In its evaluation and planning the Luftwaffe clearly placed the fighter arm behind the types of weapons which had proved the decisive tactical weapons in the Spanish battles of movement: the close-support aircraft, the Stukas, the fast bombers, the flak. Simply put, fighters were regarded as an elegant pastime, a sort of romantic luxury.

It had been shown in Spain that no bomber unit, even one equipped with relatively fast machines by the standards of the day, faster in fact than some of the opposing fighters, could survive without fighter cover in an area where enemy fighters were operating. As a result of this realization the fighter arm was expanded, but its role was defined as an escort weapon for bomber and Stuka units. The formation of a defensive fighter arm to protect cities and industry was considered superfluous, as this had been a minor consideration in the Spanish Civil War. This was to prove a bitter mistake.

In Germany many names which were later to become famous, such as Galland, Lützow, Oesau, Mölders and others, were heard for the first time.

The number of combat sorties flown by the fighter pilots in a relatively brief time was astonishingly high; Harder 297, Galland 280, Pingel 150 and Oesau 130, for example. This amassing of experience in combat was of great significance. By our estimates about 125 officers and 280 NCOs (with the rank of *Feldwebel* or *Unteroffizier*) had been with the fighter arm in Spain. Rightly so, foreign publications frequently cite this fact in explaining the Luftwaffe's success during the early years of the Second World War. Thirty-nine fighter pilots with experience in Spain were awarded the Knight's Cross or other high decoration during World War Two (out of a total of 600 Knight's Crosses awarded to fighter pilots).

J/88 scored a total of 314 confirmed air victories and a further 70 probable, but unconfirmed kills. The Legion's flak battalion was credited with 61 enemy aircraft shot down. In comparison Italian fighters claimed 903 kills, the Spanish Nationalists 294.

Only during the opening and closing phases of the civil war were the bomber units given the opportunity to perform in a strategic role. Only then, when the front was stationary while the combatants regained their breath, could they be used as intended. Industrial centers in the enemy rear, lines of communication, railway stations, power plants and other significant targets whose destruction would reduce the enemy's war-making potential, were on the list of targets.

However, as soon as another offensive "got rolling" such strategic targets lost their priority, were simply pushed aside, because progress on the ground depended to a large degree on support from the air. In this way the bombers became "flying artillery" in the truest sense of the word, but were taken away from their true role. The strategic attacks that were carried out were usually spur-of-the-moment affairs, made against critical installations located by reconnaissance aircraft just a short time before. Only a few operations, such as *Neptun*, the attacks on Gijon or the bombing of the shipping ports on the Mediterranean coast, revealed any planned, strategic thinking.

As a rule the crews of the *Kampfstaffeln* knew what lay before them day after day when an offensive was under way: bomb forward positions!

The overvaluation of the effective support provided the ground forces was to run through the history of the German bomber force during the Second World War like a red thread, forcing strategic bomber planning into the background.

With the dispatch of the *Jolanthe-Kette* to Spain the still-youthful dive-bomber arm was given an opportunity to test and develop its new techniques in action. There was no shortage of pinpoint targets, especially at the time of the arrival of the three Ju 87 A dive-bombers. Bridges over the Ebro, foot-bridges, ferry landings, railway installations, and so on, challenged the ambition of the Stuka pilots. The fact that bombing accuracy was at first poor was not due to any lack of skill on the part of the crews, rather to the fact that Stuka flying was still in its infancy. A whole series of improvements, from bombsights to release mechanisms, was required before the Ju 87 could be considered as ready for operational use.

Operating conditions in Spain were ideal for the Stukas. Concentrations of anti-aircraft guns, which were the rule during World War Two, scarcely hindered the diving *"Stupidos."* Once out of the target area there was little to fear from anti-aircraft fire. But more than anything else it was the strong fighter escort always provided the dive-bombers which kept enemy fighters at bay and allowed them to reach their targets unmolested. One can say without exaggeration that the few Stuka crews in Spain did everything they could to pass on to their parent units the lessons they had learned in Spain. The success enjoyed by the Stuka units during the first two years of the war was in no small measure based on the evaluation of the missions flown in Spain.

The limiting of the Legion's reconnaissance component to a single *Staffel* suggests that there was little to be learned from "live" reconnaissance missions. In spite of limitations on the manufacture of aircraft, the years following the First World War did not see Germany fall behind the world standard in aerial reconnaissance. On the contrary, it can be shown that in camera and developing technology Germany was somewhat ahead of the rest of the world.

German reconnaissance aircraft in Spain did nothing different than when they were on maneuvers in the Reich. They flew photo reconnaissance sorties and were occupied to a lesser extent with visual reconnaissance and artillery spotting. In the Do 17 long-range reconnaissance aircraft the crews found an eminently fast aircraft, which could easily outrun enemy fighters in a dive.

The He 45 and Hs 126 battlefield reconnaissance aircraft were usually in action where no fighter opposition was expected. As well they flew at altitudes at which they could outmaneuver attacking fighters. High-speed fighters were generally reluctant to pursue the slow, maneuverable tactical reconnaissance aircraft at low altitude due to the danger of stalling and crashing.

The naval aviators of AS/88 were out of their element in Spain. Cooperation with naval units was scarcely possible, as these were under close scrutiny. Very soon the *Staffel* found itself acting as a sort of auxiliary bomber unit, which was forced to limit its targets to the immediate coastal areas due to the type of equipment in use (floatplanes). Experience gained in such operations was of little use to the parent units in Germany. Naval aviation was simply conceived differently, and never again during the 5 Ī years of the Second World War did it encounter the primary tasks faced by AS/88 in Spain. Therefore, in spite of good success, there can be little question of the unit having learned any new lessons or gained any useful experience.

In contrast the Spanish Civil War presented the

light and heavy flak batteries of F/88 with an outstanding opportunity to test new methods of employing their guns, which would never have been tried during maneuvers. Preeminent among these, in addition to the usual engagement of aerial targets, for the first time in wartime conditions, was their use against surface targets. Once the accuracy and high rate of fire of the light and heavy guns had been demonstrated in action several times, an offensive thrust without flak support was almost inconceivable. Those gunners who failed to learn the ins and outs of rapid changes of position in Spain were almost certain never to learn. The flak units, most of which were based in Germany, learned firsthand the importance of a certain degree of mobility.

Rapid acquisition of aerial targets and range-finding, and the even faster transmission of firing data to the guns were basic requirements if enemy aircraft were to be engaged successfully. At the low altitudes commonly used in Spain, enemy bombers often passed out of a battery's effective range very quickly. Experience in cooperation between range-finding and gun sections was thus the most valuable lesson brought home from Spain by the flak artillery.

The Luftwaffe signals units in Spain were given the difficult task of establishing a reliable signals net with the most primitive means. Unique regional and provincial conditions made demands of the signals personnel which those in Germany could not have imagined. That they nevertheless managed to carry out the assignments given them speaks volumes for the improvisational skills of these soldiers.

Those most effected by conditions in Spain were undoubtedly the telephone companies; the "string pullers" learned many tricks which were to stand them in good stead in the coming campaigns.

The lessons learned by the radio and air traffic control companies were assembled and incorporated in improved, modernized service manuals. Functioning under operational conditions the light and heavy radio sections improved their air-ground and ground-ground communications skills considerably. It was an opportunity for the technical devices to prove themselves — to separate the wheat from the chaff, as it were — and they did so thoroughly. Those devices which failed to stand the test disappeared from the equipment parks of the signals units or reappeared later in modified and significantly improved form.

The ground observer companies worked out new procedures for cooperation between the observation posts in the front lines and headquarters in the rear, using 100-watt transmitters. Following many initial difficulties (sometimes with dire consequences) the importance of the aircraft recognition service was acknowledged. Aircraft spotting received official promotion in Germany and in the later war years grew to become virtually a national sport.

In general it may be stated that the relatively brief, nine month exchange of *Legion Condor* personnel gave a relatively large cadre of Luftwaffe personnel the chance to expand their military knowledge, gain confidence in their weapons and build confidence in themselves. The impact this had on the world war which was to begin in autumn 1939 cannot be overestimated.

Name Index

Appendix

Appendix A
Staffel Emblems of the Air Units

Emblem of A/88 on a Do 17 F

Emblem of A/88 on a Do 17 P

AS/88's emblem on one of the unit's He 59s

The emblem of 1. J/88, the "Marabu" Staffel, equipped with He 51s under Harro Harder.

1. J/88 "Holzauge" Staffel, with Bf 109s under Siebelt Reents.

2. J/88 "Zylinder" Staffel. This was formerly the emblem of 4. J/88 under Herwig Knüppel.

The emblem of 3. J/88 "Mickymaus" Staffel on one of the unit's He 51s.

A Bf 109 of 3. J/88 wearing the "Mickymaus" emblem.

4. J/88 "Pik-As" Staffel with He 51s under Eberhard d'Elsa.

1. K/88, the "Kometen" Staffel.

Early version of 2. K/88's Staffel emblem on a Ju 52.

The definitive form on an He 111 of 2. K/88.

The emblem of 3. K/88, worn by Ju 52s and He 111s.

4. K/88 emblem as worn by the unit's He 111s. For a brief period this was the emblem of VB/88.

The emblem worn by the Hs 123s of Stukakette/88.

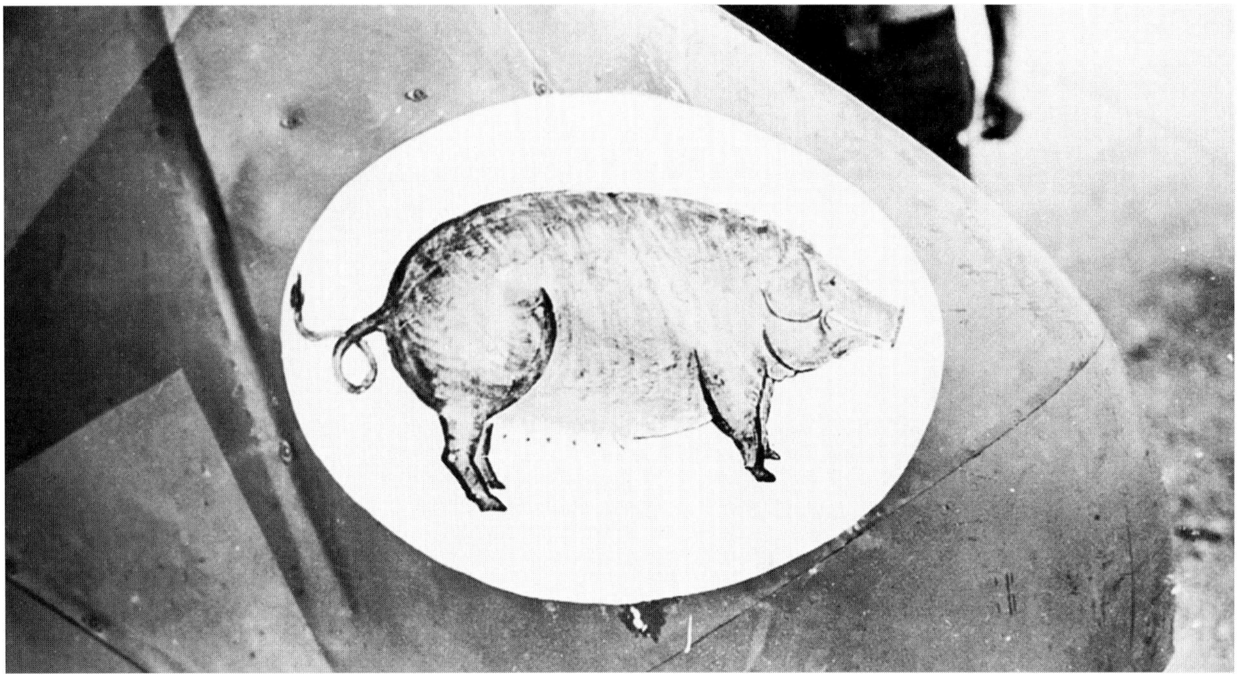

The emblem of the "Jolanthe" Stukakette, which for a time was attached to Jagdruppe 88 as 5 Staffel.

Appendix B

Unit Commanders of the Legion Condor, as of March 1939

Commander of the Legion Condor	Gen.Maj. von Richthofen
Chief-of-Staff	Oberstlt. Seidemann
A/88 Staffelkap.	Maj. Matussek
AS/88 Staffelkap.	Hptm. Smidt
J/88 Gruppenkdr.	Hptm. Grabmann
1. J/88	Hptm. Reents
2. J/88	Oblt. von Lojewski
3. J/88	Oblt. von Bonin
K/88 Gruppenkdr.	Maj. Nielsen
1. K/88	Hptm. Püttmann
2. K/88	Hptm. von Buttlar-Brandenfels
3. K/88	Hptm. Winkler
Stuka K/88	Oblt. Bohne
F/88 Battalion CO	Maj. Kretschmann
1. F/88 (88mm)	Hptm. Bundt
2. F/88 (88mm)	Hptm. Reuter
3. F/88 (88mm)	Hptm. von Jablonski
4. F/88 (20mm)	Hptm. Vogel
5. F/88 (20mm)	Oblt. Wehla
6. F/88 (Searchlight)	Oblt. Hübener
7. F/88 (Munitions Column)	Lt. Jacobi
8. F/88 (88mm)	Lt. Hacker
Ln/88 Battalion CO	Maj. Bauerschäfer
1. Ln/88 (Telephone)	Hptm. Jakisch
2. Ln/88 (Radio)	Oblt. Walkhoff
3. Ln/88 (Ground Observation)	Hptm. Schluckebier
4. Ln/88 (ATC)	Oblt. Liebelt

Appendix C

Composition of J/88

Commander	von Merhart	3.11.1936 - 18 7 1937
	Handrick	18 7 1937 - 10.9.1938
	Grabmann	10.9.1938 - end of war
	Brustellin	planned successor
1 Staffel	Palm	3.11.1936 - 6.4.1937
	Harder	6.4.1937 - 18.12.1937
	Schellmann	19.12.1937 - 2.9.1938
	Reents	2.9.1938 - end of war
2 Staffel	Lehmann	3.11.1936 - 19.3.1937
	Lützow	19.3.1937 - 6.9.1937
	Schlichting	6.9.1937 - 28.5.1938
	Kroeck	28.5.1938 - 31.10.1938
	von Lojewski	1.11.1938 - end of war
3 Staffel	Roth	3.11.1936 - 4.1937
	Pitcairn	4.1937 - 26.7.1937
	Galland	27.7.1937 - 24.5.1938
	Mölders	24.5.1938 - 5.12.1938
	von Bonin	5.12.1938 - end of war
4 Staffel	Eberhardt	6.8.1936 - 13.11.1936
	Knüppel	13.11.1936 - 1.3.1937
	Kienzle	1.3.1937 - disbanded March 1937
4 Staffel	reformed	
	d'Elsa	2.11.1937 - 17.6.1938
	disbanded	

Appendix D

Fuselage Codes of the Nationalist Air Forces

For purposes of recording by the air park individual aircraft types (and to a lesser degree whole classes of aircraft) were assigned fuselage codes. This code consisted of a one- or two-digit number, which as a rule was painted on both sides of the fuselage in front of the nationality marking, a solid black disc. A second number behind the disc indicated the aircraft's numerical position within the sequence for that type.

for example	2 • 79	2 = code for the He 51 79 = the 79th He 51
or	24 • 7	24 = code for the Hs 123 7 = the 7th Hs 123

During the early stages of the civil war the entire code was frequently placed behind the nationality marking; in these cases the two number groups were separated by a horizontal bar.

for example • 2-79 or • 24-7

Type Code

Fighters

1	•	Nieuport 52, from 1939 Fiat G-50
2	•	Heinkel He 51
3	•	Fiat C.R.32 *Chirri*
4	•	PWS-10
5	•	Heinkel He 112
6	•	Messerschmitt Bf 109
7	•	Romeo Ro-41
8	•	Heinkel He 112 V 8 and I-15 *Chato*
9	•	Arado Ar 68 E

Close-support and Low-altitude Attack Aircraft

10	•	Breguet Br. 19
11	•	Heinkel He 46 *Pava*
12	•	Romeo Ro-37
13	•	
14	•	Heinkel He 70 *Rayo*
15	•	Heinkel He 45 *Pavo*
16	•	Breda Ba-65
17	•	Aero 101 *Oca*, *Praga*, *Papagayo*
18	•	Caproni Ca-310 *Capronchino*, Vultee V-1A
19	•	Henschel Hs 126 *Super-Pava*

Bombers

20	•	Fokker F VII, Fokker F XII
21	•	Savoia-Marchetti S.M.81
22	•	Junkers Ju 52
23	•	Fiat BR-20
24	•	Henschel Hs 123 *Angelito*
25	•	Heinkel He 111
26	•	Junkers Ju 86 D
27	•	Do 17 *Bacalao*
28	•	Savoia-Marchetti S.M.79
29	•	Junkers Ju 87 *Stupido*, Stuka

Sport Aircraft

30	•	various single-engined sport aircraft: among others the Farman F 190, Monocoupe 90 A, Miles M 3 Falcon, Klemm Kl 32aXIV
31	•	various twin-engined sport aircraft: among others the G.A. ST-12 Monospar
32	•	Caproni AP-1 *Apio*
33	•	Bücker Bü 131 *Jungmann*
34	•	Breda Ba-28
35	•	Bücker Bü 133 *Jungmeister*
36	•	Arado Ar 66 C
37	•	
38	•	Gotha Go 145

Transport Aircraft

40	•	de Havilland Dragon Rapide
41	•	Airspeed Envoy
42	•	various multi-engined transport aircraft: among others the Douglas DC-2, Lockheed Electra
43	•	various single-engined transport aircraft: among others the Junkers W 34 hi, Vultee V-1A
44	•	Messerschmitt Bf 108 *Taifun*
45	•	Fokker F VII, Fokker F XII
46	•	Fieseler Fi 156 *Ciguena*
47	•	Fleetster

Seaplanes

50	•	Macchi M-41
60	•	Heinkel He 60
61	•	Savoia-Marchetti S.M.62
62	•	Cant Z-501
63	•	Fairchild
64	•	Arado Ar 95
70	•	Dornier *Wal*
71	•	Heinkel He 59 *Zapatones*
72	•	Junkers Ju 52/3m W
73	•	Cant Z-506

Captured enemy aircraft were given a number-letter combination by the Nationalists:

1W	•	I-16 *Rata*, *Mosca*
2W	•	I-15bis *Super-Chato*
3W	•	Letov S 231
4W	•	Hawker Fury
5W	•	Grumman Delfin, Goblin
16W	•	R-Z *Rasante*
17W	•	R-5 *Natascha*
20W	•	SB-2 *Katiuska*

Appendix E

Fuselage Codes of the Republican Air Forces

In contrast to the Nationalists, the Republicans chose combinations of letters as fuselage codes for their aircraft. The type code was followed by a horizontal bar and a number indicating the aircraft's number within that series.

for example	CA - 12	CA = code for the I-15 *Chato* 12 = the 12th I-15
or	BK - 46	BK = code for the SB-2 *Katiuska* 46 = the 46th SB-2

Close-support Aircraft

AD – Grumman Delfin, Goblin

Bombers

BB – Bloch MB-210
BF – Fokker F XVIII
BK – SB-2 *Katiuska*
BP – Potez 54
BV – Vultee V-1A

Fighters

CA – I-15 *Chato*
CC – I-15bis *Super-Chato*
CD – Dewoitine D 371
CE – Dewoitine D 500
CF – Fokker D 21
CL – Letov S 231
CM – Nieuport 52, I-16 *Rata*, *Mosca*
CS – Seversky P-35
CW – Dewoitine D 510

Training Aircraft

EA – Caudron C-600
EC – SAAB-10
EE – Hispano-Suiza E-30
EF – Hispano-Suiza E-34
EG – Gil-Pazo GP-1
EJ – Koolhoven FK 51
EK – Koolhoven FK 51bis
EL – Caudron C-272
EM – de Havilland D.H. 60
EN – Miles M-3, Miles M-5
EP – de Havilland D.H. 82
EQ – Monocoupe 90 A
ER – Romano R-82
EU – Morane-Saulnier MS-60, MS-140, MS-230
EW – Focke-Wulf FW 56
EX – Bücker Bü 133
EY – I-16 UTI
EZ – Hanriot H-182

Captured Aircraft

FF – Fiat C.R.32
FH – Heinkel He 111
FM – Messerschmitt Bf 109
FS – Savoia-Marchetti S.M.81

Seaplanes

HD – Dornier *Wal*
HM – Macchi M-18
HS – Savoia-Marchetti S.M.62
HV – Vickers Vildebeest

Light Bombers and Liaison Aircraft

LA – Airspeed Envoy
LB – Bellanca 28-70
LD – de Havilland D.H. 84 Dragon
LF – Fokker C-X
LG – Gourdou-Leseurre 633
LL – Aero 101
LN – R-5 *Natascha*
LR – de Havilland D.H. 89 Dragon Rapide
LY – de havilland D.H. 90 Dragonfly

Ambulance Aircraft

SF – Farman F-402
SM – Monospar ST-25 (General Aircraft)

Transport Aircraft

TA – Avia 51
TC – Caudron C-445
TD – Douglas DC-2
TF – Farman F-402
TG – Northrop Gamma
TH – de Havilland D.H. 87 B
TK – Lockheed Orion
TL – Latecoére 28
TM – General Aircraft ST-25 Monospar
TN – Northrop Delta
TP – Spartan Executive
TS – Stinson Reliant
TV – Breguet 470 T *Vulgur*

Amphibious Aircraft

XA – Fairchild 91

Appendix F - German Aircraft Types in Spain

The following list is devoted exclusively to German aircraft delivered to Spain during the Spanish Civil War.

Arado Ar 68 E
Fuselage code: 9 •
Single-seat fighter
Power plant: 1 x Jumo 210 B, 640 HP
Wingspan: 11 m Length: 9.67 m
Max. speed: 335 kph at 2,600 m
Armament: 2 fixed MG 17
1 x 5 C 10 IX bomb magazine for 5 x 10kg bombs

Several in action as twilight fighters 1937/38, flown by German as well as Spanish pilots. Three machines delivered.

Arado Ar 95 W
Fuselage code: 64 •
Multi-purpose floatplane, crew of 3
Power plant: 1 x BMW 132 Dc, 880 HP
Wingspan: 12.5 m Length: 11.1 m
Max. speed: 300 kph at 3,000 m
Armament: 1 fixed MG 17, 1 flexibly-mounted MG 15, 1 LTF 5 torpedo or 250kg bomb beneath fuselage and 6 x 50kg bombs under wings

A single example sent to AS/88 late 1938. Did not see action, purely for unit testing.

Dornier Do 17 E
Fuselage code: 27 •
High-speed bomber, crew of 3
Power plants: 2 x BMW VI/Series 9, 750 HP each
Wingspan: 18 m Length: 16.25 m
Max. speed: 315 kph at 4,000 m
Armament: 2 flexibly-mounted MG 15, 1 semi-rigid MG 15
Bombload: 750 kg

Initial deliveries early 1937 to VB/88. Handed over to A/88 when K/88 fully equipped with He 111. Ineffective bomber due to limited bombload. In action until 1939.

Dornier Do 17 F
Fuselage code: 27 •
High-speed bomber, crew of 3
Power plants: 2 x BMW VI/Series 9, 750 HP each
Wingspan: 18 m Length: 16.25 m
Max. speed: 320 kph at 4,000 m
Armament: 2 flexibly-mounted MG 15, photographic equipment

This type was delivered to A/88 in larger numbers, where it was used as a long-range reconnaissance aircraft. In action from early 1937 until the end of the war in 1939. Well-suited to its role because of its good performance.

Dornier Do 17 P
Fuselage code: 27 •
Long-range reconnaissance aircraft, crew of 3
Power plants: 2 x BMW 132/Series 1, 865 HP each
Wingspan: 18 m   Length: 16.25 m
Max. speed: 400 kph at 4,000 m
Armament: two flexibly-mounted MG 15, 1 semi-rigid MG 15 photographic equipment and four ETC 50/VIII C bomb racks under fuselage for parachute flares and photo flashbombs

A few examples arrived in Spain in autumn 1938, assigned to A/88. The Legion's fastest reconnaissance aircraft and the one best suited to night operations.

Fieseler Fi 156 A
Fuselage code: 46 •
Headquarters communications and courier aircraft, crew of 2
Power plant: 1 x Argus As 10C, 240 HP
Wingspan: 14.25 m   Length: 9.61 m
Max. speed: 175 kph at 1,000 m
Armament: none

Six machines delivered to Spain throughout 1938. Operated by S/88 and P/88. First employment of legendary *Storch*. Extremely versatile aircraft.

Heinkel He 45
Fuselage code: 15 •
Medium-range reconnaissance aircraft, crew of 2
Power plant: 1 x BMW VI U, 750 HP
Wingspan: 11.5 m   Length: 10 m
Max. speed: 250 kph at 2,000 m
Armament: 1 fixed MG 17, 1 flexibly-mounted MG 15, photographic equipment and 300 kg bombload

First deliveries to Spain to A/88 late 1936. Some later passed on to Nationalist squadrons. Stable reconnaissance aircraft for use at medium altitudes. In action until end of war.

Heinkel He 46 C
Fuselage code: 11 •
Short-range reconnaissance aircraft, crew of 2
Power plant: 1 x SAM 22 B, 650 HP
Wingspan: 14 m   Length: 9.46 m
Max. speed: 260 kph at 800 m
Armament: 1 flexibly-mounted MG 15, photographic equipment or 2 x 6 C 10 IX magazines for 12 x 10 kg bombs

Delivered in numbers beginning in October 1936. As the reconnaissance units in the Reich were re-equipping with the E version, the older C type was sent to Spain. Rather vulnerable, unstable flight characteristics, poor photographic platform. All aircraft were handed over to Nationalist squadrons.

Heinkel He 50 G
Fuselage code: ?
Dive-bomber, crew of two
Power plant: 1 x SAM 22 B, 650 HP
Wingspan: 11.5 m Length: 9.76 m
Max. speed: 230 kph at 2,000 m
Armament: 1 fixed MG 17, 1 flexibly-mounted MG 15, 2 PVC 250 bomb racks for two 250 kg bombs

Single example sent to Spain in October 1936. Tested at Seville-Tablada. Did not see action.

Heinkel He 51 B
Fuselage code: 2 •
Single-seat fighter aircraft
Power plant: 1 x BMW VI 7,3Z, 750 HP
Wingspan: 11 m Length: 8.44 m
Max. speed: 310 kph at 4,000 m
Armament: 2 fixed MG 17, 1 Elvemag 6 C 10 IX for 6 x 10 kg bombs.

First German fighter aircraft delivered to Spain. 131 delivered. Initially equal to enemy types. With the appearance of I-15 and I-16, especially the latter, it became hopelessly inferior. From then on aircraft used as close-support and low-altitude attack aircraft. Employed by German and Spanish units.

Heinkel He 59 B
Fuselage code: 71 •
Multi-purpose floatplane, crew of 4
Power plants: 2 x BMW VI U 6.0 Z, 660 HP each
Wingspan: 23.7 m Length: 17.4 m
Max. speed: 215 kph at 1,000 m
Armament: standard: 3 flexibly-mounted MG 15, in Spain: 2 flexibly-mounted MG 15, 1 flexibly-mounted Rheinmetall 20mm cannon

Air released weapons: 4 x 5 C 50 Vc magazines in fuselage for 20 x 50kg bombs, or 4 x PVC 503 racks under fuselage for 4 x 250kg bombs or 2 x 500kg bombs or 1 x LMA 1,000kg mine or 3 x S 200/V smoke devices, or 1 x PVM 1003 under fuselage for 1 x 1,000kg LMB ground mine or one rack for aerial torpedo up to 1,000 kg

Initial equipment of AS/88. Replacements delivered throughout war, total number approx. 15. Used mostly as coastal bomber although not designed for bombing role. The aircraft proved useful in its new role in spite of its inadequate performance.

Heinkel He 60 E
Fuselage code: 60 •
Multi-purpose floatplane, crew of 2
Power plant: 1 x BMW VI U/Series 8, 660 HP
Wingspan: 13.5 m Length: 11.63 m
Max. speed: 225 kph at 1,500 m
Armament: 1 fixed MG 17, 1 flexibly-mounted MG 15, 2 x 6 C 10 IX magazines for 12 x 10kg bombs or 1 x SN 40 smoke device in float installation

8 aircraft delivered. Used as maritime reconnaissance aircraft and light bombers. Not known to have participated in any notable actions.

Heinkel He 70 E/F
Fuselage code: 14 •
Multi-purpose aircraft, crew of 3
Wingspan: 14.87 m Length: 11.67 m
Max. speed: 350 kph at 2,000 m
Armament: 1 flexibly-mounted MG 15. Photographic equipment or 3 Elvemag (double) in fuselage for 6 x 50kg bombs

F version with photo equipment saw little use in Spain. Most were reequipped as E versions (light bomber). More of a high-speed nuisance aircraft than an effective bomber.

Heinkel He 111 B
Fuselage code: 25 •
Medium bomber, crew of 4
Power plants: 2 x DB 600 C, 880 HP each
Wingspan: 22.5 meters Length: 17.57 m
Max. speed: 375 kph at 4,000 m
Armament: 3 flexibly-mounted MG 15, 4 ESAC 250/IX for 4 x 250kg bombs

Sent to Spain as replacement for Ju 52. First deliveries to VB/88 in February 1937. Significant advantages compared to Ju 52 due to its higher speed and better defensive armament. Flew on with K/88 alongside later versions until the end of 1938.

Heinkel He 111 E
Fuselage code: 25 •
Medium bomber, crew of 4
Power plants: 2 x Jumo 211 A, 1,100 HP each
Wingspan: 22.5 m Length: 17.57 m
Max. speed: 395 kph at 4,000 m
Armament: 3 flexibly-mounted MG 15, 8 ESAC 250/IX for 8 x 250kg bombs

Improved performance and double the bombload of the B version. Significantly superior to enemy types. Spanish crews also trained on the aircraft. E-1 and E-3 versions in use with K/88 until March 1939.

Heinkel He 112 V
V 3
Fuselage code:5 • 1
Power plant: 1 x Jumo 210 B, 680 HP
Armament: 1 x 20mm engine-mounted cannon

V 9
Fuselage code: 8 • 2
Power plant: 1 x Jumo 210 Ea, 680 HP
Armament: 2 x MG 17 in fuselage, 2 MG FF in wings.

Two prototypes. V 4 delivered to VJ/88 at Tablada in November. Test flown by *Oblt.* Radusch; flown operationally by Radusch, Balthasar, Schultz. Written off in forced landing July 19, 1937. V 9 arrived in Spain April 1938, flown by Harro Harder.

Heinkel He 112 B-0
Fuselage code: 5 •
Single-seat fighter
Power plant: 1 x Jumo 210 Ea, 680 HP
Wingspan: 9.1 m   Length: 9.3 m
Max. speed: 410 kph at 4,700 m
Armament: 2 x MG 17 in fuselage, 2 x MG FF in wings

17 B-0 series aircraft delivered to Spain in November 1938. Equipped Spanish squadron under Garcia Pardo. No discernable advantages over Bf 109.

Henschel Hs 123 A
Fuselage code: 24 •
Single-seat dive-bomber
Power plant: BMW 132 A/Series 3, 632 HP
Wingspan: 10.5 m   Length: 8.61 m
Max. speed: 290 kph at 2,000 m
Armament: 2 fixed MG 17, 4 ETC 50/VIIIb under wings for 4 x 50kg bombs and 1 x 10 C 10 IX magazine in fuselage for 10 x 10kg bombs.

Small series (16 aircraft?) delivered to Spain. Used in action as dive-bomber and low-altitude attack aircraft. Flown by Spanish, and to a lesser extent German, pilots.

Henschel Hs 126 A
Fuselage code: 19 •
Short-range reconnaissance aircraft, crew of 2
Power plant: 1 x Bramo 323 Q/Series 2, 820 HP
Wingspan: 14.5 m Length: 10.87 m
Max. speed: 320 kph AT 2,000 m
Armament: 1 fixed MG 17, 1 flexibly-mounted Mg 15, photographic equipment or pylon on port landing gear leg for 1 x 50kg bomb or 1 x S 200/V smoke device

Six examples sent to Spain in October 1938. Used for battlefield reconnaissance, photo reconnaissance, artillery spotting. During the final phase of the civil war replaced A/88's old He 45s.

Junkers W 34 hi
Fuselage code: 43 •
Cargo and transport aircraft, crew of 2
Power plant: 1 x BMW 132 A, 660 HP
Wingspan: 18.48 m Length: 10.27 m
Max. speed: 260 kph at 1,000 m
Armament: none

Small number of aircraft used to transport personnel and material between individual *Staffeln* and headquarters of the *Legion Condor* in Spain.

Junkers Ju 52/3mg3e, /3mg4e
Fuselage code: 22 •
Improvised bomber, crew of 3
Power plants: 3 x BMW 132 A/Series 3, 660 HP each
Wingspan: 29.25 m Length: 18.9 m
Max. speed: 275 kph at 1,000 m
Armament: 2 flexibly-mounted MG 15, 3 x DSAC 250/VIII double magazines in fuselage for 6 x 250kg bombs

This trimotor, which in 1936 was still in wide use as a bomber by units of the Luftwaffe, was delivered to Spain in large numbers. By removing the bomb magazines the machine could be converted into a troop transport (Tetuan to the mainland), in which role it could carry up to 40 men. It was less suitable as a bomber, being too slow and poorly armed. In addition to the improvised bombers, the 3mg3e, which was strictly a personnel transport version) also reached Spain. The 3mg4e differed in having a reinforced undercarriage and higher all-up weight (10,000 kg) compared to the 3mg3e (9,500 kg). About 120 aircraft were delivered.

Junkers Ju 86 D
Fuselage code: 26 •
Medium bomber, crew of 4
Power plants: 2 x Jumo 205 C, 600 HP each
Wingspan: 22.5 m Length: 17.86 m
Max. speed: 320 kph at 3,000 m
Armament: 3 flexibly-mounted MG 15, 4 x ESAC 250/IX in fuselage for 4 x 250kg bombs

Four of these aircraft were sent to Spain in early 1937. Served with VB/88 for a short time before being handed over to the Nationalists. The diesel engines of the Ju 86 were trouble-prone, severely limiting the aircraft's worth as a bomber. No further deliveries.

Junkers Ju 87 A
Fuselage code: 29 •
Two-seat dive-bomber
Power plant: 1 x Jumo 210D, 640 HP
Wingspan: 13.8 m Length: 10.8 m
Max. speed: 320 kph at 3,700 m
Armament: 1 fixed MG 17, 1 flexibly-mounted MG 15, 1 x ETC 500/IX under fuselage for 1 x 500kg bomb

The Stuka's role in Spain was primarily to evaluate dive-bombing techniques. An O-Series aircraft (November 1936) was followed in mid-January by three A models. The dive-bombers were incorporated into J/88 as 5 *Staffel.* Normal load was one 250kg bomb; when armed with a 500kg weapon the aircraft had to be flown as a single-seater.

Junkers Ju 87 B
Fuselage code: 29 •
Two-seat dive-bomber
Power plant: 1 x Jumo 211D, 950 HP
Wingspan: 13.8 m Length: 11 m
Max. speed: 380 kph at 4,100 m
Armament: 2 fixed MG 171 flexibly-mounted MG 151 x ETC 500/IX under fuselage for 1 x 500kg bomb and 4 x ETC 50/VIII under wings for 4 x 50kg bombs

Five B-Series machines were sent to Spain in October 1938, to replace the A models. The dive-bombers were now placed under the command of K/88. The later version enjoyed good success, not least because of its greater bombload.

Klemm Kl 32 a XIV
Fuselage code: 30 •
Three-seat staff and courier aircraft
Power plant: 1 x Sh 14A, 150 HP
Wingspan: 12.06 m   Length: 7.21 m
Max. speed: 200 kph
Armament: none

Three machines delivered to *Legion Condor* headquarters in early 1937. Used for cross-country and courier flights.

Messerschmitt Bf 108 B
Fuselage code: 44 •
Four-seat staff and courier aircraft
Power plant: 1 x As 10 C, 240 HP
Wingspan: 10.61 m   Length: 8.29 m
Max. speed: 295 kph
Armament: none

Four *Taifuns* were sent to Spain in mid-1937 for use by S/88. The most dependable courier aircraft to see service during the Spanish Civil War.

Messerschmitt Bf 109 V
Single-seat fighter
V 3 fuselage code: 6 • 3
Power plant: 1 x Jumo 210 A, 640 HP
Armament: 1 engine-mounted MG FF 20mm cannon, two MG 17 in fuselage

V 4 fuselage code: ?
Power plant: 1 x Jumo 210 A, 610 HP
Armament: 3 x MG 17

V 5 fuselage code: ?
Power plant: 1 x Jump 210 B, 540 HP
Armament: 3 x MG 17

V 6 fuselage code: ?
Power plant: 1 x Jumo 210 B, 540 HP
Armament: 3 x MG 17

All four prototypes reached VJ/88 at Sevilla-Tablada in late 1936/early 1937, where they underwent front-line testing. Afterward the aircraft remained with the *Staffeln* of J/88.

Messerschmitt Bf 109 B
Single-seat fighter
Power plant: 1 x Jumo 210 Da, 680 HP
Wingspan: 9.9 m Length: 8.7 m
Max. speed: B-1: 440 kph at 2,700 m, B-2: 460 kph at 2,700 m
Armament: B-1: 2 x MG 17, B-2: 3 x MG 17

In March 1937 2. J/88 the first unit to receive the Bf 109 B-1 equipped with a fixed-pitch wooden propeller. The next deliveries were in April, B-2 versions with the VDM variable-pitch propeller. The Bf 109 proved a match for the Russian I-15 and I-16 fighters, and superior when equipped with the variable-pitch propeller. 39 aircraft were delivered, coded 6 • 7 to 6 • 45.

Messerschmitt Bf 109 C
Fuselage code: 6 •
Single-seat fighter
Power plant: 1 x Jumo 210 G, 700 HP
Wingspan: 9.9 m Length: 8.7 m
Max. speed: 465 kph at 4,500 m
Armament: 4 x MG 17

Follow-on version with heavier armament and more powerful engine. Increased edge in performance over enemy fighters. Best performance at an altitude of 4,500 meters. Only a small number delivered, five aircraft, coded 6 • 46 to 6 • 50

Messerschmitt Bf 109 D
Fuselage code: 6 •
Single-seat fighter
Power plant: 1 x Jumo 210 D, 680 HP
Wingspan: 9.9 m Length: 8.7 m
Max. speed: 455 kph at 4,000 m
Armament: 4 x MG 17

With its supercharger rated for 3,300 meters the Jumo 210 D of the Bf 109 d version was ideal for conditions in Spain, as most bombing sorties and air combats took place at this height. 36 aircraft delivered, coded 6 • 51 to 6 • 86.

Messerschmitt Bf 109 E
Fuselage code: 6 •
Single-seat fighter
E-1
Power plant: 1 x DB 601 A, 1,050 HP
Wingspan: 9.9 mLength: 8.8 m
Max. speed: 550 kph at 4,400 m
Armament: 4 x MG 17

E-2
Power plant: 1 x DB 601 Aa, 1,175 HP
Wingspan: 9.9 mLength: 8.8 m
Max. speed: 560 kph at 4,400 m
Armament: 2 x MG 17 in fuselage, 2 x MG FF in wings

Further increase in performance through the installation of a Daimler-Benz engine. The E-3, with the heaviest armament of any Bf 109 sent to Spain, would have given the *Super-Chatos* and *Super-Moscas* no chance. However, the aircraft never had a chance to show what it could do, as the Republican Air Force was already badly battered and the earlier fighting spirit was now lacking in the enemy pilots. 44 aircraft delivered coded 6 • 87 to 6 • 130.

Appendix G

The Most Successful Nationalist Spanish and Italian Fighter Pilots

Spain	Kills
Joachim Garcia Morato	40
Julio Salvador Diaz-Benjumea	24
Manuel Vazquez Sagastizabal	21
Aristides Garcia Lopez	17
Angel Salas Larrazabal	16
Miguel Garcia Pardo	12
Joachin Velasco Fernandez Nespral	11
Carlos Bayo Alessandri	11
Graf Rodolfo d'Henricourt (Belgium)	10
Javier Allende Isasi	7
Esteban Ibarreche Arriaga	7
Emilio O'Connor Valdivielso	6
José Larios Fernandez	6
Javier Murcia Rubio	5
Jorge Muntadas Claramunt	5
Rafael Simon Garcia	5
Abundio Cesteros Garcia	5
Antonio Manrique Garrido	5
Luis Alcocer Moreno-Abella	5
Jesus Rubio Paz	4
Ramon Senra Alvarez	4
Salvador Serra Alorda	4
Narciso Bermudez de Castro	4

The remaining 46 kills are distributed among approximately 30 pilots.

Italy	Kills
Mario Bonzano	15
Adriano Mantelli	12-15
Corrado Ricci	10/12
Guido Nobili	10
Carlo Romagnoli	9
Cenni	6
Franco Lucchini	5
Enrico degli Incenti	5

Appendix H

The Most Successful Republican Fighter Pilots

Official sources are not available. The information given here is based mostly on private sources in memoir literature and is not verifiable.

Spain	Kills
Andrés Garcia de la Calle	11
Manuel Aguirre Lopez	11
Miguel Zambudio Martinez	10
Manuel Zarauza Claver	10
Juan Comas Borras	10
José Bravo Fernandez	10
Emilio Ramirez Bravo	10
Felipe del Rio Crespo +4/23/37	7
Fransisco Tarazona Toran	6

France	
Abel Guides +6/8/37	10-11
Rayneau	5
Laboussiere	5

Yugoslavia	
Bosco Petrovic +1937	7

Russia	
Anatol Serov	13-16
Pavel Rychagov	15
Yeremenko	14
S.P. Denisov	13
V.I. Bobrov	13
Stepan Suprun	12-15
I.A. Lakeiev	12
Ahmed Amba	8
Tarsov	6
Turshanski	6

United States	
Frank Tinker	8
Albert Bäumler	4

Bulgaria	
Goronov (Sachar Sachayinov)	22??

Appendix I

Winners of the Spanish Cross in Gold with Diamonds

Awarded June 6, 1939

Oberleutnant Wilhelm Balthasar	J/88
Oberleutnant Otto Bertram	J/88
Leutnant Peter Boddem	J/88
Oberleutnant Kraft Eberhardt	J/88
Oberleutnant Wilhelm Ensslen	J/88
Leutnant Paul Fehlhaber	Ln/88
Oberleutnant Adolf Galland	J/88
Hauptmann Harro Harder	J/88
Major Martin Harlinghausen	AS/88
Leutnant Oskar Henrici	J/88
Oberleutnant Max Graf Hoyos	K/88
Oberleutnant Hans-Detlef von Kassel	A/88
Hauptmann Günther Lützow	J/88
Oberstleutnant Karl Mehnert	K/88
Hauptmann Werner Mölders	J/88
Hauptmann Rudolf Frhr. von Moreau	K/88
Hauptmann Wolfgang Neudörffer	K/88
Oberleutnant Walter Oesau	J/88
Generalmajor Wolfram Frhr. von Richthofen	S/88
Leutnant Heinz Runze	A/88
Hauptmann Wolfgang Schellmann	J/88
Hauptmann Joachim Schlichting	J/88
Oberleutnant Reinhard Seiler	J/88
General der Flieger Hugo Sperrle	S/88
Oberleutnant Bernhard Stärcke	K/88
General der Flieger Helmut Volkmann	S/88
Major Karl-Heinz Wolff	AS/88

Appendix J

Officers of Jagdgruppe J/88 (Flying Personnel)

•• = Spanish Cross in Gold with Diamonds
• = Spanish Cross in Gold with Crossed Swords
* = Knight's Cross Winner 1939-1945
† = KIA in Spain
†† = KIA in World War II

•*††	Lt. Adolph, Walter
•†	Lt. Awe, Fritz
	Major Baier
••*††	Oblt. Balthasar, Wilhelm
••*	Bertram, Otto
•*	Lt. Beyer, Erich
••	Lt. Boddem, Peter
	Oblt. Boenigk, Ernst
•	Lt. Bolz, Helmut-Felix
•*††	Oblt. von Bonin, Hubertus
•††	Oblt. von Bothmer, Dietrich
•*††	Lt. Bretnütz, Heinz
	Lt. Brockmann, Hans
•*	Lt. Brücker, Heinrich
•†	Lt. Blankennagel, Wilhelm
•†	Lt. Bötticher, Karl
††	Lt. von Cramon, Friedrich-Franz
†	Oblt. Graf Dohna, Alexander
•††	Oblt. Ebbighausen, Karl
••†	Oblt. Eberhardt, Kraft
•*††	Oblt. Ehle, Walter
•††	Lt. Ehrig, Hans-Jürgen
•	Oblt. d'Elsa, Eberhard
••††	Oblt. Ensslen, Wilhelm
•††	Lt. Ettling, Armin
•*	Oblt. Ewald, Wolfgang
•*	Lt. Fözö, Josef
••*	Oblt. Galland, Adolf
†	Lt. von Gallera, Hans-Peter
	Oblt. Gamringer, Johann
†	Lt. von Gilsa, Kurt
•	Oblt. Gläser, Fritz
•*	Hptm. Grabmann, Walter
•††	Oblt. Greisert, Karl-Heinz

Lt. Gresens, Heinz
• Lt. Goy, Rudolf
• Oblt. Haas, Hermann
• Major Handrick, Gotthard
••†† Hptm. Harder, Harro
•† Oblt. von Harling, Christian
Lt. Hasselmann, Hans
† Lt. Haupt, Martin
•†† Oblt. Heinrich, Kurt
† Lt. Hefter, Ekkehard
••† Oblt. Henrici, Oskar
•†† Oblt. Henz, Helmut
Lt. Hepe, Hans-Jürgen
† Hptm. Hering, Hubert
• Lt. Hoermann, Kurt
Oblt. Hollweg, Hermann
Lt. von Hotley, Hubertus
•†† Hptm. von Houwald, Ottheinrich
•* Lt. Ihlefeld, Herbert
Lt. Karpenkiel, Ernst-Peter
†† Hptm. von Janson, Lothar
•†† Oblt. Keidel, Wilhelm
•*†† Oblt. Keller, Lothar
Hptm. Kienitz, Walter
Oblt. Kienzle, Walter
• Lt. Klein, Alfons
† Lt. Klein, Gerhard
•†† Hptm. Knüppel, Herwig
*†† Oblt. Kollewe, Gerhard
• Oblt. Kroeck, Hubert
•†† Oblt. Kühle, Helmut
• Hptm. Lehmann, Siegfried
•†† Oblt. Lehrmann. Horst
•*†† Lt. Lippert, Wolfgang
• Oblt. von Lojewski, Alfred
* Lt. Losigkeit, Fritz
Lt. Lorbach
••*†† Hptm. Lützow, Günther
•*†† Lt. Lutz, Martin
Lt. Maurer, Walter
•*†† Oblt. Mayer, Hans-Karl
• Major von Merhart, Hubertus
•† Lt. Michaelis, Manfred
Oblt. von Minnigerode, Albrecht
••*†† Hptm. Mölders, Werner
• Oblt. Müller, Kurt
• Oblt. Neumann, Eduard
••*†† Oblt. Oesau, Walter
• Hptm. Palm, Werner
•* Oblt. Pingel, Rolf
• Oblt. Pitcairn, Douglas
• Oblt. Priebe, Eckehardt
•* Oblt. Radusch, Günther
•†† Oblt. Rech, Horst
•*†† Oblt. Redlich, Karl-Wolfgang
• Hptm. Reents, Siebelt
•† Lt. Rehahn, Paul
•†† Rempel, Edgar
•*†† Oblt. Resch, Rudolf
•† Lt. Reutter, Ernst
* Lt. Roedel, Gustav
•* Lt. Rossiwall, Theodor
• Oblt. Roth, Jürgen
*†† Hptm. Rubensdörffer, Walter
••† Lt. Runze, Heinz
†† Oblt. Rutsch, Gerhard
†† Oblt. Sandmann, Karl-Heinz
†† Lt. Scharnhorst, Artur
•†† Lt. Schelcher, Ekkehard
••*†† Hptm. Schellmann, Wolfgang
• Oblt. Schlaffer, Urban
••* Hptm. Schlichting, Joachim
Oblt. Schmoller-Haldy, Hans
• Oblt. Scholz, Günther
• Oblt. Schulze-Blank, Günther
•*†† Oblt. Schumann, Heinz
•†† Lt. Schumann, August-Wilhelm
••* Lt. Seiler, Reinhard
* Lt. Sochatzky, Kurt
Lt. Stehle, Adelwald
•†† Lt. Strößner, Rolf
• Oblt. Strümpell, Hennig
• Lt. Strümpell, Kurt
•*†† Oblt. Tietzen, Horst
•* Hptm. Trautloft, Hannes
• Oblt. Unger, Rudolf
• Lt. Ursinus, Werner
*†† Oblt. Wandel, Joachim
• Oblt. Weyert, Gerhard
*†† Oblt. Wilcke, Wolf-Dietrich
Hptm. Winterer, Otto-Hans
•†† Oblt. Woitke, Erich

Appendix K

NCO's of Jagdgruppe J/88 (Flying Personnel)

*Spanish Cross

Uffz. Bartels, Ernst
Uffz. Bartsch, Ulrich
Uffz. Bauer, Josef
Uffz. Beurer, Hermann
Uffz. Biegert, Hermann
Uffz. Boer
Uffz. Borchers, Adolf*
Ofw. Braunschweiger, Heinz
Uffz. Braunshirn, Georg
Uffz. Brucks, Helmut
Uffz. Buhl, Adolf
Uffz. Droste
Fw. Fenske, Walter
Uffz. Fischer
Fw. Flegel, Norbert
Fw. Fleischmann
Uffz. Franz, Albert
Uffz. Freund
Uffz. Gerstmann, Waldemar
Uffz. Giehl, Erich
Uffz. Gödecke, Willi
Uffz. Grassheuser, Georg
Ofw. Grimmling
Uffz. Grosse
Uffz. Halupczek
Uffz. Harbach
Fw. Heilmayer, Franz
Fw. Helw, Alfred
Uffz. Herber
Uffz. Herzog, Gerhard
Uffz. Hester, Andreas
Uffz. Hien
Ofw. Hillmann
Uffz. Höneß, Guido
Uffz. Holitzke
Uffz. Jaenisch, Franz
Uffz. Jecke
Uffz. Jeschke
Uffz. Keller, Peter
Uffz. Kiening
Fw. Kley, Erwin
Uffz. Kneiding, Kurt
Uffz. Kolb, Karl
Uffz. Kolbow, Hans*
Uffz. König
Uffz. Kowalski
Fw. Krahl, Karl-Heinz*
Uffz. Kroessmann, Heinz
Uffz. van Kueck, Karl
Uffz. Küll
Fw. Kuhlmann, Erich
Uffz. Kurz, Anton
Uffz. Lenz
Uffz. Leyerer, Walter
Uffz. Lohrer
Uffz. März
Ofw. Menge, Robert
Uffz. Metz, Karlheinz
Uffz. Meyer, Willi
Uffz. Mratzek, Ernst
Ofw. Müller
Uffz. Nirminger, Hans
Ofw. Otte, Walter
Ofw. Prestele, Ignaz
Ufw. Polenz, Otto
Uffz. Quasinowski, Ernst
Uffz. Rabeneck, Fritz
Fw. Riedinger
Ofw. Ries, Hans
Uffz. Rochel, Kurt
Fw. Rückert, Emil
Uffz. Sawallisch, Erwin
Uffz. Schob, Herbert*
Uffz. Schulz, Max
Uffz. Schulze
Fw. Schweikart
Fw. Seliger
Uffz. Seufert, Bernhard
Ofw. Sigmund, Leo
Uffz. Staege, Wilhelm
Uffz. Stange, Hermann
Uffz. Stark, Alfred
Uffz. Stegemann
Uffz. Supke
Uffz. Szuggar, Willy
Uffz. Terry, Ernst
Ufw. Torner, Heinrich
Fhr. Tornow, Heinz
Uffz. Vielhaber, Heinrich
Ofw. Wilfert, Karl
Uffz. Wilmsen, August
Uffz. Windemuth, Heinrich

Ogefr. Erb, Hans **Ju 52**
Uffz. Ogaza, Hubert **Ju 52**

Appendix L

Combat Score Listing of Jagdgruppe J/88

No.	Name	Date	Staffel	Type	Kills
1	Oblt. Eberhardt	8/25/36		Breguet 19	1
2	Oblt. Trautloft	8/25/36		Breguet 19	1
3	Oblt. Knüppel	8/26/36		Breguet 19	1
4	Oblt. Eberhardt	8/26/36		Breguet 19	2
5	Oblt. Knüppel	8/27/36		Nieuport 46	2
	Oblt. Eberhardt	8/29/36		Potez	3
6	Oblt. Eberhardt	8/30/36		Potez	4
7	Oblt. Trautloft	8/30/36		Potez	2
8	Oblt. Knüppel	8/30/36		Potez	3
9	Oblt. Trautloft	9/1/36		Nieuport 46	3
10	Lt. von Houwald	9/5/36		Nieuport 46	1
11	Lt. von Houwald	9/5/36		Breguet 19	2
12	Oblt. Knüppel	9/5/36		Nieuport 46	4
13	Oblt. Eberhardt	9/6/36		Potez	5
14	Oblt. Knüppel	9/6/36		Potez	5
	Oblt. Knüppel	9/17/36		Nieuport 46	6
15	Lt. von Houwald	9/26/36		Vickers	3
16	Oblt. Hefter	9/26/36		Breguet 19	1
17	Oblt. Klein	9/26/36		Breguet 19	1
18	Oblt. Eberhardt	9/30/36		Potez	6
19	Oblt. Trautloft	9/30/36		Potez	4
20	Lt. Henrici	10/19/36		Nieuport 46	1
21	Lt. Henrici	10/19/36		Breguet 19	2
22	Oblt. Strümpell	10/19/36		Nieuport 46	1
23	Lt. von Houwald	10/19/36		Nieuport 46	4
24	Lt. Henrici	10/19/36		Fokker	3
25	Uffz. Sawallisch	11/13/36		Curtiss	1
26	Uffz. Mratzek	11/13/36		Curtiss	1
27	Oblt. Strümpell	11/13/36		Curtiss	2
28	Oblt. Knüppel	11/13/36		Curtiss	7
29	Lt. von Bothmer	11/13/36		Curtiss	1
	Lt. Henrici	11/13/36		Curtiss	4
	Oblt. Eberhardt	11/13/36		Curtiss	7
30	Lt. Rehahn	12/8/36	4.	Breguet 19	1
31	Oblt. Trautloft	12/8/36		Rata	5
32	Lt. von Bothmer	12/8/36		Rata	2
33	Lt. von Gilsa	12/12/36		SB-2	1
34	Lt. Rehahn	12/12/36		SB-2	2
35	Uffz. Sawallisch	12/12/36	4.	SB-2	2
36	Uffz. Gödecke	12/12/36		SB-2	1
	Oblt. Knüppel	12/12/36		SB-2	8
37	Hptm. Palm	12/16/36	1.	Boeing	1
38	Uffz. Sawallisch	1/4/37	4.	Curtiss	3
39	Lt. von Houwald	1/4/37	2.	Boeing	5
40	Oblt. Harder	1/4/37	1.	Curtiss	1
	Oblt. Balthasar	1/20/37		Rata	1
41	Uffz. Hepe	2/12/37	1.	Boeing	1
42	Oblt. Lützow	4/6/37	2.	Curtiss	1
43	Lt. Radusch	4/22/37	2.	Curtiss	1
44	Fw. Heilmayer	4/22/37	2.	Curtiss	1
	Hptm. von Janson	4/22/37	2.	Curtiss	1

No.	Name	Date	Staffel	Type	Kills
45	Oblt. Lützow	5/22/37	2.	Curtiss	2
46	Oblt. Lützow	5/28/37	2.	Curtiss	3
47	Fw. Braunschweiger	5/28/37	1.	Curtiss	1
	Lt. Pingel	6/5/37	2.	Curtiss	1
48	Uffz. Höneß	7/8/37	2.	SB-2	1
49	Lt. Pingel	7/8/37	2.	SB-2	2
50	Lt. Pingel	7/12/37	2.	SB-2	3
51	Lt. Pingel	7/12/37	2.	Rata	4
52	Uffz. Höneß	7/12/37	2.	Praga	
53	Uffz. Höneß	7/12/37	2.	Praga	
54	Fw. Boddem	7/12/37	2.	Rata	1
	Fw. Buhl	7/12/37	2.	Rata	1
55	Fw. Boddem	7/13/37	2.	Rata	2
	Fw. Braunschweiger	7/13/37	2.	Rata	2
	Ofw. Hillmann	7/13/37	2.	Rata	1
56	Lt. Pingel	7/16/37	2.	Rata	5
	Ofw. Hillmann	7/17/37	2.	Rata	2
57	Ofw. Hillmann	7/18/37	2.	Rata	3
58	Fw. Boddem	7/21/37	2.	SB-2	3
59	Fw. Boddem	7/25/37	2.	Rata	4
60	Fw. Boddem	8/13/37	2.	Rata	5
61	Lt. Rempel	8/15/37	2.	Rata	1
62	Fw. Boddem	8/17/37	2.	Curtiss	6
63	Fw. Boddem	8/17/37	2.	Rata	7
	Fw. Flegel	8/17/37	2.	Rata	1
64	Oblt. Lützow	8/18/37	2.	Curtiss	4
65	Lt. Boddem	8/18/37	2.	Curtiss	8
	Fw. Flegel	8/18/37	2.	Curtiss	2
66	Oblt. Lützow	8/22/37	2.	Rata	5
67	Lt. Pingel	8/22/37	2.	Rata	6
68	Fw. Flegel	8/22/37	2.	Rata	3
69	Ofw. Seiler	8/26/37	2.	Curtiss	1
70	Uffz. Schulz	8/27/37	2.	Curtiss	1
71	Oblt. Harder	8/27/37	1.	SB-2	2
72	Ofw. Seiler	9/4/37	2.	Rata	2
73	Lt. Neumann	9/4/37	3.	Curtiss	1
74	Lt. Boddem	9/6/37	2.	Rata	9
75	Oblt. Harder	9/7/37	1.	French Dual Engine	3
76	Oblt. Harder	9/9/37	1.	Nieuport	4
77	Oblt. Harder	9/9/37	1.	Curtiss	5
78	Lt. Brücker	9/9/37	2.	Rata	1
	Lt. Boddem	9/9/37	2.	Curtiss	10
	Hptm. Handrick	9/9/37	Stab	Curtiss	1
79	Oblt. Harder	9/15/37	1.	Curtiss	6
80	Oblt. Schlichting	9/23/37	2.	Rata	1
81	Lt. Woitke	9/27/37	1.	Rata	1
82	Oblt. Harder	9/27/37	1.	Rata	7
83	Oblt. Harder	9/27/37	1.	Rata	8
84	Oblt. Harder	9/28/37	1.	Rata	9
85	Lt. Woitke	9/30/37	1.	Rata	2
	Fw. Flegel	9/30/37	2.	Curtiss	4
86	Oblt. Harder	10/13/37	1.	Rata	10
87	Ofw. Sugmund	10/13/37	1.	Curtiss	1
88	Oblt. Schlichting	11/29/37	2.	Rata	2
89	Uffz. Rochel	11/29/37	2.	Rata	1
90	Ofw. Seiler	11/29/37	2.	Rata	3
91	Lt. Greisert	11/30/37	2.	Rata	1
92	Uffz. Stange	11/30/37	2.	Rata	1

No.	Name	Date	Staffel	Type	Kills
93	Uffz. Staege	11/30/37	2.	Rata	1
94	Hptm. Harder	12/5/37	1.	Curtiss	11
95	Lt. Adolph	12/30/37	1.	Curtiss	1
96	Ofw. Prestele	12/30/37	1.	Rata	1
97	Uffz. Terry	12/30/37	1.	Curtiss	1
98	Ofw. Prestele	1/5/38	1.	Rata	2
99	Ofw. Seiler	1/12/38	2.	SB-2	4
100	Uffz. Staege	1/12/38	2.	SB-2	2
101	Oblt. Schellmann	1/18/38	1.	Rata	1
102	Lt. Woitke	1/18/38	1.	Rata	3
103	Oblt. Balthasar	1/20/38	1.	Rata	2
104	Uffz. Rochel	1/20/38	2.	Curtiss	2
105	Ofw. Seiler	1/22/38	2.	Rata	5
106	Uffz. Lohrer	2/5/38	2.	Rata	1
107	Uffz. Stange	2/6/38	2.	Rata	2
108	Lt. Mayer	2/7/38	1.	SB-2	1
109	Lt. Mayer	2/7/38	1.	Rata	2
110	Ofw. Prestele	2/7/38	1.	SB-2	3
111	Ofw. Seiler	2/7/38	2.	SB-2	6
112	Ofw. Seiler	2/7/38	2.	SB-2	7
113	Uffz. Quasinowski	2/7/38	1.	SB-2	1
114	Uffz. Terry	2/7/38	1.	SB-2	2
115	Oblt. Schlichting	2/7/38	2.	Rata	3
116	Oblt. Balthasar	2/7/38	2.	SB-2	3
117	Oblt. Balthasar	2/7/38	2.	SB-2	4
118	Oblt. Balthasar	2/7/38	2.	SB-2	5
119	Oblt. Balthasar	2/7/38	2.	SB-2	6
120	Uffz. Stange	2/19/38	2.	Curtiss	3
121	Lt. Awe	2/21/38	1.	Rata	1
122	Lt. Mayer	2/21/38	1.	Rata	3
123	Lt. Woitke	2/21/38	1.	Rata	4
124	Oblt. Schlichting	2/21/38	2.	Rata	4
125	Lt. Rempel	2/21/38	2.	Rata	2
126	Uffz. Ihlefeld	2/21/38	2.	Rata	1
127	Uffz. Rochel	2/21/38	2.	Rata	3
128	Lt. Seiler	2/22/38	2.	Curtiss	8
129	Lt. Seiler	2/22/38	2.	Curtiss	9
130	Oblt. Schellmann	3/8/38	1.	Curtiss	2
131	Lt. Awe	3/8/38	1.	Curtiss	2
132	Ofw. Prestele	3/10/38	1.	Curtiss	4
133	Uffz. Rochel	3/10/38	2.	Rata	4
134	Oblt. Schlichting	3/10/38	2.	Rata	5
135	Lt. Ettling	3/13/38	2.	Curtiss	1
136	Uffz. Ihlefeld	3/13/38	2.	Curtiss	2
137	Lt. Awe	3/24/38	1.	Curtiss	3
138	Oblt. Schellmann	3/24/38	1.	Curtiss	3
139	Uffz. Stark	3/24/38	1.	Curtiss	1
140	Lt. Mayer	3/29/38	1.	Curtiss	4
141	Uffz. Ihlefeld	5/11/38	2.	Rata	3
142	Lt. Priebe	5/14/38	1.	Rata	1
143	Uffz. Rochel	5/18/38	2.	Rata	5
144	Hptm. Handrick	5/18/38	Stab	Rata	2
	Uffz. Ihlefeld	5/18/38	2.	Rata	4
	Uffz. Seufert	5/18/38	2.	Rata	1
145	Lt. Heinrich	6/2/38	2.	SB-2	1
146	Lt. Heinrich	6/2/38	2.	SB-2	2
147	Lt. Heinrich	6/2/38	2.	SB-2	3
148	Uffz. Meyer	6/2/38	2.	SB-2	1

No.	Name	Date	Staffel	Type	Kills
149	Uffz. Ihlefeld	6/2/38	2.	SB-2	5
150	Uffz. Seufert	6/10/38	2.	Rata	2
151	Uffz. Rochel	6/10/38	2.	Rata	6
152	Lt. Mayer	6/10/38	1.	SB-2	5
	Lt. Heinrich	6/10/38	2.	Rata	4
153	Lt. Neumann	6/11/38	Stab	Rata	2
154	Uffz. Staege	6/13/38	2.	Curtiss	3
155	Uffz. Seufert	6/13/38	2.	Curtiss	3
156	Lt. Ewald	6/13/38	2.	Rata	1
157	Lt. Keller	6/13/38	1.	Curtiss	1
158	Oblt. Schellmann	6/13/38	1.	Rata	4
159	Uffz. Kuhlmann	6/13/38	1.	Curtiss	1
	Lt. Maurer	6/13/38	1.	Curtiss	1
	Oblt. Müller	6/13/38	1.	Curtiss	1
	Lt. Mayer	6/13/38	1.	Rata	6
160	Fw. Kuhlmann	6/14/38	1.	Curtiss	2
161	Oblt. Schellmann	6/25/38	1.	Rata	5
	Fw. Ihlefeld	6/25/38	2.	Rata	6
162	Lt. Keidel	7/12/38	2.	Curtiss	1
163	Fw. Ihlefeld	7/12/38	2.	Curtiss	7
164	Lt. Oesau	7/15/38	Stab	Curtiss	1
165	Fw. Ihlefeld	7/15/38	2.	Curtiss	8
166	Fw. Ihlefeld	7/15/38	2.	Curtiss	9
167	Lt. Lippert	7/15/38	3.	Curtiss	1
168	Oblt. Müller	7/15/38	1.	Curtiss	2
169	Lt. Keller	7/15/38	1.	Curtiss	2
170	Fw. Kuhlmann	7/15/38	1.	Curtiss	3
171	Uffz. Quasinowski	7/15/38	1.	Curtiss	2
172	Oblt. Mölders	7/15/38	3.	Curtiss	1
173	Oblt. Mölders	7/17/38	3.	Curtiss	2
174	Uffz. Bauer	7/17/38	3.	Curtiss	1
175	Uffz. Bauer	7/17/38	3.	Curtiss	2
176	Lt. Resch	7/17/38	2.	Curtiss	1
177	Lt. Oesau	7/17/38	Stab	Curtiss	2
178	Uffz. Quasinowski	7/17/38	1.	Curtiss	3
179	Lt. Oesau	7/18/38	Stab	Rata	3
180	Uffz. Quasinowski	7/18/38	1.	Rata	4
181	Oblt. Schellmann	7/18/38	1.	Rata	6
	Fw. Kuhlmann	7/18/38	1.	Rata	4
182	Lt. Tietzen	7/19/38	3.	Rata	1
183	Oblt. Mölders	7/19/38	3.	Rata	3
184	Ogfr. Hien	7/19/38	3.	Rata	1
185	Lt. Ebbighausen	7/19/38	3.	Rata	1
	Lt. Goy	7/19/38	3.	Rata	1
186	Oblt. Schellmann	7/20/38	1.	Rata	7
187	Oblt. Schellmann	7/20/38	1.	Rata	8
188	Uffz. Brucks	7/20/38	1.	Rata	1
	Lt. Oesau	7/20/38	Stab	Curtiss	4
189	Fw. Menge	7/23/38	1.	Rata	1
190	Lt. Lippert	7/23/38	3.	Rata	2
	Uffz. Braunshirn	7/23/38	2.	Rata	1
	Uffz. Boer	7/23/38	3.	Curtiss	1
	Lt. Oesau	7/27/38	Stab	SB-2	5
191	Uffz. Jaenisch	8/1/38	3.	Curtiss	1
192	Uffz. Bauer	8/1/38	3.	Curtiss	3
193	Oblt. Ebbighausen	8/1/38	3.	Curtiss	2
194	Oblt. Kroeck	8/2/38	2.	Rata	1
195	Uffz. Brucks	8/12/38	1.	SB-2	2

No.	Name	Date	Staffel	Type	Kills
196	Hptm. Schellmann	8/12/38	1.	SB-2	9
197	Lt. Bertram	8/12/38	1.	Rata	1
198	Hptm. Schellmann	8/12/38	1.	SB-2	10
199	Lt. Lippert	8/14/38	3.	Rata	3
200	Lt. Bertram	8/14/38	1.	Rata	2
201	Hptm. Schellmann	8/14/38	1.	Rata	11
202	Uffz. Szuggar	8/14/38	1.	Rata	1
203	Uffz. Hien	8/14/38	3.	Rata	2
204	Uffz. Hien	8/14/38	3.	Rata	3
205	Uffz. Szuggar	8/14/38	1.	Rata	2
206	Lt. Bertram	8/15/38	1.	Rata	3
207	Uffz. Kuell	8/15/38	2.	Curtiss	1
208	Lt. Oesau	8/15/38	Stab	Curtiss	6
209	Uffz. Kuell	8/19/38	2.	Rata	2
210	Oblt. Keller	8/19/38	1.	Rata	3
211	Oblt. Mölders	8/19/38	3.	Rata	4
212	Lt. Scholz	8/19/38	3.	Rata	1
213	Hptm. Schellmann	8/20/38	1.	Rata	12
214	Lt. Oesau	8/20/38	Stab	Rata	7
215	Lt. Bertram	8/23/38	1.	Rata	4
216	Oblt. Müller	8/23/38	1.	Rata	3
217	Lt. Ensslen	8/23/38	2.	Curtiss	1
218	Oblt. Mölders	8/23/38	3.	SB-2	5
	Uffz. Hien	8/31/38	3.	Rata	4
219	Lt. Ensslen	9/5/38	2.	Curtiss	2
	Lt. Bertram	9/7/38	1.	Rata	5
	Lt Bertram	9/7/38	1.	Rata	6
220	Oblt. Mölders	9/9/38	3.	Rata	6
221	Oblt. Mölders	9/13/38	3.	Rata	7
	Lt. Fözö	9/18/38	3.	Rata	1
222	Lt. Ensslen	9/20/38	2.	Rata	3
	Lt. Tietzen	9/20/38	1.	Rata	2
	Lt. Tietzen	9/20/38	1.	Rata	3
	Lt. Keidel	9/20/38	2.		2
223	Hptm. Grabmann	9/23/38	Stab	SB-2	1
224	Oblt. Mölders	9/23/38	3.	Rata	8
225	Uffz. März	9/23/38	3.	Rata	1
226	Hptm. Grabmann	9/23/38	Stab	Curtiss	2
227	Hptm. Grabmann	9/23/38	Stab	Rata	3
228	Uffz. Braunshirn	9/23/38	2.	SB-2	2
229	Lt. Goy	9/23/38	3.	Rata	2
230	Lt. Goy	9/23/38	2.	Rata	3
	Lt. Bertram	9/23/38	1.	Rata	7
	Oblt. Mölders	9/23/38	3.	Rata	Not Confirmed
231	Uffz. Schob	9/24/38	2.	Rata	1
232	Lt. Bertram	9/27/38	1.	Rata	8
233	Oblt. Unger	9/27/38	1.	Rata	1
234	Lt. Tietzen	9/27/38	1.	Rata	4
235	Lt. Tietzen	9/27/38	1.	Rata	5
236	Lt. Bertram	10/4/38	1.	Curtiss	9
237	Lt. Lippert	10/4/38	3.	Rata	4
238	Uffz. Szuggar	10/4/38	1.	Curtiss	3
239	Lt. Ehrig	10/7/38	1.	Rata	1
240	Fw. Menge	10/7/38	1.	Rata	2
241	Hptm. Grabmann	10/10/38	Stab	SB-2	4
242	Oblt. Mölders	10/10/38	3.	Rata	9
243	Oblt. Gamringer	10/10/38	3.	SB-2	1
244	Uffz. Schob	10/13/38	2.	Rata	2

No.	Name	Date	Staffel	Type	Kills
245	Hptm. Grabmann	10/15/38	Stab	Rata	5
246	Oblt. Mölders	10/15/38	3.	Rata	10
247	Oblt. Mölders	10/15/38	3.	Rata	11
248	Lt. Oesau	10/15/38	Stab	Rata	8
249	Hptm. Mölders	10/31/38	3.	Rata	12
250	Hptm. Mölders	10/31/38	3.	Rata	13
251	Lt. Fözö	10/31/38	3.	Rata	2
252	Fw. Fleischmann	10/31/38	3.	Rata	1
253	Fw. Fleischmann	10/31/38	3.	Rata	2
254	Lt. Lutz	10/31/38	2.	Rata	1
255	Lt. Schumann	10/31/38	2.	Curtiss	1
256	Uffz. Braunshirn	10/31/38	2.	Curtiss	3
257	Uffz. Kiening	10/31/38	3.	Rata	1
	Lt. Rossiwall	10/31/38	3.	Rata	1
258	Fw. Menge	11/1/38	1.	Curtiss	3
	Uffz. März	11/2/38	3.	Rata	2
259	Hptm. Mölders	11/3/38	3.	Rata	14
260	Lt. Oesau	11/3/38	Stab	Rata	9
261	Uffz. Braunshirn	11/3/38	2.	Curtiss	4
262	Ogfr. Freund	11/3/38	2.	Curtiss	1
263	Uffz. Schob	11/3/38	2.	Rata	3
	Hptm. Grabmann	11/3/38	Stab	Rata	6
264	Uffz, März	11/4/38	3.	Rata	3
265	Ofw. Menge	11/5/38	1.	Rata	4
	Lt.Redlich	11/5/38	2.	Rata	1
	?	11/5/38	2.		
266	Lt. Bretnütz	11/6/38	2.	Curtiss	1
267	Braunshirn	11/6/38	2.	Curtiss	5
	Lt. Bolz	11/8/38	3.		1
268	Uffz. Kolb	11/12/38	1.	Rata	1
269	Fw. Fleischmann	11/12/38	3.	Curtiss	3
270	Uffz. Fischer	11/12/38	1.	Rata	1
271	Uffz. Szuggar	11/12/38	1.	Rata	4
272	Uffz. Schob	11/16/38	2.	SB-2	4
	Lt. Bolz	11/16/38	3.	SB-2	2
273	Lt. Rossiwell	12/20/38	3.	Rata	2
274	Lt. Tietzemen	12/21/38	1.	Rata	6
275	Lt. Schumann	12/28/38	2.	Rata	2
276	Lt. Ensslen	12/28/38	2.	SB-2	4
277	Fw. Schott	12/28/38	2.	Rata	1
278	Lt. Bretnütz	12/28/38	2.	SB-2	2
279	Lt. Redlich	12/28/38	2.	SB-2	2
280	Lt. Ensslen	12/28/38	2.	Rata	5
281	Lt. Lippert	12/29/38	3.	Curtiss	5
282	Oblt. von Bonin	12/29/38	3.	Rata	1
283	Uffz. Freund	12/29/38	3.	Rata	2
284	Lt. Tietzen	12/29/38	1.	Rata	7
285	Oblt. von Lojewski	12/30/38	2.	Curtiss	
286	Uffz. Schob	12/30/38	2.	Rata	5
287	Lt. Hormann	12/30/38	Stab	Rata	1
288	Lt. Ensslen	12/30/38	2.	Rata	6
289	Fw. Schott	12/30/38	2.	Curtiss	2.
290	Lt. Schumann	12/30/38	2.	Rata	3
291	Fw. Schott	12/31/38	2.	Rata	3
292	Lt. Ensslen	1/1/39	2.	Rata	7
	Uffz. Szuggar	1/3/39	1.	Curtiss	5
	Lt. Redlich	1/4/39	2.	SB-2	3
293	Hptm. Grabmann	1/4/39	Stab	Curtiss	7

No.	Name	Date	Staffel	Type	Kills
294	Oblt. Ebbighausen	1/5/39	Stab	Rata	3
295	Oblt. Ensslen	1/9/39	2.	Rata	8
296	Oblt. von Bonin	1/17/39	3.	Rata	2
297	Fhr. Tornow	1/17/39	3.	Rata	1
298	Lt. Fözö	1/17/39	3.	Rata	3
299	Ofw. Müller	1/17/39	3.	Rata	1
300	Oblt. Bolz	1/21/39	3.	Curtiss	3
301	Ofw. Müller	1/21/39	3.	Curtiss	2
	Uffz. Schob	1/22/39	2.	Curtiss	6
302	Oblt. von Bonin	2/3/39	3.	Curtiss	3
303	Fhr. Tornow	2/3/39	3.	Curtiss	2
	Lt. Schumann	2/4/39	2.	Curtiss	4
304	Oblt. Ensslen	2/5/39	2.	Curtiss	9
	Hptm. Rubensdörffer	2/5/39	Stab	Curtiss	1
	Lt. Redlich	2/5/39	2.	Curtiss	4
305	Hptm. Reents	2/6/39	1.	Curtiss	1
306	Uffz. Nirminger	2/6/39	1.	Reconnaissance A/C	1
307	Uffz. Halupczek	2/6/39	1.	Curtiss	1
308	Uffz. Herzog	2/6/39		Curtiss	1
309					
310					
311					
312					
313					
314	Oblt. von Bonin	3/6/39	3.	Curtiss	4

The dates of victories 309-313 are unknown. It seems quite certain that these five were scored by:

Oblt. von Lojewski
Uffz. Windemuth
Uffz. König
Ofw. Grimmling
Uffz. Metz

Note: The victories accompanied by a number were officially confirmed during the civil war. Which of the remaining victories were subsequently confirmed is not known.

In our research we came across a number of victories for which details were unavailable:

Oblt. Balthasar	1 Rata, end of December 1937/January 1938
Ofw. Braunschweiger	1
Uffz. Droste	3
Hptm. Handrick	3
Oblt. Kaldrack	3 possible reconnaissance A/C
Oblt. Mayer	2

List of Pilots with Victories

* Spanish Cross +KIA or accidental death during civil war

	Name	Victories
*	Lt. Adolph, Walter	1
+	Lt. Awe, Fritz	3
*	Oblt. Balthasar, Wilhelm	7
	Uffz. Bauer, Josef	3
*	Oblt. Bertram, Otto	9
	Lt. Boddem, Peter	10
	Uffz. Boer	1
	Oblt. Bolz, Helmut-Felix	3
*	Oblt. von Bonin, Hubertus	4
	Oblt. von Bothmer, Dietrich	2

	Ofw. Braunschweiger, Heinz	3
	Uffz. Braunshirn, Georg	5
*	Lt. Bretnütz, Heinz	2
	Uffz. Brucks, Helmut	2
*	Lt. Brücker, Heinrich	1
	Uffz. Buhl, Adolf	1
	Uffz. Droste	3
	Oblt. Ebbighausen, Karl	3
+	Eberhardt, Kraft	7
	Lt. Ehrig, Hans-Jürgen	1
	Oblt. Ensslen, Wilhelm	9
	Lt. Ettling, Armin	1
*	Oblt. Ewald, Wolfgang	1
	Uffz. Fischer	1
	Fw. Flegel, Norbert	4
	Fw. Fleischmann	3
*	Lt. Födö, Josef	3
	Uffz. Freund	2
	Oblt. Gamringer, Johann	1
+	Lt. von Gilsa, Kurt	1
	Uffz. Gödecke, Willi	1
	Lt. Goy, Rudolf	3
*	Hptm. Grabmann, Walter	7
	Oblt. Greisert, Karl-Heinz	1
	Ofw. Grimmling	1
	Hptm. Handrick, Gotthard	5
	Uffz. Halupczek	1
	Hptm. Harder, Harro	11
+	Lt. Hefter, Ekkehard	1
	Fw. Heilmayer, Franz	1
	Oblt. Heinrich, Kurt	4
+	Henrici, Oskar	4
	Lt. Hepe, Hans-Jürgen	1
	Uffz. Herzog, Gerhard	1
	Uffz. Hien	4
	Ofw. Hillmann	3
+	Uffz. Höneß, Guido	3
	Lt. Hörmann, Kurt	1
	Hptm. von Houwald, Ottheinrich	5
*	Lt. Ihlefeld, Herbert	9
	Uffz. Jaenisch, Franz	1
	Hptm. von Janson, Lothar	1
*	Oblt. Kaldrack, Rolf	3
	Oblt. Keidel, Wilhelm	2
*	Oblt. Keller, Lothar	3
	Uffz. Kiening	1
	Lt. Klein, Alfons	1
	Hptm. Knüppel, Herwig	8
	Uffz. Kolb, Karl	1
	Uffz. König	1
	Oblt. Kroeck, Hubert	1
	Uffz. Küll	2
	Fw. Kuhlmann, Erich	4
*	Lt. Lippert, Wolfgang	5
	Uffz. Lohrer	1
	Oblt. von Lojewski, Alfred	2
*	Hptm. Lützow, Günther	5
*	Lt. Lutz, Martin	1
	Uffz. März	3
	Lt. Maurer, Walter	1
*	Oblt. Mayer, Hans-Karl	8
	Ofw. Menge, Robert	4
	Uffz. Metz, Karlheinz	1
	Uffz. Meyer, Willi	1
*	Hptm. Mölders, Werner	14
+	Uffz. Mratzek, Ernst	1
	Oblt. Müller, Kurt	3
	Ofw. Müller	2
	Oblt. Neumann, Eduard	2
+	Uffz. Nirminger, Hans	1
*	Oblt. Oesau, Walter	9
	Hptm. Palm, Werner	1
*	Oblt. Pingel, Rolf	6
	Ofw. Prestele, Ignaz	4
	Oblt. Priebe, Eckehardt	1
	Uffz. Quasinowski, Ernst	4
*	Oblt. Radusch, Günther	1
*	Oblt. Redlich, Karl-Wolfgang	4
	Hptm. Reents, Siebelt	1
+	Lt. Rehahn, Paul	2
	Lt. Rempel, Edgar	2
*	Oblt. Resch, Rudolf	1
	Uffz. Rochel, Kurt	6
*	Lt. Rossiwall, Theodor	2
*	Hptm. Rubensdörffer, Walter	1
	Uffz. Sawallisch, Erwin	3
*	Hptm. Schellmann, Wolfgang	12
*	Hptm. Schlichting, Joachim	5
*	Uffz. Schob, Herbert	6
	Oblt. Scholz, Günther	1
	Fw. Schott	3
	Uffz. Schulz, Max	1
	Lt. Schumann, Aug. Wilhelm	4
*	Lt. Seiler, Reinhard	9
	Uffz. Seufert, Bernhard	3
	Ofw. Sigmund, Leo	1
	Uffz. Staege, Wilhelm	3
	Uffz. Stange, Hermann	3
	Uffz. Stark, Alfred	1
	Oblt. Strümpell, Hennig	2
	Uffz. Szuggar, Willy	5
	Uffz. Terry, Ernst	2
*	Oblt. Tietzen, Horst	7
	Fhr. Tornow, Heinz	2
*	Hptm. Trautloft, Hannes	5
	Oblt. Unger, Rudolf	1
+	Uffz. Windemuth, Heinrich	1
	Oblt. Woitke, Erich	4

Appendix M
Legion Condor Casualty Listing

I • Kampfgruppe K/88

A) Killed while on an operational mission as a result of enemy action or accident

Date	Name	Region	Cause
8/15/36	Uffz. Schulze, Helmut	Jerez de la Frontera	Ju 52 crash
8/15/36	Uffz. Zech, Herbert	Jerez de la Frontera	Ju 52 crash
11/4/36	Lt. Kolbitz, Oskar	Getafe	shot down in aerial combat
12/8/36	Oblt. Liegnitz, Heinz	Arenas de S. Pedro	shot down
12/8/36	Lt. Hornschuh, Werner	Arenas de S. Pedro	shot down
12/8/36	Uffz. Harjes, Wilhelm	Alcala de Henares	shot down in aerial combat
12/8/36	Uffz. Ullmann, Josef	Arenas de S. Pedro	shot down
12/8/36	Ogefr. Seitz, Johann	Arenas de S. Pedro	shot down
1/4/37	Ofw. Hermann, Adolf	Bilbao	shot down in aerial combat
1/4/37	Fw. Barowski, Herbert	Bilbao	shot down in aerial combat
1/4/37	Uffz. Ziepek, Paul	Bilbao	shot down in aerial combat
1/4/37	Gefr. Schüll, Hans	Bilbao	shot down in aerial combat
2/23/37	Lt. Kaufmann, Rudolf	Andujar	shot down
2/23/37	Uffz. Bowitz, Gerhard	Andujar	shot down
2/23/37	Uffz. Sieken, Heinrich	Andujar	shot down
3/9/37	Uffz. Dallmann, Heinrich	Bejar	aircraft crash
4/18/37	Oblt. Sobotka, Hans	Bilbao	shot down in aerial combat
4/18/37	Uffz. Hoffmeister, Otto	Bilbao	shot down in aerial combat
4/18/37	Uffz. Müller, Friedrich	Bilbao	shot down in aerial combat
6/18/37	Uffz. Gorski, Leo	Burgos	bomb explosion
6/18/37	Uffz. Link, Richard	Burgos	bomb explosion
6/22/37	Fw. Götze, Fritz	Burgos	bomb explosion
7/25/37	Lt. Falk, Leo	Valdemorillo	shot down in aerial combat
7/25/37	Fw. Übelhack, Georg	Valdemorillo	shot down in aerial combat
7/25/37	Uffz. Berndt, Fritz	Valdemorillo	shot down in aerial combat
7/25/37	Uffz. Brötzmann, Walter	Valdemorillo	shot down in aerial combat
7/25/37	Uffz. Heyer, August	Valdemorillo	shot down in aerial combat
9/21/37	Uffz. Held, Claus	Reinosa	flew into mountain
9/21/37	Ogefr. Ness, Bruno	Reinosa	flew into mountain
9/21/37	Ogefr. Nokler, Franz	Reinosa	flew into mountain
9/24/37	Ogefr. Sembach, Willi	Gijon	fatally wounded in aerial combat
9/24/37	Lt. König, Ernst	Pontejos	emergency landing
9/24/37	Lt. Meyer, Heinrich	Pontejos	emergency landing
9/24/37	Uffz. Niebuhr, Franz	Pontejos	emergency landing
9/24/37	Ogefr. Brettmeier, Karl	Pontejos	emergency landing
10/7/37	Lt. Stallamann, Heinrich	Gijon	shot down by anti-aircraft fire
10/7/37	Uffz. Hartig, Rudolf	Gijon	shot down by anti-aircraft fire
10/7/37	Uffz. Uhrmeister, Karl	Gijon	shot down by anti-aircraft fire
12/10/37	Lt. Beucke, Friedrich Karl	Candasnos	shot down
12/10/37	Lt. Klein, Heinrich	Candasnos	shot down
12/10/37	Fw. Bergmann, Anton	Candasnos	shot down
12/10/37	Uffz. Brühl, Fritz	Candasnos	shot down
12/10/37	Ogefr. Ehlen, Alois	Canasnos	shot down
1/16/38	Ogefr. Martner, Thomas	Teruel	shot down in aerial combat
4/2/38	Lt. Hoyer, Herbert	Alfaro	collided with another He 111 before landing and crashed
4/2/38	Fw. Hoyer, Walter	Alfaro	collided with another He 111 before landing and crashed
4/2/38	Fw. Brüggemann, Herbert	Alfaro	collided with another He 111 before landing and crashed
4/2/38	Ogefr. Kondziela, Kurt	Alfaro	collided with another He 111 before landing and crashed
5/29/38	Lt. Kostlin, Karl	Sanjorge	shot down by anti-aircraft fire

Date	Name	Region	Cause
8/20/38	Lt. Willer, Heinz	Gandesa	shot down by anti-aircraft fire
10/1/38	Uffz. Pacht, Gerhard	Corbera	shot down by anti-aircraft fire
10/16/38	Oblt. von Janson, Thilo	Fatarella	aircraft exploded mid-air
10/16/38	Lt. Rodel, Emil	Fatarella	aircraft exploded mid-air
10/16/38	Uffz. Hoevener, Heinrich	Fatarella	aircraft exploded mid-air
12/4/38	Uffz. Achade, Gustav	over water	shot down
1/4/39	Uffz. Albrecht, Bruno	Tarragona	shot down
1/4/39	Uffz. von Prondzynski, Horst	Tarragona	shot down
1/17/39	Uffz. Meiling, Horst	Ocejo	shot down
1/25/39	Lt. Meister, Walter	Barcelona	shot down by anti-aircraft fire
1/29/39	Lt. Bötker, Claus	Arrens	flew into mountain at night
1/29/39	Uffz. Seiler, Fritz	Arrens	flew into mountain at night
1/29/39	Uffz. Möller, Armin	Arrens	flew into mountain at night
1/29/39	Uffz. Adler, Otto	Arrens	flew into mountain at night
2/5/39	Uffz. Brückers, Walter	Cervia	flew into mountain
2/5/39	Uffz. Hoffmann, Willi	Cervia	flew into mountain
2/5/39	Uffz. Schnabel, Rudolf	Cervia	flew into mountain
3/12/39	Obstlt. Härle, Friedrich	Madrid	explosion of bombload
3/12/39	Oblt. Pawelcik	Madrid	explosion of bombload
3/12/39	Ofw. Kollenda, Rudolf	Madrid	explosion of bombload
3/12/39	Ofw. Lange, Walter	Madrid	explosion of bombload
3/12/39	Uffz. Schrödel, Hans	Madrid	explosion of bombload
3/12/39	Uffz. Buttner, Harry	Madrid	explosion of bombload

B) Killed as the result of an accident

1/17/37	Flieger Jentsch, Alfred	Sierra Gredos	aircraft crash
9/21/37	Uffz. Marting, Egon	San Miguel	flew into mountain
11/13/37	Lt. Plate, Siegfried	Burgos	auto accident
11/16/37	Ogefr. Lehmann, Willi	Santander	auto accident
11/28/37	Uffz. Lütgeduhme, Karl	Burgo de Osma	weapons accident
12/23/37	Uffz. Kurz, Anton	Leon	aircraft crash
1/8/38	Uffz. Schick, Paul	Lerma	flew into mountain
1/8/38	Ogefr. Hoster, Erwin	Lerma	flew into mounatain
4/16/38	Lt. Siemson, Andreas	Monasterio	flew into mountain
4/16/38	Ogefr. Schmalfuß, Fritz	Monasterio	flew into mountain
4/16/38	Uffz. Kruschbersky, Oswald	Monasterio	flew into mountain
4/16/38	Uffz. Spieler, Rudolf	Monasterio	flew into mountain
4/16/38	Uffz. Matz, Albert	Monasterio	flew into mountain
4/16/38	Ogefr. Frielingsdorf, Erich	Monasterio	flew into mountain
12/16/38	Fw. Poppenhagen, Herbert	Zaragoza	auto accident
12/25/38	Uffz. Stöver, Gustav	Burgos	air accident
1/27/39	Uffz. Kollig, Gustav	Zaragoza	air accident
2/5/39	Ogefr. Penderak, Karl	Tarragona	auto accident
4/13/39	Uffz. Mais, Günther	San Rafael	auto accident
4/22/38	Uffz. Langrock, Kurt	San Rafael	auto accident

C) Died following illness

1/26/37	Gefr. Becker, Kurt	Sevilla
1/14/38	Fw. Wolf, Helmut	Germany
2/25/38	Ogefr. Hildebrand, Wilhelm	Alfaro
3/21/38	Lt. Schiller, Wolfgang	Zaragoza

II • Jagdgruppe J/88

A) Killed while on an operational mission as a result of enemy action or accident

9/28/36	Lt. Hefter, Ekkehard	Vitoria	crashed as the result of engine failure
11/13/36	Oblt. Eberhardt, Kraft	Casa de Campo	shot down in aerial combat
11/13/36	Lt. Henrici, Oscar	Alcoron	shot down in aerial combat

Date	Name	Region	Cause
1/6/37	Lt. von Gallera, Hans-Peter	Madrid	shot down in aerial combat
1/6/37	Uffz. Kneiding, Kurt	Madrid	shot down in aerial combat
2/11/37	Oblt. Rehahn, Paul	Caceres	crash
3/25/37	Uffz. Rückert, Konrad	Aravaca	shot down while making a low-level attack
4/1/37	Lt. Blankenagel, August Wilhelm	Vitoria	shot down while making a low-level attack
4/6/37	Oblt. von Harling, Christian	Ochandiano	shot while being captured
4/6/37	Dolm. Freese, Paul	Ochandiano	shot while being captured
6/11/37	Uffz. Wilmsen, August	Bilbao	shot down while making a low-level attack
7/12/37	Uffz. Höneß, Guido	Villaverde	shot down in aerial combat
7/24/37	Lt. Reuter, Ernst-Friedrich	Brunete	shot down by anti-aircraft fire
1/1/38	Lt. Runze, Heinz	Teruel	shot down by anti-aircraft fire
1/18/38	Lt. Klein, Gerhard	Teruel	shot down by anti-aircraft fire
2/19/38	Ufw. Torner, Heinrich	Valdecebro	shot down by anti-aircraft fire
3/11/38	Oblt. Graf zu Dohna, Alexander	Sastago	shot down in aerial combat
3/30/38	Hptm. Hering, Hubertus	Alcarraz	mid-air collision
3/30/38	Lt. Michaelis, Manfred	Alcarraz	mid-air collision
4/4/38	Lt. Awe, Fritz	Zaragoza	mid-air collision
5/4/38	Uffz. Hester, Andreas	Albocacer	shot down by anti-aircraft fire
6/2/38	Lt. Haupt, Martin	Culla	shot down by anti-aircraft fire
6/8/38	Lt. Beyer, Erich	Castellon	shot down by anti-aircraft fire
10/17/38	Uffz. Selk, Alfred	Zaragoza	killed by bomb fragments
1/29/39	Lt. Bötticher, Karl August	Mollet	shot down by anti-aircraft fire
2/6/39	Ufw. Windemuth, Heinrich	Vilajuiga	shot down while making a low-level attack

B) Killed as the result of an accident

Date	Name	Region	Cause
4/30/37	Oblt. von Gilsa, Kurt	MIA over water	missing on flight from Sevilla to Rome
4/30/37	Uffz. Mratzek, Ernst	MIA over water	missing on flight from Sevilla to Rome
5/11/39	Uffz. Nirminger, Hans	Leon	air accident

C) Died following illness

Date	Name	Region
1/20/37	Uffz. Grassheuser, Georg	Avila
11/21/37	Mont. Wengler, Heinz	Burgos
6/7/38	Ogefr. Lesky, Willi	Vigo
10/20/38	Ogefr. Schäfer, Rudolf	Zaragoza
10/29/38	Ogefr. Bienert, Hermann	Zaragoza

III • Aufklärungsgruppe A/88 (Reconnaissance)

A) Killed while on an operational mission as a result of enemy action or accident

Date	Name	Region	Cause
6/16/37	Lt. Gottanka, Siegfried	Miravalles	shot down
6/16/37	Lt. Hildemann, Helmut	Miravalles	shot down
6/16/37	Uffz. Heerschlag, Fritz	Miravalles	shot down
7/10/37	Lt. von Posser, Hans	Brunete	shot down
7/10/37	Ogefr. Reinhold, Roland	Brunete	shot down
9/4/37	Oblt. von Kessel, Hans-Detlef	Llanes	shot down by anti-aircraft fire
9/4/37	Uffz. Hein, Ernst	Llanes	shot down by anti-aircraft fire
9/4/37	Uffz. Schnell, Waldemar	Llanes	shot down by anti-aircraft fire
9/4/37	Ogefr. Krüger, Waldemar	Llanes	shot down by anti-aircraft fire
9/4/37	Lt. Krocker, Gerhard	Llanes	shot down by anti-aircraft fire
9/4/37	Uffz. Heil, Hermann	Llanes	shot down by anti-aircraft fire
9/11/37	Gefr. Leske, Stanislaus	Burgos	crash landing
9/22/37	Lt. Kemper, Hans	Santander	crash
10/22/37	Lt. Schwanengel, Friedrich	Aviles	shot down by anti-aircraft fire
4/7/38	Lt. Kendel, Max	Cubels	shot down by anti-aircraft fire
4/7/38	Uffz. Birkhofen, Paul	Cubels	shot down by anti-aircraft fire
4/7/38	Uffz. v.d. Driesch, Willi	Cubels	shot down by anti-aircraft fire
4/7/38	Ogefr. Fiedler, Erich	Cubels	shot down by anti-aircraft fire
8/5/38	Uffz. Lehmann, Otto	Flix	shot down by anti-aircraft fire

Date	Name	Region	Cause

B) Killed as the result of an accident

Date	Name	Region	Cause
3/22/37	Gefr. Matschek, Gustav	Pejar	auto accident
2/15/38	Uffz. Brückner, Heinz	Leon	weapons accident
1/31/39	Ogefr. Knogler, Johann	Montblanch	motorcycle accident

C) Died following illness

Date	Name	Region	Cause
1/28/37	Ogefr. Hoffmann, Oskar	Sevilla	

IV • Aufklärungsgruppe See AS/88

A) Killed while on an operational mission as a result of enemy action or accident

Date	Name	Region	Cause
1/13/37	Uffz. Kahl, Harald	Pollensa	crashed into sea on night mission
2/5/37	Lt. Leicht, Dieter	Malaga	shot down in aerial combat
4/9/37	Gefr. Papendick, Siegfried	Malaga	killed by bomb fragments
3/21/38	Oblt. Jürgens, Hajo	Cambrils	aircraft explosion in mid-air
3/21/38	Lt. Zunker, Karl	Cambrils	aircraft explosion in mid-air
3/21/38	Uffz. Keitzel, Kurt	Cambrils	aircraft explosion in mid-air
12/31/38	Oblt. Printz, Carl-Friedrich	Valls	shot down
12/31/38	Lt. Schmidt, Otto	Valls	shot down
12/31/38	Uffz. Jeck, Paul	Valls	shot down
12/31/38	Uffz. Bulling, Walter	Valls	shot down
12/31/38	Insp. Müller, Ludwig	Valls	shot down

B) Killed as the result of an accident

Date	Name	Region	Cause
1/1/39	Oblt. Poeschel	Unknown	crashed due to icing
1/1/39	Lt. Schöbel	Unknown	crashed due to icing
1/1/39	Funker Zervas	Unknown	crashed due to icing
1/1/39	Fw. Herold	Unknown	crashed due to icing

C) Died following illness

Date	Name	Region	Cause
12/15/38	Lt. Fritsch, Wilhelm	Palma Mallorca	

V • Flakabteilung F/88

A) Killed while on an operational mission as a result of enemy action or accident

Date	Name	Region	Cause
1/14/37	Gefr. Eppert, Rudolf	Villafranca	small arms fire
4/22/37	Gefr. Rettemaier, Karl	Urbina	explosion
4/4/37	Gefr. Creutz, Emil	Vitoria	explosion
4/20/37	Gefr. Fischer, Johann	Vitoria	explosion
6/12/37	Uffz. Claus, Felix	Munguia	bombing attack
6/12/37	Uffz. Steeg, Richard	Munguia	bombing attack
6/12/37	Gefr. Hoffmann, Martin	Munguia	bombing attack
6/12/37	Uffz. Bauer, Friedrich	Munguia	bombing attack
8/15/37	Gefr. Otto, Hermann	Alar del Rey	shot by Spanish soldier
9/11/37	Gefr. Kohlheim, Georg	Llanes	shell fragments
12/28/37	Uffz. Florezack, Ludwig	Bezas	bombing attack
12/30/37	Gefr. Finger, Heinrich	Teruel	head wound
1/5/38	Uffz. Lampe, Arno	Teruel	explosion of shell
6/26/38	Gefr. Horn, Ehrhardt	Villareal	
7/2/38	Kan. Müller, Walter	Bechi	small arms fire
7/6/38	Uffz. Bauer, Wolfgang	Castellon	small arms fire
7/8/38	Fw. Vandrey, Erich	Castellon	artillery fire
1/11/39	Gefr. Knohr, Herbert-Joachim	Espluga Francoli	artillery fire

Date	Name	Region	Cause
1/11/39	Ogefr. Plewe, Erwin	Espluga, Francoli	artillery fire
1/12/39	Ogefr. Sordon, Georg	Espluga Francoli	artillery fire
2/4/39	Ogefr. Hüsemann, Heinrich	Roda	small arms fire

B) Killed as the result of an accident

12/24/36	Gefr. Schäfer, Konrad	Madrid	weapons accident
1/17/37	Uffz. Hensen, Otto	Sierra Gredos	aircraft crash
4/15/37	Gefr. Zschetzsching, Erich	Agueda	weapons accident
4/30/37	Ofw. Gaus, Gustav	Unknown	aircraft crash during flight from Sevilla to Rome
7/14/37	Dolm. Wolf, Felix	Santo Domingo	auto accident
4/9/38	Ogefr. Bode, Siegfried	Alcaraz	motorcycle accident
6/6/38	Ogefr. Simon, Alfred	Benasal	hand grenade explosion
8/23/38	Uffz. Henke, Werner	San Rafael	auto accident
12/25/38	Ogefr. Conrad, Richard	Burgos	aircraft crash
2/19/39	Ogefr. Coburger, Helmut	Sabadell	crash
3/28/39	Ogefr. Remke, Heinrich	Orgaz	explosion of munitions truck

C) Died following illness

4/10/37	Gefr. Hilger, Gerhard	Grinon	

VI • Nachrichtenabteilung LN/88 (Signal Battalion)

A) Killed while on an operational mission as a result of enemy action or accident

6/11/37	Lt. Fehlhaber, Paul	Bilbao	killed by artillery fire
6/11/37	Uffz. Aldag, Wilhelm	Bilbao	killed by artillery fire
6/11/37	Techn. Wiegand, Oscar	Bilbao	killed by artillery fire
6/11/37	Uffz. Oblau, Willi	Bilbao	killed by artillery fire
4/23/38	Gefr. Franke, Martin	Alcanar	murdered by Republicans
11/2/38	Ogefr. Scharl, Georg	Corbera	shell fragments
1/3/39	Ogefr. Uhlig, Liebreich	Cubells	low-level attack
1/3/39	Gefr. Markus, Helmut	Cubells	low-level attack
1/3/39	Dolm. Buntrock, Hermann	Cubells	low-level attack
1/28/39	Lt. Jochmann, Karl-Heinz	Mollet	shot while in captivity
1/28/39	Dolm. Behrmann, Johann	Mollet	shot while in captivity
1/28/39	Stgefr. Eckert, Walter	Mollet	shot while in captivity

B) Killed as the result of an accident

1/4/37	Ogefr. Uhlig, Wilhelm	San Fernando	auto accident
4/30/37	Lt. Gieseke, Hans	Unknown	aircraft crash during flight from Sevilla to Rome
4/30/37	Uffz. Demant, Herbert	Unknown	aircraft crash during flight from Sevilla to Rome
4/30/37	Uffz. Ossenkopp, Ernst	Unknown	aircraft crash during flight from Sevilla to Rome
7/11/37	Uffz. Altenstädter, Hermann	San Martin	suicide
2/12/38	Ogefr. Ottsen, Ludwig	Teruel	hand grenade explosion
4/5/38	Uffz. Mertens, Alex	Corella	auto accident
6/20/38	Ogefr. Striegan, Josef	Zaragoza	drowned while swimming
6/21/38	Uffz. Wolf, Franz	Zarauz	weapons accident
7/22/38	Uffz. Vetterlein, Gerhard	Zaragoza	auto accident
8/22/38	Dolm. Hoster, Paul	Benicarlo	drowned while swimming
9/3/38	Gefr. Weigelt, Karl	Zaragoza	auto accident
9/7/38	Ogefr. Huster, Rudolf	Vinaroz	auto accident
10/10/38	Gefr. Müller, Lothar	Corella	weapons accident
10/20/38	Stgefr. Quinque, Herbert	Alcanar	auto accident

Date	Name	Region	Cause
11/27/38	Uffz. Hintelmann, Walter	Deva	auto accident
12/25/38	Handw. Schmitz, Hermann	Burgos	aircraft crash
12/25/38	Feuerw. Hentschel, Bernhard	Burgos	aircraft crash
12/25/38	Dolm. Laux, Kurt	Burgos	aircraft crash
2/21/39	Uffz. Hanke, Heinz	Zaragoza	auto accident
2/24/39	Oblt. Lessmann, Lothar	Roubillon (France)	aircraft crash
2/24/39	Ofw. Uhl, Walter	Roubillon (France)	aircraft crash
2/24/39	Uffz, Grünewald, Hermann	Roubillon (France)	aircraft crash
2/24/39	Uffz. Wöhlecke, Willi	Roubillon (France)	aircraft crash
2/24/39	Lt. Bodden, Wilhelm	Roubillon (France)	aircraft crash
2/24/39	Fw. Timmler, Paul	Roubillon (France)	aircraft crash
2/24/39	Uffz. Hagl, Michael	Roubillon (France)	aircraft crash
2/24/39	Uffz. Kubnick, Werner	Roubillon (France)	aircraft crash
2/24/39	Uffz. Regenhardt, Erich	Roubillon (France)	aircraft crash
4/8/39	Oblt. Dickoré	Zaragoza	aircraft crash
4/8/39	Lt. Weyer	Zaragoza	aircraft crash
4/8/39	Fw. Gall	Zaragoza	aircraft crash
4/8/39	Uffz. Kaluza	Zaragoza	aircraft crash

C) Died following illness

7/23/37	Gefr. Knecht, Eberhard	Germany
3/11/38	Gefr. Neisse, Herbert	Germany
6/27/38	Uffz. Schilling, Ernst	Zaragoza

VII • Stab S/88

A) Killed while on an opertional mission as a result of enemy action or accident

10/12/37	Ogefr. Grempel, Walter	Cangas de Onis	small arms fire
3/20/38	Ogefr. Schuller, Alois	Escatron	shot while in captivity
?	Ogefr. Imping, Gerhard	?	shot while in captivity

B) Killed as the result of an accident

6/6/37	Obstlt. Evers, Walter	Salamanca
5/15/37	Funker Bastein, Karl-Heinz	Germany
5/15/37	Oblt. Ohlhorst	Salamanca
1/24/39	Dolm. Bönesch, Julius	Burgos
1/24/39	Dolm. Farwig, Hans-Günther	Burgos

VIII • Technical Services (Depot) P/88

A) Killed while on an operational mission as a result of enemy action or accident

1/17/37	Uffz. Fischer, Josef	Sierra Gredos	aircraft crash
1/17/37	Uffz. Schuhmann, Wilhelm	Sierra Gredos	aircraft crash
1/17/37	Gefr. May, Konrad	Sierra Gredos	aircraft crash
6/9/37	Ogefr. Graber, Willi	Plasencia	auto accident
11/14/37	Gefr. Möhlmann, Alois	Burgos	motorcycle accident
12/15/37	Gefr. Schmidt, Wilhelm	Sevilla	struck by propeller

B) Killed as the result of an accident

6/4/38	Ogefr. Dunkelmann, Heinrich	Germany

IX • Panzerabteilung (Imker)

A) Killed while on an operational mission as a result of enemy action or accident

Date	Name	Region	Cause
5/12/37	Uffz. Butz, Adalbert	Murga	head wound
5/23/37	Gefr. Hol, Karl	Durango	killed trying to destroy enemy tank
7/24/37	Lt. von Morner, Hans-Hannibal	Brunete	KIA
8/31/37	Uffz. Wohlgemuth, Fritz	Munorodero	KIA
11/3/37	Uffz. Scheuern, Georg	Burgos	stomach wound
3/25/37	Gefr. Geisel, Karl	Bujaraloz	KIA
11/14/37	Oblt. Trippe, Gustav	Fatarella	auto accident

B) Killed as the result of an accident

Date	Name	Region	Cause
10/11/36	Uffz. Kempe, Paul	Caceres	auto accident
12/14/36	Gefr. Szymanski, Heinrich	Madrid	auto accident
1/22/37	Gefr. Schäfer, Karl	Cubas	weapons accident
1/26/37	Uffz. Schneider, Paul	Germany	as the result of motorcycle accident
3/29/37	Gefr. Mayer, Oskar	San Martin	auto accident
4/30/37	Schirrm. Jaskulla, Paul	Unknown	aircraft crash during flight from Sevilla to Rome
7/24/37	Uffz. Schaumburg, Walter	San Roque	weapons accident
8/6/37	Funker Noack, Kurt	Reinosa	auto accident
9/22/38	Funker Senifert, Helmut	Zaragoza	suicide
12/15/38	Dolm. Hübner, Willy	Zaragoza	auto accident
4/7/39	Fw. Hardt, Georg	Monasterio	auto accident
4/7/39	Fw. Bosselmann, Kurt	Monasterio	auto accident
4/7/39	Fw. Spranger, Rudolf	Monasterio	auto accident
4/7/39	Fw. Mittelsdorp, Heinrich	Monasterio	auto accident

C) Died following illness

Date	Name	Region
4/2/37	Ogefr. Förster, Karl-Heinz	Cubas
7/1/37	Uffz. Blume, Wilhelm	Germany
7/24/37	Uffz. Balewski, Otto	Cubas
8/1/37	Ogefr. Wolf, Richard	Burgos
1/10/38	Uffz. Hinners, Heinrich	Burgos
3/3/38	Dolm. Paege, Wilhelm	Burgos
9/29/38	Funker Börflet, Hans	Zaragoza

X • Naval (Anker)

A) Killed while on an operational mission as a result of enemy action or accident

Date	Name	Region
3/6/38	Mont. Jensen, Jürgen	Cartagena

B) Killed as the result of an accident

Date	Name	Region	Cause
1/17/37	Korv.Kptn. Mayhöfer, Richard	Sierra Gredos	aircraft crash
4/30/37	Freg.Kptn. Fuhrke, Manfred	Unknown	aircraft crash during flight from Sevilla to Rome
5/12/37	Waffenm. Vülcher, Walter	Mallorca	auto accident
4/8/39	Funker Scharl	Zaragoza	aircraft crash

VNA GRANDE LIBRE

PLVS VLTRA

Ejercito Espanol

En atención a los méritos contraidos en Operaciones de Guerra por Capitan Hermann Hogeback

S. E. el Jefe del Estado y Generalísimo de los Ejércitos Nacionales ha tenido á bien concederle la Medalla de Sufrimientos por la Patria

Y para que conste y para satisfacción del interesado, expido en nombre de S. E. el presente diploma en Burgos a 4 de Mayo de 1939, Año de la Victoria.

El Ministro de Defensa Nacional

Fidel Dávila

MINISTERIO DE DEFENSA NACIONAL

dibujo Herrero

Award certificate issued to Hermann Hogeback with the Spanish Wound Badge.

Award certificate issued to Ignaz Prestele with the "Medalla Militar."

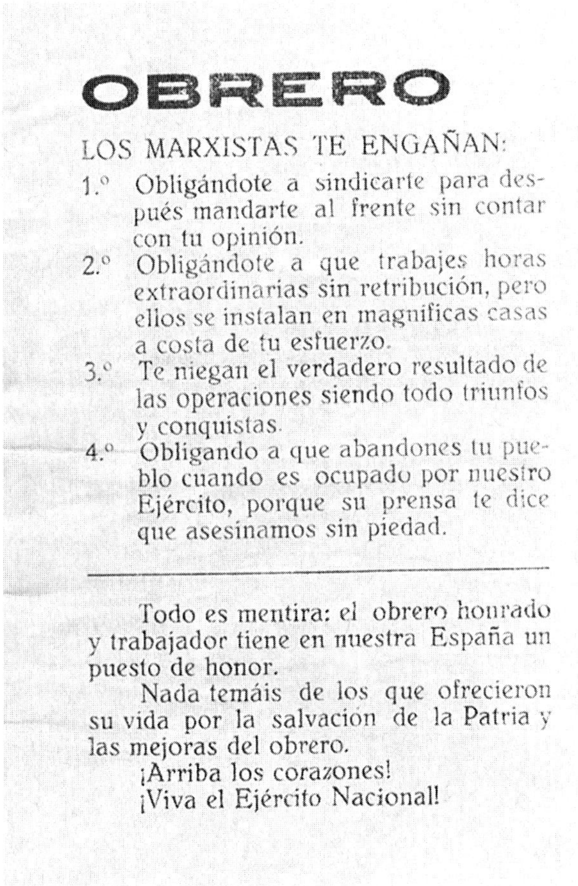

OBRERO

LOS MARXISTAS TE ENGAÑAN:

1.º Obligándote a sindicarte para después mandarte al frente sin contar con tu opinión.

2.º Obligándote a que trabajes horas extraordinarias sin retribución, pero ellos se instalan en magníficas casas a costa de tu esfuerzo.

3.º Te niegan el verdadero resultado de las operaciones siendo todo triunfos y conquistas.

4.º Obligando a que abandones tu pueblo cuando es ocupado por nuestro Ejército, porque su prensa te dice que asesinamos sin piedad.

Todo es mentira: el obrero honrado y trabajador tiene en nuestra España un puesto de honor.

Nada temáis de los que ofrecieron su vida por la salvación de la Patria y las mejoras del obrero.

¡Arriba los corazones!

¡Viva el Ejército Nacional!

WORKER
THE MARXISTS ARE DECEIVING YOU

1. You are forced to organize into syndicates and then sent to the front without first being asked your opinion.

2. You are forced to work overtime without pay; they, however, live in first-class houses at your expense.

3. They are withholding from you what is really going on at the front and speak only of victories and captures.

4. You are forced to leave your villages when they are occupied by our troops because their press maintains that we murder without pity.

All lies: In our Spain the honest, decent worker holds a position of honor.

Fear nothing from those who have risked their lives for the salvation of our fatherland and the improvement of the lot of the worker.

Lift up your hearts!

Long live the National Army!

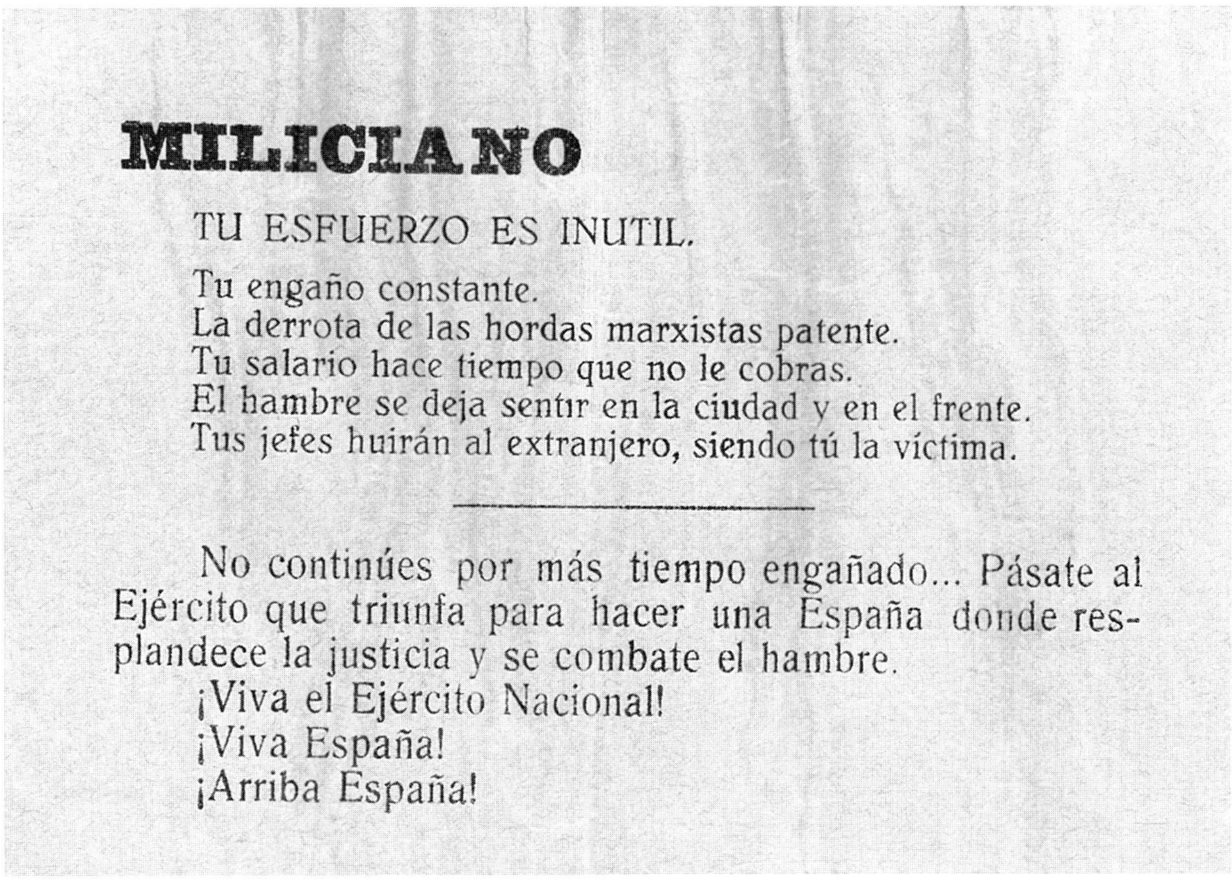

MILICIANO

TU ESFUERZO ES INUTIL.

Tu engaño constante.
La derrota de las hordas marxistas patente.
Tu salario hace tiempo que no le cobras.
El hambre se deja sentir en la ciudad y en el frente.
Tus jefes huirán al extranjero, siendo tú la víctima.

No continúes por más tiempo engañado... Pásate al Ejército que triunfa para hacer una España donde resplandece la justicia y se combate el hambre.

¡Viva el Ejército Nacional!
¡Viva España!
¡Arriba España!

Two leaflets dropped by Nationalist aircraft over Republican territory.

Menu cover from a dinner held in honor of the German and Italian fliers.

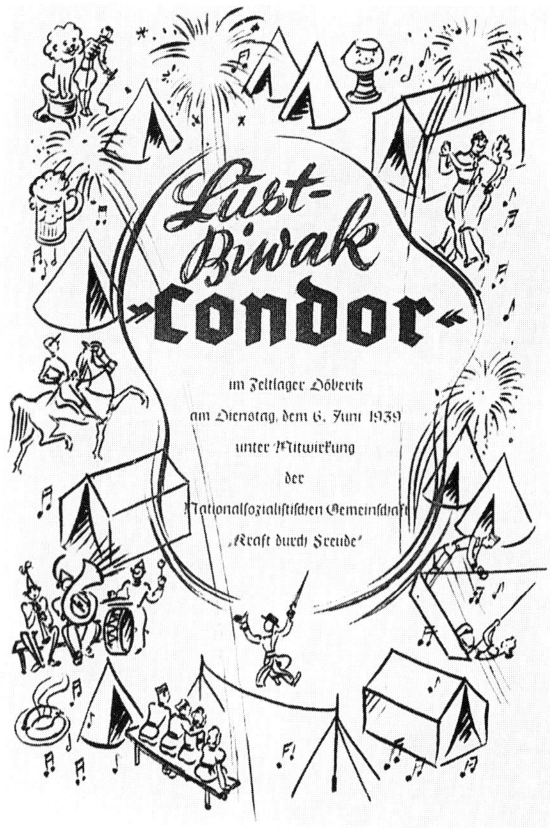

Program title page for activities in the Döberitz tent camp on the evening of June 6, 1939.

Almost twenty years later. The former officers mess at La Cenia airfield, photographed in 1957.

Bibliography

Published Works:

Beumelburg, W., *Kampf un Spanien*, Oldenburg, 1939
Bley, W., *Das Buch der Spanienflieger*, Leipzig, 1939
Die Wehrmacht, *Wir kämpften in Spanien* (SH), Berlin, 1939
Forell, F.V., *Mölders und seine Männer*, Graz, 1941
Galland, A., *Die Ersten und die Letzten*, Darmstadt, 1953
Green & Fricker, *The Air Forces of the World*, London, 1958
Hoffmann, K.O., *Geschichte der LN-Truppe*, Neckargemünd, 1965
Koch, K.H., *Flak*, Bad Nauheim, 1965
Kohl, H., *Deutsche Flieger über Spanien*, Berlin, 1939
Kühne, H., *Pasaremos*, Berlin (Ost), 1970
Kropp, A., *So kämpften deutsche Spanien*, Berlin, 1939
Larrazabal, J., *Air War Over Spain*, London, 1974
Legion Condor, *Deutsche kämpfen in Spanien*, Berlin, 1939
L.N. 88, *Wir von der L.N./88*, Zarazoga, 1938
Mason, H.M., *Die Luftwaffe 1918-1945*, Vienna
Merkes, M., *Die deutsche Politik im Spanischen Bürgerkrieg,* Bonn, 1969
Obermaier, E., *Die Ritterkreuzträger der Luftwaffe*, Band 1, Mainz, 1966
Oven, W.v., *Hitler und der Spanische Bürgerkrieg*, Tübingen, 1978
Ries, K., *Luftwaffen-Story*, Mainz, 1974
Shores, Chr., *Spanish Civil War Air Forces*, London, 1977
Stackelberg, K.G.v., *Legion Condor*, Berlin, 1938
Tinker, F.G., *Some Still Alive*, 1938
Trautloft, H., *Als Jadflieger in Spanien*, Berlin, 1939

Unpublished Works:

War Diary compiled by Hptm. T. Christ, adjutant to the Legion Condor General Staff

Diary Records by:
Balthasar, Bertram, Harder, Lützow, Priebe, Schellmann, Trautloft

Author's Archives

Additional Luftwaffe Titles from Schiffer Military History

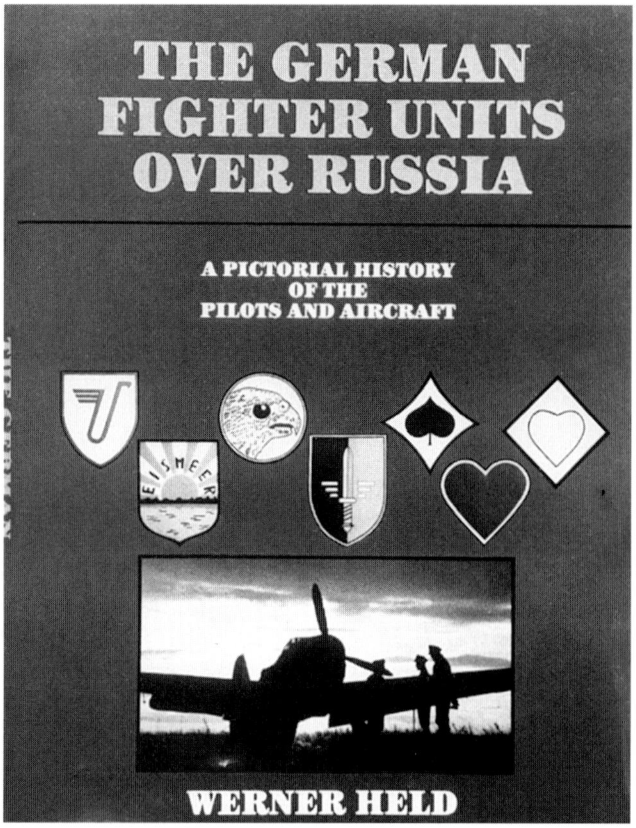

Luftwaffe Rudder Markings • 1936-1945
Karl Ries & Ernst Obermaier

Six Months To Oblivion
Werner Girbig

GERMAN FIGHTERS IN WORLD WAR II

The Day Fighters
Werner Held

The Night Fighters
Werner Held/Holger Nauroth